J. A. Dehner sj

*The Origin of Consciousness
in the Breakdown of the Bicameral Mind*

Julian Jaynes

THE ORIGIN
OF CONSCIOUSNESS
IN THE BREAKDOWN OF
THE BICAMERAL MIND

HOUGHTON MIFFLIN COMPANY

Boston

Library of Congress Cataloging in Publication Data

Jaynes, Julian.
    The origin of consciousness in the breakdown of the bicam-
eral mind.

    Includes bibliographical references and index.
    1. Consciousness. 2. Consciousness — History. I. Title.
BF311.J36   128'.2   76–28748
ISBN 0–395–20729–0

Printed in the United States of America

v   10   9   8

See last page of book for credits.

PREFACE

THE CENTRAL IDEAS of this inquiry were first summarized publicly in an Invited Address to the American Psychological Association in Washington in September 1969. Since then, I have been something of an itinerant lecturer, various parts of this work having been given at colloquia and lectures at various places. The resulting attention and discussion have been very helpful.

Book I presents these ideas as I arrived at them.
Book II examines the historical evidence.
Book III makes deductions to explain some modern phenomena.

Originally, I had planned a Book IV to complete the central positions of my theory. This will now become a separate volume, to be published shortly.

PRINCETON UNIVERSITY, 1976

CONTENTS

PREFACE   V

INTRODUCTION: The Problem of Consciousness   I

Book I
The Mind of Man

1. The Consciousness of Consciousness   21
2. Consciousness   48
3. The Mind of Iliad   67
4. The Bicameral Mind   84
5. The Double Brain   100
6. The Origin of Civilization   126

Book II
The Witness of History

1. Gods, Graves, and Idols   149
2. Literate Bicameral Theocracies   176
3. The Causes of Consciousness   204
4. A Change of Mind in Mesopotamia   223
5. The Intellectual Consciousness of Greece   255
6. The Moral Consciousness of the Khabiru   293

Book III
Vestiges of the Bicameral Mind in the Modern World

1. The Quest for Authorization   317
2. Of Prophets and Possession   339
3. Of Poetry and Music   361
4. Hypnosis   379
5. Schizophrenia   404
6. The Auguries of Science   433

INDEX   447

*The Origin of Consciousness
in the Breakdown of the Bicameral Mind*

INTRODUCTION

The Problem of Consciousness

O, WHAT A WORLD of unseen visions and heard silences, this insubstantial country of the mind! What ineffable essences, these touchless rememberings and unshowable reveries! And the privacy of it all! A secret theater of speechless monologue and prevenient counsel, an invisible mansion of all moods, musings, and mysteries, an infinite resort of disappointments and discoveries. A whole kingdom where each of us reigns reclusively alone, questioning what we will, commanding what we can. A hidden hermitage where we may study out the troubled book of what we have done and yet may do. An introcosm that is more myself than anything I can find in a mirror. This consciousness that is myself of selves, that is everything, and yet nothing at all — what is it?

And where did it come from?

And why?

Few questions have endured longer or traversed a more perplexing history than this, the problem of consciousness and its place in nature. Despite centuries of pondering and experiment, of trying to get together two supposed entities called mind and matter in one age, subject and object in another, or soul and body in still others, despite endless discoursing on the streams, states, or contents of consciousness, of distinguishing terms like intuitions, sense data, the given, raw feels, the sensa, presentations and representations, the sensations, images, and affections of structuralist introspections, the evidential data of the scientific positivist, phenomenological fields, the apparitions of Hobbes, the phenomena of Kant, the appearances of the idealist, the elements of Mach, the phanera of Peirce, or the category errors of Ryle, in spite of all of these, the problem of consciousness is still with us. Something about it keeps returning, not taking a solution.

It is the difference that will not go away, the difference between what others see of us and our sense of our inner selves and the deep feelings that sustain it. The difference between the you-and-me of the shared behavioral world and the unlocatable location of things thought about. Our reflections and dreams, and the imaginary conversations we have with others, in which never-to-be-known-by-anyone we excuse, defend, proclaim our hopes and regrets, our futures and our pasts, all this thick fabric of fancy is so absolutely different from handable, standable, kickable reality with its trees, grass, tables, oceans, hands, stars — even brains! How is this possible? How do these ephemeral existences of our lonely experience fit into the ordered array of nature that somehow surrounds and engulfs this core of knowing?

Men have been conscious of the problem of consciousness almost since consciousness began. And each age has described consciousness in terms of its own theme and concerns. In the golden age of Greece, when men traveled about in freedom while slaves did the work, consciousness was as free as that. Heraclitus, in particular, called it an enormous space whose boundaries, even by traveling along every path, could never be found out.[1] A millennium later, Augustine among the caverned hills of Carthage was astonished at the "mountains and hills of my high imaginations," "the plains and caves and caverns of my memory" with its recesses of "manifold and spacious chambers, wonderfully furnished with unnumberable stores."[2] Note how the metaphors of mind are the world it perceives.

The first half of the nineteenth century was the age of the great geological discoveries in which the record of the past was written in layers of the earth's crust. And this led to the popularization of the idea of consciousness as being in layers which

---

[1] Diels, Fragment, 45.
[2] *Confessions*, 9:7; 10:26, 65.

recorded the past of the individual, there being deeper and deeper layers until the record could no longer be read. This emphasis on the unconscious grew until by 1875 most psychologists were insisting that consciousness was but a small part of mental life, and that unconscious sensations, unconscious ideas, and unconscious judgments made up the majority of mental processes.[3]

In the middle of the nineteenth century chemistry succeeded geology as the fashionable science, and consciousness from James Mill to Wundt and his students, such as Titchener, was the compound structure that could be analyzed in the laboratory into precise elements of sensations and feelings.

And as steam locomotives chugged their way into the pattern of everyday life toward the end of the nineteenth century, so they too worked their way into the consciousness of consciousness, the subconscious becoming a boiler of straining energy which demanded manifest outlets and when repressed pushed up and out into neurotic behavior and the spinning camouflaged fulfillments of going-nowhere dreams.

There is not much we can do about such metaphors except to state that that is precisely what they are.

Now originally, this search into the nature of consciousness was known as the mind-body problem, heavy with its ponderous philosophical solutions. But since the theory of evolution, it has bared itself into a more scientific question. It has become the problem of the origin of mind, or, more specifically, the origin of consciousness in evolution. Where can this subjective experience which we introspect upon, this constant companion of hosts of associations, hopes, fears, affections, knowledges, colors, smells, toothaches, thrills, tickles, pleasures, distresses, and desires — where and how in evolution could all this wonderful tapestry of inner experience have evolved? How can we derive this inwardness out of mere matter? And if so, when?

[3] For a statement of this effect, see G. H. Lewes, *The Physical Basis of Mind* (London: Trübner, 1877), p. 365.

This problem has been at the very center of the thinking of the twentieth century. And it will be worthwhile here to briefly look at some of the solutions that have been proposed. I shall mention the eight that I think are most important.

Consciousness as a Property of Matter

The most extensive possible solution is attractive mostly to physicists. It states that the succession of subjective states that we feel in introspection has a continuity that stretches all the way back through phylogenetic evolution and beyond into a fundamental property of interacting matter. The relationship of consciousness to what we are conscious of is not fundamentally different from the relationship of a tree to the ground in which it is rooted, or even of the gravitational relationship between two celestial bodies. This view was conspicuous in the first quarter of this century. What Alexander called compresence or Whitehead called prehension provided the groundwork of a monism that moved on into a flourishing school called Neo-Realism. If a piece of chalk is dropped on the lecture table, that interaction of chalk and table is different only in complexity from the perceptions and knowledges that fill our minds. The chalk knows the table just as the table knows the chalk. That is why the chalk stops at the table.

This is something of a caricature of a very subtly worked out position, but it nevertheless reveals that this difficult theory is answering quite the wrong question. We are not trying to explain how we interact with our environment, but rather the particular experience that we have in introspecting. The attractiveness of this kind of neo-realism was really a part of an historical epoch when the astonishing successes of particle physics were being talked of everywhere. The solidity of matter was being dissolved into mere mathematical relationships in space, and this seemed like the same unphysical quality as the relationship of individuals conscious of each other.

Consciousness as a Property of Protoplasm

The next most extensive solution asserts that consciousness is not in matter *per se;* rather it is the fundamental property of all living things. It is the very irritability of the smallest one-celled animals that has had a continuous and glorious evolution up through coelenterates, the protochordates, fish, amphibians, reptiles, and mammals to man.

A wide variety of nineteenth- and twentieth-century scientists, including Charles Darwin and E. B. Titchener, found this thesis unquestionable, initiating in the first part of this century a great deal of excellent observation of lower organisms. The search for rudimentary consciousnesses was on. Books with titles such as *The Animal Mind* or *The Psychic Life of Micro-Organisms* were eagerly written and eagerly read.[4] And anyone who observes amoebas hunting food or responding to various stimuli, or paramecia avoiding obstacles or conjugating, will know the almost passionate temptation to apply human categories to such behavior.

And this brings us to a very important part of the problem — our sympathy and identification with other living things. Whatever conclusions we may hold on the matter, it is certainly a part of our consciousness to 'see' into the consciousness of others, to identify with our friends and families so as to imagine what they are thinking and feeling. And so if animals are behaving such as we would in similar situations, so well are we trained in our human sympathies that it requires a particular vigor of mind to suppress such identifications when they are not warranted. The explanation for our imputing consciousness to protozoa is simply that we make this common and misleading identification. Yet the explanation for their behavior resides entirely in physical chemistry, not in introspective psychology.

Even in animals with synaptic nervous systems, the tendency

---

[4] By Margaret Floy Washburn, a Titchenerian, and by Alfred Binet respectively. The real classic in the field of early evolved animals is H. S. Jennings, *Behavior of the Lower Organisms* (New York: Macmillan, 1906).

to read consciousness into their behavior comes more from ourselves than from our observations. Most people will identify with a struggling worm. But as every boy who has baited a fish hook knows, if a worm is cut in two, the front half with its primitive brain seems not to mind as much as the back half, which writhes in 'agony'.[5] But surely if the worm felt pain as we do, surely it would be the part with the brain that would do the agonizing. The agony of the tail end is our agony, not the worm's; its writhing is a mechanical release phenomenon, the motor nerves in the tail end firing in volleys at being disconnected from their normal inhibition by the cephalic ganglion.

Consciousness as Learning

To make consciousness coextensive with protoplasm leads, of course, to a discussion of the criterion by which consciousness can be inferred. And hence a third solution, which states that consciousness began not with matter, nor at the beginning of animal life, but at some specific time after life had evolved. It seemed obvious to almost all the active investigators of the subject that the criterion of when and where in evolution consciousness began was the appearance of associative memory or learning. If an animal could modify its behavior on the basis of its experience, it must be having an experience; it must be conscious. Thus, if one wished to study the evolution of consciousness, one simply studied the evolution of learning.

This was indeed how I began my search for the origin of consciousness. My first experimental work was a youthful attempt to produce signal learning (or a conditional response) in an especially long suffering mimosa plant. The signal was an intense light; the response was the drooping of a leaf to a care-

---

[5] Since an earthworm 'writhes' from the tactile stimulation of simply being handled, the experiment is best performed with a razor blade as the worm is crawling over some hard ground or a board. The unbelieving and squeamish may suppress their anguish with the consciousness that they are helping the worm population (and therefore the robin population) since both ends regenerate.

which harasses the artist, the sweet thorn of justice which fierces the rebel from the eases of life, or the thrill of exultation with which we hear of true acts of that now difficult virtue of courage, of cheerful endurance of hopeless suffering — are these really derivable from matter? Or even continuous with the idiot hierarchies of speechless apes?

The chasm *is* awesome. The emotional lives of men and of other mammals are indeed marvelously similar. But to focus upon the similarity unduly is to forget that such a chasm exists at all. The intellectual life of man, his culture and history and religion and science, is different from anything else we know of in the universe. That is fact. It is as if all life evolved to a certain point, and then in ourselves turned at a right angle and simply exploded in a different direction.

The appreciation of this discontinuity between the apes and speaking civilized ethical intellectual men has led many scientists back to a metaphysical view. The interiority of consciousness just could not in any sense be evolved by natural selection out of mere assemblages of molecules and cells. There has to be more to human evolution than mere matter, chance, and survival. Something must be added from outside of this closed system to account for something so different as consciousness.

Such thinking began with the beginning of modern evolutionary theory, particularly in the work of Alfred Russel Wallace, the codiscoverer of the theory of natural selection. Following their twin announcements of the theory in 1858, both Darwin and Wallace struggled like Laocoöns with the serpentine problem of human evolution and its encoiling difficulty of consciousness. But where Darwin clouded the problem with his own naiveté, seeing only continuity in evolution, Wallace could not do so. The discontinuities were terrifying and absolute. Man's conscious faculties, particularly, "could not possibly have been developed by means of the same laws which have determined the progressive development of the organic world in general, and also of man's physical organism."[8] He felt the evidence showed that some metaphysical force had directed evolution at three different points: the beginning of life, the beginning of consciousness, and the beginning of civilized culture. Indeed, it is partly because Wallace insisted on spending the latter part of his life searching in vain among the séances of spiritualists for evidence of such metaphysical imposition that his name is not as well known as is Darwin's as the discoverer of evolution by natural selection. Such endeavors were not acceptable to the scientific Establishment. To explain consciousness by metaphysical imposition seemed to be stepping outside the rules of natural science. And that indeed was the problem, how to explain consciousness in terms of natural science alone.

The Helpless Spectator Theory

In reaction to such metaphysical speculations, there grew up through this early period of evolutionary thinking an increasingly materialist view. It was a position more consistent with straight natural selection. It even had inherent in it that acrid pessimism that is sometimes curiously associated with really hard science. This doctrine assures us consciousness does nothing at all, and in fact can do nothing. Many tough-minded experimentalists still agree with Herbert Spencer that such a downgrading of consciousness is the only view that is consistent with straight evolutionary theory. Animals are evolved; nervous systems and their mechanical reflexes increase in complexity; when some unspecified degree of nervous complexity is reached, consciousness appears, and so begins its futile course as a helpless spectator of cosmic events.

What we do is completely controlled by the wiring diagram of the brain and its reflexes to external stimuli. Consciousness is not

---

[8] *Darwinism, an Exposition of the Theory of Natural Selection* (London: Macmillan, 1889), p. 475; see also Wallace's *Contributions to the Theory of Natural Selection*, Ch. 10.

more than the heat given off by the wires, a mere epiphenomenon. Conscious feelings, as Hodgson put it, are mere colors laid
on the surface of a mosaic which is held together by its stones,
not by the colors.[9] Or as Huxley insisted in a famous essay, "we
are conscious automata."[10] Consciousness can no more modify
the working mechanism of the body or its behavior than can the
whistle of a train modify its machinery or where it goes. Moan as
it will, the tracks have long ago decided where the train will go.
Consciousness is the melody that floats from the harp and cannot pluck its strings, the foam struck raging from the river that
cannot change its course, the shadow that loyally walks step for
step beside the pedestrian, but is quite unable to influence his
journey.

It is William James who has given the best discussion of the
conscious automaton theory.[11] His argument here is a little like
Samuel Johnson's downing philosophical idealism by kicking a
stone and crying, "I refute it thus!" It is just plain inconceivable
that consciousness should have *nothing to do* with a business
which it so faithfully attends. If consciousness is the mere impo-
tent shadow of action, why is it more intense when action is most
hesitant? And why are we least conscious when doing something
most habitual? Certainly this seesawing relationship between
consciousness and actions is something that any theory of consciousness *must* explain.

Emergent Evolution

The doctrine of emergent evolution was very specifically wel-
comed into court to rescue consciousness from this undignified

[9] Shadworth Hodgson, *The Theory of Practice* (London: Longmans Green, 1870),
1:416.
[10] And volitions merely *symbols* of brain-states. T. H. Huxley, *Collected Essays*
(New York: Appleton, 1896), Vol. 1, p. 244.
[11] William James, *Principles of Psychology* (New York: Holt, 1890), Vol. 1, Ch.
5), but also see William McDougall, *Body and Mind* (London: Methuen, 1911),
Chs. 11, 12.

position as a mere helpless spectator. It was also designed to explain scientifically the observed evolutionary discontinuities that had been the heart of the metaphysical imposition argument. And when I first began to study it some time ago, I, too, felt with a shimmering flash how everything, the problem of consciousness and all, seemed to shiveringly fall into accurate and wonderful place.

Its main idea is a metaphor: Just as the property of wetness cannot be derived from the properties of hydrogen and oxygen alone, so consciousness emerged at some point in evolution in a way underivable from its constituent parts.

While this simple idea goes back to John Stuart Mill and G. H. Lewes, it was Lloyd Morgan's version in his *Emergent Evolution* of 1923 that really captured the cheering. This book is a thoroughgoing scheme of emergent evolution vigorously carried all the way back into the physical realm. All the properties of matter have emerged from some unspecified forerunner. Those of complex chemical compounds have emerged from the conjunction of simpler chemical components. Properties distinctive of living things have emerged from the conjunctions of these complex molecules. And consciousness emerged from living things. New conjunctions bring about new kinds of relatedness which bring about new emergents. So the new emergent properties are in each case effectively related to the systems from which they emerge. In fact, the new relations emergent at each higher level guide and sustain the course of events distinctive of that level. Consciousness, then, emerges as something genuinely new at a critical stage of evolutionary advance. When it has emerged, it guides the course of events in the brain and has causal efficacy in bodily behavior.

The whoop with which this antireductionist doctrine was greeted by the majority of prominent biological and comparative psychologists, frustrated dualists all, was quite undignified. Biologists called it a new Declaration of Independence from physics and chemistry. "No longer can the biologist be bullied into suppressing observed results because they are not discovered nor expected from work on the non-living. Biology becomes a science in its own right." Prominent neurologists agreed that now we no longer had to think of consciousness as merely dancing an assiduous but futile attendance upon our brain processes.[12] The origin of consciousness seemed to have been pointed at in such a way as to restore consciousness to its usurped throne as the governor of behavior and even to promise new and unpredictable emergents in the future.

But had it? If consciousness emerged in evolution, when? In what species? What kind of a nervous system is necessary? And as the first flush of a theoretical breakthrough waned, it was seen that nothing about the problem had really changed. It is these specifics that need to be answered. What is wrong about emergent evolution is not the doctrine, but the release back into old comfortable ways of thinking about consciousness and behavior, the license that it gives to broad and vacuous generalities.

Historically, it is of interest here to note that all this dancing in the aisles of biology over emergent evolution was going on at the same time that a stronger, less-educated doctrine with a rigorous experimental campaign was beginning its robust conquest of psychology. Certainly one way of solving the problem of consciousness and its place in nature is to deny that consciousness exists at all.

Behaviorism

It is an interesting exercise to sit down and try to be conscious of what it means to say that consciousness does not exist. History has not recorded whether or not this feat was attempted by the early behaviorists. But it has recorded everywhere and in large

[12] The quote here is from H. S. Jennings and the paraphrase from C. Judson Herrick. For these and other reactions to emergent evolution, see F. Mason, *Creation by Evolution* (London: Duckworth, 1928) and W. McDougall, *Modern Materialism and Emergent Evolution* (New York: Van Nostrand, 1929).

the enormous influence which the doctrine that consciousness does not exist has had on psychology in this century.

And this is behaviorism. Its roots rummage far back into the musty history of thought, to the so-called Epicureans of the eighteenth century and before, to attempts to generalize tropisms from plants to animals to man, to movements called Objectivism, or more particularly, Actionism. For it was Knight Dunlap's attempt to teach the latter to an excellent but aweless animal psychologist, John B. Watson, that resulted in a new word, Behaviorism.[13] At first, it was very similar to the helpless spectator theory we have already examined. Consciousness just was not important in animals. But after a World War and a little invigorating opposition, behaviorism charged out into the intellectual arena with the snorting assertion that consciousness is nothing at all.

What a startling doctrine! But the really surprising thing is that, starting off almost as a flying whim, it grew into a movement that occupied center stage in psychology from about 1920 to 1960. The external reasons for the sustained triumph of such a peculiar position are both fascinating and complex. Psychology at the time was trying to wriggle out of philosophy into a separate academic discipline and used behaviorism to do so. The immediate adversary of behaviorism, Titchenerian introspectionism, was a pale and effete opponent, based as it was on a false analogy between consciousness and chemistry. The toppled idealism after World War I created a revolutionary age demanding new philosophies. The intriguing successes of physics and general technology presented both a model and a means that seemed more compatible with behaviorism. The world was weary and

---

[13] For a less *ad hominem* picture of the beginnings of behaviorism, see John C. Burnham, "On the origins of behaviorism." *Journal of the History of the Behavioral Sciences*, 1968, 4: 143–151. And for a good discussion, Richard Herrnstein's "Introduction to John B. Watson's Comparative Psychology" in *Historical Conceptions of Psychology*, M. Henle, J. Jaynes, and J. J. Sullivan, eds. (New York: Springer, 1974), 98–115.

wary of subjective thought and longed for objective fact. And in America objective fact was pragmatic fact. Behaviorism provided this in psychology. It allowed a new generation to sweep aside with one impatient gesture all the worn-out complexities of the problem of consciousness and its origin. We would turn over a new leaf. We would make a fresh start.

And the fresh start was a success in one laboratory after another. But the single inherent reason for its success was not its truth, but its program. And what a truly vigorous and exciting program of research it was! with its gleaming stainless-steel promise of reducing all conduct to a handful of reflexes and conditional responses developed from them, of generalizing the spinal reflex terminology of stimulus and response and reinforcement to the puzzles of headed behavior and so seeming to solve them, of running rats through miles and miles of mazes into more fascinating mazes of objective theorems, and its pledge, its solemn pledge to reduce thought to muscle twitches and personality to the woes of Little Albert.[14] In all this there was a heady excitement that is difficult to relate at this remove. Complexity would be made simple, darkness would be made light, and philosophy would be a thing of the past.

From the outside, this revolt against consciousness seemed to storm the ancient citadels of human thought and set its arrogant banners up in one university after another. But having once been a part of its major school, I confess it was not really what it seemed. Off the printed page, behaviorism was only a refusal to talk about consciousness. Nobody really believed he was not conscious. And there was a very real hypocrisy abroad, as those interested in its problems were forcibly excluded from academic psychology, as text after text tried to smother the unwanted problem from student view. In essence, behaviorism was a method, not the theory that it tried to be. And as a method, it

---

[14] The unfortunate subject of Watson's experiments on conditioned fear.

exorcised old ghosts. It gave psychology a thorough house cleaning. And now the closets have been swept out and the cupboards washed and aired, and we are ready to examine the problem again.

Consciousness as the Reticular Activating System

But before doing so, one final approach, a wholly different approach, and one that has occupied me most recently, the nervous system. How often in our frustrations with trying to solve the mysteries of mind do we comfort our questions with anatomy, real or fancied, and think of a thought as a particular neuron or a mood as a particular neurotransmitter! It is a temptation born of exasperation with the untestableness and vagueness of all the above solutions. Away with these verbal subtleties! These esoteric poses of philosophy and even the paper theories of behaviorists are mere subterfuges to avoid the very material we are talking about! Here we have an animal — make him a man if you will — here he is on the table of our analysis. If he is conscious, it has to be here, right here in him, in the brain in front of us, not in the presumptuous inklings of philosophy back in the incapable past! And today we at last have the techniques to explore the nervous system directly, brain to brain. Somewhere here in a mere three-and-a-half pound lump of pinkish-gray matter, the answer has to be.

All we have to do is to find those parts of the brain that are responsible for consciousness, then trace out their anatomical evolution, and we will solve the problem of the origin of consciousness. Moreover, if we study the behavior of present-day species corresponding to various stages in the development of these neurological structures, we will be able at last to reveal with experimental exactness just what consciousness basically is.

Now this sounds like an excellent scientific program. Ever since Descartes chose the brain's pineal body as the seat of consciousness and was roundly refuted by the physiologists of his day, there has been a fervent if often superficial search for where in the brain consciousness exists.[15] And the search is still on.

At the present, a plausible nominee for the neural substrate of consciousness is one of the most important neurological discoveries of our time. This is that tangle of tiny internuncial neurons called the reticular formation, which has long lain hidden and unsuspected in the brainstem. It extends from the top of the spinal cord through the brainstem on up into the thalamus and hypothalamus, attracting collaterals from sensory and motor nerves, almost like a system of wire-taps on the communication lines that pass near it. But this is not all. It also has direct lines of command to half a dozen major areas of the cortex and probably all the nuclei of the brainstem, as well as sending fibers down the spinal cord where it influences the peripheral sensory and motor systems. Its function is to sensitize or "awaken" selected nervous circuits and desensitize others, such that those who pioneered in this work christened it "the waking brain."[16]

The reticular formation is also often called by its functional name, the reticular activating system. It is the place where general anesthesia produces its effect by deactivating its neurons. Cutting it produces permanent sleep and coma. Stimulating it through an implanted electrode in most of its regions wakes up a sleeping animal. Moreover, it is capable of grading the activity of most other parts of the brain, doing this as a reflection of its own internal excitability and the titer of its neurochemistry. There are exceptions, too complicated for discussion here. But they are not such as to diminish the exciting idea that this disordered network of short neurons that connect up with the entire brain, this central transactional core between the strictly sensory and motor systems of classical neurology, is the long-sought answer to the whole problem.

* * *

[15] I have discussed this at greater length in my paper, "The Problem of Animate Motion in the Seventeenth Century," *Journal of the History of Ideas,* 1970, 31 : 219–234.

[16] See H. W. Magoun, *The Waking Brain* (Springfield, Illinois: Thomas, 1958).

If we now look at the evolution of the reticular formation, asking if it could be correlated with the evolution of consciousness, we find no encouragement whatever. It turns out to be one of the oldest parts of the nervous system. Indeed, a good case could be made that this is the very oldest part of the nervous system, around which the more orderly, more specific, and more highly evolved tracts and nuclei developed. The little that we at present know about the evolution of the reticular formation does not seem to indicate that the problem of consciousness and its origin will be solved by such a study.

Moreover, there is a delusion in such reasoning. It is one that is all too common and unspoken in our tendency to translate psychological phenomena into neuro-anatomy and chemistry. We can only know in the nervous system what we have known in behavior first. Even if we had a complete wiring diagram of the nervous system, we still would not be able to answer our basic question. Though we knew the connections of every tickling thread of every single axon and dendrite in every species that ever existed, together with all its neurotransmitters and how they varied in its billions of synapses of every brain that ever existed, we could still never — *not ever* — from a knowledge of the brain alone know if that brain contained a consciousness like our own. We first have to start from the top, from some conception of what consciousness is, from what our own introspection is. We have to be sure of that, before we can enter the nervous system and talk about its neurology.

We must therefore try to make a new beginning by stating what consciousness is. We have already seen that this is no easy matter, and that the history of the subject is an enormous confusion of metaphor with designation. In any such situation, where something is so resistant to even the beginnings of clarity, it is wisdom to begin by determining *what that something is not*. And that is the task of the next chapter.

BOOK ONE

The Mind of Man

CHAPTER 1

The Consciousness
of Consciousness

WHEN ASKED the question, what is consciousness? we become conscious of consciousness. And most of us take this consciousness of consciousness to be what consciousness is. This is not true.

In being conscious of consciousness, we feel it is the most self-evident thing imaginable. We feel it is the defining attribute of all our waking states, our moods and affections, our memories, our thoughts, attentions, and volitions. We feel comfortably certain that consciousness is the basis of concepts, of learning and reasoning, of thought and judgment, and that it is so because it records and stores our experiences as they happen, allowing us to introspect on them and learn from them at will. We are also quite conscious that all this wonderful set of operations and contents that we call consciousness is located somewhere in the head.

On critical examination, all of these statements are false. They are the costume that consciousness has been masquerading in for centuries. They are the misconceptions that have prevented a solution to the problem of the origin of consciousness. To demonstrate these errors and show what consciousness is not, is the long but I hope adventurous task of this chapter.

The Extensiveness of Consciousness

To begin with, there are several uses of the word consciousness which we may immediately discard as incorrect. We have for example the phrase "to lose consciousness" after receiving a blow on the head. But if this were correct, we would then have no word for those somnambulistic states known in the clinical literature where an individual is clearly not conscious and yet is responsive to things in a way in which a knocked-out person is not. Therefore, in the first instance we should say that the person suffering a severe blow on the head loses both consciousness and what I am calling reactivity, and they are therefore different things.

This distinction is also important in normal everyday life. We are constantly reacting to things without being conscious of them at the time. Sitting against a tree, I am always reacting to the tree and to the ground and to my own posture, since if I wish to walk, I will quite unconsciously stand up from the ground to do so.

Immersed in the ideas of this first chapter, I am rarely conscious even of where I am. In writing, I am reacting to a pencil in my hand since I hold on to it, and am reacting to my writing pad since I hold it on my knees, and to its lines since I write upon them, but I am only conscious of what I am trying to say and whether or not I am being clear to you.

If a bird bursts up from the copse nearby and flies crying to the horizon, I may turn and watch it and hear it, and then turn back to this page without being conscious that I have done so.

In other words, reactivity covers all stimuli my behavior takes account of in any way, while consciousness is something quite distinct and a far less ubiquitous phenomenon. We are conscious of what we are reacting to only from time to time. And whereas reactivity can be defined behaviorally and neurologically, consciousness at the present state of knowledge cannot.

But this distinction is much more far-reaching. We are continually reacting to things in ways that have no phenomenal component in consciousness whatever. Not at any time. In seeing any object, our eyes and therefore our retinal images are reacting to the object by shifting twenty times a second, and yet

we see an unshifting stable object with no consciousness whatever of the succession of different inputs or of putting them
together into the object. An abnormally small retinal image of
something in the proper context is automatically seen as something at a distance; we are not conscious of making the correc-
tion. Color and light contrast effects, and other perceptual
constancies all go on every minute of our waking and even
dreaming experience without our being in the least conscious of
them. And these instances are barely touching the multitude of
processes which by the older definitions of consciousness one
might expect to be conscious of, but which we definitely are not.
I am here thinking of Titchener's designation of consciousness as
"the sum total of mental processes occurring now." We are now
very far from such a position.

But let us go further. Consciousness is a much smaller part of
our mental life than we are conscious of, because we cannot be
conscious of what we are not conscious of. How simple that is to
say; how difficult to appreciate! It is like asking a flashlight in a
dark room to search around for something that does not have any
light shining upon it. The flashlight, since there is light in whatever direction it turns, would have to conclude that there is light
everywhere. And so consciousness can seem to pervade all mentality when actually it does not.

The timing of consciousness is also an interesting question.
When we are awake, are we conscious all the time? We think
so. In fact, we are sure so! I shut my eyes and even if I try not to
think, consciousness still streams on, a great river of contents in
a succession of different conditions which I have been taught to
call thoughts, images, memories, interior dialogues, regrets,
wishes, resolves, all interweaving with the constantly changing
pageant of exterior sensations of which I am selectively aware.
Always the continuity. Certainly this is the feeling. And whatever we're doing, we feel that our very self, our deepest of deep

identity, is indeed this continuing flow that only ceases in sleep between remembered dreams. This is our experience. And many thinkers have taken this spirit of continuity to be the place to start from in philosophy, the very ground of certainty which no one can doubt. Cogito, ergo sum.

But what could this continuity mean? If we think of a minute as being sixty thousand milliseconds, are we conscious for every one of those milliseconds? If you still think so, go on dividing the time units, remembering that the firing of neurons is of a finite order — although we have no idea what that has to do with our sense of the continuity of consciousness. Few persons would wish to maintain that consciousness somehow floats like a mist above and about the nervous system completely ununited to any earthly necessities of neural refractory periods.

It is much more probable that the seeming continuity of consciousness is really an illusion, just as most of the other metaphors about consciousness are. In our flashlight analogy, the flashlight would be conscious of being on only when it is on. Though huge gaps of time occurred, providing things were generally the same, it would seem to the flashlight itself that the light had been continuously on. We are thus conscious less of the time than we think, because we cannot be conscious of when we are not conscious. And the feeling of a great uninterrupted stream of rich inner experiences, now slowly gliding through dreamy moods, now tumbling in excited torrents down gorges of precipitous insight, or surging evenly through our nobler days, is what it is on this page, a metaphor for how subjective consciousness seems to subjective consciousness.

But there is a better way to point this out. If you close your left eye and stare at the left margin of this page, you are not at all conscious of a large gap in your vision about four inches to the right. But, still staring with your right eye only, take your finger and move it along a line of print from the left margin to the right, and you will see the top of it disappear into this gap and then reappear on the other side. This is due to a two-millimeter gap on the nasal side of the retina where the optic nerve fibers are gathered together and leave the eye for the brain.[1] The interesting thing about this gap is that it is not so much a blind spot as it is usually called; it is a non-spot. A blind man sees his darkness.[2] But you cannot see any gap in your vision at all, let alone be conscious of it in any way. Just as the space around the blind spots is joined without any gap at all, so consciousness knits itself over its time gaps and gives the illusion of continuity.

Examples of how little we are conscious of our everyday behavior can be multiplied almost anywhere we look. Playing the piano is a really extraordinary example.[3] Here a complex array of various tasks is accomplished all at once with scarcely any consciousness of them whatever: two different lines of near hieroglyphics to be read at once, the right hand guided to one and the left to the other; ten fingers assigned to various tasks, the fingering solving various motor problems without any awareness, and the mind interpreting sharps and flats and naturals into black and white keys, obeying the timing of whole or quarter or sixteenth notes and rests and trills, one hand perhaps in three beats to a measure while the other plays four, while the feet are softening or slurring or holding various other notes. And all this

[1] A better technique of noticing the blind spot is to take two pieces of paper about a half-inch square, and while holding them about a foot and a half in front of you, fixate on one with one eye, and move the other piece of paper out on the same side until it disappears.

[2] Except when the cause of blindness is in the brain. For example, soldiers wounded in one or the other occipital areas of the cortex, with large parts of the visual field destroyed, are not conscious of any alteration in their vision. Looking straight ahead, they have the illusion of seeing a complete visual world, as you or I do.

[3] This example with similar phrasing was used by W. B. Carpenter to illustrate his "unconscious cerebration," probably the first important statement of the idea in the nineteenth century. It was first described in the fourth edition of Carpenter's *Human Physiology* in 1852, but more extensively in his later works, as in his influential *Principles of Mental Physiology* (London: Kegan Paul, 1874), Book 2, Ch. 13.

time the performer, the conscious performer, is in a seventh heaven of artistic rapture at the results of all this tremendous business, or perchance lost in contemplation of the individual who turns the leaves of the music book, justly persuaded he is showing her his very soul! Of course consciousness usually has a role in the learning of such complex activities, but not necessarily in their performance, and that is the only point I am trying to make here.

Consciousness is often not only unnecessary; it can be quite undesirable. Our pianist suddenly conscious of his fingers during a furious set of arpeggios would have to stop playing. Nijinsky somewhere says that when he danced, it was as if he were in the orchestra pit looking back at himself; he was not conscious of every movement, but of how he was looking to others. A sprinter may be conscious of where he is relative to the others in the race, but he is certainly not conscious of putting one leg in front of the other; such consciousness might indeed cause him to trip. And anyone who plays tennis at my indifferent level knows the exasperation of having his service suddenly 'go to pieces' and of serving consecutive double faults! The more doubles, the more conscious one becomes of one's motions (and of one's disposition!) and the worse things get.[4]

Such phenomena of exertion are not to be explained away on the basis of physical excitement, for the same phenomena in regard to consciousness occur in less strenuous occupations. Right at this moment, you are not conscious of how you are sitting, of where your hands are placed, of how fast you are reading, though even as I mentioned these items, you were. And as you read, you are not conscious of the letters or even of the words or even of the syntax or the sentences and punctuation,

[4] The present writer improvises on the piano, and his best playing is when he is not conscious of the performance side as he invents new themes or developments, but only when he is somnambulistic about it and is conscious of his playing only as if he were another person.

but only of their meaning. As you listen to an address, phonemes disappear into words and words into sentences and sentences disappear into what they are trying to say, into meaning. To be conscious of the elements of speech is to destroy the intention of the speech.

And also on the production side. Try speaking with a full consciousness of your articulation as you do it. You will simply stop speaking.

And so in writing, it is as if the pencil or pen or typewriter itself spells the words, spaces them, punctuates properly, goes to the next line, does not begin consecutive sentences in the same way, determines that we place a question here, an exclamation there, even as we ourselves are engrossed in what we are trying to express and the person we are addressing.

For in speaking or writing we are not really conscious of what we are actually doing at the time. Consciousness functions in the decision as to what to say, how we are to say it, and when we say it, but then the orderly and accomplished succession of phonemes or of written letters is somehow done for us.

Consciousness Not a Copy of Experience

Although the metaphor of the blank mind had been used in the writings ascribed to Aristotle, it is really only since John Locke thought of the mind as a *tabula rasa* in the seventeenth century that we have emphasized this recording aspect of consciousness, and thus see it crowded with memories that can be read over again in introspection. If Locke had lived in our time, he would have used the metaphor of a camera rather than a slate. But the idea is the same. And most people would protest emphatically that the chief function of consciousness is to store up experience, to copy it as a camera does, so that it can be reflected upon at some future time.

So it seems. But consider the following problems: Does the

door of your room open from the right or the left? Which is your second longest finger? At a stoplight, is it the red or the green that is on top? How many teeth do you see when brushing your teeth? What letters are associated with what numbers on a telephone dial? If you are in a familiar room, without turning around, write down all the items on the wall just behind you, and then look.

I think you will be surprised how little you can retrospect in consciousness on the supposed images you have stored from so much previous attentive experience. If the familiar door suddenly opened the other way, if another finger suddenly grew longer, if the red light were differently placed, or you had an extra tooth, or the telephone were made differently, or a new window latch had been put on the window behind you, you would know it immediately, showing that you all along '*knew*', but not consciously so. Familiar to psychologists, this is the distinction between recognition and recall. What you can consciously recall is a thimbleful to the huge oceans of your actual knowledge.

Experiments of this sort demonstrate that conscious memory is not a storing up of sensory images, as is sometimes thought. Only if you have at some time consciously noticed your finger lengths or your door, have at some time counted your teeth, though you have observed these things countless times, can you remember. Unless you have particularly noted what is on the wall or recently cleaned or painted it, you will be surprised at what you have left out. And introspect upon the matter. Did you not in each of these instances ask what *must* be there? Starting with ideas and reasoning, rather than with any image? Conscious retrospection is not the retrieval of images, but the retrieval of what you have been conscious of before,[5] and the reworking of these elements into rational or plausible patterns.

* * *

[5] See in this connection the discussion of Robert S. Woodworth in his *Psychological Issues* (New York: Columbia University Press, 1939), Ch. 7.

Let us demonstrate this in another way. Think, if you will, of when you entered the room you are now in and when you picked up this book. Introspect upon it and then ask the question: are the images of which you have copies the actual sensory fields as you came in and sat down and began reading? Don't you have an image of yourself coming through one of the doors, perhaps even a bird's-eye view of one of the entrances, and then perhaps vaguely see yourself sitting down and picking up the book? Things which you have never experienced except in this intro-spection! And can you retrieve the sound fields around the event? Or the cutaneous sensations as you sat, took the pressure off your feet, and opened this book? Of course, if you go on with your thinking you can also rearrange your imaginal retrospection such that you do indeed 'see' entering the room just as it might have been; and 'hear' the sound of the chair and the book open-ing, and 'feel' the skin sensations. But I suggest that this has a large element of created imagery — what we shall call narratiz-ing a little later — of what the experience should be like, rather than what it actually was like.

Or introspect on when you last went swimming: I suspect you have an image of a seashore, lake, or pool which is largely a retrospection, but when it comes to yourself swimming, lo! like Nijinsky in his dance, you are seeing yourself swim, something that you have never observed at all! There is precious little of the actual sensations of swimming, the particular waterline across your face, the feel of the water against your skin, or to what extent your eyes were underwater as you turned your head to breathe.[6] Similarly, if you think of the last time you slept out of doors, went skating, or — if all else fails — did something that you regretted in public, you tend not to see, hear, or feel things as you actually experienced them, but rather to re-create them in objective terms, seeing yourself in the setting as if you were

[6] An example taken from Donald Hebb's provocative discussion, "The mind's eye," *Psychology Today*, 1961, 2.

somebody else. Looking back into memory, then, is a great deal invention, seeing yourself as others see you. Memory is the medium of the must-have-been. Though I have no doubt that in any of these instances you could by inference invent a subjective view of the experience, even with the conviction that it was the actual memory.

Consciousness Not Necessary for Concepts

A further major confusion about consciousness is the belief that it is specifically and uniquely the place where concepts are formed. This is a very ancient idea: that we have various concrete conscious experiences and then put the similar ones together into a concept. This idea has even been the paradigm of a slew of experiments by psychologists who thought they were thus studying concept formation.

Max Müller, in one of his fascinating discussions in the last century, brought the problem to a point by asking, whoever saw a tree? "No one ever saw a tree, but only this or that fir tree, or oak tree, or apple tree . . . Tree, therefore, is a concept, and as such can never be seen or perceived by the senses."[7] Particular trees alone were outside in the environment, and only in consciousness did the general concept of tree exist.

Now the relation between concepts and consciousness could have an extensive discussion. But let it suffice here simply to show that there is no necessary connection between them. When Müller says no one has ever seen *a* tree, he is mistaking what he knows about an object for the object itself. Every weary wayfarer after miles under the hot sun has seen *a* tree. So has every cat, squirrel, and chipmunk when chased by a dog. The bee has a concept of a flower, the eagle a concept of a sheer-faced rocky

[7] Max Müller, *The Science of Thought* (London: Longmans Green, 1887), 78–79. Eugenio Rignano in his *The Psychology of Reasoning* (New York: Harcourt, Brace, 1923), p. 108f., makes a similar criticism to mine.

ledge, as a nesting thrush has a concept of a crotch of upper branch awninged with green leaves. Concepts are simply classes of behaviorally equivalent things. Root concepts are prior to experience. They are fundamental to the aptic structures that allow behavior to occur at all.[8] Indeed what Müller should have said was, no one has ever been *conscious* of *a* tree. For consciousness, indeed, not only is *not* the repository of concepts; it does not usually work with them at all! When we consciously think of *a* tree, we are indeed conscious of a particular tree, of the fir or the oak or the elm that grew beside our house, and let it stand for the concept, just as we can let a concept word stand for it as well. In fact, one of the great functions of language is to let the word stand for a concept, which is exactly what we do in writing or speaking about conceptual material. And we must do this because concepts are usually not in consciousness at all.

Consciousness Not Necessary for Learning

A third important misconception of consciousness is that it is the basis for learning. Particularly for the long and illustrious series of Associationist psychologists through the eighteenth and nineteenth centuries, learning was a matter of ideas in consciousness being grouped by similarity, contiguity, or occasionally some other relationship. Nor did it matter whether we were speaking of a man or an animal; all learning was "profiting from experience" or ideas coming together in consciousness — as I said in the Introduction. And so contemporary common knowledge, without realizing quite why, has culturally inherited the notion that consciousness is necessary for learning.

The matter is somewhat complex. It is also unfortunately

---

[8] *Aptic structures* are the neurological basis of aptitudes that are composed of an innate evolved aptic paradigm plus the results of experience in development. The term is the heart of an unpublished essay of mine and is meant to replace such problematic words as *instincts*. They are organizations of the brain, always partially innate, that make the organism apt to behave in a certain way under certain conditions.

disfigured in psychology by a sometimes forbidding jargon, which is really an overgeneralization of the spinal-reflex terminology of the nineteenth century. But, for our purposes, we may consider the laboratory study of learning to have been of three central kinds, the learning of signals, skills, and solutions. Let us take up each in turn, asking the question, is consciousness necessary?

Signal learning (or classical or Pavlovian conditioning) is the simplest example. If a light signal immediately followed by a puff of air through a rubber tube is directed at a person's eye about ten times, the eyelid, which previously blinked only to the puff of air, will begin to blink to the light signal alone, and this becomes more and more frequent as trials proceed.[9] Subjects who have undergone this well-known procedure of signal learning report that it has no conscious component whatever. Indeed, consciousness, in this example the intrusion of voluntary eye blinks to try to assist the signal learning, blocks it from occurring.

In more everyday situations, the same simple associative learning can be shown to go on without any consciousness that it has occurred. If a distinct kind of music is played while you are eating a particularly delicious lunch, the next time you hear the music you will like its sounds slightly more and even have a little more saliva in your mouth. The music has become a signal for pleasure which mixes with your judgment. And the same is true for paintings.[10] Subjects who have gone through this kind of test in the laboratory, when asked why they liked the music or paintings better after lunch, could not say. They were not conscious they had learned anything. But the really interesting thing here is that if you know about the phenomenon beforehand and

[9] G. A. Kimble, "Conditioning as a function of the time between conditioned and unconditioned stimuli," *Journal of Experimental Psychology*, 1947, 37: 1–15.

[10] These studies are those of Gregory Razran and are discussed on page 232 of his *Mind in Evolution* (Boston: Houghton Mifflin, 1971). They are discussed critically in relation to the whole problem of unintentional learning by T. A. Ryan, *Intentional Behavior* (New York: Ronald Press, 1970), pp. 235–236.

are conscious of the contingency between food and the music or painting, the learning does not occur. Again, consciousness actually *reduces* our learning abilities of this type, let alone not being necessary for them.

As we saw earlier in the performance of skills, so in the learning of skills, consciousness is indeed like a helpless spectator, having little to do. A simple experiment will demonstrate this fact. Take a coin in each hand and toss them both, crossing them in the air in such a way that each coin is caught by the opposite hand. This you can learn in a dozen trials. As you do, ask, are you conscious of everything you do? Is consciousness necessary at all? I think you will find that learning is much better described as being 'organic' rather than conscious. Consciousness takes you into the task, giving you the goal to be reached. But from then on, apart perhaps from fleeting neurotic concerns about your abilities at such tasks, it is as if the learning is done for you. Yet the nineteenth century, taking consciousness to be the whole architect of behavior, would have tried to explain such a task as consciously recognizing the good and bad motions, and by free choice repeating the former and dropping out the latter!

The learning of complex skills is no different in this respect. Typewriting has been extensively studied, it generally being agreed in the words of one experimenter "that all adaptations and short cuts in methods were unconsciously made, that is, fallen into by the learners quite unintentionally. The learners suddenly noticed that they were doing certain parts of the work in a new and better way."[11]

In the coin-tossing experiment, you may have even discovered that consciousness if present impeded your learning. This is a very common finding in the learning of skills, just as we saw it was in their performance. Let the learning go on without your being too conscious of it, and it is all done more smoothly and

[11] W. F. Book, *The Psychology of Skill* (New York: Gregg, 1925).

efficiently. Sometimes too much so, for, in complex skills like typing, one may learn to consistently type 'hte' for 'the'. The remedy is to reverse the process by consciously practicing the mistake 'hte', whereupon contrary to the usual idea of 'practice makes perfect', the mistake drops away — a phenomenon called negative practice.

In the common motor skills studied in the laboratory as well, such as complex pursuit-rotor systems or mirror-tracing, the subjects who are asked to be very conscious of their movements do worse.[12] And athletic trainers whom I have interviewed are unwittingly following such laboratory-proven principles when they urge their trainees not to think so much about what they are doing. The Zen exercise of learning archery is extremely explicit on this, advising the archer not to think of himself as drawing the bow and releasing the arrow, but releasing himself from the consciousness of what he is doing by letting the bow stretch itself and the arrow release itself from the fingers at the proper time.

Solution learning (or instrumental learning or operant conditioning) is a more complex case. Usually when one is acquiring some solution to a problem or some path to a goal, consciousness plays a very considerable role in setting up the problem in a certain way. But consciousness is not necessary. Instances can be shown in which a person has no consciousness whatever of either the goal he is seeking or the solution he is finding to achieve that goal.

Another simple experiment can demonstrate this. Ask someone to sit opposite you and to say words, as many words as he can think of, pausing two or three seconds after each of them for you to write them down. If after every plural noun (or adjective, or abstract word, or whatever you choose) you say "good" or "right" as you write it down, or simply "mmm-hmm" or smile, or repeat the plural word pleasantly, the frequency of plural nouns (or

[12] H. L. Waskom, "An experimental analysis of incentive and forced application and their effect upon learning," *Journal of Psychology*, 1936, 2: 393–408.

whatever) will increase significantly as he goes on saying words. The important thing here is that the subject is not aware that he is learning anything at all.[13] He is not conscious that he is trying to find a way to make you increase your encouraging remarks, or even of his solution to that problem. Every day, in all our conversations, we are constantly training and being trained by each other in this manner, and yet we are never conscious of it.

Such unconscious learning is not confined to verbal behavior. Members of a psychology class were asked to compliment any girl at the college wearing red. Within a week the cafeteria was a blaze of red (and friendliness), and none of the girls was aware of being influenced. Another class, a week after being told about unconscious learning and training, tried it on the professor. Every time he moved toward the right side of the lecture hall, they paid rapt attention and roared at his jokes. It is reported that they were almost able to train him right out the door, he remaining unaware of anything unusual.[14]

The critical problem with most of these studies is that if the subject decided beforehand to look for such contingencies, he would of course be conscious of what he was learning to do. One way to get around this is to use a behavioral response which is imperceptible to the subject. And this has been done, using a very small muscle in the thumb whose movements are imperceptible to us and can only be detected by an electrical recording apparatus. The subjects were told that the experiments were concerned with the effect of intermittent unpleasant noise com-

13 J. Greenspoon, "The reinforcing effect of two spoken sounds on the frequency of two responses," *American Journal of Psychology*, 1955, 68: 409–416. But there is considerable controversy here, particularly in the order and wording of postexperimental questions. There may even be a kind of tacit contract between subject and experimenter. See Robert Rosenthal, *Experimenter Effects in Behavioral Research* (New York: Appleton-Century-Crofts, 1966). In this controversy, I presently agree with Postman that the learning occurs *before* the subject becomes conscious of the reinforcement contingency, and indeed that consciousness would not occur unless this had been so. L. Postman and L. Sassenrath, "The automatic action of verbal rewards and punishment," *Journal of General Psychology*, 1961, 65: 109–136.

14 W. Lambert Gardiner, *Psychology: A Story of a Search* (Belmont, California: Brooks/Cole, 1970), p. 76.

bined with music upon muscle tension. Four electrodes were placed on their bodies, the only real one being the one over the small thumb muscle, the other three being dummy electrodes. The apparatus was so arranged that whenever the imperceptible thumb-muscle twitch was electrically detected, the unpleasant noise was stopped for 15 seconds if it was already sounding, or delayed for 15 seconds if was not turned on at the time of the twitch. In all subjects, the imperceptible thumb twitch that turned off the distressing noise increased in rate without the subjects' being the slightest bit conscious that they were learning to turn off the unpleasant noise.[15]

Thus, consciousness is not a necessary part of the learning process, and this is true whether it be the learning of signals, skills, or solutions. There is, of course, much more to say on this fascinating subject, for the whole thrust of contemporary research in behavior modification is along these lines. But, for the present, we have simply established that the older doctrine that conscious experience is the substrate of all learning is clearly and absolutely false. At this point, we can at least conclude that it is possible — possible I say — to conceive of human beings who are not conscious and yet can learn and solve problems.

Consciousness Not Necessary for Thinking

As we go from simple to more complicated aspects of mentality, we enter vaguer and vaguer territory, where the terms we use become more difficult to travel with. Thinking is certainly one of these. And to say that consciousness is not necessary for thinking makes us immediately bristle with protest. Surely thinking is the very heart and bone of consciousness! But let us go slowly

[15] R. F. Hefferline, B. Keenan, R. A. Harford, "Escape and avoidance conditioning in human subjects without their observation of the response," *Science*, 1959, 130: 1338–1339. Another study which shows unconscious solution learning very clearly is that of J. D. Keehn: "Experimental Studies of the Unconscious: operant conditioning of unconscious eye blinking," *Behavior Research and Therapy*, 1967, 5: 95–102.

here. What we would be referring to would be that type of free associating which might be called thinking-about or thinking-of, which, indeed, always seems to be fully surrounded and immersed in the image-peopled province of consciousness. But the matter is really not that clear at all.

Let us begin with the type of thinking that ends in a result to which may be predicated the terms right or wrong. This is what is commonly referred to as making judgments, and is very similar to one extreme of solution learning that we have just discussed.

A simple experiment, so simple as to seem trivial, will bring us directly to the heart of the matter. Take any two unequal objects, such as a pen and pencil or two unequally filled glasses of water, and place them on the desk in front of you. Then, partly closing your eyes to increase your attention to the task, pick up each one with the thumb and forefinger and judge which is heavier. Now introspect on everything you are doing. You will find yourself conscious of the feel of the objects against the skin of your fingers, conscious of the slight downward pressure as you feel the weight of each, conscious of any protuberances on the sides of the objects, and so forth. And now the actual judging of which is heavier. Where is that? Lo! the very act of judgment that one object is heavier than the other is not conscious. It is somehow just given to you by your nervous system. If we call that process of judgment thinking, we are finding that such thinking is not conscious at all. A simple experiment, yes, but extremely important. It demolishes at once the entire tradition that such thought processes are the structure of the conscious mind.

This type of experiment came to be studied extensively back at the beginning of this century in what came to be known as the Würzburg School. It all began with a study by Karl Marbe in 1901, which was very similar to the above, except that small weights were used.[16] The subject was asked to lift two weights

---

[16] K. Marbe, *Experimentell-Psychologische Untersuchungen uber das Urteil, eine Einleitung in die Logik* (Leipzig: Engelmann, 1901).

in front of him, and place the one that was heavier in front of the experimenter, who was facing him. And it came as a startling discovery both to the experimenter himself and to his highly trained subjects, all of them introspective psychologists, that the process of judgment itself was never conscious. Physics and psychology always show interesting contrasts, and it is one of the ironies of science that the Marbe experiment, so simple as to seem silly, was to psychology what the so-difficult-to-set-up Michaelson-Morley experiment was to physics. Just as the latter proved that the ether, that substance supposed to exist throughout space, did not exist, so the weight-judgment experiment showed that judging, that supposed hallmark of consciousness, did not exist in consciousness at all.

But a complaint can be lodged here. Maybe in lifting the objects the judging was all happening so fast that we forgot it. After all, in introspecting we always have hundreds of words to describe what happens in a few seconds. (What an astonishing fact that is!) And our memory fades as to what just happened even as we are trying to express it. Perhaps this was what was occurring in Marbe's experiment, and that type of thinking called judging could be found in consciousness, after all, if we could only remember.

This was the problem as Watt faced it a few years after Marbe.[17] To solve it, he used a different method, word associations. Nouns printed on cards were shown to the subject, who was to reply by uttering an associate word as quickly as he could. It was not free association, but what is technically called partially constrained: in different series the subject was required to associate to the visual word a superordinate (e.g., oak-tree), coordinate (oak-elm), or subordinate (oak-beam); or a whole (oak-forest), a part (oak-acorn), or another part of a common whole

[17] H. J. Watt, "Experimentelle Beitrage zur einer Theorie des Denkens," *Archiv für geschite der Psychologie,* 1905, 4: 289–436.

(oak-path). The nature of this task of constrained associations made it possible to divide the consciousness of it into four periods: the instructions as to which of the constraints it was to be (e.g., superordinate), the presentation of the stimulus noun (e.g., oak), the search for an appropriate association, and the spoken reply (e.g., tree). The introspecting observers were asked to confine themselves first to one period and then to another, and thus get a more accurate account of consciousness in each.

It was expected that the precision of this fractionation method would prove Marbe's conclusions wrong, and that the consciousness of thinking would be found in Watt's third period, the period of the search for the word that would suit the particular constrained association. But nothing of the sort happened. It was the third period that was introspectively blank. What seemed to be happening was that thinking was automatic and not really conscious once a stimulus word had been given, and, previous to that, the particular type of association demanded had been adequately understood by the observer. This was a remarkable result. Another way of saying it is that *one does one's thinking before one knows what one is to think about.* The important part of the matter is the instruction, which allows the whole business to go off automatically. This I shall shorten to the term *struction*, by which I mean it to have the connotation of both instruction and construction.[18]

Thinking, then, is not conscious. Rather, it is an automatic process following a struction and the materials on which the struction is to operate.

But we do not have to stay with verbal associations; any type of problem will do, even those closer to voluntary actions. If I say to

[18] The terms *set, determining tendency,* and *struction* need to be distinguished. A set is the more inclusive term, being an engaged aptic structure which in mammals can be ordered from a general limbic component of readiness to a specific cortical component of a determining tendency, the final part of which in humans is often a struction.

myself, I shall think about an oak in summer, that is a struction, and what I call thinking about is really a file of associated images cast up on the shores of my consciousness out of an unknown sea, just like the constrained associations in Watt's experiment.

If we have the figures 6 and 2, divided by a vertical line, 6|2, the ideas produced by such a stimulus will be eight, four, or three, according to whether the struction prescribed is addition, subtraction, or division. The important thing is that the struction itself, the process of addition, subtraction, or division, disappears into the nervous system once it is given. But it is obviously there 'in the mind' since the same stimulus can result in any of three different responses. And that is something we are not in the least aware of, once it is put in motion.

Suppose we have a series of figures such as the following:

What is the next figure in this series? How did you arrive at your answer? Once I have given you the struction, you automatically 'see' that it is to be another triangle. I submit that if you try to introspect on the process by which you came up with the answer you are not truly retrieving the processes involved, but inventing what you think they must have been by giving yourself another struction to that effect. In the task itself, all you were really conscious of was the struction, the figures before you on the page, and then the solution.

Nor is this different from the case of speech which I mentioned earlier. When we speak, we are not really conscious either of the search for words, or of putting the words together into phrases, or of putting the phrases into sentences. We are only conscious of the ongoing series of structions that we give ourselves, which then, automatically, without any consciousness whatever, result in speech. The speech itself we can be conscious of as it is produced if we wish, thus giving some feedback to result in further structions.

So we arrive at the position that the actual process of thinking, so usually thought to be the very life of consciousness, is not conscious at all and that only its preparation, its materials, and its end result are consciously perceived.

Consciousness Not Necessary for Reason

The long tradition of man as the rational animal, the tradition that enthroned him as *Homo sapiens,* rests in all its pontifical generality on the gracile assumption that consciousness is the seat of reason. Any discussion of such an assumption is embarrassed by the vagueness of the term reason itself. This vagueness is the legacy we have from an older 'faculty' psychology that spoke of a 'faculty' of reason, which was of course situated 'in' consciousness. And this forced deposition of reason and consciousness was further confused with ideas of truth, of how we ought to reason, or logic — all quite different things. And hence logic was supposed to be the structure of conscious reason confounding generations of poor scholars who knew perfectly well that syllogisms were not what was on their side of introspection.

Reasoning and logic are to each other as health is to medicine, or — better — as conduct is to morality. Reasoning refers to a gamut of natural thought processes in the everyday world. Logic is how we ought to think if objective truth is our goal — and the everyday world is very little concerned with objective truth. Logic is the science of the justification of conclusions we have reached by natural reasoning. My point here is that, for such natural reasoning to occur, consciousness is not necessary. The very reason we need logic at all is because most reasoning is not conscious at all.

Consider to begin with the many phenomena we have already established as going on without consciousness which can be called elementary kinds of reasoning. Choosing paths, words, notes, motions, the perceptual corrections in size and color constancies — all are primitive kinds of reasoning that go on without any prod, nudge, or even glance of consciousness.

Even the more standard types of reasoning can occur without consciousness. A boy, having observed on one or more past occasions that a particular piece of wood floats on a particular pond, will conclude directly in a new instance that another piece of wood will float on another pond. There is no collecting together of past instances in consciousness, and no necessary conscious process whatever when the new piece of wood is seen directly as floating on the new pond. This is sometimes called reasoning from particulars, and is simply expectation based on generalization. Nothing particularly extraordinary. It is an ability common to all the higher vertebrates. Such reasoning is the structure of the nervous system, not the structure of consciousness.

But more complex reasoning without consciousness is continually going on. Our minds work much faster than consciousness can keep up with. We commonly make general assertions based on our past experiences in an automatic way, and only as an afterthought are we sometimes able to retrieve any of the past experiences on which an assertion is based. How often we reach sound conclusions and are quite unable to justify them! Because reasoning is not conscious. And consider the kind of reasoning that we do about others' feelings and character, or in reasoning out the motives of others from their actions. These are clearly the result of automatic inferences by our nervous systems in which consciousness is not only unnecessary, but, as we have seen in the performance of motor skills, would probably hinder the process.[19]

Surely, we exclaim, this cannot be true of the highest processes of intellectual thought! Surely there at last we will come to

[19] Such instances were early recognized as not conscious and were called "automatic inference" or "common sense." Discussions can be found in Sully, Mill, and other nineteenth-century psychologists.

the very empire of consciousness, where all is spread out in a golden clarity and all the orderly processes of reason go on in a full publicity of awareness. But the truth has no such grandeur. The picture of a scientist sitting down with his problems and using conscious induction and deduction is as mythical as a unicorn. The greatest insights of mankind have come more mysteriously. Helmholtz had his happy thoughts which "often enough crept quietly into my thinking without my suspecting their importance . . . in other cases they arrived suddenly, without any effort on my part . . . they liked especially to make their appearance while I was taking an easy walk over wooded hills in sunny weather!"[20]

And Gauss, referring to an arithmetical theorem which he had unsuccessfully tried to prove for years, wrote how "like a sudden flash of lightning, the riddle happened to be solved. I myself cannot say what was the conducting thread which connected what I previously knew with what made my success possible."[21]

And the brilliant mathematician Poincaré was particularly interested in the manner in which he came upon his own discoveries. In a celebrated lecture at the Société de Psychologie in Paris, he described how he set out on a geologic excursion: "The incidents of the journey made me forget my mathematical work. Having reached Coutances, we entered an omnibus to go some place or other. At the moment when I put my foot on the step, the idea came to me, without anything in my former thoughts seeming to have paved the way for it, the transformation I had used to define the Fuchsian functions were identical with those of non-Euclidian geometry!"[22]

It does seem that it is in the more abstract sciences, where the materials of scrutiny are less and less interfered with by everyday

[20] As quoted by Robert S. Woodworth, *Experimental Psychology* (New York: Holt, 1938), p. 818.

[21] As quoted by Jacques Hadamard, *The Psychology of Invention in the Mathematical Field* (Princeton: Princeton University Press, 1945), p. 15.

[22] Henri Poincaré, "Mathematical creation," in his *The Foundations of Science*, G. Bruce Halsted, trans. (New York: The Science Press, 1913), p. 387.

experience, that this business of sudden flooding insights is most obvious. A close friend of Einstein's has told me that many of the physicist's greatest ideas came to him so suddenly while he was shaving that he had to move the blade of the straight razor very carefully each morning, lest he cut himself with surprise. And a well-known physicist in Britain once told Wolfgang Köhler, "We often talk about the three B's, the Bus, the Bath, and the Bed. That is where the great discoveries are made in our science."

The essential point here is that there are several stages of creative thought: first, a stage of preparation in which the problem is consciously worked over; then a period of incubation without any conscious concentration upon the problem; and then the illumination which is later justified by logic. The parallel between these important and complex problems and the simple problems of judging weights or the circle-triangle series is obvious. The period of preparation is essentially the setting up of a complex struction together with conscious attention to the materials on which the struction is to work. But then the actual process of reasoning, the dark leap into huge discovery, just as in the simple trivial judgment of weights, has no representation in consciousness. Indeed, it is sometimes almost as if the problem had to be forgotten to be solved.

The Location of Consciousness

The final fallacy which I wish to discuss is both important and interesting, and I have left it for the last because I think it deals the coup de grâce to the everyman theory of consciousness. Where does consciousness take place?

Everyone, or almost everyone, immediately replies, in my head. This is because when we introspect, we seem to look inward on an inner space somewhere behind our eyes. But what on earth do we mean by 'look'? We even close our eyes sometimes to introspect even more clearly. Upon what? Its spatial character seems unquestionable. Moreover we seem to move or at least 'look' in different directions. And if we press ourselves too strongly to further characterize this space (apart from its imagined contents), we feel a vague irritation, as if there were something that did not want to be known, some quality which to question was somehow ungrateful, like rudeness in a friendly place.

We not only locate this space of consciousness inside our own heads. We also assume it is there in others'. In talking with a friend, maintaining periodic eye-to-eye contact (that remnant of our primate past when eye-to-eye contact was concerned in establishing tribal hierarchies), we are always assuming a space behind our companion's eyes into which we are talking, similar to the space we imagine inside our own heads where we are talking from.

And this is the very heartbeat of the matter. For we know perfectly well that there is no such space in anyone's head at all! There is nothing inside my head or yours except physiological tissue of one sort or another. And the fact that it is predominantly neurological tissue is irrelevant.

Now this thought takes a little thinking to get used to. It means that we are continually inventing these spaces in our own and other people's heads, knowing perfectly well that they don't exist anatomically; and the location of these 'spaces' is indeed quite arbitrary. The Aristotelian writings,[23] for example, located consciousness or the abode of thought in and just above the heart, believing the brain to be a mere cooling organ since it was insensitive to touch or injury. And some readers will not have found this discussion valid since they locate their thinking selves somewhere in the upper chest. For most of us, however, the habit of locating consciousness in the head is so ingrained that it

---

[23] It is so obvious that the writings ascribed to Aristotle were not written by the same hand that I prefer this designation.

is difficult to think otherwise. But, actually, you could, as you remain where you are, just as well locate your consciousness around the corner in the next room against the wall near the floor, and do your thinking there as well as in your head. Not really just as well. For there are very good reasons why it is better to imagine your mind-space inside of you, reasons to do with volition and internal sensations, with the relationship of your body and your 'I' which will become apparent as we go on.

That there is no phenomenal necessity in locating consciousness in the brain is further reinforced by various abnormal instances in which consciousness seems to be outside the body. A friend who received a left frontal brain injury in the war regained consciousness in the corner of the ceiling of a hospital ward looking down euphorically at himself on the cot swathed in bandages. Those who have taken lysergic acid diethylamide commonly report similar out-of-the-body or exosomatic experiences, as they are called. Such occurrences do not demonstrate anything metaphysical whatever; simply that locating consciousness can be an arbitrary matter.

Let us not make a mistake. When I am conscious, I am always and definitely using certain parts of my brain inside my head. But so am I when riding a bicycle, and the bicycle riding does not go on inside my head. The cases are different of course, since bicycle riding has a definite geographical location, while consciousness does not. In reality, consciousness has no location whatever except as we imagine it has.

Is Consciousness Necessary?

Let us review where we are, for we have just found our way through an enormous amount of ramous material which may have seemed more perplexing than clarifying. We have been brought to the conclusion that consciousness is not what we generally think it is. It is not to be confused with reactivity. It is not involved in hosts of perceptual phenomena. It is not involved in the performance of skills and often hinders their execution. It need not be involved in speaking, writing, listening, or reading. It does not copy down experience, as most people think. Consciousness is not at all involved in signal learning, and need not be involved in the learning of skills or solutions, which can go on without any consciousness whatever. It is not necessary for making judgments or in simple thinking. It is not the seat of reason, and indeed some of the most difficult instances of creative reasoning go on without any attending consciousness. And it has no location except an imaginary one! The immediate question therefore is, does consciousness exist at all? But that is the problem of the next chapter. Here it is only necessary to conclude that consciousness does not make all that much difference to a lot of our activities. If our reasonings have been correct, it is perfectly possible that there could have existed a race of men who spoke, judged, reasoned, solved problems, indeed did most of the things that we do, but who were not conscious at all. This is the important and in some ways upsetting notion that we are forced to conclude at this point. Indeed I have begun in this fashion, and place great importance on this opening chapter, for unless you are here convinced that a civilization without consciousness is possible, you will find the discussion that follows unconvincing and paradoxical.

CHAPTER 2

Consciousness

T HUS HAVING CHISELED away some of the major misconceptions about consciousness, what then have we left? If consciousness is not all these things, if it is not so extensive as we think, not a copy of experience, or the necessary locus of learning, judgment, or even thought, what is it? And as we stare into the dust and rubble of the last chapter, hoping Pygmalion-like to see consciousness newly step forth pure and pristine out of the detritus, let us ramble out and around the subject a little way as the dust settles, talking of different things.

Metaphor and Language

Let us speak of metaphor. The most fascinating property of language is its capacity to make metaphors. But what an understatement! For metaphor is not a mere extra trick of language, as it is so often slighted in the old schoolbooks on composition; it is the very constitutive ground of language. I am using metaphor here in its most general sense: the use of a term for one thing to describe another because of some kind of similarity between them or between their relations to other things. There are thus always two terms in a metaphor, the thing to be described, which I shall call the *metaphrand*, and the thing or relation used to elucidate it, which I shall call the *metaphier*. A metaphor is always a known metaphier operating on a less known metaphrand.[1] I have coined these hybrid terms simply to echo multiplication where a multiplier operates on a multiplicand.

It is by metaphor that language grows. The common reply to the question "what is it?" is, when the reply is difficult or the experience unique, "well, it is like — ." In laboratory studies, both children and adults describing nonsense objects (or metaphrands) to others who cannot see them use extended metaphiers that with repetition become contracted into labels.[2] This is the major way in which the vocabulary of language is formed. The grand and vigorous function of metaphor is the generation of new language as it is needed, as human culture becomes more and more complex.

A random glance at the etymologies of common words in a dictionary will demonstrate this assertion. Or take the naming of various fauna and flora in their Latin indicants, or even in their wonderful common English names, such as stag beetle, lady's-slipper, darning needle, Queen Anne's lace, or buttercup. The human body is a particularly generative metaphier, creating previously unspeakable distinctions in a throng of areas. The *head* of an army, table, page, bed, ship, household, or nail, or of steam or water; the *face* of a clock, cliff, card, or crystal; the *eyes* of needles, winds, storms, targets, flowers, or potatoes; the *brow* of a hill; the *cheeks* of a vise; the *teeth* of cogs or combs; the *lips* of pitchers, craters, augers; the *tongues* of shoes, boardjoints, or railway switches; the *arm* of a chair or the sea; the *leg* of a table, compass, sailor's voyage, or cricket field; and so on and on. Or

[1] This distinction is not connotatively the same as I. A. Richards' 'tenor' and 'vehicle'. See his *Philosophy of Rhetoric* (New York: Oxford University Press, 1936), pp. 96, 120–121. Nor as Christine Brooke-Rose's 'proper' and 'metaphor' terms, both of which make the matter too literary. See her *A Grammar of Metaphor* (London: Secker and Warburg, 1958), the first chapter of which is a good historical introduction to the subject.

[2] See S. Glucksberg, R. M. Krauss, and R. Weisberg, "Referential communication in nursery school children: Method and some preliminary findings," *Journal of Experimental Child Psychology*, 1966, 3: 333–342.

the *foot* of this page. Or the *leaf* you will soon turn. All of these concrete metaphors increase enormously our powers of perception of the world about us and our understanding of it, and literally create new objects. Indeed, language is an organ of perception, not simply a means of communication.

This is language moving out synchronically (or without reference to time) into the space of the world to describe it and perceive it more and more definitively. But language also moves in another and more important way, diachronically, or through time, and behind our experiences on the basis of aptic structures in our nervous systems to create abstract concepts whose referents are not observables except in a metaphorical sense. And these too are generated by metaphor. This is indeed the nub (knob), heart, pith, kernel, core, marrow, etc. of my argument, which itself is a metaphor and 'seen' only with the mind's 'eye'.

In the abstractions of human relations, the skin becomes a particularly important metaphier. We get or stay 'in touch' with others who may be 'thick-' or 'thin-skinned' or perhaps 'touchy' in which case they have to be 'handled' carefully lest we 'rub' them the wrong way; we may have a 'feeling' for another person with whom we may have a 'touching' experience.[3]

The concepts of science are all of this kind, abstract concepts generated by concrete metaphors. In physics, we have force, acceleration (to increase one's steps), inertia (originally an indolent person), impedance, resistance, fields, and now charm. In physiology, the metaphier of a machine has been at the very center of discovery. We understand the brain by metaphors to everything from batteries and telegraphy to computers and holograms. Medical practice is sometimes dictated by metaphor. In the eighteenth century, the heart in fever was like a boiling pot, and so bloodletting was prescribed to reduce its fuel. And even today, a great deal of medicine is based upon the military meta-

[3] See Ashley Montagu, *Touching* (New York: Columbia University Press, 1971).

phor of defense of the body against attacks of this or that. The very concept of law in Greek derives from *nomos*, the word for the foundations of a building. To be liable, or bound in law, comes from the Latin *ligare*, meaning to bind with cord.

In early times, language and its referents climbed up from the concrete to the abstract on the steps of metaphors, even, we may say, created the abstract on the bases of metaphors.

It is not always obvious that metaphor has played this all-important function. But this is because the concrete metaphiers become hidden in phonemic change, leaving the words to exist on their own. Even such an unmetaphorical-sounding word as the verb 'to be' was generated from a metaphor. It comes from the Sanskrit *bhu*, "to grow, or make grow," while the English forms 'am' and 'is' have evolved from the same root as the Sanskrit *asmi*, "to breathe." It is something of a lovely surprise that the irregular conjugation of our most nondescript verb is thus a record of a time when man had no independent word for 'existence' and could only say that something 'grows' or that it "breathes."[4] Of course we are not conscious that the concept of being is thus generated from a metaphor about growing and breathing. Abstract words are ancient coins whose concrete images in the busy give-and-take of talk have worn away with use.

Because in our brief lives we catch so little of the vastnesses of history, we tend too much to think of language as being solid as a dictionary, with a granite-like permanence, rather than as the rampant restless sea of metaphor which it is. Indeed, if we consider the changes in vocabulary that have occurred over the last few millennia, and project them several millennia hence, an interesting paradox arises. For if we ever achieve a language that has the power of expressing everything, then metaphor will

[4] A paraphrase of Phillip Wheelwright in his *The Burning Fountain* (Bloomington: Indiana University Press, 1954).

no longer be possible. I would not say, in that case, my love is like a red, red rose, for love would have exploded into terms for its thousands of nuances, and applying the correct term would leave the rose metaphorically dead.

The lexicon of language, then, is a finite set of terms that by metaphor is able to stretch out over an infinite set of circumstances, even to creating new circumstances thereby.

(Could consciousness be such a new creation?)

Understanding as Metaphor

We are trying to understand consciousness, but what are we really trying to do when we try to understand anything? Like children trying to describe nonsense objects, so in trying to understand a thing we are trying to find a metaphor for that thing. Not just any metaphor, but one with something more familiar and easy to our attention. Understanding a thing is to arrive at a metaphor for that thing by substituting something more familiar to us. And the feeling of familiarity is the feeling of understanding.

Generations ago we would understand thunderstorms perhaps as the roaring and rumbling about in battle of superhuman gods. We would have reduced the racket that follows the streak of lightning to familiar battle sounds, for example. Similarly today, we reduce the storm to various supposed experiences with friction, sparks, vacuums, and the imagination of bulgeous banks of burly air smashing together to make the noise. None of these really exist as we picture them. Our images of these events of physics are as far from the actuality as fighting gods. Yet they act as the metaphor and they feel familiar and so we say we understand the thunderstorm.

So, in other areas of science, we say we understand an aspect of nature when we can say it is similar to some familiar theoretical model. The terms theory and model, incidentally, are sometimes used interchangeably. But really they should not be. A theory is a relationship of the model to the things the model is supposed to represent. The Bohr model of the atom is that of a proton surrounded by orbiting electrons. It is something like the pattern of the solar system, and that is indeed one of its metaphoric sources. Bohr's *theory* was that all atoms were similar to his *model*. The theory, with the more recent discovery of new particles and complicated interatomic relationships, has turned out not to be true. But the model remains. A model is neither true nor false; only the theory of its similarity to what it represents.

A theory is thus a metaphor between a model and data. And understanding in science is the feeling of similarity between complicated data and a familiar model.

If understanding a thing is arriving at a familiarizing metaphor for it, then we can see that there always will be a difficulty in understanding consciousness. For it should be immediately apparent that there is not and cannot be anything in our immediate experience that is like immediate experience itself. There is therefore a sense in which we shall never be able to understand consciousness in the same way that we can understand things that we are conscious of.

Most of the errors about consciousness that we have been studying have been errors of attempted metaphors. We spoke of the notion of consciousness being a copy of experience coming out of the explicit metaphor of a schoolboy's slate. But of course no one really meant consciousness copies experience; it was as if it did. And we found on analysis, of course, that it did no such thing.

And even the idea behind that last phrase, that consciousness does anything at all, even that is a metaphor. It is saying that consciousness is a person behaving in physical space who does things, and this is true only if 'does' is a metaphor as well. For to *do* things is some kind of behavior in a physical world by a living body. And also in what 'space' is the metaphorical 'doing' being done? (Some of the dust is beginning to settle.) This 'space' too must be a metaphor of real space. All of which is reminiscent of our discussion of the location of consciousness, also a metaphor. Consciousness is being thought of as a thing, and so like other things must have a location, which, as we saw earlier, it does not actually have in the physical sense.

I realize that my argument here is becoming fairly dense. But before coming out into the clearing, I wish to describe what I shall mean by the term *analog*. An analog is a model, but a model of a special kind. It is not like a scientific model, whose source may be anything at all and whose purpose is to act as an hypothesis of explanation or understanding. Instead, an analog is at every point generated by the thing it is an analog of. A map is a good example. It is not a model in the scientific sense, not a hypothetical model like the Bohr atom to explain something unknown. Instead, it is constructed from something well known, if not completely known. Each region of a district of land is allotted a corresponding region on the map, though the materials of land and map are absolutely different and a large proportion of the features of the land have to be left out. And the relation between an analog map and its land is a metaphor. If I point to a location on a map and say, "There is Mont Blanc and from Chamonix we can reach the east face this way," that is really a shorthand way of saying, "The relations between the point labeled 'Mont Blanc' and other points is similar to the actual Mont Blanc and its neighboring regions."

The Metaphor Language of Mind

I think it is apparent now, at least dimly, what is emerging from the debris of the previous chapter. I do not now feel myself proving my thesis to you step by step, so much as arranging in your mind certain notions so that, at the very least, you will not be immediately estranged from the point I am about to make. My procedure here in what I realize is a difficult and overtly diffuse part of this book is to simply state in general terms my conclusion and then clarify what it implies.

Subjective conscious mind is an analog of what is called the real world. It is built up with a vocabulary or lexical field whose terms are all metaphors or analogs of behavior in the physical world. Its reality is of the same order as mathematics. It allows us to shortcut behavioral processes and arrive at more adequate decisions. Like mathematics, it is an operator rather than a thing or repository. And it is intimately bound up with volition and decision.

Consider the language we use to describe conscious processes. The most prominent group of words used to describe mental events are visual. We 'see' solutions to problems, the best of which may be 'brilliant', and the person 'brighter' and 'clear-headed' as opposed to 'dull', 'fuzzy-minded', or 'obscure' solutions. These words are all metaphors and the mind-space to which they apply is a metaphor of actual space. In it we can 'approach' a problem, perhaps from some 'viewpoint', and 'grapple' with its difficulties, or seize together or 'com-prehend' parts of a problem, and so on, using metaphors of behavior to invent things to do in this metaphored mind-space.

And the adjectives to describe physical behavior in real space are analogically taken over to describe mental behavior in mind-space when we speak of our minds as being 'quick,' 'slow', 'agitated' (as when we cogitate or co-agitate), 'nimble-witted', 'strong-' or 'weak-minded.' The mind-space in which these metaphorical activities go on has its own group of adjectives; we can be 'broad-minded', 'deep', 'open', or 'narrow-minded'; we can be 'occupied'; we can 'get something off our minds', 'put something out of mind', or we can 'get it', let something 'penetrate', or 'bear', 'have', 'keep', or 'hold' it in mind.

As with a real space, something can be at the 'back' of our

mind, in its 'inner recesses', or 'beyond' our mind, or 'out' of our mind. In argument we try to 'get things through' to someone, to 'reach' their 'understanding' or find a 'common ground', or 'point out', etc., all actions in real space taken over analogically into the space of the mind.

But what is it we are making a metaphor of? We have seen that the usual function of metaphor is a wish to designate a particular aspect of a thing or to describe something for which words are not available. That thing to be designated, described, expressed, or lexically widened is what we have called the metaphrand. We operate upon this by some similar, more familiar thing, called a metaphier. Originally, of course, the purpose was intensely practical, to designate an arm of the sea as a better place for shellfish, or to put a head on a nail that it might better hold a board to a stanchion. The metaphiers here were arm and head, and the metaphrands a particular part of the sea and particular end of the nail that already existed. Now when we say mind-space is a metaphor of real space, it is the real 'external' world that is the metaphier. But if metaphor generates consciousness rather than simply describes it, what is the metaphrand?

Paraphiers and Paraphrands

If we look more carefully at the nature of metaphor (noticing all the while the metaphorical nature of almost everything we are saying), we find (even the verb "find"!) that it is composed of more than a metaphier and a metaphrand. There are also at the bottom of most complex metaphors various associations or attributes of the metaphier which I am going to call *paraphiers*. And these paraphiers project back into the metaphrand as what I shall call the *paraphrands* of the metaphrand. Jargon, yes, but absolutely necessary if we are to be crystal clear about our referents.

Some examples will show that the unraveling of metaphor into these four parts is really quite simple, as well as clarifying what otherwise we could not speak about.

Consider the metaphor that the snow blankets the ground. The metaphrand is something about the completeness and even thickness with which the ground is covered by snow. The metaphier is a blanket on a bed. But the pleasing nuances of this metaphor are in the paraphiers of the metaphier, blanket. These are something about warmth, protection, and slumber until some period of awakening. These associations of blanket then automatically become the associations or paraphrands of the original metaphrand, the way the snow covers the ground. And we thus have created by this metaphor the idea of the earth sleeping and protected by the snow cover until its awakening in spring. All this is packed into the simple use of the word 'blanket' to pertain to the way snow covers the ground.

Not all metaphors, of course, have such generative potential. In that often-cited one that a ship plows the sea, the metaphrand is the particular action of the bow of the ship through the water, and the metaphier is plowing action. The correspondence is exact. And that is the end of it.

But if I say the brook sings through the woods, the similarity of the metaphrand of the brook's bubbling and gurgling and the metaphier of (presumably) a child singing is not at all exact. It is the paraphiers of joy and dancingness becoming the paraphrands of the brook that are of interest.

Or in the many-poemed comparison of love to a rose, it is not the tenuous correspondence of metaphrand and metaphier but the paraphrands that engage us, that love lives in the sun, smells sweet, has thorns when grasped, and blooms for a season only. Or suppose I say less visually and so more profoundly something quite opposite, that my love is like a tinsmith's scoop, sunk past its gleam in the meal-bin.[5] The immediate correspondence here

[5] From "Mossbawn (for Mary Heaney)" by Seumas Heaney, *North* (London: Faber, 1974).

of metaphrand and metaphier, of being out of casual sight, is trivial. Instead, it is the paraphrands of this metaphor which create what could not possibly be there, the enduring careful shape and hidden shiningness and holdingness of a lasting love deep in the heavy manipulable softnesses of mounding time, the whole simulating (and so paraphranding) sexual intercourse from a male point of view. Love has not such properties except as we generate them by metaphor.

Of such poetry is consciousness made. This can be seen if we return to some of the metaphors of mind we have earlier looked at. Suppose we are trying to solve some simple problem such as the circle-triangle series in the previous chapter. And suppose we express the fact that we have obtained the solution by exclaiming that at last we 'see' what the answer is, namely, a triangle.

This metaphor may be analyzed just as the blanket of snow or the singing brook. The metaphrand is obtaining the solution, the metaphier is sight with the eyes, and the paraphiers are all those things associated with vision that then create paraphrands, such as the mind's 'eye', 'seeing the solution *clearly*', etc., and, most important, the paraphrand of a 'space' in which the 'seeing' is going on, or what I am calling mind-space, and 'objects' to 'see.'

I do not mean this brief sketch to stand in for a real theory of how consciousness was generated in the first place. That problem we shall come to in Book II. Rather I intend only to suggest the possibility that I hope to make plausible later, that consciousness is the work of lexical metaphor. It is spun out of the concrete metaphiers of expression and their paraphiers, projecting paraphrands that exist only in the functional sense. Moreover, it goes on generating itself, each new paraphrand capable of being a metaphrand on its own, resulting in new metaphiers with their paraphiers, and so on.

Of course this process is not and cannot be as haphazard as I am making it sound. The world is organized, highly organized, and the concrete metaphiers that are generating consciousness thus generate consciousness in an organized way. Hence the similarity of consciousness and the physical-behavioral world we are conscious of. And hence the structure of that world is echoed — though with certain differences — in the structure of consciousness.

One last complication before going on. A cardinal property of an analog is that the way it is generated is not the way it is used — obviously. The map-maker and map-user are doing two different things. For the map-maker, the metaphrand is the blank piece of paper on which he operates with the metaphier of the land he knows and has surveyed. But for the map-user, it is just the other way around. The land is unknown; it is the land that is the metaphrand, while the metaphier is the map which he is using, by which he understands the land.

And so with consciousness. Consciousness is the metaphrand when it is being generated by the paraphrands of our verbal expressions. But the functioning of consciousness is, as it were, the return journey. Consciousness becomes the metaphier full of our past experience, constantly and selectively operating on such unknowns as future actions, decisions, and partly remembered pasts, on what we are and yet may be. And it is by the generated structure of consciousness that we then understand the world.

What kinds of things can we say about that structure? Here I shall briefly allude to only the most important.

The Features of Consciousness

1. *Spatialization.* The first and most primitive aspect of consciousness is what we already have had occasion to refer to, the paraphrand of almost every mental metaphor we can make, the mental space which we take over as the very habitat of it all. If I ask you to think of your head, then your feet, then the breakfast

you had this morning, and then the Tower of London, and then the constellation of Orion, these things have the quality of being spatially separated; and it is this quality I am here referring to. When we introspect (a metaphor of seeing into something), it is upon this metaphorical mind-space which we are constantly renewing and 'enlarging' with each new thing or relation consciousized.

In Chapter 1, we spoke of how we invent mind-space inside our own heads as well as the heads of others. The word invent is perhaps too strong except in the ontological sense. We rather assume these 'spaces' without question. They are a part of what it is to be conscious and what it is to assume consciousness in others.

Moreover, things that in the physical-behavioral world do not have a spatial quality are made to have such in consciousness. Otherwise we cannot be conscious of them. This we shall call spatialization.

Time is an obvious example. If I ask you to think of the last hundred years, you may have a tendency to excerpt the matter in such a way that the succession of years is spread out, probably from left to right. But of course there is no left or right in time. There is only before and after, and these do not have any spatial properties whatever — except by analog. You cannot, absolutely cannot think of time except by spatializing it. Consciousness is always a spatialization in which the diachronic is turned into the synchronic, in which what has happened in time is excerpted and seen in side-by-sideness.

This spatialization is characteristic of all conscious thought. If you are now thinking of where in all the theories of mind my particular theory fits, you are first habitually 'turning' to your mind-space where abstract things can be 'separated out' and 'put beside' each other to be 'looked at' — as could never happen physically or in actuality. You then make the metaphor of theories as concrete objects, then the metaphor of a temporal succession of such objects as a synchronic array, and thirdly, the metaphor of the characteristics of theories as physical character- istics, all of some degree so they can be 'arranged' in a kind of order. And you then make the further expressive metaphor of 'fit'. The actual behavior of fitting, of which 'fit' here is the analog in consciousness, may vary from person to person or from culture to culture, depending on personal experience of arranging things in some kind of order, or of fitting objects into their receptacles, etc. The metaphorical substrate of thought is thus sometimes very complicated, and difficult to unravel. But every conscious thought that you are having in reading this book can by such an analysis be traced back to concrete actions in a concrete world.

2. *Excerption.* In consciousness, we are never 'seeing' any- thing in its entirety. This is because such 'seeing' is an analog of actual behavior; and in actual behavior we can only see or pay attention to a part of a thing at any one moment. And so in consciousness. We excerpt from the collection of possible atten- tions to a thing which comprises our knowledge of it. And this is all that it is possible to do since consciousness is a metaphor of our actual behavior.

Thus, if I ask you to think of a circus, for example, you will first have a fleeting moment of slight fuzziness, followed perhaps by a picturing of trapeze artists or possibly a clown in the center ring. Or, if you think of the city which you are now in, you will excerpt some feature, such as a particular building or tower or crossroads. Or if I ask you to think of yourself, you will make some kind of excerpts from your recent past, believing you are then thinking of yourself. In all these instances, we find no difficulty or particular paradox in the fact that these excerpts are not the things themselves, although we talk as if they were. Actually we are never conscious of things in their true nature, only of the excerpts we make of them.

The variables controlling excerption are deserving of much

more thought and study. For on them the person's whole consciousness of the world and the persons with whom he is interacting depend. Your excerptions of someone you know well are heavily associated with your affect toward him. If you like him, the excerpts will be the pleasant things; if not, the unpleasant. The causation may be in either direction.

How we excerpt other people largely determines the kind of world we feel we are living in. Take for example one's relatives when one was a child. If we excerpt them as their failures, their hidden conflicts, their delusions, well, that is one thing. But if we excerpt them at their happiest, in their idiosyncratic delights, it is quite another world. Writers and artists are doing in a controlled way what happens 'in' consciousness more haphazardly.

Excerption is distinct from memory. An excerpt of a thing is in consciousness the representative of the thing or event to which memories adhere, and by which we can retrieve memories. If I wish to remember what I was doing last summer, I first have an excerption of the time concerned, which may be a fleeting image of a couple of months on the calendar, until I rest in an excerption of a particular event, such as walking along a particular riverside. And from there I associate around it and retrieve memories about last summer. This is what we mean by reminiscence, and it is a particular conscious process which no animal is capable of. Reminiscence is a succession of excerptions. Each so-called association in consciousness is an excerption, an aspect or image, if you will, something frozen in time, excerpted from the experience on the basis of personality and changing situational factors.[6]

3. *The Analog 'I'*. A most important 'feature' of this metaphor 'world' is the metaphor we have of ourselves, the analog 'I', which can 'move about' vicariously in our 'imagination', 'doing'

---

[6] Individual differences and changes in the excerptions with age or health are an exceedingly interesting study. For example, if we are depressed or suffering, the excerptions of the world in consciousness change dramatically.

things that we are not actually doing. There are of course many uses for such an analog 'I'. We imagine 'ourselves' 'doing' this or that, and thus 'make' decisions on the basis of imagined 'outcomes' that would be impossible if we did not have an imagined 'self' behaving in an imagined 'world'. In the example in the section on spatialization, it was not your physical behavioral self that was trying to 'see' where my theory 'fits' into the array of alternative theories. It was your analog 'I'.

If we are out walking, and two roads diverge in a wood, and we know that one of them comes back to our destination after a much more circuitous route, we can 'traverse' that longer route with our analog 'I' to see if its vistas and ponds are worth the longer time it will take. Without consciousness with its vicarial analog 'I', we could not do this.

4. *The Metaphor 'Me'.* The analog 'I' is, however, not simply that. It is also a *metaphor 'me'*. As we imagine ourselves strolling down the longer path we indeed catch 'glimpses' of 'ourselves', as we did in the exercises of Chapter 1, where we called them autoscopic images. We can both look out from within the imagined self at the imagined vistas, or we can step back a bit and see ourselves perhaps kneeling down for a drink of water at a particular brook. There are of course quite profound problems here, particularly in the relationship of the 'I' to the 'me'. But that is another treatise. And I am only indicating the nature of the problem.

5. *Narratization.* In consciousness, we are always seeing our vicarial selves as the main figures in the stories of our lives. In the above illustration, the narratization is obvious, namely, walking along a wooded path. But it is not so obvious that we are constantly doing this whenever we are being conscious, and this I call narratization. Seated where I am, I am writing a book and this fact is imbedded more or less in the center of the story of my life, time being spatialized into a journey of my days and years.

New situations are selectively perceived as part of this ongoing story, perceptions that do not fit into it being unnoticed or at least unremembered. More important, situations are chosen which are congruent to this ongoing story, until the picture I have of myself in my life story determines how I am to act and choose in novel situations as they arise.

The assigning of causes to our behavior or saying why we did a particular thing is all a part of narratization. Such causes as reasons may be true or false, neutral or ideal. Consciousness is ever ready to explain anything we happen to find ourselves doing. The thief narratizes his act as due to poverty, the poet his as due to beauty, and the scientist his as due to truth, purpose and cause inextricably woven into the spatialization of behavior in consciousness.

But it is not just our own analog 'I' that we are narratizing; it is everything else in consciousness. A stray fact is narratized to fit with some other stray fact. A child cries in the street and we narratize the event into a mental picture of a lost child and a parent searching for it. A cat is up in a tree and we narratize the event into a picture of a dog chasing it there. Or the facts of mind as we can understand them into a theory of consciousness.

6. *Conciliation.* A final aspect of consciousness I wish to mention here is modeled upon a behavioral process common to most mammals. It really springs from simple recognition, where a slightly ambiguous perceived object is made to conform to some previously learned schema, an automatic process sometimes called *assimilation*. We assimilate a new stimulus into our conception or schema about it, even though it is slightly different. Since we never from moment to moment see or hear or touch things in exactly the same way, this process of assimilation into previous experience is going on all the time as we perceive our world. We are putting things together into recognizable objects on the basis of the previously learned schemes we have of them.

Now assimilation consciousized is *conciliation*. A better term
for it might be compatibilization, but that seems something too
rococo. What I am designating by conciliation is essentially doing
in mind-space what narratization does in mind-time or spatialized
time. It brings things together as conscious objects just as narratization brings things together as a story. And this fitting together
into a consistency or probability is done according to rules built up
in experience.

In conciliation we are making excerpts or narratizations compatible with each other, just as in external perception the new
stimulus and the internal conception are made to agree. If we are
narratizing ourselves as walking along a wooded path, the succession of excerpts is automatically made compatible with such a
journey. Or if in daydreaming two excerpts or narratizations happen to begin occurring at the same time, they are fused or con-
ciliated.

If I ask you to think of a mountain meadow and a tower at the
same time, you automatically conciliate them by having the tower
rising from the meadow. But if I ask you to think of the mountain
meadow and an ocean at the same time, conciliation tends not
to occur and you are likely to think of one and then the other.
You can only bring them together by a narratization. Thus there
are principles of compatibility that govern this process, and such
principles are learned and are based on the structure of the
world.

Let me summarize as a way of 'seeing' where we are and the
direction in which our discussion is going. We have said that
consciousness is an operation rather than a thing, a repository, or
a function. It operates by way of analogy, by way of constructing
an analog space with an analog 'I' that can observe that space,
and move metaphorically in it. It operates on any reactivity,
excerpts relevant aspects, narratizes and conciliates them together in a metaphorical space where such meanings can be

manipulated like things in space. Conscious mind is a spatial analog of the world and mental acts are analogs of bodily acts. Consciousness operates only on objectively observable things. Or, to say it another way with echoes of John Locke, there is nothing in consciousness that is not an analog of something that was in behavior first.

This has been a difficult chapter. But I hope I have sketched out with some plausibility that the notion of consciousness as a metaphor-generated model of the world leads to some quite definite deductions, and that these deductions are testable in our own everyday conscious experience. It is only, of course, a beginning, a somewhat rough-hewn beginning, which I hope to develop in a future work. But it is enough to return now to our major inquiry of the origin of it all, saving further amplification of the nature of consciousness itself for later chapters.

If consciousness is this invention of an analog world on the basis of language, paralleling the behavioral world even as the world of mathematics parallels the world of quantities of things, what then can we say about its origin?

We have arrived at a very interesting point in our discussion, and one that is completely contradictory to all of the alternative solutions to the problem of the origin of consciousness which we discussed in the introductory chapter. For if consciousness is based on language, then it follows that it is of a much more recent origin than has heretofore been supposed. Consciousness come after language! The implications of such a position are extremely serious.

CHAPTER 3

The Mind of Iliad

THERE IS an awkward moment at the top of a Ferris wheel when, having come up the inside curvature, where we are facing into a firm structure of confident girders, suddenly that structure disappears, and we are thrust out into the sky for the outward curve down.

Such perhaps is the present moment. For all the scientific alternatives that we faced into in the Introduction, including my own prejudgments about the matter, all assured us that consciousness was evolved by natural selection back somewhere in mammalian evolution or before. We felt assured that at least some animals were conscious, assured that consciousness was related in some important way to the evolution of the brain and probably its cortex, assured certainly that early man was conscious as he was learning language.

These assurances have now disappeared, and we seem thrust out into the sky of a very new problem. If our impressionistic development of a theory of consciousness in the last chapter is even pointing in the right direction, then consciousness can only have arisen in the human species, and that development must have come after the development of language.

Now if human evolution were a simple continuity, our procedure at this point would normally be to study the evolution of language, dating it as best we could. We would then try to trace out human mentality thereafter until we reached the goal of our inquiry, where we could claim by some criterion or other that here at last is the place and the date of the origin and beginning of consciousness.

But human evolution is not a simple continuity. Into human history around 3000 B.C. comes a curious and very remarkable practice. It is a transmutation of speech into little marks on stone or clay or papyrus (or pages) so that speech can be seen rather than just heard, and seen by anybody, not just those within earshot at the time. So before pursuing the program of the preceding paragraph, we should first try to date the origin of consciousness either before or after the invention of such seen speech by examining its earliest examples. Our present question then is: what is the mentality of the earliest writings of mankind?

As soon as we go back to the first written records of man to seek evidence for the presence or absence of a subjective conscious mind, we are immediately beset with innumerable technical problems. The most profound is that of translating writings that may have issued from a mentality utterly different from our own. And this is particularly problematic in the very first human writings. These are in hieroglyphics, hieratic, and cuneiform, all — interestingly enough — beginning about 3000 B.C. None of these is entirely understood. When the subjects are concrete, there is little difficulty. But when the symbols are peculiar and undetermined by context, the amount of necessary guesswork turns this fascinating evidence of the past into a Rorschach test in which modern scholars project their own subjectivity with little awareness of the importance of their distortion. The indications here as to whether consciousness was present in the early Egyptian dynasties and in the Mesopotamian cultures are thus too ambiguous for the kind of concerned analysis which is required. We shall return to these questions in Book II.

The first writing in human history in a language of which we have enough certainty of translation to consider it in connection with my hypothesis is the Iliad. Modern scholarship regards this revenge story of blood, sweat, and tears to have been developed by a tradition of bards or *aoidoi* between about 1230 B.C. when, according to inferences from some recently found Hittite tablets,[1] the events of the epic occurred and about 900 or 850 B.C., when it came to be written down. I propose here to regard the poem as a psychological document of immense importance. And the question we are to put to it is: What is mind in the Iliad?

The Language of the Iliad

The answer is disturbingly interesting. There is in general no consciousness in the Iliad. I am saying 'in general' because I shall mention some exceptions later. And in general therefore, no words for consciousness or mental acts. The words in the Iliad that in a later age come to mean mental things have different meanings, all of them more concrete. The word *psyche*, which later means soul or conscious mind, is in most instances life-substances, such as blood or breath: a dying warrior bleeds out his *psyche* onto the ground or breathes it out in his last gasp. The *thumos*, which later comes to mean something like emotional soul, is simply motion or agitation. When a man stops moving, the *thumos* leaves his limbs. But it is also somehow like an organ itself, for when Glaucus prays to Apollo to alleviate his pain and to give him strength to help his friend Sarpedon, Apollo hears his prayer and "casts strength in his *thumos*" (Iliad, 16:529). The *thumos* can tell a man to eat, drink, or fight. Diomedes says in one place that Achilles will fight "when the *thumos* in his chest tells him to and a god rouses him" (9:702f.). But it is not really an organ and not always localized; a raging ocean has *thumos*. A word of somewhat similar use is *phren*, which is always localized anatomi-

1 V. R. d'A. Desborough, *The Last Mycenaeans and Their Successors: An Archeological Survey, c. 1200–c. 1000* B.C. (Oxford, Clarendon Press, 1964).

cally as the midriff, or sensations in the midriff, and is usually used in the plural. It is the *phrenes* of Hector that recognize that his brother is not near him (22:296); this means what we mean by "catching one's breath in surprise". It is only centuries later that it comes to mean mind or 'heart' in its figurative sense.

Perhaps most important is the word *noos* which, spelled as *nous* in later Greek, comes to mean conscious mind. It comes from the word *noeein*, to see. Its proper translation in the Iliad would be something like perception or recognition or field of vision. Zeus "holds Odysseus in his *noos*." He keeps watch over him.

Another important word, which perhaps comes from the doubling of the word *meros* (part), is *mermera*, meaning in two parts. This was made into a verb by adding the ending *-izo*, the common suffix which can turn a noun into a verb, the resulting word being *mermerizein*, to be put into two parts about something. Modern translators, for the sake of a supposed literary quality in their work, often use modern terms and subjective categories which are not true to the original. *Mermerizein* is thus wrongly translated as to ponder, to think, to be of divided mind, to be troubled about, to try to decide. But essentially it means to be in conflict about two actions, not two thoughts. It is always behavioristic. It is said several times of Zeus (20:17, 16:647), as well as of others. The conflict is often said to go on in the *thumos*, or sometimes in the *phrenes*, but never in the *noos*. The eye cannot doubt or be in conflict, as the soon-to-be-invented conscious mind will be able to.

These words are in general, and with certain exceptions, the closest that anyone, authors or characters or gods, usually get to having conscious minds or thoughts. We shall be entering the meaning of these words more carefully in a later chapter.

There is also no concept of will or word for it, the concept developing curiously late in Greek thought. Thus, Iliadic men have no will of their own and certainly no notion of free will.

Indeed, the whole problem of volition, so troubling, I think, to modern psychological theory, may have had its difficulties because the words for such phenomena were invented so late.

A similar absence from Iliadic language is a word for body in our sense. The word *soma*, which in the fifth century B.C. comes to mean body, is always in the plural in Homer and means dead limbs or a corpse. It is the opposite of *psyche*. There are several words which are used for various parts of the body, and, in Homer, it is always these parts that are referred to, and never the body as a whole.[2] So, not surprisingly, the early Greek art of Mycenae and its period shows man as an assembly of strangely articulated limbs, the joints underdrawn, and the torso almost separated from the hips. It is graphically what we find again and again in Homer, who speaks of hands, lower arms, upper arms, feet, calves, and thighs as being fleet, sinewy, in speedy motion, etc., with no mention of the body as a whole.

Now this is all very peculiar. If there is no subjective consciousness, no mind, soul, or will, in Iliadic men, what then initiates behavior?

The Religion of the Early Greeks

There is an old and general idea that there was no true religion in Greece before the fourth century B.C.[3] and that the gods in the Homeric poems are merely a "gay invention of poets," as it has been put by noted scholars.[4] The reason for this erroneous view is that religion is being thought of as a system of ethics, as a kind

[2] Bruno Snell, *The Discovery of Mind*, T. G. Rosenmeyer, trans. (Cambridge: Harvard University Press, 1953). I was well along into the ideas and material of this chapter before knowing of Snell's parallel work on Homeric language. Our conclusions, however, are quite different.

[3] Except E. R. Dodds in his superb book *The Greeks and the Irrational* (Berkeley: University of California Press, 1951).

[4] For example, Maurice Bowra, *Tradition and Design in the Iliad* (Oxford: Clarendon Press, 1930), p. 222.

of bowing down to external gods in an effort to behave virtuously. And indeed in this sense the scholars are right. But to say that the gods in the Iliad are merely the inventions of the authors of the epic is to completely misread what is going on.

The characters of the Iliad do not sit down and think out what to do. They have no conscious minds such as we say we have, and certainly no introspections. It is impossible for us with our subjectivity to appreciate what it was like. When Agamemnon, king of men, robs Achilles of his mistress, it is a god that grasps Achilles by his yellow hair and warns him not to strike Agamemnon (1:197ff.). It is a god who then rises out of the gray sea and consoles him in his tears of wrath on the beach by his black ships, a god who whispers low to Helen to sweep her heart with homesick longing, a god who hides Paris in a mist in front of the attacking Menelaus, a god who tells Glaucus to take bronze for gold (6:234ff.), a god who leads the armies into battle, who speaks to each soldier at the turning points, who debates and teaches Hector what he must do, who urges the soldiers on or defeats them by casting them in spells or drawing mists over their visual fields. It is the gods who start quarrels among men (4:437ff.) that really cause the war (3:164ff.), and then plan its strategy (2:56ff.). It is one god who makes Achilles promise not to go into battle, another who urges him to go, and another who then clothes him in a golden fire reaching up to heaven and screams through his throat across the bloodied trench at the Trojans, rousing in them ungovernable panic. In fact, the gods take the place of consciousness.

The beginnings of action are not in conscious plans, reasons, and motives; they are in the actions and speeches of gods. To another, a man seems to be the cause of his own behavior. But not to the man himself. When, toward the end of the war, Achilles reminds Agamemnon of how he robbed him of his mistress, the king of men declares, "Not I was the cause of this act, but Zeus, and my portion, and the Erinyes who walk in darkness:

they it was in the assembly put wild *ate* upon me on that day
when I arbitrarily took Achilles' prize from him, so what could I
do? Gods always have their way." (19:86–90). And that this
was no particular fiction of Agamemnon's to evade responsibility
is clear in that this explanation is fully accepted by Achilles, for
Achilles also is obedient to his gods. Scholars who in comment-
ing on this passage say that Agamemnon's behavior has become
"alien to his ego,"[5] do not go nearly far enough. For the question
is indeed, what is the psychology of the Iliadic hero? And I
am saying that he did not have any ego whatever.

Even the poem itself is not wrought by men in our sense. Its
first three words are *Menin aedie Thea*, Of wrath sing, O Goddess! And the entire epic which follows is the song of the goddess
which the entranced bard 'heard' and chanted to his iron-age listeners among the ruins of Agamemnon's world.

If we erase all our preconceptions about poetry and act toward
the poem as if we had never heard of poetry before, the abnormal
quality of the speech would immediately arrest us. We call it
meter nowadays. But what a different thing, these steady hexameters of pitch stresses, from the looser jumble of accents in
ordinary dialogue! The function of meter in poetry is to drive the
electrical activity of the brain, and most certainly to relax the
normal emotional inhibitions of both chanter and listener. A
similar thing occurs when the voices of schizophrenics speak in
scanning rhythms or rhyme. Except for its later accretions, then,
the epic itself was neither consciously composed nor consciously
remembered, but was successively and creatively changed with
no more awareness than a pianist has of his improvisation.

Who then were these gods that pushed men about like robots
and sang epics through their lips? They were voices whose
speech and directions could be as distinctly heard by the Iliadic
heroes as voices are heard by certain epileptic and schizophrenic

[5] Among others, Martin P. Nilsson, *A History of Greek Religion* (New York:
Norton, 1964).

patients, or just as Joan of Arc heard her voices. The gods were organizations of the central nervous system and can be regarded as personae in the sense of poignant consistencies through time, amalgams of parental or admonitory images. The god is a part of the man, and quite consistent with this conception is the fact that the gods never step outside of natural laws. Greek gods cannot create anything out of nothing, unlike the Hebrew god of Genesis. In the relationship between the god and the hero in their dialectic, there are the same courtesies, emotions, persuasions as might occur between two people. The Greek god never steps forth in thunder, never begets awe or fear in the hero, and is as far from the outrageously pompous god of Job as it is possible to be. He simply leads, advises, and orders. Nor does the god occasion humility or even love, and little gratitude. Indeed, I suggest that the god-hero relationship was — by being its progenitor — similar to the referent of the ego-superego relationship of Freud or the self-generalized other relationship of Mead. The strongest emotion which the hero feels toward a god is amazement or wonder, the kind of emotion that we feel when the solution of a particularly difficult problem suddenly pops into our heads, or in the cry of eureka! from Archimedes in his bath.

The gods are what we now call hallucinations. Usually they are only seen and heard by the particular heroes they are speaking to. Sometimes they come in mists or out of the gray sea or a river, or from the sky, suggesting visual auras preceding them. But at other times, they simply occur. Usually they come as themselves, commonly as mere voices, but sometimes as other people closely related to the hero.

Apollo's relation to Hector is particularly interesting in this regard. In Book 16, Apollo comes to Hector as his maternal uncle; then in Book 17 as one of his allied leaders; and then later in the same book as his dearest friend from abroad. The dénouement of the whole epic comes when it is Athene who, after telling Achilles to kill Hector, then comes to Hector as his dearest brother, Deïphobus. Trusting in him as his second, Hector challenges Achilles, demands of Deïphobus another spear, and turns to find nothing is there. We would say he has had an hallucination. So has Achilles. The Trojan War was directed by hallucinations. And the soldiers who were so directed were not at all like us. They were noble automatons who knew not what they did.

The Bicameral Mind

The picture then is one of strangeness and heartlessness and emptiness. We cannot approach these heroes by inventing mind-spaces behind their fierce eyes as we do with each other. Iliadic man did not have subjectivity as do we; he had no awareness of his awareness of the world, no internal mind-space to introspect upon. In distinction to our own subjective conscious minds, we can call the mentality of the Myceneans a *bicameral mind*. Volition, planning, initiative is organized with no consciousness whatever and then 'told' to the individual in his familiar language, sometimes with the visual aura of a familiar friend or authority figure or 'god', or sometimes as a voice alone. The individual obeyed these hallucinated voices because he could not 'see' what to do by himself.

The evidence for the existence of such a mentality as I have just proposed is not meant to rest solely on the Iliad. It is rather that the Iliad suggests the hypothesis that in later chapters I shall attempt to prove or refute by examining the remains of other civilizations of antiquity. Nevertheless, it would be persuasive at this time to bring up certain objections to the preceding which will help clarify some of the issues before going on.

Objection: Is it not true that some scholars have considered the poem to be entirely the invention of one man, Homer, with no historical basis whatever, even doubting whether Troy ever existed at all, in spite of Schliemann's famous discoveries in the nineteenth century?

Reply: This doubt has recently been put to rest by the discovery of Hittite tablets, dating from 1300 B.C., which clearly refer to the land of the Achaeans and their king, Agamemnon. The catalogue of Greek places that send ships to Troy in Book 2 corresponds remarkably closely to the pattern of settlement which archaeology has discovered. The treasures of Mycenae, once thought to be fairy tales in the imagination of a poet, have been dug out of the silted ruins of the city. Other details mentioned in the Iliad, the manners of burial, the kinds of armor, such as the precisely described boars'-tusk helmet, have been unearthed in sites relevant to the poem. There is thus *no* question of its historical substrate. The Iliad is *not* imaginative creative literature and hence not a matter for literary discussion. It is history, webbed into the Mycenaean Aegean, to be examined by psychohistorical scientists.

The problem of single or multiple authorship of the poem has been endlessly debated by classical scholars for at least a century. But this establishment of an historical basis, even of artifacts mentioned in the poem, must indicate that there were many intermediaries who verbally transmitted whatever happened in the thirteenth century to succeeding ages. It is thus more plausible to think of the creation of the poem as part of this verbal transmission than as the work of a single man named Homer in the ninth century B.C. Homer, if he existed, may simply have been the first *aoidos* to be transcribed.

Objection: Even if this is so, what basis is there to suppose that an epic poem, whose earliest manuscript that we know of is a recension from Alexandrian scholars of the fourth or third century B.C., which obviously must have existed in many forms, and as we read it today was put together out of them, how can a poem of this sort be regarded as indicative of what the actual Mycenaeans of the thirteenth century B.C. were like?

Reply: This very serious objection is made even stronger by certain discrepancies between the descriptions in the poem and plausibility. The disappointing mounds of grassy rubble identified today by archaeologists as the city of Priam cover but a few acres, while the Iliad counts its defenders at 50,000 men. Even the trivial is sometimes moved up by hyperbole into impossibility: the shield of Ajax, if it were made of seven oxhides and a layer of metal, would have weighed almost 300 pounds. History has definitely been altered. The siege lasts ten years, an absolutely impossible duration given the problems of supply on both sides.

There are two general periods during which such alterations of the original history could have occurred: the verbal transmission period from the Trojan War to the ninth century B.C., when the Greek alphabet comes into existence and the epic is written down, and the literate period thereafter up to the time of the scholars of Alexandria in the third and second centuries B.C. whose put-together recension is the version we have today. As to the second period, there can be no doubt that there would be differences among various copies, and that extra parts and variations, even events belonging to different times and places, could have been drawn into the vortex of this one furious story. But all these additions were probably kept in check both by the transcribers' reverence for the poem at this time, as is indicated in all other Greek literature, and by the requirements of public performances. These were held at various sites, but particularly at the Panathenaea every four years at Athens, where the Iliad was devoutly chanted along with the Odyssey to vast audiences by the so-called *rhapsodes*. It is probable therefore that with the exception of some episodes which contemporary scholars believe are late additions (such as the ambushing of Dolon and the references to Hades), the Iliad as we have it is very similar to what was first written down in the ninth century B.C.

But further back in the dim obscurities of earlier time stand the shadowy aoidoi. And it is they certainly who successively altered the original history. Oral poetry is a very different species from written poetry.[6] The way we read it and judge it must be completely different. Composition and performance are not separate; they are simultaneous. And each new composing of the Iliad down the swift generations was on the basis of auditory memory and traditional bardic formulae, each aoidos with set phrases of varying lengths filling out the unremembered hexameters and with set turns of plot filling out unremembered action. And this was over the three or four centuries following the actual war. The Iliad, then, is not so much a reflection of the social life of Troy as it is of several stages of social development from that time up to the literate period. Treated as a sociological document, the objection is sustained.

But as a psychological document, the case is quite different. Whence these gods? And why their particular relationship to the individuals? My argument has stressed two things, *the lack of mental language and the initiation of action by the gods.* These are not archaeological matters. Nor are they matters likely to have been invented by the aoidoi. And any theory about them has to be a psychological theory about man himself. The only other alternative is the following.

Objection: Are we not making a great deal out of what might be merely literary style? That the gods are mere poetic devices of the aoidoi to make the action vivid, devices which may indeed go back to the earliest bards of Mycenae?

Reply: This is the well-known problem of the gods and their overdetermination of the action. The gods seem to us quite unnecessary. Why are they there? And the common solution is as above, that they are a poetic device. The divine machinery duplicates natural conscious causations simply to present them in concrete pictorial form, because the aoidoi were without the refinements of language to express psychological matters.

[6] See Milman Parry, *Collected Papers* (New York, Oxford University Press, 1971). I wish to thank both Randall Warner and Judith Griessman for discussion on some of these points.

Not only is there no reason to believe that the aoidoi had any conscious psychology they were trying to express, such a notion is quite foreign to the whole texture of the poem. The Iliad is about *action* and it is full of action — constant action. It really is *about* Achilles' acts and their consequences, not about his mind. And as for the gods, the Iliadic authors and the Iliadic characters all agree in the acceptance of this divinely managed world. To say the gods are an artistic apparatus is the same kind of thing as to say that Joan of Arc told the Inquisition about her voices merely to make it all vivid to those who were about to condemn her.

It is not that the vague general ideas of psychological causation appear first and then the poet gives them concrete pictorial form by inventing gods. It is, as I shall show later in this essay, just the other way around. And when it is suggested that the inward feelings of power or inward monitions or losses of judgment are the germs out of which the divine machinery developed, I return that the truth is just the reverse, that the presence of voices which had to be obeyed were the absolute prerequisite to the conscious stage of mind in which it is the self that is responsible and can debate within itself, can order and direct, and that the creation of such a self is the product of culture. In a sense, we have become our own gods.

Objection: If the bicameral mind existed, one might expect utter chaos, with everybody following his own private hallucinations. The only possible way in which there could be a bicameral civilization would be that of a rigid hierarchy, with lesser men hallucinating the voices of authorities over them, and those authorities hallucinating yet higher ones, and so on to the kings and their peers hallucinating gods. Yet the Iliad does not present any such picture with its concentration on the heroic individual.

Reply: This is a very telling objection that puzzled me for a long time, particularly as I studied the history of other bicameral civilizations in which there was not the freedom for individual action that there was in the social world of the Iliad.

The missing pieces in the puzzle turn out to be the well-known

Linear B Tablets from Knossos, Mycenae, and Pylos. They were written directly in what I am calling the bicameral period. They have long been known, yet long resistant to the most arduous labors of cryptographers. Recently, however, they have been deciphered and shown to contain a syllabic script, the earliest written Greek used only for record purposes.[7] And it gives us an outline picture of Mycenaean society much more in keeping with the hypothesis of a bicameral mind: hierarchies of officials, soldiers, or workers, inventories of goods, statements of goods owed to the ruler and particularly to gods. The actual world of the Trojan War, then, was in historical fact much closer to the rigid theocracy which the theory predicts than to the free individuality of the poem.

Moreover, the very structure of the Mycenaean state is profoundly different from the loose assemblage of warriors depicted in the Iliad. It is indeed quite similar to the contemporary divinely ruled kingdoms of Mesopotamia (as described later in this essay, particularly in II.2). These records in Linear B call the head of the state the *wanax*, a word which in later classical Greek is only used for gods. Similarly, the records call the land occupied by his state as his *temenos*, a word which later is used only for land sacred to the gods. The later Greek word for king is *basileus*, but the term in these tablets denotes a much less important person. He is more or less the first servant of the *wanax*, just as in Mesopotamia the human ruler was really the steward of the lands 'owned' by the god he heard in hallucination — as we shall see in II.2. The material from the Linear B tablets is difficult to piece together, but they do reveal the hierarchical and leveled nature of centralized palace civilizations which the succession of poets who composed the Iliad in the oral tradition completely ignored.

---

[7] M. C. F. Ventris and J. Chadwick, *Documents in Mycenaean Greek* (Cambridge: Cambridge University Press, 1973). A summary of this material and its relationship to archaeological finds may be found in T. B. L. Webster, *From Mycenae to Homer* (London: Methuen, 1958).

This loosening of the social structure in the fully developed Iliad may in part have been caused by the bringing together of other much later stories into the main theme of the Trojan War. One of the most telling pieces of evidence that the Iliad is a composite of different compositions is the large number of inconsistencies in the poem, some in very close proximity. For example, when Hector is withdrawing from the battle, one line (6:117) says, "The black hide beat upon his neck and ankles." This can only be the early Mycenaean body-shield. But the next line refers to "The rim which ran round the outside of the bossed shield," and this is a very different kind and a much later type of shield. Obviously, the second line was added by a later poet who in his auditory trance was not even visualizing what he was saying.

Further Qualifications

Indeed, since this is the chaotic period when the bicameral mind breaks down and consciousness begins (as we shall see in a later chapter), we might expect the poem to reflect both this breakdown of civil hierarchies as well as more subjectification side by side with the older form of mentality. As it is, I have in the previous pages omitted certain discrepancies to the theory which I regard as such incursions. These outcroppings of something close to subjective consciousness occur in parts of the Iliad regarded by scholars as later additions to the core poem.[8]

Book 9, for example, which was written and added to the poem only after the great migration of the Achaeans into Asia Minor, contains references to human deception unlike any in the other books. Most of these occur in the great, long rhetorical reply of Achilles to Odysseus about Agamemnon's treatment of him (9:344, 371, and 375). In particular is Achilles' slur on Agamemnon: "Hateful to me as the gates of Hades is the man who

[8] I am here drawing on Walter Leaf, *A Companion to the Iliad* (London: Macmillan, 1892), pp. 170–173.

hides one thing in his heart and speaks another." (9:3123f.). This is definitely an indication of subjective consciousness. So also may be the difficult-to-translate optative constructions of Helen (3:173ff.; 6:344ff.) or the apparent reminiscence of Nestor (1:260ff.).

There are also two extraordinary places in the text where first Agenor (21:553) and then Hector (22:99) talk to themselves. The fact that these two speeches occur late in the poem, in close proximity, have highly inappropriate content (they contradict the previous characterizations of the speakers), and use some identical phrases and lines, all suggest that they are formulaic insertions into the story by the same aoidos at a later time.[9] But not much later. For they are sufficiently unusual to surprise even their speakers. After these soliloquies, both heroes exclaim precisely the same astonished words, "But wherefore does my life say this to me?" If, indeed, such talks to oneself were common, as they would be if their speakers were really conscious, there would be no cause for surprise. We shall have occasion to return to these instances when we discuss in more detail how consciousness arose.[10]

The main point of this chapter is that the earliest writing of men in a language that we can really comprehend, when looked at objectively, reveals a very different mentality from our own. And this must, I think, be accepted as true. Such instances of narratization, analog behavior, or mind-space as occasionally occur are regarded by scholars as of later authorship. The bulk of the poem is consistent in its lack of analog consciousness and points back to a very different kind of human nature. Since we know that Greek culture very quickly became a literature of

[9] Even Leaf, p. 356, regards these two passages as spurious.

[10] A further analysis might be made, establishing dates for the various parts of the poem as they are thought by some scholars to have been assembled around the much shorter core poem, and then demonstrating that the frequencies of occurrence of these subjective outcroppings increase with recency.

consciousness, we may regard the Iliad as standing at the great turning of the times, and a window back into those unsubjective times when every kingdom was in essence a theocracy and every man the slave of voices heard whenever novel situations occurred.

CHAPTER 4

The Bicameral Mind

W E ARE conscious human beings. We are trying to understand human nature. The preposterous hypothesis we have
come to in the previous chapter is that at one time human nature
was split in two, an executive part called a god, and a follower
part called a man. Neither part was conscious. This is almost
incomprehensible to us. And since we are conscious, and wish to
understand, we wish to reduce this to something familiar in our
experience, as we saw was the nature of understanding in Chapter 2. And this is what I shall attempt in the present chapter.

THE BICAMERAL MAN

Very little can be said to make the man side of it seem familiar to
us, except by referring back to the first chapter, to remember all
the things we do without the aid of consciousness. But how
unsatisfying is a list of nots! Somehow we still wish to identify
with Achilles. We still feel that there must, there absolutely *must*
be something he feels inside. What we are trying to do is to
invent a mind-space and a world of analog behaviors in him just
as we do in ourselves and our contemporaries. And this invention, I say, is not valid for Greeks of this period.

Perhaps a metaphor of something close to that state might be
helpful. In driving a car, I am not sitting like a back-seat driver
directing myself, but rather find myself committed and engaged

with little consciousness.[1] In fact my consciousness will usually be involved in something else, in a conversation with you if you happen to be my passenger, or in thinking about the origin of consciousness perhaps. My hand, foot, and head behavior, however, are almost in a different world. In touching something, I am touched; in turning my head, the world turns to me; in seeing, I am related to a world I immediately obey in the sense of driving on the road and not on the sidewalk. And I am not conscious of any of this. And certainly not logical about it. I am caught up, unconsciously enthralled, if you will, in a total interacting reciprocity of stimulation that may be constantly threatening or comforting, appealing or repelling, responding to the changes in traffic and particular aspects of it with trepidation or confidence, trust or distrust, while my consciousness is still off on other topics.

Now simply subtract that consciousness and you have what a bicameral man would be like. The world would happen to him and his action would be an inextricable part of that happening with no consciousness whatever. And now let some brand-new situation occur, an accident up ahead, a blocked road, a flat tire, a stalled engine, and behold, our bicameral man would not do what you and I would do, that is, quickly and efficiently swivel our consciousness over to the matter and narratize out what to do. He would have to wait for his bicameral voice which with the stored-up admonitory wisdom of his life would tell him nonconsciously what to do.

THE BICAMERAL GOD

But what were such auditory hallucinations like? Some people find it difficult to even imagine that there can be mental voices

[1] I owe the idea of this example to Erwin W. Straus' insightful essay, "Phenomenology of Hallucinations," in L. J. West, ed., *Hallucinations* (New York: Grune and Stratton, 1962), pp. 220–232.

that are heard with the same experiential quality as externally produced voices. After all, there is no mouth or larynx in the brain!

Whatever brain areas are utilized, it is absolutely certain that such voices do exist and that experiencing them is just like hearing actual sound. Further, it is highly probable that the bicameral voices of antiquity were in quality very like such auditory hallucinations in contemporary people. They are heard by many completely normal people to varying degrees. Often it is in times of stress, when a parent's comforting voice may be heard.

Or in the midst of some persisting problem. In my late twenties, living alone on Beacon Hill in Boston, I had for about a week been studying and autistically pondering some of the problems in this book, particularly the question of what knowledge is and how we can know anything at all. My convictions and misgivings had been circling about through the sometimes precious fogs of epistemologies, finding nowhere to land. One afternoon I lay down in intellectual despair on a couch. Suddenly, out of an absolute quiet, there came a firm, distinct loud voice from my upper right which said, "Include the knower in the known!" It lugged me to my feet absurdly exclaiming, "Hello?" looking for whoever was in the room. The voice had had an exact location. No one was there! Not even behind the wall where I sheepishly looked. I do not take this nebulous profundity as divinely inspired, but I do think that it is similar to what was heard by those who have in the past claimed such special selection.

Such voices may be heard by perfectly normal people on a more continuing basis. After giving lectures on the theory in this book, I have been surprised at members of the audience who have come up afterwards to tell me of their voices. One young biologist's wife said that almost every morning as she made the beds and did the housework, she had long, informative, and pleasant conversations with the voice of her dead grandmother in which the grandmother's voice was actually heard. This came as something of a shock to her alarmed husband, for she had never previously mentioned it, since "hearing voices" is generally supposed to be a sign of insanity. Which, in distressed people, of course, it is. But because of the dread surrounding this disease, the actual incidence of auditory hallucinations in normal people on such a continuing basis is not known.

The only extensive study was a poor one done in the last century in England.[2] Only hallucinations of normal people when they were in good health were counted. Of 7717 men, 7.8 percent had experienced hallucinations at some time. Among 7599 women, the figure was 12 percent. Hallucinations were most frequent in subjects between twenty and twenty-nine years of age, the same age incidentally at which schizophrenia most commonly occurs. There were twice as many visual hallucinations as auditory. National differences were also found. Russians had twice as many hallucinations as the average. Brazilians had even more because of a very high incidence of auditory hallucinations. Just why is anyone's conjecture. One of the deficiencies of this study, however, is that in a country where ghosts are exciting gossip, it is difficult to have accurate criteria of what is actually seen and heard as an hallucination. There is an important need for further and better studies of this sort.[3]

Hallucinations in Psychotics

It is of course in the distress of schizophrenia that auditory hallucinations similar to bicameral voices are most common and best studied. This is now a difficult matter. At a suspicion of hallucinations, distressed psychotics are given some kind of chemotherapy such as Thorazine, which specifically eliminates hallucinations. This procedure is at least questionable, and may be done not for the patient, but for the hospital which wishes to

[2] Henry Sidgewick et al., "Report on the census of hallucinations," *Proceedings of the Society for Psychical Research*, 1894, 34: 25–394.

[3] An example of what not to do may be found in D. J. West, "A mass-observation questionnaire on hallucinations," *Journal of the Society for Psychical Research*, 1948, 34: 187–196.

eliminate this rival control over the patient. But it has never been shown that hallucinating patients are more intractable than others. Indeed, as judged by other patients, hallucinating schizophrenics are more friendly, less defensive, more likable, and have more positive expectancies toward others in the hospital than nonhallucinating patients.[4] And it is possible that even when the effect is apparently negative, hallucinated voices may be helpful to the healing process.

At any rate, since the advent of chemotherapy the incidence of hallucinatory patients is much less than it once was. Recent studies have revealed a wide variation among different hospitals, ranging from 50 percent of psychotics in the Boston City Hospital, to 30 percent in a hospital in Oregon[5] and even lower in hospitals with long-term patients under considerable sedation. Thus, in what follows, I am leaning more heavily on some of the older literature in the psychoses, such as Bleuler's great classic, *Dementia Praecox*, in which the hallucinatory aspect of schizophrenia in particular is more clearly seen.[6] This is important if we are to have an idea of the nature and range of the bicameral voices heard in the early civilizations.

The Character of the Voices

The voices in schizophrenia take any and every relationship to the individual. They converse, threaten, curse, criticize, consult, often in short sentences. They admonish, console, mock, command, or sometimes simply announce everything that's happen-

---

[4] P. M. Lewinsohn, "Characteristics of patients with hallucinations," *Journal of Clinical Psychology*, 1968, 24: 423.

[5] P. E. Nathan, H. F. Simpson, and M. M. Audberg, "A systems analytic model of diagnosis II. The diagnostic validity of abnormal perceptual behavior," *Journal of Clinical Psychology*, 1969, 25: 115–136.

[6] Eugen Bleuler, *Dementia Praecox or The Group of Schizophrenias*, Joseph Zinkin, trans. (New York: International Universities Press, 1950). Other sources for the sections to follow include my own observations and interviews with patients, works footnoted on subsequent pages, various chapters in L. J. West, and miscellaneous case reports.

ing. They yell, whine, sneer, and vary from the slightest whisper to a thunderous shout. Often the voices take on some special peculiarity, such as speaking very slowly, scanning, rhyming, or in rhythms, or even in foreign languages. There may be one particular voice, more often a few voices, and occasionally many. As in bicameral civilizations, they are recognized as gods, angels, devils, enemies, or a particular person or relative. Or occasionally they are ascribed to some kind of apparatus reminiscent of the statuary which we will see was important in this regard in bicameral kingdoms.

Sometimes the voices bring patients to despair, commanding them to do something and then viciously reproaching them after the command is carried out. Sometimes they are a dialogue, as of two people discussing the patient. Sometimes the roles of pro and con are taken over by the voices of different people. The voice of his daughter tells a patient: "He is going to be burnt alive!" While his mother's voice says: "He will not be burnt!"[7] In other instances, there are several voices gabbling all at once, so that the patient cannot follow them.

Their Locality and Function

In some cases, particularly the most serious, the voices are not localized. But usually they are. They call from one side or another, from the rear, from above and below; only rarely do they come from directly in front of the patient. They may seem to come from walls, from the cellar and the roof, from heaven and from hell, near or far, from parts of the body or parts of the clothing. And sometimes, as one patient put it, "they assume the nature of all those objects through which they speak — whether they speak out of walls, or from ventilators, or in the woods and fields."[8] In some patients there is a tendency to associate the good consoling voices with the upper right, while bad voices

---

[7] Bleuler, p. 97f.

[8] T. Hennell, *The Witnesses* (London: Davis, 1938), p. 182.

come from below and to the left. In rare instances, the voices seem to the patient to come from his own mouth, sometimes feeling like foreign bodies bulging up in his mouth. Sometimes the voices are hypostasized in bizarre ways. One patient claimed that a voice was perched above each of his ears, one of which was a little larger than the other, which is reminiscent of the *ka*'s and the way they were depicted in the statues of the pharaohs of ancient Egypt, as we shall see in a subsequent chapter.

Very often the voices criticize a patient's thoughts and actions. Sometimes they forbid him to do what he was just thinking of doing. And sometimes this occurs even before the patient is aware of his intention. One intelligent paranoid who came from the Swiss canton of Thurgau harbored hostile feelings toward his personal attendant. As the latter stepped into his room, the voice said in its most reproachful tone before the patient had done anything, "There you have it! A Thurgauer beats up a perfectly decent private attendant!"[9]

Of immense importance here is the fact that the nervous system of a patient makes simple perceptual judgments of which the patient's 'self' is not aware. And these, as above, may then be transposed into voices that seem prophetic. A janitor coming down a hall may make a slight noise of which the patient is not conscious. But the patient hears his hallucinated voice cry out, "Now someone is coming down the hall with a bucket of water." Then the door opens, and the prophecy is fulfilled. Credence in the prophetic character of the voices, just as perhaps in bicameral times, is thus built up and sustained. The patient then follows his voices alone and is defenseless against them. Or else, if the voices are not clear, he waits, catatonic and mute, to be shaped by them or, alternatively, by the voices and hands of his attendants.

Usually the severity of schizophrenia oscillates during hospitalization and often the voices come and go with the undulations of the illness. Sometimes they occur only when the patients are

9 Bleuler, p. 98.

doing certain things, or only in certain environments. And in many patients, before the present-day chemotherapy, there was no single waking moment free from them. When the illness is most severe, the voices are loudest and come from outside; when least severe, voices often tend to be internal whispers; and when internally localized, their auditory qualities are sometimes vague. A patient might say, "They are not at all real voices but merely reproductions of the voices of dead relatives." Particularly intelligent patients in mild forms of the illness are often not sure whether they are actually hearing the voices or whether they are only compelled to think them, like "audible thoughts," or "soundless voices," or "hallucinations of meanings."

Hallucinations *must* have some innate structure in the nervous system underlying them. We can see this clearly by studying the matter in those who have been profoundly deaf since birth or very early childhood. For even they can — somehow — experience auditory hallucinations. This is commonly seen in deaf schizophrenics. In one study, 16 out of 22 hallucinating, profoundly deaf schizophrenics insisted they had *heard* some kind of communication.[10] One thirty-two-year-old woman, born deaf, who was full of self-recrimination about a therapeutic abortion, claimed she *heard* accusations from God. Another, a fifty-year-old congenitally deaf woman, heard supernatural voices which proclaimed her to have occult powers.

The Visual Component

Visual hallucinations in schizophrenia occur less commonly, but sometimes with extreme clarity and vividness. One of my schizophrenic subjects, a vivacious twenty-year-old writer of folk songs, had been sitting in a car for a long time, anxiously waiting for a friend. A blue car coming along the road suddenly, oddly,

---

[10] J. D. Rainer, S. Abdullah, and J. C. Altshuler, "Phenomenology of hallucinations in the deaf" in *Origin and Mechanisms of Hallucinations*, Wolfram Keup, ed. (New York: Plenum Press, 1970), pp. 449–465.

slowed, turned rusty brown, then grew huge gray wings and slowly flapped over a hedge and disappeared. Her greater alarm, however, came when others in the street behaved as if nothing extraordinary had happened. Why? Unless all of them were somehow in league to hide their reactions from her. And why should that be? It is often the narratization of such false events by consciousness, fitting the world in around them in a rational way, that brings on other tragic symptoms.

It is interesting that profoundly deaf schizophrenics who do not have auditory hallucinations often have visual hallucinations of sign language. A sixteen-year-old girl who became deaf at the age of eight months indulged in bizarre communication with empty spaces and gesticulated to the walls. An older, congenitally deaf woman communicated with her hallucinated boyfriend in sign language. Other deaf patients may appear to be in constant communication with imaginary people using a word salad of signs and finger spelling. One thirty-five-year-old deaf woman, who lost her hearing at the age of fourteen months, lived a life of unrestrained promiscuity alternating with violent temper outbursts. On admission, she explained in sign language that every morning a spirit dressed in a white robe came to her, saying things in sign language which were at times frightening and which set the pace of her mood for the day. Another deaf patient would spit at empty space, saying that she was spitting at the angels who were lurking there. A thirty-year-old man, deaf since birth, more benignly, would see little angels and Lilliputian people around him and believed he had a magic wand with which he could achieve almost anything.

Occasionally, in what are called acute twilight states, whole scenes, often of a religious nature, may be hallucinated even in broad daylight, the heavens standing open with a god speaking to the patient. Or sometimes writing will appear before a patient as before Nebuchadnezzar. A paranoid patient saw the word *poison* in the air at the very moment when the attendant made him take his medicine. In other instances, the visual hallucinations may be fitted into the real environment, with figures walking about the ward, or standing above the doctor's head, even as I suggest Athene appeared to Achilles. More usually, when visual hallucinations occur with voices, they are merely shining light or cloudy fog, as Thetis came to Achilles or Yahweh to Moses.

The Release of the Gods

If we are correct in assuming that schizophrenic hallucinations are similar to the guidances of gods in antiquity, then there should be some common physiological instigation in both instances. This, I suggest, is simply stress. In normal people, as we have mentioned, the stress threshold for release of hallucinations is extremely high; most of us need to be over our heads in trouble before we would hear voices. But in psychosis-prone persons, the threshold is somewhat lower; as in the girl I described, only anxious waiting in a parked car was necessary. This is caused, I think, by the buildup in the blood of breakdown products of stress-produced adrenalin which the individual is, for genetical reasons, unable to pass through the kidneys as fast as a normal person.

During the eras of the bicameral mind, we may suppose that the stress threshold for hallucinations was much, much lower than in either normal people or schizophrenics today. The only stress necessary was that which occurs when a change in behavior is necessary because of some novelty in a situation. Anything that could not be dealt with on the basis of habit, any conflict between work and fatigue, between attack and flight, any choice between whom to obey or what to do, anything that required any decision at all was sufficient to cause an auditory hallucination.

It has now been clearly established that decision-making (and I would like to remove every trace of conscious connotation from the word 'decision') is precisely what stress is. If rats have to cross an electric grid each time they wish to get food and water, such rats develop ulcers.[11] Just shocking the rats does not do this to them. There has to be the pause of conflict or the decision-making stress of whether to cross a grid or not to produce this effect. If two monkeys are placed in harnesses, in such a way that one of the monkeys can press a bar at least once every twenty seconds to avoid a periodic shock to both monkeys' feet, within three or four weeks the decision-making monkey will have ulcers, while the other, equally shocked monkey will not.[12] It is the pause of unknowingness that is important. For if the experiment is so arranged that an animal can make an effective response and receive immediate feedback of his success, executive ulcers, as they are often called, do not occur.[13]

So Achilles, repulsed by Agamemnon, in decision-stress by the gray sea, hallucinates Thetis out of the mists. So Hector, faced with the decision-suffering of whether to go outside the walls of Troy to fight Achilles or stay within them, in the stress of the decision hallucinates the voice that tells him to go out. The divine voice ends the decision-stress before it has reached any considerable level. Had Achilles or Hector been modern executives, living in a culture that repressed their stress-relieving gods, they too might have collected their share of our psychosomatic diseases.

THE AUTHORITY OF SOUND

We must not leave this subject of the hallucinatory mechanism without facing up to the more profound question of why such

[11] W. L. Sawrey and J. D. Weisz, "An experimental method of producing gastric ulcers," *Journal of Comparative and Physiological Psychology*, 1956, 49: 269–270.

[12] J. V. Brady, R. W. Porter, D. G. Conrad, and J. W. Mason, "Avoidance behavior and the development of gastro-duodenal ulcers," *Journal of the Experimental Analysis of Behavior*, 1958, 1: 69–72.

[13] J. M. Weiss, "Psychological Factors in Stress and Disease," *Scientific American*, 1972, 226: 106.

voices are believed, why obeyed. For believed as objectively real, they are, and obeyed as objectively real in the face of all the evidence of experience and the mountains of common sense. Indeed, the voices a patient hears are more real than the doctor's voice. He sometimes says so. "If that is not a real voice, then I can just as well say that even you are not now really talking to me," said one schizophrenic to his physicians. And another when questioned replied:

> Yes, Sir. I hear voices distinctly, even loudly; they interrupt us at this moment. It is more easy for me to listen to them than to you. I can more easily believe in their significance and actuality, and they do not ask questions.[14]

That he alone hears the voices is not of much concern. Sometimes he feels he has been honored by this gift, singled out by divine forces, elected and glorified, and this even when the voice reproaches him bitterly, even when it is leading him to death. He is somehow face to face with elemental auditory powers, more real than wind or rain or fire, powers that deride and threaten and console, powers that he cannot step back from and see objectively.

One sunny afternoon not long ago, a man was lying back in a deck chair on the beach at Coney Island. Suddenly, he heard a voice so loud and clear that he looked about at his companions, certain that they too must have heard the voice. When they acted as if nothing had happened, he began to feel strange and moved his chair away from them. And then

> . . . suddenly, clearer, deeper, and even louder than before, the deep voice came at me again, right in my ear this time, and getting me tight and shivery inside. "Larry Jayson, I told you before you weren't any good. Why are you sitting here making believe you are as good as anyone else when you're not? Whom are you fooling?"

[14] Hennell, pp. 181–182.

The deep voice was so loud and so clear, everyone must have heard it. He got up and walked slowly away, down the stairs of the boardwalk to the stretch of sand below. He waited to see if the voice came back. It did, its words pounding in this time, not the way you hear any words, but deeper,

> . . . as though all parts of me had become ears, with my fingers hearing the words, and my legs, and my head too. "You're no good," the voice said slowly, in the same deep tones. "You've never been any good or use on earth. There is the ocean. You might just as well drown yourself. Just walk in, and keep walking."
>
> As soon as the voice was through, I knew by its cold command, I had to obey it.[15]

The patient walking the pounded sands of Coney Island heard his pounding voices as clearly as Achilles heard Thetis along the misted shores of the Aegean. And even as Agamemnon "had to obey" the "cold command" of Zeus, or Paul the command of Jesus before Damascus, so Mr. Jayson waded into the Atlantic Ocean to drown. Against the will of his voices, he was saved by life-guards and brought to Bellevue Hospital, where he recovered to write of this bicameral experience.

In some less severe cases, the patients, when accustomed to the voices, can learn to be objective toward them and to attenuate their authority. But almost all autobiographies of schizophrenic patients are consistent in speaking of the unquestioning submission, at least at first, to the commands of the voices. Why should this be so? Why should such voices have such authority either in Argos, on the road to Damascus, or the shores of Coney Island?

Sound is a very special modality. We cannot handle it. We cannot push it away. We cannot turn our backs to it. We can close our eyes, hold our noses, withdraw from touch, refuse to taste. We cannot close our ears though we can partly muffle

[15] L. N. Jayson, *Mania* (New York: Funk and Wagnall, 1937), pp. 1–3.

them. Sound is the least controllable of all sense modalities, and it is this that is the medium of that most intricate of all evolutionary achievements, language. We are therefore looking at a problem of considerable depth and complexity.

The Control of Obedience

Consider what it is to listen and understand someone speaking to us. In a certain sense we have to become the other person; or rather, we let him become part of us for a brief second. We suspend our own identities, after which we come back to ourselves and accept or reject what he has said. But that brief second of dawdling identity is the nature of understanding language; and if that language is a command, the identification of understanding becomes the obedience. To hear is actually a kind of obedience. Indeed, both words come from the same root and therefore were probably the same word originally. This is true in Greek, Latin, Hebrew, French, German, Russian, as well as in English, where 'obey' comes from the Latin *obedire*, which is a composite of *ob* + *audire*, to hear facing someone.[16]

The problem is the control of such obedience. This is done in two ways.

The first but less important is simply by spatial distance. Think, if you will, of what you do when hearing someone else talk to you. You adjust your distance to some culturally established standard.[17] When the speaker is too close, it seems he is trying to control your thoughts too closely. When too far, he is not controlling them enough for you to understand him comfortably. If you are from an Arabian country, a face-to-face distance of less than twelve inches is comfortable. But in more northern

[16] Straus, p. 229.

[17] For those interested in pursuing this subject, see Edward T. Hall's *The Hidden Dimension* (New York: Doubleday, 1966), which stresses the cultural differences, and Robert Sommer's *Personal Space: The Behavioral Basis of Design* (Englewood Cliffs, New Jersey: Prentice-Hall, 1969), which examines spatial behavior in depth.

countries, the conversation distance most comfortable is almost twice that, a cultural difference, which in social exchanges can result in a variety of international misunderstandings. To converse with someone at less than the usual distance means at least an attempted mutuality of obedience and control, as, for example, in a love relationship, or in the face-to-face threatening of two men about to fight. To speak to someone within that distance is to attempt to truly dominate him or her. To be spoken to within that distance, and there remain, results in the strong tendency to accept the authority of the person who is speaking.

The second and more important way that we control other people's voice-authority over us is by our opinions of them. Why are we forever judging, forever criticizing, forever putting people in categories of faint praise or reproof? We constantly rate others and pigeonhole them in often ridiculous status hierarchies simply to regulate their control over us and our thoughts. Our personal judgments of others are filters of influence. If you wish to release another's language power over you, simply hold him higher in your own private scale of esteem.

And now consider what it is like if neither of these methods avail, because there is no person there, no point of space from which the voice emanates, a voice that you cannot back off from, as close to you as everything you call you, when its presence eludes all boundaries, when no escape is possible — flee and it flees with you — a voice unhindered by walls or distances, undiminished by muffling one's ears, nor drowned out with anything, not even one's own screaming — how helpless the hearer! And if one belonged to a bicameral culture, where the voices were recognized as at the utmost top of the hierarchy, taught you as gods, kings, majesties that owned you, head, heart, and foot, the omniscient, omnipotent voices that could not be categorized as beneath you, how obedient to them the bicameral man!

The explanation of volition in subjective conscious men is still a profound problem that has not reached any satisfactory solution. But in bicameral men, this *was* volition. Another way to say it is that volition came as a voice that was in the nature of a neurological command, in which the command and the action were not separated, in which to hear was to obey.

CHAPTER 5

The Double Brain

WHAT HAPPENS in the brain of a bicameral man? Anything as important in the history of our species as a completely different kind of mentality existing only a hundred generations ago *demands* some statement of what is going on physiologically. How is it possible? Given this profoundly subtle structure of nerve cells and fibers inside our skulls, how could that structure have been organized so that a bicameral mentality was possible? This is the great question of the present chapter.

Our first approach to an answer is obvious. Since the bicameral mind is mediated by speech, the speech areas of the brain must be concerned in some important way.

Now in discussing these areas, and throughout this chapter, and indeed in the rest of this essay, I shall be using terms suitable only to right-handed people, in order to avoid a certain clumsiness of expression. Thus, it is the left cerebral hemisphere of the brain, controlling the right side of the body, which in right-handed people contains the speech areas. It is therefore commonly called the dominant hemisphere, while the right hemisphere, controlling the left side of the body, is commonly called the nondominant. I shall be speaking as if the left hemisphere were dominant in all of us. Actually, however, left-handed persons have a variety of degrees of lateral dominance, some being completely switched (the right hemisphere doing what the left usually does), others not, and still others with

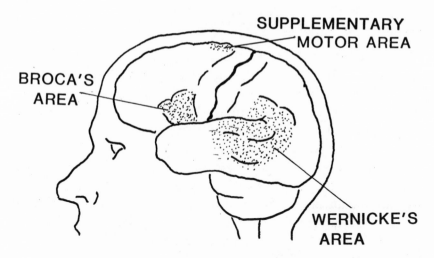

The three speech areas of the left hemisphere have different functions and values. The supplementary motor area is mostly involved
in articulation; Broca's area in articulation, vocabulary, inflection,
and grammar; and Wernicke's area in vocabulary, syntax, meaning,
and understanding speech.

mixed dominance. But being exceptional, only 5 percent of the
population, they can be left out of the present discussion.

The speech areas then are three, all on the left hemisphere in
the great majority of mankind.[1] They are: (1) the supplementary motor cortex, on the very top of the left frontal lobe, removal
of which by surgery produces a loss of speech which clears up in
several weeks; (2) Broca's area, lower down at the back of the
left frontal lobe, the removal of which produces a loss of speech
which is sometimes permanent and sometimes not; and (3)
Wernicke's area, chiefly the posterior part of the left temporal
lobe with parts of the parietal area, any large destruction of

[1] I am here following the late Wilder Penfield and Lamar Roberts, *Speech and
Brain-Mechanisms* (Princeton: Princeton University Press, 1959), the traditional
authority although some of it is out of date in the present explosion of knowledge
in this area.

which after a certain age produces a permanent loss of meaningful speech.

It is thus Wernicke's area that is the most indispensable to normal speech. As we might expect, the cortex in Wernicke's area is quite thick with large, widely spaced cells, indicating considerable internal and external connections. While there is some disagreement as to its precise boundaries,[2] there is none about its importance to meaningful communication.

Of course it is extremely hazardous thinking to isomorphize between a conceptual analysis of a psychological phenomenon and its concomitant brain structure, yet this is what we cannot avoid doing. And among these three areas on the left hemisphere, or even in their more subtle interrelationships, it is difficult to imagine a duplication of some speech function to the extent and separation which my theory of the bicameral mind would demand.

Let us sit down with this problem a moment. Speech areas all on the left side. Why? One intriguing puzzle which has long fascinated me and anyone else who has considered the evolution of all this is why language function should be represented in only one hemisphere. Most other important functions are bilaterally represented. This redundancy in everything else is a biological advantage to the animal, since, if one side is injured, the other side can compensate. Why then was not language? Language, that most urgent and significant of skills, the pre-emptory and exigent ground of social action, the last communicant thread on which life itself in the post-glacial millennia must often have depended! Why was not this without-which-nothing of human culture represented on both hemispheres?

The problem drifts off into even more mystery when we remember that the neurological structure necessary for language

[2] Joseph Bogen with his usual helpfulness has taken the time to point out to me the slipperiness of the evidence for just what regions are to be included in Wernicke's area. I am also indebted to my former student, Stevan Harnad, for invaluable discussion on many of these issues.

exists in the right hemisphere as well as the left. In a child, a major lesion of Wernicke's area on the left hemisphere, or of the underlying thalamus which connects it to the brainstem, produces transfer of the whole speech mechanism to the right hemisphere. A very few ambidextrous people actually do have speech on both hemispheres. Thus the usually speechless right hemisphere can under certain conditions become a language hemisphere, just like the left.

And a further range of the problem is what *did* happen in the right hemisphere as the aptic structures for language were evolving in the left? Just consider those areas on the right hemisphere corresponding to the speech areas of the left: what is their function? Or, more particularly, what is their important function, *since it must have been such to preclude its development as an auxiliary speech area?* If we stimulate such areas on the right hemisphere today, we do not get the usual "aphasic arrest" (simply the stopping of ongoing speech) which occurs when the normal language areas of the left hemisphere are stimulated. And because of this apparent lack of function, it has often been concluded that large portions of the right hemisphere are simply unnecessary. In fact, large amounts of right hemisphere tissue, including what corresponds to Wernicke's area, and even in some instances the entire hemisphere, have been cut out in human patients because of illness or injury, with surprisingly little deficit in mental function.

The situation then is one where the areas on the right hemisphere that correspond to the speech areas have seemingly no easily observable major function. Why this relatively less essential part of the brain? Could it be that these silent 'speech' areas on the right hemisphere had some function at an earlier stage in man's history that now they do not have?

The answer is clear if tentative. The selective pressures of evolution which could have brought about so mighty a result are those of the bicameral civilizations. The language of men was involved with only one hemisphere in order to leave the other free for the language of gods.

If so, we might expect that there would have to be certain tracts by which the bicameral voices would relate between the right nondominant temporal lobe and the left. The major interconnection between the hemispheres is of course the huge corpus callosum of over two million fibers. But the temporal lobes in men have their own private callosum, so to speak, the much smaller anterior commissures. In rats and dogs, the anterior commissures connect the olfactory parts of the brain. But in men, as seen in my rather imprecise sketch, this transverse band of fibers collects from most of the temporal lobe cortex but particularly the middle gyrus of the temporal lobe included in Wernicke's area, and then squeezes into a tract only slightly more than one eighth of an inch in diameter as it plunges over the amygdala across the top of the hypothalamus toward the other temporal lobe. Here then, I suggest, is the tiny bridge across which came the directions which built our civilizations and founded

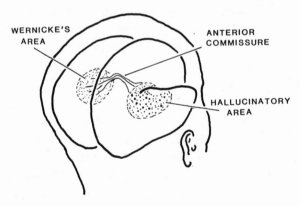

WERNICKE'S AREA   ANTERIOR COMMISSURE

HALLUCINATORY AREA

In ancient times, what corresponds to Wernicke's area on the right hemisphere may have organized admonitory experience and coded it into 'voices' which were then 'heard' over the anterior commissure by the left or dominant hemisphere.

the world's religions, where gods spoke to men and were obeyed because they were human volition.[3]

There are two forms in which this hypothesis can be specified.

The stronger form, and the one I favor because it is simpler and more specific (and thus more easily verified or disconfirmed by empirical investigation), is that the speech of the gods was directly organized in what corresponds to Wernicke's area on the right hemisphere and 'spoken' or 'heard' over the anterior commissures to or by the auditory areas of the left temporal lobe. (Note how I can only express this metaphorically, personifying the right temporal lobe as a person speaking or the left temporal lobe as a person listening, both being equivalent and both literally false.) Another reason I am inclined to this stronger form is its very rationality in terms of getting processed information or thought from one side of the brain to the other. Consider the evolutionary problem: billions of nerve cells processing complex experience on one side and needing to send the results over to the other through the much smaller commissures. Some code would have to be used, some way of reducing very complicated processing into a form that could be transmitted through the fewer neurons particularly of the anterior commissures. And what better code has ever appeared in the evolution of animal nervous systems than human language? Thus in the stronger form of our model, auditory hallucinations exist as such in a linguistic manner because that is the most efficient method of getting complicated cortical processing from one side of the brain to the other.

The weaker form of the hypothesis is more vague. It states that the articulatory qualities of the hallucination were of left hemisphere origin like the speech of the person himself, but that

[3] I do not mean to imply that the bicameral transmission was the only function of the anterior commissure. This commissure interconnects most of the two temporal lobes, including a good part of the posterior portion of the inferior temporal convolution. This region is fed by a strong system of fibers sweeping down from the occipital lobe and is centrally important to visual gnostic functions. See E. G. Ettlinger, *Functions of the Corpus Callosum* (Boston: Little, Brown, 1965).

its sense and direction and different relation to the person were due to right temporal lobe activity sending excitation over the anterior commissures and probably the splenium (the back part of the corpus callosum) to the speech areas of the left hemisphere, and 'heard' from there.

At the present time, it does not really matter which form of the hypothesis we take. The central feature of both is that the amalgamating of admonitory experience was a right hemisphere function and it was excitation in what corresponds to Wernicke's area on the right hemisphere that occasioned the voices of the gods.

The evidence to support this hypothesis may be brought together as five observations: (1) that both hemispheres are able to understand language, while normally only the left can speak; (2) that there is some vestigial functioning of the right Wernicke's area in a way similar to the voices of gods; (3) that the two hemispheres under certain conditions are able to act almost as independent persons, their relationship corresponding to that of the man-god relationship of bicameral times; (4) that contemporary differences between the hemispheres in cognitive functions at least echo such differences of function between man and god as seen in the literature of bicameral man; and (5) that the brain is more capable of being organized by the environment than we have hitherto supposed, and therefore could have undergone such a change as from bicameral to conscious man mostly on the basis of learning and culture.

The rest of this chapter will be devoted to these five observations.

1. *That Both Hemispheres Understand Language*

The gods, I have said with some presumption, were amalgams of admonitory experience, made up of meldings of whatever commands had been given the individual. Thus, while the divine areas would not have to be involved in speech, they would have to be involved in hearing and in understanding language. And this is the case even today. We do in fact understand language with both hemispheres. Stroke patients who have hemorrhages on the left side of the cortex cannot speak, but still can understand.[4] If sodium amytal is injected into the left carotid artery leading to the left hemisphere (the Wada test), the entire hemisphere is anesthetized, leaving only the right hemisphere working; but the subject still can follow directions.[5] Tests on commissurotomized patients (which I shall describe more fully in a moment) demonstrate considerable understanding by the right hemisphere.[6] Named objects can usually be retrieved by the left hand, and verbal commands obeyed by the left hand. Even when the entire left hemisphere, the speech hemisphere, remember, is removed in human patients suffering from glioma, the remaining right hemisphere immediately after the operation seems to understand the surgeon's questions, though unable to reply.[7]

2. *That There Exists Vestigial Godlike Function in the Right Hemisphere*

If the preceding model is correct, there might be some residual indication, no matter how small, of the ancient divine function of the right hemisphere. We can, indeed, be more specific here. Since the voices of the gods did not, of course, entail articulate

[4] This is a general observation — true of cases I have interviewed personally.

[5] The Wada test is presently part of presurgical procedures before brain surgery in the Montreal Neurological Institute. See J. Wada and T. Rasmussen, "Intracarotid Injection of Sodium Amytal for the Lateralization of Cerebral Speech Dominance," *Journal of Neurosurgery*, 1960, 17: 266–282.

[6] M. S. Gazzaniga, J. E. Bogen, R. W. Sperry, "Laterality effects in somesthesis following cerebral commissurotomy in man," *Neuropsychologia*, 1: 209–215. See also Stuart Dimond's excellent discussion of the problem in his *The Double Brain* (Edinburgh and London: Churchill Livingstone, 1972), p. 84.

[7] Aaron Smith, "Speech and other functions after left (dominant) hemispherectomy," *Journal of Neurology Neurosurgical Psychiatry*, 29: 467–471.

speech, did not entail the use of the larynx and mouth, we can rule out what corresponds to Broca's area and the supplementary motor area, to a certain extent, and concentrate on what corresponds to Wernicke's area or the posterior part of the temporal lobe on the right or so-called nondominant side. If we stimulate it in this location, would we hear then the voices of the gods as of yore? Or some remnant of them? Something that would allow us to think that three thousand years ago its function was that of the divine direction of human affairs?

We may recall that this was indeed the very area which had been stimulated by Wilder Penfield in a famous series of studies a few years ago.[8] Let me describe them in some detail.

These observations were made on some seventy patients with a diagnosis of epilepsy caused by lesions somewhere in the temporal lobe. As a preliminary to the removal of the damaged brain tissue by surgery, various points on the surface of the temporal lobe were stimulated with a gentle electric current. The intensity of the stimulation was approximately the least current needed to excite tingling in the thumb by stimulation of the appropriate motor area. If it be objected that the phenomena resulting from this stimulation are corrupted by the presence of some focal area of gliosis, or sclerosis, or meningo-cerebral cicatrix, all typically found in such patients, I think such objections would be dissipated by reviewing the original report. These abnormalities, when found, were circumscribed in location and were not in any way influencing the responses of the subject as they were being stimulated.[9] It can thus be assumed with some confidence that the results of these studies are representative of what would be found in normal individuals.

In the great majority of these cases, it was the right temporal

[8] Wilder Penfield and Phanor Perot, "The brain's record of auditory and visual experience: a final summary and discussion," *Brain*, 1963, 86: 595–702.

[9] Though presumably the particular aura of the epilepsy had been occasioned by the spread of cortical excitation from the lesion to these same areas.

lobe that was stimulated, particularly the posterior part of the temporal lobe toward its superior convolution, Wernicke's area on the right side. A remarkable series of responses from the patients was obtained. This is, to repeat myself, the point at which we might expect to hear the gods of antiquity calling to us again, as if from the other part of our bicameral minds. Would these patients hear some vestiges of the ancient divinities?

Here are some representative data.

When stimulated in this region, Case 7, a twenty-year-old college student, cried out, "Again I hear voices, I sort of lost touch with reality. Humming in my ears and a small feeling like a warning." And when stimulated again, "Voices, the same as before. I was just losing touch with reality again." When asked, he replied that he could not understand what the voices were saying. They sounded "hazy."

In the majority of cases, the voices were similarly hazy. Case 8, a twenty-six-year-old housewife, stimulated in approximately the same area, said there seemed to be a voice a way, way off. "It sounded like a voice saying words but it was so faint I couldn't get it." Case 12, a twenty-four-year-old woman, stimulated at successive points of the superior gyrus of the posterior temporal lobe, said, "I could hear someone talking, murmuring or something." And then further on, "There was talking or murmuring, but I cannot understand it." And then stimulated about three quarters of an inch along the gyrus, she was at first silent, and then gave a loud cry. "I heard the voices and then I screamed. I had a feeling all over." And then stimulated a little back toward the first stimulations, she began to sob. "That man's voice again! The only thing I know is that my father frightens me a lot." She did not recognize the voice as her father's; it only reminded her of him.

Some patients heard music, unrecognized melodies that could be hummed to the surgeon (Cases 4 and 5). Others heard relatives, particularly their mothers. Case 32, a twenty-two-year-old woman, heard her mother and father talking and singing, and then stimulated on another point, her mother "just yelling."

Many patients heard the voices as emanating from strange and unknown places. Case 36, a twenty-six-year-old woman, stimulated somewhat anteriorly on the superior gyrus of the right temporal lobe, said, "Yes, I heard voices down along the river somewhere — a man's voice and a woman's voice, calling." When asked how she could tell it was down along the river, she said, "I think I saw the river." When asked what river, she said, "I do not know, it seems to be one I was visiting when I was a child." And at other stimulation points, she heard voices of people calling from building to building somewhere. And at an adjacent point, the voice of a woman calling in a lumberyard, though she insisted that she had "never been around any lumber-yard."

When the voices were located as coming from one side or the other, as rarely happened, it was from the contralateral side. Case 29, a twenty-five-year-old man, stimulated in the middle of the right temporal gyrus, said, "Someone telling me in my left ear, 'Sylvère, Sylvère!' It could have been my brother."

The voices and the music, whether garbled or recognized, were experienced as actually heard, and the visual hallucinations were experienced as actually seen, just as Achilles experienced Thetis, or Moses heard Yahweh out of the burning bush. Case 29, the same as above, when stimulated again, also saw "someone speaking to another and he mentioned the name, but I could not understand it." And when asked whether he saw the person he replied, "It was just like a dream." And when asked further if the person was there, he said, "Yes, sir, about where the nurse with the eyeglasses is sitting over there."

In some slightly older patients, only exploratory stimulation produced an hallucination. A thirty-four-year-old French-Canadian, Case 24, after previous stimulations had produced nothing, when stimulated on the posterior part of the middle gyrus of the right temporal lobe, suddenly said, "Wait a minute, I see someone!" And then about an inch higher, "Oui, là, là, là! It was he, he came, that fool!" And then stimulated somewhat higher though still within what corresponds to Wernicke's area on the right side, "There, there, j'entend! It is just that somebody wanted to speak to me, and he was going, 'vite, vite, vite!'

But at younger ages, there is a definite suggestion that hallucinations caused by stimulating the right temporal lobe are more striking, vivid, and admonitory. A fourteen-year-old boy (Case 34) saw two men sitting in armchairs singing at him. A fourteen-year-old girl, Case 15, when stimulated on the superior posterior gyrus of the right temporal lobe, cried out, "Oh, everybody is shouting at me again, make them stop!" The stimulus duration was two seconds; the voices lasted eleven seconds. She explained, "They are yelling at me for doing something wrong, everybody is yelling." At all stimulation points along the posterior temporal lobe of the right hemisphere, she heard yelling. And even when stimulated an inch and a half posterior to the first point, she cried out, "There they go, yelling at me; stop them!" And the voices coming from just one stimulation lasted twenty-one seconds.

I should not give the impression that it is all this simple. I have selected these cases. In some patients, there was no response at all. Occasionally such experiences involved autoscopic illusions such as we referred to in I.2. A further complication is that stimulation of corresponding points on the left or usually dominant hemisphere may also result in similar hallucinations. In other words, such phenomena are not confined to the right temporal lobe. But the instances of response to stimulation on the left are much less frequent and occur with less intensity.

The important thing about almost all these stimulation-caused experiences is their *otherness*, their opposition from the self, rather than the self's own actions or own words. With a few exceptions, the patients never experienced eating, talking, sex, running, or playing. In almost all instances, the subject was passive and being acted upon, exactly as a bicameral man was acted upon by his voices.

Being acted upon by what? Penfield and Perot think it is simply past experience, flashbacks to earlier days. They try to explain the failure of recognition so consistently observed as mere forgetfulness. They assume that these were actual specific memories that with more time during the operation could have been pushed into full recognition. In fact, their questions to the patients during stimulation were guided by this hypothesis. Sometimes, indeed, the patient did become specific in his replies. But far more representative of the data as a whole is the patients' persistence under questioning that these experiences could not be called memories.

Because of this, and because of the general absence of personal active images, which are the usual kind of memories that we have, I suggest that the conclusions of Penfield and Perot are incorrect. These areas of the temporal lobe are not "the brain's record of auditory and visual experience," nor are they its retrieval, but combinations and amalgamations of certain aspects of that experience. The evidence does not, I think, warrant the assertion that these areas "play in adult lives some role in the subconscious recall of past experience, making it available for present interpretation." Rather the data lead away from this, to hallucinations that distill particularly admonition experiences, and perhaps become embodied or rationalized into actual experiences in those patients who reported them on being questioned.

3. *That the Two Hemispheres Can Behave Independently*

In our brain model of the bicameral mind, we have assumed that the god part and the man part behaved and thought somewhat independently. And if we now say that the duality of this ancient mentality is represented in the duality of the cerebral hemispheres, is this not personifying parts of the brain without warrant? Is it possible to think of the two hemispheres of the brain almost as two individuals, only one of which can overtly speak, while both can listen and both understand?

The evidence that this is plausible comes from another group of epileptics. These are the dozen or so neurosurgical patients who have undergone complete commissurotomy, the cutting down the midline of all interconnections between the two hemispheres.[10] This so-called split-brain operation (which it is not — the deeper parts of the brain are still connected) usually cures the otherwise untreatable epilepsy by preventing the spread of abnormal neural excitation over the whole cortex. Immediately after operation, some patients lose speech for up to two months, while others have no problem whatever — no one knows why. Perhaps each of us has a slightly different relationship between our hemispheres. Recovery is gradual, all patients showing short-term memory deficits (perhaps due to the cutting of the small hippocampal commissures), some orientation problems, and mental fatigue.

Now the astonishing thing is that such patients after a year or so of recovery do not feel any different from the way they felt before the operation. They sense nothing wrong. At the present time they are watching television or reading the paper with no complaints about anything peculiar. Nor does an observer notice anything different about them.

But under rigorous control of sensory input, fascinating and important defects are revealed.

[10] The literature on these patients of Joseph E. Bogen is still expanding. I would recommend his classical papers, particularly "The other side of the brain, II: An appositional mind," *Bulletin of the Los Angeles Neurological Society*, 1969, 34 (3): 135–162. For a discussion by one of the pioneers in hemispheric research, R. W. Sperry, "Hemisphere Deconnection and Unity in Conscious Awareness," *American Psychologist*, 1968, 23: 723–733. And for a readable account by the man whose ingenuity devised ways of testing these patients, read Michael Gazzaniga's *The Bisected Brain* (New York: Appleton-Century-Crofts, 1970).

As you look at anything, say, the middle word of this line of print, all the words to the left are seen only by the right hemisphere, and all the words to the right only by the left. With the connections between the hemispheres intact, there is no particular problem in co-ordinating the two, although it really is astonishing that we can read at all. But if you had your hemispheric connections cut, the matter would be very different. Starting at the middle of this line, all the print to your right would be seen as before and you would be able to read it off almost as usual. But all the print and all the page to your left would be a blank. Not a blank really, but a nothing, an absolute nothing, far more nothing than any nothing you can imagine. So much nothing that you would not even be conscious that there was nothing there, strange as it seems. Just as in the phenomenon of the blind spot, the 'nothing' is somehow 'filled in', 'stitched together', as if nothing were wrong with nothing. Actually, however, all that nothing would be in your other hemisphere which would be seeing all that 'you' were not, all the print to the left, and seeing it perfectly well. But since it does not have articulated speech, it cannot say that it sees anything. It is as if 'you' — whatever that means — were 'in' your left hemisphere and now with the commissures cut could never know or be conscious of what a quite different person, once also 'you', in the other hemisphere was seeing or thinking about. Two persons in one head.

This is one of the ways these commissurotomized patients are tested. The patient fixates on the center of a translucent screen; photographic slides of objects projected on the left side of the screen are thus seen only by the right hemisphere and cannot be reported verbally, though the patient can use his left hand (controlled by the right hemisphere) to point to a matching picture or search out the object among others, even while insisting vocally that he did not see it.[11] Such stimuli seen by the right nondomi-

11 M. S. Gazzaniga, J. E. Bogen, and R. W. Sperry, "Observations on visual perception after disconnection of the cerebral hemispheres in man," *Brain*, 8: 221–236, 1965.

nant hemisphere alone are there imprisoned, and cannot be 'told' to the left hemisphere where the language areas are because the connections have been cut. The only way we know that the right hemisphere has this information at all is to ask the right hemisphere to use its left hand to point it out — which it can readily do.

If two different figures are flashed simultaneously to the right and left visual fields, as, for example, a "dollar sign" on the left and a "question mark" on the right, and the subject is asked to draw what he saw, using the left hand out of sight under a screen, he draws the dollar sign. But asked what he has just drawn out of sight, he insists it was the question mark. In other words, the one hemisphere does not know what the other hemisphere has been doing.

Again, if the name of some object, like the word 'eraser', is flashed to the left visual field, the subject is then able to search out an eraser from among a collection of objects behind a screen using only the left hand. If the subject is then asked what the item is behind the screen after it has been selected correctly, 'he' in the left hemisphere cannot say what the dumb 'he' of the right hemisphere is holding in his left hand. Similarly, the left hand can do this if the word 'eraser' is spoken, but the talking hemisphere does not know when the left hand has found the object. This shows, of course, what I have said earlier, that both hemispheres understand language, but it has never been possible to find out the extent of language understanding in the right hemisphere previously.

Further, we find that the right hemisphere is able to understand complicated definitions. Flashing "shaving instrument" onto the left visual field and so into the right hemisphere, the left hand points to a razor, or with "dirt remover" to soap, and with "inserted in slot machines" to a twenty-five-cent piece.[12]

Moreover, the right hemisphere in these patients can respond emotionally without the left talking hemisphere knowing what it

[12] M. S. Gazzaniga and R. W. Sperry, "Language after section of the cerebral commissures," *Brain*, 1967, 90: 131–148.

is all about. If among a series of neutral geometric figures being flashed to the right and left visual fields at random, which means respectively into the left and right hemispheres, and then a picture of a nude girl by surprise is flashed on the left side going into the right hemisphere, the patient (really the patient's left hemisphere) says that it saw nothing or just a flash of light. But the grinning, blushing, and giggling during the next minute contradicts what the speech hemisphere has just said. Asked what all the grinning is about, the left or speech hemisphere replies that it has no idea.[13] These facial expressions and blushings, incidentally, are not confined to one side of the face, being mediated through the deep interconnections of the brainstem. The expression of affect is not a cortical matter.

Similarly with other sensory modalities. Odors presented to the right nostril and so to the right hemisphere (olfactory fibers do not cross) in these patients cannot be named by the talking hemisphere, though the latter can say very well whether the smell is pleasant or unpleasant. The patient may even grunt, make aversive reactions, or exclaim "Phew!" to a stench, but cannot say verbally whether it is garlic, cheese, or decayed matter.[14] The same odors presented to the left nostril can be named and described perfectly well. What this means is that the emotion of disgust gets across to the speaking hemisphere through the intact limbic system and brainstem, while the more specific information processed by the cortex does not.

Indeed, there is some indication that it is the right hemisphere that commonly triggers the emotional reactions of displeasure from the limbic system and brainstem. In test situations, where the speechless right hemisphere is made to know the correct answer, and then hears the left dominant hemisphere making

---

[13] R. W. Sperry, "Hemisphere Deconnection."
[14] H. W. Gordon and R. W. Sperry, "Olfaction following surgical disconnection of the hemisphere in man," *Proceedings of the Psychonomic Society*, 1968.

obvious verbal mistakes, the patient may frown, wince, or shake his head. It is not simply a way of speaking to say that the right hemisphere is annoyed at the erroneous vocal responses of the other. And so perhaps the annoyance of Pallas Athene when she grasped Achilles by his yellow hair and twisted him away from murdering his king (Iliad, 1:197). Or the annoyance of Yahweh with the iniquities of his people.

Of course there is a difference. Bicameral man had all his commissures intact. But I shall suggest later that it is possible for the brain to be so reorganized by environmental changes that the inferences of my comparison here are not entirely foolish. At any rate, the studies of these commissurotomy patients demonstrate conclusively that the two hemispheres can function so as to seem like two independent persons, which in the bicameral period were, I suggest, the individual and his god.

4. That Hemispheric Differences in Cognitive Function Echo the Differences of God and Man

If this brain model of the bicameral mind is correct, it would predict decided differences in cognitive function between the two hemispheres. Specifically, we would expect that these functions necessary for the man-side would be in the left or dominant hemisphere, and those functions necessary to the gods would be more emphasized in the right hemisphere. Moreover, there is no reason not to think that the residuals of these different functions at least are present in the brain organization of contemporary man.

The function of the gods was chiefly the guiding and planning of action in novel situations. The gods size up problems and organize action according to an ongoing pattern or purpose, resulting in intricate bicameral civilizations, fitting all the disparate parts together, planting times, harvest times, the sorting out of commodities, all the vast putting together of things in a grand design, and the giving of the directions to the neurological man in his verbal analytical sanctuary in the left hemisphere. We might thus predict that one residual function of the right hemisphere today would be an organizational one, that of sorting out the experiences of a civilization and fitting them together into a pattern that could 'tell' the individual what to do. Perusal of various speeches of gods in the Iliad, the Old Testament, or other ancient literatures is in agreement with this. Different events, past and future, are sorted out, categorized, synthesized into a new picture, often with that ultimate synthesis of metaphor. And these functions should, therefore, characterize the right hemisphere.

Clinical observations are consistent with this hypothesis. From the commissurotomized patients of a few pages past, we know that the right hemisphere with its left hand is excellent at sorting out and categorizing shapes, sizes, and textures. From brain-damaged patients, we know that damage to the right hemisphere interferes with spatial relations and with gestalt, synthetic tasks.[15] Mazes are problems in which various elements of a spatial pattern must be organized in learning. Patients in whom the right temporal lobe has been removed find learning the pathways of visual and tactile mazes almost impossible, while patients with lesions of equal extent on the left temporal lobe have little difficulty.[16]

Another task involving the organization of parts into a spatial pattern is Koh's Block Test, commonly used in many intelligence tests. The subject is shown a simple geometric pattern, and asked to duplicate it with blocks that have its elements painted on them. Most of us can do it easily. But patients with brain lesions

[15] H. Hecaen, "Clinical Symptomatology in Right and Left Hemispheric Lesions," in *Interhemispheric Relations and Cerebral Dominance*, V. B. Mountcastle, ed. (Baltimore: Johns Hopkins Press, 1962).

[16] Brenda Milner, "Visually guided maze learning in man: effects of bilateral, frontal, and unilateral cerebral lesions," *Neuropsychologia*, 1965, 3: 317–338.

in the right hemisphere find this extremely difficult, so much so that the test is used to diagnose right hemisphere damage. In the commissurotomy patients referred to earlier, the right hand often cannot succeed at all in putting the design together with the blocks. The left hand, in a sense the hand of the gods, has no problem whatever. In some of the commissurotomy patients, the left hand had even to be held back by the observer as it tried to help the right hand in its fumbling attempts at this simple task.[17] The inference has thus been drawn from these and other studies that the right hemisphere is more involved in synthetic and spatial-constructive tasks while the left hemisphere is more analytic and verbal. The right hemisphere, perhaps like the gods, sees parts as having a meaning only within a context; it looks at wholes. While the left or dominant hemisphere, like the man side of the bicameral mind, looks at parts themselves.

These clinical results have been confirmed in normal people in what promises to be the first of many future studies.[18] EEG electrodes were placed over the temporal and parietal lobes on both sides of normal subjects who were then given various tests. When asked to write various kinds of letters involving verbal and analytic abilities, the EEG records show low-voltage fast waves over the left hemisphere, denoting that the left hemisphere is doing the work, while slow alpha waves (seen on both hemispheres in a resting subject with the eyes closed) are seen over the right hemisphere, indicating that it is not doing the work. When such subjects are given spatial synthetic tests, such as Koh's Block Test as used in the clinical studies above, the reverse is found. It is now the right hemisphere that is doing the work.

Further deductions can be made about what particular functions might be residual in the right hemisphere by considering

[17] R. W. Sperry, Film presented at Princeton, February 1971.
[18] David Galin and R. E. Ornstein, "Lateral specialization of cognitive mode: an EEG study," *Psychophysiology*, 1972, 9: 412–418.

These faces are mirror images of each other. Stare at the nose of each. Which face is happier?

what it is that the divine voices of the bicameral mind would have to do in particular situations. To sort out and synthesize experience into directives to action, the gods would have to make certain kinds of recognitions. Throughout the speeches of gods in ancient literature, such recognitions are common. I do not mean recognitions of individuals in particular, but more generally of types of people, of classifications, as well as of individuals. One important judgment for a human being of any century is the recognition of facial expression, particularly in regard to friendly or unfriendly intent. If a bicameral man saw an unrecognized man coming toward him, it would be of considerable survival value for the god-side of his mentality to decide if the person was of friendly or unfriendly intent.

The adjoining figure is an experiment I designed about ten years ago out of such a supposition. The two faces are mirror images of each other. I have so far asked almost a thousand people which face looks happier. Quite consistently, about 80 percent of right-handed people chose the bottom face with the smile going up on their left. They were thus judging the face with their right hemispheres, assuming, of course, that they were glancing at the center of the face. This result can be made stronger by tachistoscopic presentation. With the focal point in the center and flashed at one tenth of a second, the bottom face always looks happier to right-handed persons.

An alternative hypothesis, of course, is that this tendency to judge facial expression by the left visual field is a carry-over of reading from left to right. And in our cultures it certainly enhances the effect. But that the hemispheric explanation is at the bottom of it is suggested by the results for left-handed people. Fifty-five percent of left-handers chose the upper face as happier, suggesting that it was the left hemisphere making the judgment. And this cannot be understood on the reading-direction hypothesis. Also, in people who are completely left-lateralized, left-handed in every way, the likelihood of seeing the top face as happier seems to be much higher.

Recently we have made a similar finding, using photographs of an actor expressing sadness, happiness, disgust, and surprise.[19] Our subjects, carefully screened for right-handedness, first stared at the fixation point in a tachistoscope, then were presented with one photograph flashed for a few milliseconds in the central position, and then with another either in the right or left visual field for the same duration. The subjects were asked to say whether the photographs were the same or different, and the time taken to make this decision was recorded. Most of the subjects were able to match facial expressions more correctly and in less time when the face was presented on the left and hence to the right hemisphere. In a control condition, scrambled pictures of the same facial expressions (which were really nonsense patterns) also could be matched more quickly and correctly when presented on the left, but not nearly as well as the facial expressions themselves.

Recent clinical evidence is in clear agreement. Failure to recognize faces, not just facial expressions, is much more frequently associated with damage to the right hemisphere than to the left. In clinical testing, the patient is asked to match the frontal view of a face with three-quarter views of the same face

[19] These experiments were done by Jack Shannon. We are both grateful to Stevan Harnad for his criticism and suggestions.

under different lighting conditions. Patients with lesions in the right hemisphere find this extremely difficult in comparison with normal subjects or patients who have lesions in the left hemisphere.[20] Recognition of both faces and facial expression is therefore primarily a right hemisphere function.

And to tell friend from non-friend in novel situations was one of the functions of a god.

6. *A New Look at the Brain*

How, it may be argued, can such a system as this, a brain structured into what I have called a bicameral mind, this substrate of human civilization for thousands of years, involving such loci as we have mentioned in the model, how can its function change over so short a period of time, such that the admonitory voices are heard no more and that we have this new organization called consciousness? While the amount of genocide going on in the world during these changes was enough to allow some natural selection and evolution, I in no way wish to rest the case upon that. Such natural selection as did occur during these periods of the development of consciousness certainly assisted in its perpetuation, but could not be said to have evolved consciousness out of the bicameral mind in the sense that a seal's flipper is evolved out of an ancestral paw.

A true understanding of the situation requires a different view of the brain from that which was usual a few decades ago. Its emphasis is the brain's plasticity, its redundant representation of psychological capacities within a specialized center or region, the multiple control of psychological capacities by several centers either paired bilaterally or as what Hughlings Jackson recognized as "rerepresentations" of a function lying at successively higher

---

[20] H. Hecaen and R. Angelergues, "Agnosia for Faces (Prosopagnosia)," *Archives of Neurology* 7: 92–100, 1962; A. L. Benton and M. W. Allen, "Impairment in Facial Recognition in Patients with Cerebral Disease," *Cortex*, 1968, 4: 345–358.

and phylogenetically younger levels of the nervous system.[21] The organization of the mammalian brain in this fashion allows for those experimental phenomena brought together under the rubric of "recovery of function." Its emphasis gives a view of the brain much more plastic than usual, with a dramatic surplus of neurons such that, for example, 98 percent of the optic tracts can be cut in the cat, and brightness and pattern discrimination will remain.[22] The brain teems with redundant centers, each of which may exert direct influence on a final common pathway, or modulate the operation of others, or both, their arrangements able to assume many forms and degrees of coupling between constituent centers.

All this redundant representation in multiple control gives us the notion of a much more changeable kind of brain than the earlier neurologists described. A particular behavior or group of behaviors engage a host of similar neurons in a given center and may call into play several different centers arranged in various patterns of inhibition and facilitation, depending upon their evolutionary status. And the tightness of the coupling between centers varies tremendously from one function to another.[23] In other words, the amount of changeableness that the locus of cortical functions can undergo is different among different functions, but that such changeableness is a pronounced feature of the higher mammalian brain is becoming more and more apparent. The biological purpose or selective advantage of such redundant representation and multiple control and its resulting plasticity is twofold: it protects the organism against the effects of brain damage, and, perhaps more important, it provides an

21 Hughlings Jackson, "Evolution and Dissolution of the Nervous System," in *Selected Writings of John Hughlings Jackson*, J. Taylor, ed. (London: Staples Press, 1958), 2: 45–75.

22 R. Galambos, T. T. Norton, and G. P. Fromer, "Optic tract lesions sparing pattern vision in cats," *Experimental Neurology*, 1967, 18: 18–25.

23 I am paraphrasing the superb recent review of this problem by Burton Rosner, "Brain functions," *Annual Review of Psychology*, 1970, 21: 555–594.

organism of far greater adaptability to the constantly changing environmental challenges. I am thinking here of such challenges as characterize the successive glaciations of primate man's existence, and, of course, that even greater challenge of the breakdown of the bicameral mind to which man adapted with consciousness.

But this does not mean just that adult man's behavior is less rigid than his forebear's, though this is of course true. More important, it provides an organism where the early developmental history of the individual can make a great difference in how the brain is organized. Some years ago, an idea such as this would have seemed very far-fetched indeed. But the increasing tide of research has eroded any rigid concept of the brain, and has emphasized the remarkable degree to which the brain can compensate for any structures missing either by injury or by congenital malformation. Many studies show that brain injury to animals in infancy may make little difference in adult behavior, while similar injury to adults may have profound changes. We have already noted that early injury to the left hemisphere usually results in the switch of the entire speech mechanism to the right hemisphere.

One of the most astonishing of the cases that demonstrate this resiliency of the brain is that of a thirty-five-year-old man who died of an abdominal malignancy. At autopsy, it was revealed that he had a congenital absence of the hippocampal fimbria, the fornix, septum pellucidum, and the mass intermedia thalami, with an abnormally small hippocampus and abnormally small hippocampal and dentate gyri. In spite of these remarkable abnormalities, the patient had always displayed an "easygoing" personality and had even led his class in school![24]

Thus, the growing nervous system compensates for genetic or environmental damage by following other but less preferred de-

[24] P. W. Nathan and M. C. Smith, "Normal mentality associated with a maldeveloped Rhinencephalon," *Journal of Neurology, Neurosurgery and Psychiatry*, 1950, 13: 191–197, as cited in Rosner.

velopmental paths which utilize intact tissue. In adults, with development completed, this is no longer possible. The normally preferred modes of neural organization have already been achieved. It is only in early development that such reorganization of the systems of multiple control can take place. And this is definitely true of the relationship between the hemispheres so central to this discussion.[25]

With this as a background, I do not see the difficulty in considering that, in the bicameral epochs, what corresponds to Wernicke's area on the right nondominant hemisphere had its strict bicameral function, whereas after a thousand years of psychological reorganization in which such bicamerality was discouraged when it appeared in early development, such areas function in a different way. And similarly, it would be wrong to think that whatever the neurology of consciousness now may be, it is set for all time. The cases we have discussed indicate otherwise, that the function of brain tissue is not inevitable, and that perhaps different organizations, given different developmental programs, may be possible.

[25] R. E. Saul and R. W. Sperry, "Absence of commissurotomy symptoms with agenesis of the corpus callosum," *Neurology*, 1968, 18: 307; D. L. Reeves and C. B. Carville, "Complete agenesis of corpus callosum: report of four cases," *Bulletin of Los Angeles Neurological Society*, 1938, 3: 169–181.

CHAPTER 6

The Origin of Civilization

B UT WHEREFORE should there be such a thing as the bicameral mind? And why are there gods? What can be the origin of things divine? And if the organization of the brain in bicameral times was as I have suggested in the previous chapter, what could the selective pressures in human evolution have been to bring about so mighty a result?

The speculative thesis which I shall try to explain in this chapter — and it is very speculative — is simply an obvious corollary from what has gone before. The bicameral mind is a form of social control and it is that form of social control which allowed mankind to move from small hunter-gatherer groups to large agricultural communities. The bicameral mind with its controlling gods was evolved as a final stage of the evolution of language. And in this development lies the origin of civilization.

Let us begin by looking at what we mean by social control.

THE EVOLUTION OF GROUPS

Mammals in general show a wide variety of social groupings, all the way from the solitariness of certain predatory animals to the very close social cohesiveness of others. The latter animals are the more preyed upon, and a social group is itself a genetic adaptation for protection against predators. The structure of herds in ungulates is relatively simple, utilizing precise genetically given anatomical and behavioral signals that are all evolved for group protection. Primates have a similar vulnerability, and for the same reason are evolved to live in close association with others. In dense protective forests, the social group may be as small as six, as in gibbons, while on the more exposed terrains, the group may be up to eighty, as in the Cape baboons.[1] In exceptional ecologies, the group size may be even larger.

It is the group then that evolves. When dominant individuals give a warning cry or run, others of the group flee without looking for the source of danger. It is thus the experience of one individual and his dominance that is an advantage to the whole group. Individuals do not generally respond even to basic physiological needs except within the whole pattern of the group's activity. A thirsty baboon, for example, does not leave the group and go seeking water; it is the whole group that moves or none. Thirst is satisfied only within the patterned activity of the group. And so it is with other needs and situations.

The important thing for us here is that this social structure depends upon the communication between the individuals. Primates have therefore evolved a tremendous variety of complex signals: tactile communication ranging from mounting and grooming to various kinds of embracing, nuzzling, and fingering; sounds ranging from assorted grunts, barks, screeching, and yakking, all grading into each other; nonvocal signals such as grinding teeth or beating branches;[2] visual signals in a variety of facial expressions, the threatening, direct eye-to-eye gaze, eyelid fluttering in baboons in which the brows are raised and the lids are lowered to expose their pale color against the darker background

[1] Irven DeVore and K. R. L. Hall, "Baboon Ecology," Ch. 2 in *Primate Behavior*, I. DeVore, ed. (New York: Holt, Rinehart and Winston, 1965), pp. 20–52.

[2] K. R. L. Hall, "The sexual, agonistic, and derived social behaviour patterns of the wild chacma baboon, *Papio ursinus*," *Proceedings of the Zoological Society*, London, 1962, 139: 283–327.

of the face, together with a yawn that bares the teeth aggres-
sively; various postural signals such as lunging, head jerking,
feinting with the hands, and all these in various constellations.[3]

This huge redundant complexity of signaling is essentially devoted to the requisites of the group, its organization into patterns
of dominance and subordination, the maintenance of peace, re-
production, and care for the young. Except for signifying potential group danger, primate signals rarely apply to events outside
the group, such as the presence of food or water.[4] They are
totally within group affairs and are not evolved to give environmental information in the way human languages are.

Now this is what we start with. Within a specific ecology, for
most species, it is this communication system that limits the size
of the group. Baboons are able to achieve groups as high as
eighty or more because they have a strict geographical structure
as they move about on the open plains, with dominant hierarchies being maintained within each circle of the group. But in
general the usual primate group does not exceed thirty or forty, a
limit determined by the communication necessary for the dominance hierarchy to work.

In gorillas, for example, the dominant male, usually the largest
silver-backed male, together with all the females and young,
occupies the central core of each group of about twenty, the other
males tending to be peripheral. The diameter of a group at any
given moment rarely exceeds 200 feet, as every animal remains
attentive to the movements of others in the dense forest environment.[5] The group moves when the dominant male stands motion-

---

[3] Peter Marler, "Communication in monkeys and apes," Ch. 16, in *Primate Behavior*.

[4] As is known in some birds. See M. Konishi, "The role of auditory feedback in
the vocal behavior of the domestic fowl," *Zeitschrift für Tierpsychologie*, 1963, 20:
349–367.

[5] G. Schaller, *The Mountain Gorilla: Ecology and Behavior* (Chicago: University
of Chicago Press, 1963).

less with his legs spread and faces a certain direction. The other members of the group then crowd around him, and the troop moves off on its leisurely day's journey of about a third of a mile. The important thing here is that the complex channels of communication are open between the top of the dominance hierarchy and all the rest.

There is no reason to think that early man from the beginning of the genus *Homo* two million years ago lived any differently. Such archaeological evidence as has been obtained indicates the size of a group to be about thirty.[6] This number, I suggest, was limited by the problem of social control and the degree of openness of the communication channels between individuals.[7] And it is the problem of this limitation of group size which the gods may have come into evolutionary history to solve.

But first we must consider the evolution of language as the necessary condition for there to be gods at all.

THE EVOLUTION OF LANGUAGE

When Did Language Evolve?

It is commonly thought that language is such an inherent part of the human constitution that it must go back somehow through the tribal ancestry of man to the very origin of the genus *Homo*, that is, for almost two million years. Most contemporary linguists of my acquaintance would like to persuade me that this is true. But with this view, I wish to totally and emphatically

---

[6] Glynn L. Isaac, "Traces of Pleistocene Hunters: An East African Example," in *Man the Hunter*, Richard B. Lee and Irven DeVore, eds. (Chicago: Aldine Press, 1968).

[7] This group size is approximately the same for modern tribal hunters when they are nomadic. But the case is not the same. See Joseph B. Birdsell, "On population structure in generalized hunting and collecting populations," *Evolution*, 1958, 12: 189–205.

disagree. If early man, through these two million years, had even a primordial speech, why is there so little evidence of even simple culture or technology? For there is precious little archaeologically up to 40,000 B.C., other than the crudest of stone tools.

Sometimes the reaction to a denial that early man had speech is, how then did man function or communicate? The answer is very simple: just like all other primates, with an abundance of visual and vocal signals which were very far removed from the syntactical language that we practice today. And when I even carry this speechlessness down through the Pleistocene Age, when man developed various kinds of primitive pebble choppers and hand axes, again my linguist friends lament my arrogant ignorance and swear oaths that in order to transmit even such rudimentary skills from one generation to another, there had to be language. But consider that it is almost impossible to describe chipping flints into choppers in language. This art was transmitted solely by imitation, exactly the same way in which chimpanzees transmit the trick of inserting straws into ant hills to get ants. It is the same problem as the transmission of bicycle riding; does language assist at all?

Because language *must* make dramatic changes in man's attention to things and persons, because it allows a transfer of information of enormous scope, it must have developed over a period that shows archaeologically that such changes occurred. Such a one is the late Pleistocene, roughly from 70,000 B.C. to 8000 B.C. This period was characterized climactically by wide variations in temperature, corresponding to the advance and retreat of glacial conditions, and biologically by huge migrations of animals and man caused by these changes in weather. The hominid population exploded out of the African heartland into the Eurasian subarctic and then into the Americas and Australia. The population around the Mediterranean reached a new high and took the lead in cultural innovation, transferring man's cultural and biological focus from the tropics to the middle latitudes.[8] His fires, caves, and furs created for man a kind of transportable microclimate that allowed these migrations to take place.

We are used to referring to these people as late Neanderthalers. At one time they were thought to be a separate species of man supplanted by Cro-Magnon man around 35,000 B.C. But the more recent view is that they were part of the general human line, which had great variation, a variation that allowed for an increasing pace of evolution, as man, taking his artificial climate with him, spread into these new ecological niches. More work needs to be done to establish the true patterns of settlement, but the most recent emphasis seems to be on its variation, some groups continually moving, others making seasonal migrations, and others staying at a site all the year round.[9]

I am emphasizing the climate changes during this last glacial age because I believe these changes were the basis of the selective pressures behind the development of language through several stages.

Calls, Modifiers, and Commands

The first stage and the *sine qua non* of language is the development out of incidental calls of *intentional calls,* or those which tend to be repeated unless turned off by a change in behavior of the recipient. Previously in the evolution of primates, it was only postural or visual signals such as threat postures which were intentional. Their evolution into auditory signals was made necessary by the migration of man into northern climates, where there was less light both in the environment and in the dark caves where man made his abode, and where visual signals could

[8] See J. D. Clark, "Human ecology during the Pleistocene and later times in Africa south of the Sahara," *Current Anthropology,* 1960, 1: 307–324.

[9] See Karl W. Butzer, *Environment and Archaeology: An Introduction to Pleistocene Geography* (Chicago: Aldine Press, 1964), p. 378.

not be seen as readily as on the bright African savannahs. This evolution may have begun as early as the Third Glaciation Period or possibly even before. But it is only as we are approaching the increasing cold and darkness of the Fourth Glaciation in northern climates that the presence of such vocal intentional signals gave a pronounced selective advantage to those who possessed them.

I am here summarizing a theory of language evolution which I have developed more fully and with more caution elsewhere.[10] It is not intended as a definitive statement of what occurred in evolution so much as a rough working hypothesis to approach it. Moreover, the stages of language development that I shall describe are not meant to be necessarily discrete. Nor are they always in the same order in different localities. The central assertion of this view, I repeat, is that *each new stage of words literally created new perceptions and attentions, and such new perceptions and attentions resulted in important cultural changes which are reflected in the archaeological record.*

The first real elements of speech were the final sounds of intentional calls differentiating on the basis of intensity. For example, a danger call for immediately present danger would be exclaimed with more intensity, changing the ending phoneme. An imminent tiger might result in 'wahee!' while a distant tiger might result in a cry of less intensity and so develop a different ending such as 'wahoo'. It is these endings, then, that become the first modifiers meaning 'near' and 'far'. And the next step was when these endings, 'hee' and 'hoo', could be separated from the particular call that generated them and attached to some other call with the same indication.

The crucial thing here is that the differentiation of vocal qualifiers had to precede the invention of the nouns which they modified, rather than the reverse. And what is more, this stage of speech had to remain for a long period until such modifiers

---

[10] Julian Jaynes, "The evolution of language in the Late Pleistocene," *Annals of the New York Academy of Sciences*, Vol. 280, 1976, in press.

became stable. This slow development was also necessary so that the basic repertoire of the call system was kept intact to perform its intentional functions. This age of modifiers perhaps lasted up to 40,000 B.C., where we find archaeologically retouched hand axes and points.

The next stage might have been an age of commands, when modifiers, separated from the calls they modify, now can modify men's actions themselves. Particularly as men relied more and more on hunting in the chilled climate, the selective pressure for such a group of hunters controlled by vocal commands must have been immense. And we may imagine that the invention of a modifier meaning 'sharper' as an instructed command could markedly advance the making of tools from flint and bone, resulting in an explosion of new types of tools from 40,000 B.C. up to 25,000 B.C.

Nouns

Once a tribe has a repertoire of modifiers and commands, the necessity of keeping the integrity of the old primitive call system can be relaxed for the first time, so as to indicate the referents of the modifiers or commands. If 'wahee!' once meant an imminent danger, with more intensity differentiation, we might have 'wak ee!' for an approaching tiger, or "wab ee!' for an approaching bear. These would be the first sentences with a noun subject and a predicative modifier, and they may have occurred somewhere between 25,000 and 15,000 B.C.

These are not arbitrary speculations. The succession from modifiers to commands and, only when these become stable, to nouns is no arbitrary succession. Nor is the dating entirely arbitrary. Just as the age of modifiers coincides with the making of much superior tools, so the age of nouns for animals coincides with the beginning of drawing animals on the walls of caves or on horn implements.

The next stage is the development of thing nouns, really a carry-over from the preceding. And just as life nouns began animal drawings, so nouns for things beget new things. This period corresponds, I suggest, to the invention of pottery, pendants, ornaments, and barbed harpoons and spearheads, the last two tremendously important in spreading the human species into more difficult climates. From fossil evidence we know factually that the brain, particularly the frontal lobe in front of the central sulcus, was increasing with a rapidity that still astonishes the modern evolutionist. And by this time, perhaps what corresponds to the Magdalenian culture, the language areas of the brain as we know them had developed.

The Origin of Auditory Hallucinations

At this point, let us consider another problem in the origin of gods, the origin of auditory hallucinations. That there is a problem here comes from the very fact of their undoubted existence in the contemporary world, and their inferred existence in the bicameral period. The most plausible hypothesis is that verbal hallucinations were a side effect of language comprehension which evolved by natural selection as a method of behavioral control.

Let us consider a man commanded by himself or his chief to set up a fish weir far upstream from a campsite. If he is not conscious, and cannot therefore narratize the situation and so hold his analog 'I' in a spatialized time with its consequences fully imagined, how does he do it? It is only language, I think, that can keep him at this time-consuming all-afternoon work. A Middle Pleistocene man would forget what he was doing. But lingual man would have language to remind him, either repeated by himself, which would require a type of volition which I do not think he was then capable of, or, as seems more likely, by a repeated 'internal' verbal hallucination telling him what to do.

To someone who has not fully understood the previous chapters, this type of suggestion will sound extremely strange and far-fetched. But if one is facing directly and conscientiously the problem of tracing out the development of human mentality, such suggestions are necessary and important, even though we cannot at the present time think how we can substantiate them. Behavior more closely based on aptic structures (or, in an older terminology, more 'instinctive') needs no temporal priming. But learned activities with no consummatory closure do need to be maintained by something outside of themselves. This is what verbal hallucinations would supply.

Similarly, in fashioning a tool, the hallucinated verbal command of "sharper" enables nonconscious early man to keep at his task alone. Or an hallucinated term meaning "finer" for an individual grinding seeds on a stone quern into flour. It was indeed at this point in human history that I believe articulate speech, under the selective pressures of *enduring* tasks, began to become unilateral in the brain, to leave the other side free for these hallucinated voices that could maintain such behavior.

The Age of Names

This has been an all too brief sketch of what must have been involved in the evolution of language. But before there could be gods, one further step had to be taken, the invention of that most important social phenomenon — names.

It is somehow startling to realize that names were a particular invention that must have come into human development at a particular time. When? What changes might this make in human culture? It is, I suggest, as late as the Mesolithic era, about 10,000 B.C. to 8000 B.C. when names first occurred. This is the period of man's adaptation to the warmer postglacial environment. The vast sheet of ice has retreated to the latitude of Copenhagen, and man keys in to specific environmental situations, to grassland hunting, to life in the forest, to shellfish collecting, or to the exploitation of marine resources combined with terrestrial hunting. Such living is characterized by a much greater stability of population, rather than the necessary mobility of the hunting groups which preceded them with their large mortality. With these more fixed populations, with more fixed relationships, longer life-spans, and probably larger numbers in the group which had to be distinguished, it is not difficult to see both the need and the likelihood of a carry-over of nouns into names for individual persons.

Now, once a tribe member has a proper name, he can in a sense be recreated in his absence. 'He' can be thought about, using 'thought' here in a special nonconscious sense of fitting into language structures. While there had been earlier graves of a sort, occasionally somewhat elaborate, this is the first age in which we find ceremonial graves as a common practice. If you think of someone close to you who has died, and then suppose that he or she had no name, in what would your grief consist? How long could it last? Previously, man, like other primates, had probably left his dead where they fell, or else hidden them from view with stones, or in some instances roasted and eaten them.[11] But just as a noun for an animal makes that relationship a much more intense one, so a name for a person. And when the person dies, the name still goes on, and hence the relationship, almost as in life, and hence burial practices and mourning. The Mesolithic midden-dwellers of Morbihan, for example, buried their dead in skin cloaks fastened by bone pins and sometimes crowned them with stag antlers and protected them with stone slabs.[12] Other graves from the period show burials with little crowns, or various ornaments, or possibly flowers in carefully excavated places, all, I suggest, the result of the invention of names.

But a further change occurs with names. Up to this time auditory hallucinations had probably been casually anonymous and

[11] As at Choukoutien during the Middle Pleistocene and later in the Croatian cave of Krapina. See Grahame Clark and Stewart Piggott, *Prehistoric Societies* (London: Hutchinson, 1965), p. 61.

[12] Grahame Clark, *The Stone Age Hunters* (New York: McGraw-Hill, 1967), p. 105.

not in any sense a significant social interaction. But once a specific hallucination is recognized with a name, as a voice originating from a particular person, a significantly different thing is occurring. The hallucination is now a social interaction with a much greater role in individual behavior. And a further problem here is just how hallucinated voices were recognized, as whom, and if there were many, how sorted out. Some light on these questions comes from the autobiographical writings of schizophrenic patients. But not enough to pursue the matter here. We are greatly in need of specific research in this area of schizophrenic experience to help us in understanding Mesolithic man.

The Advent of Agriculture

We are now at the threshold of the bicameral period, for the mechanism of social control which can organize large populations of men into a city is at hand. Everyone agrees that the change from a hunting and gathering economy to a food-producing economy by the domestication of plants and animals is the gigantic step that made civilization possible. But there is wide disagreement as to its causes and the means by which it came about.

The traditional theory emphasizes the fact that when the glaciers covered most of Europe during the Late Pleistocene, the whole area from the Atlantic coast across North Africa and the Near East to the Zagros Mountains in Iran enjoyed such an abundant rainfall that it was indeed a vast procreant Eden, luxuriant with plant life ample to support a wide range of fauna, including Paleolithic man. But the recession of the polar ice cap moved these Atlantic rain-winds northward, and the entire Near East became increasingly arid. The wild food-plants and the game on which man had preyed were no longer sufficient to allow him to live by simple food-gathering, and the result was that many tribes emigrated out of the area into Europe, while those who remained — in the words of Pumpelly, who originated this hypothesis from his own excavations — "concentrating on the oases and forced to conquer new means of support, began to utilize the native plants; and from among these he learned to use seeds of different grasses growing on the dry land and in marshes at the mouths of larger streams on the desert."[13] And this view has been followed by a series of more recent authors, including Childe,[14] as well as Toynbee,[15] who called this supposed desiccation of the Near East environment the "physical challenge" to which agricultural civilization was the response.

Recent evidence[16] shows that there was no such extensive desiccation, and that agriculture was not economically 'forced' on anyone. I have been placing an overwhelming importance on language in the development of human culture in Mesolithic times and I would do so here as well. As we saw in Chapter 3, language allows the metaphors of things to increase perception and attention, and so to give new names to things of new importance. It is, I think, this added linguistic mentality, surrounded as it was in the Near East by a fortuitous grouping of suitable domesticates, wild wheats and wild barley, whose native distribution overlaps with the much broader habitats of the herd animals of southwestern Asia, goats, sheep, cattle, and wild pigs, that resulted in agriculture.

THE FIRST GOD

Let us look more directly for a moment at the best defined and most fully studied Mesolithic culture, the Natufian, named after the Wadi en-Natuf in Israel, where the first of the sites was

[13] R. Pumpelly, *Explorations in Turkestan: Expedition of 1904: Prehistoric Civilizations of Anau* (Washington: Carnegie Institution, 1908), pp. 65–66.

[14] V. G. Childe, *The Most Ancient East*, 4th ed. (London: Routledge and Kegan Paul, 1954).

[15] A. J. Toynbee, *A Study of History* (London: Oxford University Press, 1962), Vol. 1, pp. 304–305.

[16] Butzer, p. 416.

found. In 10,000 B.C., like their Paleolithic predecessors, the Natufians were hunters, about five feet tall, often living in the mouths of caves, were skillful in working bone and antler and in chipping retouched blades and burins out of flint, drew animals almost as well as the artists of the cave drawings of Lascaux, and wore perforated shells or animal teeth as ornaments.

By 9000 B.C., they are burying their dead in ceremonial graves and adopting a more settled life. The latter is indicated by the first signs of structural building, such as the paving and walling of platforms with much plaster, and cemeteries sometimes large enough for eighty-seven burials, a size unknown in any previous age. It is, as I have suggested, the age of names, with all that it implies.

It is the open-air Natufian settlement at Eynan which shows this change most dramatically.[17] Discovered in 1959, this heavily investigated site is about a dozen miles north of the Sea of Galilee on a natural terrace overlooking the swamps and pools of Lake Huleh. Three successive permanent towns dating from about 9000 B.C. have been carefully excavated. Each town comprised about fifty round stone houses with reed roofs, with diameters up to 23 feet. The houses were arranged around an open central area where many bell-shaped pits had been dug and plastered for the storage of food. Sometimes these pits were reused for burials.

Now here is a *very* significant change in human affairs. Instead of a nomadic tribe of about twenty hunters living in the mouths of caves, we have a *town* with a population of at least 200 persons. It was the advent of agriculture, as attested by the abundance of sickle blades, pounders and pestles, querns and mortars, recessed in the floor of each house, for the reaping and preparation of cereals and legumes, that made such permanence and population possible. Agriculture at this time was exceedingly

[17] See J. Perrot, "Excavations at Eynan, 1959 season," *Israel Exploration Journal,* 1961, 10: 1; James Mellaart, *Earliest Civilizations of the Near East* (New York: McGraw-Hill, 1965), Ch. 2; Clark and Piggott, p. 150ff.

primitive and only a supplement to the wide variety of animal
fauna — wild goats, gazelles, boars, fox, hare, rodents, birds,
fish, tortoises, crustaceans, mussels, and snails — which, as carbon-
dated remains show, were the significant part of the diet.

The Hallucinogenic King

A town! Of course it is not impossible that one chief could
dominate a few hundred people. But it would be a consuming
task if such domination had to be through face-to-face encounters
repeated every so often with each individual, as occurs in those
primate groups that maintain strict hierarchies.

I beg you to recall, as we try to picture the social life of Eynan,
that these Natufians were not conscious. They could not narratize and had no analog selves to 'see' themselves in relation to
others. They were what we could call signal-bound, that is, responding each minute to cues in a stimulus-response manner,
and controlled by those cues.

And what were the cues for a social organization this large?
What signals were the social control over its two or three hundred inhabitants?

I have suggested that auditory hallucinations may have
evolved as a side effect of language and operated to keep individuals persisting at the longer tasks of tribal life. Such hallucinations began in the individual's hearing a command from himself
or from his chief. There is thus a very simple continuity between
such a condition and the more complex auditory hallucinations
which I suggest were the cues of social control in Eynan and
which originated in the commands and speech of the king.

Now we must not make the error here of supposing that these
auditory hallucinations were like tape recordings of what the king
had commanded. Perhaps they began as such. But after a time
there is no reason not to suppose that such voices could 'think'
and solve problems, albeit, of course, unconsciously. The 'voices'

heard by contemporary schizophrenics 'think' as much and often more than they do. And thus the 'voices' which I am supposing were heard by the Natufians could with time improvise and 'say' things that the king himself had never said. Always, however, we may suppose that all such novel hallucinations were strictly tied in consistency to the person of the king himself. This is not different from ourselves when we inherently know what a friend is likely to say. Thus each worker, gathering shellfish or trapping small game or in a quarrel with a rival or planting seed where the wild grain had previously been harvested, had within him the voice of his king to assist the continuity and utility to the group of his labors.

The God-King

We have decided that the occasion of an hallucination was stress, as it is in our contemporaries. And if our reasonings have been correct, we may be sure that the stress caused by a person's death was far more than sufficient to trigger his hallucinated voice. Perhaps this is why, in so many early cultures, the heads of the dead were often severed from the body, or why the legs of the dead were broken or tied up, why food is so often in the graves, or why there is evidence so often of a double burial of the same corpse, the second being in a common grave after the voices have stopped.

If this were so for an ordinary individual, how much more so for a king whose voice even while living ruled by hallucination. We might therefore expect a very special accordance given to the house of this unmoving man whose voice is still the cohesion of the entire group.

At Eynan, still dating about 9000 B.C., the king's tomb — the first such ever found (so far) — is a quite remarkable affair. The tomb itself, like all the houses, was circular, about 16 feet in diameter. Inside, two complete skeletons lay in the center extended on their backs, with legs detached after death and bent out of position. One wore a headdress of dentalia shells and was presumed to have been the king's wife. The other, an adult male, presumably the king, was partly covered with stones and partly propped up on stones, his upright head cradled in more stones, facing the snowy peaks of Mount Hermon, thirty miles away.

At some later time, soon after or years later, we do not know, the entire tomb was surrounded by a red-ochered wall or parapet. Then, without disturbing its two motionless inhabitants, large flat stones were paved over the top, roofing them in. Then, on the roof a hearth was built. Another low circular wall of stones was built still later around the roof-hearth, with more paving stones on top of that, and three large stones surrounded by smaller ones set in the center.

I am suggesting that the dead king, thus propped up on his pillow of stones, was in the hallucinations of his people still giving forth his commands, and that the red-painted parapet and

The first god: the dead king of Eynan propped up on a pillow of stones in about 9000 B.C., as discovered by excavations in 1959.

its top tier of a hearth were a response to the decomposition of the body, and that, for a time at least, the very place, even the smoke from its holy fire, rising into visibility from furlongs around, was, like the gray mists of the Aegean for Achilles, a source of hallucinations and of the commands that controlled the Mesolithic world of Eynan.

This was a paradigm of what was to happen in the next eight millennia. The king dead is a living god. The king's tomb is the god's house, the beginning of the elaborate god-house or temples which we shall look at in the next chapter. Even the two-tiered formation of its structure is prescient of the multitiered ziggurats, of the temples built on temples, as at Eridu, or the gigantic pyramids by the Nile that time in its majesty will in several thousand years unfold.

We should not leave Eynan without at least mentioning the difficult problem of succession. Of course, we have next to nothing to go on in Eynan. But the fact that the royal tomb contained previous burials that had been pushed aside for the dead king and his wife suggests that its former occupants may have been earlier kings. And the further fact that beside the hearth on the second tier above the propped-up king was still another skull suggests that it may have belonged to the first king's successor, and that gradually the hallucinated voice of the old king became fused with that of the new. The Osiris myth that was the power behind the majestic dynasties of Egypt had perhaps begun.

The king's tomb as the god's house continues through the millennia as a feature of many civilizations, particularly in Egypt. But, more often, the king's-tomb part of the designation withers away. This occurs as soon as a successor to a king continues to hear the hallucinated voice of his predecessor during his reign, and designates himself as the dead king's priest or servant, a pattern that is followed throughout Mesopotamia. In place of the tomb is simply a temple. And in place of the corpse is a statue, enjoying even more service and reverence, since it does not decompose.

We shall be discussing these idols, or replacements for the corpses of kings, more fully in the next two chapters. They are important. Like the queen in a termite nest or a beehive, the idols of a bicameral world are the carefully tended centers of social control, with auditory hallucinations instead of pheromones.

The Success of Civilization

Here then is the beginning of civilization. Rather abruptly, archaeological evidence for agriculture such as the sickle blades and pounding and milling stones of Eynan appear more or less simultaneously in several other sites in the Levant and Iraq around 9000 B.C., suggesting a very early diffusion of agriculture in the Near Eastern highlands. At first, this is as it was at Eynan, a stage in which incipient agriculture and, later, animal domestication were going on within a dominant food-collecting economy.[18]

But by 7000 B.C., agriculture has become the primary subsistence of farming settlements found in assorted sites in the Levant, the Zagros area, and southwestern Anatolia. The crops consisted of einkorn, emmer, and barley, and the domesticated animals were sheep, goats, and sometimes pigs. By 6000 B.C., farming communities spread over much of the Near East. And by 5000 B.C., the agricultural colonization of the alluvial valleys of the Tigris-Euphrates and Nile was rapidly spreading, swelling populations into an intensive cultural landscape.[19] Cities of 10,000 inhabitants, as at Merinde on the western edge of the Nile delta, were not uncommon.[20] The great dynasties of Ur and of Egypt begin their mighty impact on history. The date 5000 B.C.,

[18] See R. J. Braidwood, "Levels in pre-history: A model for the consideration of the evidence," in *Evolution After Darwin*, S. Tax, ed. (Chicago: University of Chicago Press, 1960), Vol. 2, pp. 143–151.

[19] Butzer, p. 464.

[20] See K. W. Butzer, "Archaeology and geology in ancient Egypt," *Science*, 1960, 132: 1617–1624.

or perhaps five hundred years earlier, is also the beginning of what is known to geologists as the Holocene Thermal Maximum, lasting to approximately 3000 B.C., in which the world's climate, particularly as revealed by pollen studies, was considerably warmer and moister than today, allowing even further agricultural dispersal into Europe and northern Africa, as well as more productive agriculture in the Near East. And in this immensely complex civilizing of mankind, the evidence, I think, suggests that the *modus operandi* of it all was the bicameral mind.

It is to that evidence that we now turn.

BOOK TWO

The Witness of History

CHAPTER 1

Gods, Graves, and Idols

C IVILIZATION is the art of living in towns of such size that everyone does not know everyone else. Not a very inspiring definition, perhaps, but a true one. We have hypothesized that it is the social organization provided by the bicameral mind that made this possible. In this and the ensuing chapter, I am attempting to integrate without excessive particularization the worldwide evidence that such a mentality did in fact exist wherever and whenever civilization first began.

While the matter is in much current debate, the view I am adopting is that civilization began independently in various sites in the Near East, as described in the previous chapter, then spread along the valleys of the Tigris and Euphrates rivers, into Anatolia and the valley of the Nile; then into Cyprus, Thessaly, and Crete; and then somewhat later by diffusion into the Indus River valley and beyond, and into the Ukraine and Central Asia; then, partly by diffusion and partly spontaneously, along the Yangtze; then independently in Mesoamerica; and again, partly by diffusion and partly independently, in the Andean highlands. In each of these areas, there was a succession of kingdoms all with similar characteristics that, somewhat prematurely, I shall call bicameral. While there were certainly other bicameral kingdoms in the history of the world, perhaps along the margins of the Bay of Bengal or the Malay peninsular, in Europe, certainly in central Africa by diffusion from Egypt, and possibly among the North

American Indians during the so-called Missouri Period, too little has been recovered of these civilizations to be of assistance in checking out the main hypothesis.

Given the theory as I have outlined it, I suggest that there are several outstanding archaeological features of ancient civilizations which can only be understood on this basis. These silent features are the subject of this chapter, the literate civilizations of Mesopotamia and Egypt being reserved for the next.

THE HOUSES OF GODS

Let us imagine ourselves coming as strangers to an unknown land and finding its settlements all organized on a similar plan: ordinary houses and buildings grouped around one larger and more magnificent dwelling. We would immediately assume that the large magnificent dwelling was the house of the prince who ruled there. And we might be right. But in the case of older civilizations, we would not be right if we supposed such a ruler was a person like a contemporary prince. Rather he was an hallucinated presence, or, in the more general case, a statue, often at one end of his superior house, with a table in front of him where the ordinary could place their offerings to him.

Now, whenever we encounter a town or city plan such as this, with a central larger building that is not a dwelling and has no other practical use as a granary or barn, for example, and particularly if the building contains some kind of human effigy, we may take it as evidence of a bicameral culture or of a culture derived from one. This criterion may seem fatuous, simply because it is the plan of many towns today. We are so used to the town plan of a church surrounded by lesser houses and shops that we see nothing unusual. But our contemporary religious and city architecture is partly, I think, the residue of our bicameral past. The church or temple or mosque is still called the House of

God. In it, we still speak to the god, still bring offerings to be placed on a table or altar before the god or his emblem. My purpose in speaking in this objective fashion is to defamiliarize this whole pattern, so that standing back and seeing civilized man against his entire primate evolution, we can see that such a pattern of town structure *is* unusual and not to be expected from our Neanderthal origins.

From Jericho to Ur

With but few exceptions, the plan of human group habitation from the end of the Mesolithic up to relatively recent eras is of a god-house surrounded by man-houses. In the earliest villages,[1] such as the excavated level of Jericho corresponding to the ninth millennium B.C., such a plan is not entirely clear and is perhaps debatable. But the larger god-house at Jericho, surrounded by what were lesser dwellings, at a level corresponding to the seventh millennium B.C., with its perhaps columned porchway leading into a room with niches and curvilinear annexes, defies doubt as to its purpose. It is no longer the tomb of a dead king whose corpse is propped up on stones. The niches housed nearly life-sized effigies, heads modeled naturalistically in clay and set on canes or bundles of reeds and painted red. Of similar hallucinogenic function may have been the ten human skulls, perhaps of dead kings, found at the same site, with features realistically modeled in plaster and white cowrie shells inserted for eyes. And the Hacilar culture in Anatolia of about 7000 B.C. also had human crania set up on floors, suggesting similar bicameral control to hold the members of the culture together in their food-producing and protection enterprise.

---

[1] General sources consulted here include Grahame Clark and Stuart Piggott, *Prehistoric Societies* (London: Hutchinson, 1965); James Mellaart, *Earliest Civilizations of the Near East* (New York: McGraw-Hill, 1965); and Grahame Clark, *World Prehistory: A New Outline* (Cambridge: Cambridge University Press, 1969).

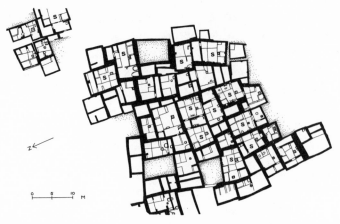

Plan of building-level VI B at Çatal Hüyük, about 6000 B.C. Note
that there is a shrine signified by S in almost every household.

The largest Neolithic site in the Near East is the 32-acre Çatal
Hüyük, of which only one or two acres have been as yet excavated. Here the arrangement was slightly different. Excavations
at levels dating from about 6000 B.C. show that almost every
house had a series of four to five rooms nestled around a god's
room. Numerous groups of statues in stone or baked clay have
been found within these god's rooms.

At Eridu, five centuries later, god-houses were set on mud-brick
platforms, which were the origin of ziggurats. In a long central
room, the god-idol on a platform at one end looked at an offering
table at the other. And it is this Eridu sequence of sanctuaries up
to the Ubaid culture in southern Iraq which, spreading over the
whole of Mesopotamia around 4300 B.C., lays the foundations of
the Sumerian civilization and its Babylonian successor which I
consider in the next chapter. With cities of many thousands
came the building of the huge monumental god-houses which
characterize and dominate cities from then on, perhaps being
hallucinogenic aids to everyone for miles around. To stand even
today under such mountainous ziggurats as that of Ur, still heav-
ing up above the excavated ruins of its once bicameral civiliza-

tion, with its ramps of staircases rising to but half the height it once had, and to imagine its triple tier of temples on top rising into the sun is to feel the grip such architecture alone can have upon one's mentality.

A Hittite Variation

The Hittites in the center of their capital, Hattusas, now Bŏghazköy in central Turkey,[2] had four huge temples with great granite sanctuaries that projected beyond the main façades of the limestone walls to obtain lateral lighting for some huge idols.

But, perhaps taking the place of a ziggurat, that is, of a high place that could be seen wherever lands were being farmed, is the beautiful outdoor mountain shrine of Yazilikaya just above the city, its sanctuary walls streaming with reliefs of gods.[3] That the mountains themselves were hallucinatory to the Hittites is indicated by relief sculptures still clearly visible on the rocks within the sanctuary, showing the usual stereotyped drawings of mountains topped with the heads and headdresses used for gods. As the Psalmist sings, "I will lift up mine eyes unto the hills whence cometh my help."

On one of the faces of this mountain temple, the robed king is carved in profile. Just behind him in the stone relief towers a god with a much loftier crown; the god's right arm is outstretched, showing the king the way, while the god's left arm is hugged around the king's neck and grasps the king's right wrist firmly. It is testament to an emblem of the bicameral mind.

The depicting of gods in long files, unique I think to the Hit-

[2] The Hittites may be an example of a group of nomadic tribes learning a bicameral civilization from their neighbors. It is the sudden intrusion of brightly decorated polychrome pottery among the burnished monochrome pottery of the Cappadocian plateau in the archaelogical record dating about 2100 B.C. that is taken to be the indication of their arrival, probably from the steppes of southern Russia.

[3] Good photographs of Yazilikaya may be seen in Ch. 3 of Seton Lloyd, *Early Highland Peoples of Anatolia* (New York: McGraw-Hill, 1967). An explanatory discussion may be found in Ekron Akurgal, *Ancient Civilizations and Ruins of Turkey* (Istanbul, 1969).

Rock relief at Yazilikaya, about 1250 B.C. The god Sharruma holds his steward-king, Tudhaliys, in his embrace. The pretzel-like hieroglyph for deity is seen both as the head in the god's ideogram on the upper left and repetitively on the god's crown. It is also seen in the king's ideogram on the upper right, indicating, I think, that the king too was 'heard' in hallucination by his subjects.

tites, suggests a solution to an old problem in Hittite research. This is the translation of the important word *pankush*. Scholars originally interpreted it as signifying the whole human community, perhaps some sort of national assembly. But other texts have forced a revision of this to some kind of an elite. A further possibility, I suggest, is that it indicates the whole community of these many gods, and, particularly, the choice-decisions in which all the bicameral voices were in agreement. The fact that during the last century or so of Hittite rule, from around 1300 B.C., no mention of the *pankush* appears in any text could indicate their collective silence and the beginning of the troublous change toward subjectivity.

Olmec and Maya

The earliest bicameral kingdoms of America are also characterized by these huge, otherwise useless centrally located buildings: the queer-shaped clumsy Olmec pyramid at La Venta of
about 500 B.C. with its corridor of lesser mounds smothering
mysterious jaguar-face mosaics; or the rash of great temple pyramids constructed about 200 B.C.[4] The largest of them, the gigantic pyramid of the sun at Teotihuacan (literally "Place of the
Gods") has a greater cubic content than any in Egypt, being an
eighth of a mile long on each side, and higher than a twenty-story
building.[5] A room for a god on its summit was reached by
systems of steep stairs. And on top of the god-room, tradition
states, there was a gigantic statue of the sun. A processional way
flanked by other pyramids leads toward it, and, for miles around
on the Mexican plateau, one can still see the remains of a great
city, houses for priests, numerous courtyards, and smaller buildings, all of one story so that from anywhere in the city one could
see the great pyramidal houses of gods.[6]

Beginning somewhat later, but co-temporaneous with Teotihuacan, are the many Maya cities in the Yucatan peninsula[7]
showing the same bicameral architecture, each city centering
upon steeply rising pyramids topped with god-houses and richly
decorated with Olmec-type jaguar masks and other murals and
carvings, in which an endless variety of dragons with human
faces crawl fiercely through the intricate stone decoration. Ex-
ceptionally interesting is the fact that some of the pyramids

[4] See in this connection C. A. Burland, *The Gods of Mexico* (London: Eyre and
Spottiswoode, 1967); and also G. H. S. Bushnell, *The First Americans: The Pre-
Columbian Civilizations* (New York: McGraw-Hill, 1968).

[5] It was constructed of nearly 3 million tons of clay adobes, thus requiring a
tremendous number of man-hours. For a way of understanding such hand labor
(Mesoamerica did not have the wheel), see p. 427.

[6] See S. Linne, *Archaeological Researches at Teotihuacan, Mexico* (Stockholm:
Ethnographic Museum of Sweden, 1934); also Miguel Covarrubias, *Indian Art of
Mexico and Central America* (New York: Knopf, 1957).

[7] See Victor W. von Hagen, *World of the Maya* (New York: New American
Library, 1960).

contain burials as in Egypt, perhaps indicating a phase in which the king was a god. In front of these Mayan pyramids are usually stelae carved with the figures of gods and glyphic inscriptions which have yet to be fully understood. Since this kind of writing is always in connection with religious images, it is possible that the hypothesis of the bicameral mind may assist in unwinding their mysteries.

I also think that the curious unhospitable sites on which Mayan cities were often built and their sudden appearance and disappearance can best be explained on the basis that such sites and movements were commanded by hallucinations which in certain periods could be not only irrational but downright punishing — as was Jahweh sometimes to his people, or Apollo (through the Delphic Oracle) to his, by siding with the invaders of Greece (see III.1, III.2, n. 12).

Occasionally, there are actual depictions of the bicameral act. On two stone reliefs from Santa Lucia Cotz umalhaupa, a non-Mayan site on the Pacific slope of Guatemala, this is very clearly the case. A man is shown prostrate on the grass being spoken to by two divine figures, one half-human, half-deer, and the other a death figure. That this is an actual bicameral scene is clear from modern observations of the so-called *chilans* or prophets of the area. Even today, they hallucinate voices while face down in this identical posture, although it is thought by some that such contemporary hallucinations are aided by eating peyote.[8]

Andean Civilizations

The half dozen or so civilizations of the Andes that precede the Inca are even more lost in the overgrowth of time.[9] The earliest,

[8] J. Erik S. Thompson, *Maya History and Religion* (Norman: University of Oklahoma Press, 1970), p. 186. Peyote, incidentally, was used by most Mesoamerican Indians when their bicamerality was breaking down. The exceptions were the Maya and they are the only ones to have any kind of writing. Is it possible that 'reading' or hallucinating from glyphs functioned for the Maya as did hallucinogenic peyote for others?

[9] This is partly due to the fact that a new bicameral civilization in an area tends to obliterate the remains of its predecessor. Bicameral gods are jealous gods.

Kotosh, dating before 1800 B.C., is centered about a rectangular god-house built on a stepped platform 25 feet high on a large mound, where it was surrounded by the remains of other buildings. Its interior walls had a few tall rectangular niches in each, in one of which was a pair of crossed hands modeled in plaster, perhaps part of a larger idol, now dust. How similar to Jericho five millennia earlier!

While it is possible that Kotosh was the work of migrants from Mexico, the next civilization, the Chavin, beginning about 1200 B.C., shows decided Olmec features: the cultivation of maize, a number of pottery characteristics, and the jaguar theme in its religious sculpture. At Chavin itself in the north highlands, a great platformlike temple, honeycombed with passages, houses an impressive idol in the form of a prismatic mass of granite carved in low relief to represent a human being with a jaguar head.[10] Following them, the Mochicas,[11] ruling the northern Peruvian desert from A.D. 400 to 1000, built huge pyramids for their gods, towering in front of walled enclosures which probably contained the cities, as can be seen today in the Chicama valley near Trujillo.[12]

Then on the bleak uplands near Lake Titicaca from A.D. 1000 to 1300 came the great empire of Tiahuanaco, with an even larger stone-faced pyramid, set about with giant pillarlike gods weeping tears (why?) of condor heads and snake heads.[13]

Then the Chimu, on an even vaster scale. Its capital of Chan-

[10] The next culture, the Paracas, from about 400 B.C. to A.D. 400, is a mysterious anomaly. They left no building sites, only 400 or so brightly robed mummies in deep subterranean caverns on the Paracas peninsular.

[11] So-called. As in all these early civilizations we have no idea what they called themselves.

[12] Aerial views of their cities look very similar to those of Mesopotamia in the bicameral period. Other cultures, such as the Ica Nazca, also existed at the same time to the south. Little, however, remains except the mysterious lines and figures, some running for miles in length in the dry valleys of Nazca, and gigantic bird or insect outlines, acres in area, for which no one can suggest an explanation.

[13] So complete and swift was their collapse around A.D. 1300, perhaps due to over-expansion (see II.3 for reasons why bicameral kingdoms are unstable), that 250 years later, after the European invasion, no one had heard anything about them.

Chan, covering eleven square miles, was walled off into ten great compounds, each a city in miniature with its own pyramid, its own palacelike structure, its own irrigated areas, reservoirs, and cemeteries. Precisely what these neighboring separated walled compounds could mean in the light of the bicameral hypothesis is a fascinating problem for research.

The Golden Realm of the Incas

And then the Incas themselves, like a synthesis of Egypt and Assyria. At least at the beginning of their power about A.D. 1200, their realm was suggestive of a god-king type of bicameral kingdom. But within a century, the Incas had conquered all before them, perhaps thereby weakening their own bicamerality, as did Assyria in another age and another clime.

The Inca empire at the time of its conquest by Pizarro was perhaps a combination of things bicameral and things protosubjective. This meeting was probably the closest thing there is to a clash between the two mentalities this essay is about. On the subjective side was the vast empire which, if we suppose it was administered with the horizontal and vertical social mobility such an administration demands today,[14] would be very difficult to control in a purely bicameral fashion. From hearsay reports, it is believed that conquered chiefs were allowed to retain their titles, and their sons sent to Cuzco for training and perhaps held as hostages, a difficult conception in a bicameral world. Conquered peoples seem to have retained their own speech, although all officials had to learn the religious language, Quechua.

But on the bicameral side, there are a large number of features which are most certainly bicameral in origin, even though they may have been acted out partially through the inertia of tradition, as the small city-state of Cuzco on the upper reaches of the Amazon exploded into this Roman empire of the Andes. The

[14] J. H. Rowe, "Inca Culture at the time of the Spanish Conquest," in J. H. Steward, *Handbook of South American Indians,* Vol. 2 (Washington, D.C., 1946–50).

Inca himself was the god-king, a pattern so similar to Egypt's that less conservative historians of American antiquity have felt that there must have been some diffusion. But I suggest that given man, language, and cities organized on a bicameral basis, there are only certain fixed patterns into which history can fit.

The king was divine, a descendant of the sun, the creator-god of land and earth, of people, of the sun's sweat (gold) and the moon's tears (silver). Before him, even his highest lords might tremble with such awe as to shake them from their feet,[15] an awe that is impossible for modern psychology to appreciate. His daily life was deep in elaborate ritual. His shoulders were mantled in quilts of fresh bat-webs, and his head circled with a fringe of red tassels, like a curtain before his eyes to protect his lords from too awesome a view at his unwatchable divinity. When the Inca died, his concubines and personal servants first drank and danced, and then were eagerly strangled to join him on his journey to the sun, just as had previously happened in Egypt, Ur, and China. The Inca's body was mummified and placed in his house, which thereafter became a temple. A life-sized golden statue was made of him sitting on his golden stool as in his life, and served daily with food as in the kingdoms of the Near East.

While it is possible that the sixteenth-century Inca and his hereditary aristocracy were walking through bicameral roles established in a much earlier truly bicameral kingdom, even as perhaps the Emperor Hirohito, the divine sun god of Japan, does to this day, the evidence suggests that it was much more than this. The closer an individual was to the Inca, the more it seems his mentality was bicameral. Even the gold and jeweled spools which the top of the hierarchy, including the Inca, wore in their ears, sometimes with images of the sun on them, may have indicated that those same ears were hearing the voice of the sun.

[15] As reported by Pedro Pizarro, a cousin of the Conquistador, quoted by V. W. von Hagen, *Realm of the Incas*, p. 113.

But perhaps most suggestive of all is the manner in which this huge empire was conquered.[16] The unsuspicious meekness of the surrender has long been the most fascinating problem of the European invasions of America. The fact that it occurred is clear, but the record as to why is grimy with supposition, even in the superstitious Conquistadors who later recorded it. How could an empire whose armies had triumphed over the civilizations of half a continent be captured by a small band of 150 Spaniards in the early evening of November 16, 1532?

It is possible that it was one of the few confrontations between subjective and bicameral minds, that for things as unfamiliar as Inca Atahualpa was confronted with — these rough, milk-skinned men with hair drooling from their chins instead of from their scalps so that their heads looked upside down, clothed in metal, with avertive eyes, riding strange llamalike creatures with silver hoofs, having arrived like gods in gigantic huampus tiered like Mochican temples over the sea which to the Inca was unsailable — that for all this there were no bicameral voices coming from the sun, or from the golden statues of Cuzco in their dazzling towers. Not subjectively conscious, unable to deceive or to narratize out the deception of others,[17] the Inca and his lords were captured like helpless automatons. And as its people mechanically watched, this shipload of subjective men stripped the gold sheathing from the holy city, melted down its golden images and all the treasures of the Golden Enclosure, its fields of golden corn with stems and leaves all cunningly wrought in gold, murdered its living god and his princes, raped its unprotesting women, and, narratizing their Spanish futures, sailed away with the yellow metal into the subjective conscious value system from which they had come.

It is a long way from Eynan.

---

[16] For a detailed readable recent account, see John Hemming, *The Conquest of the Incas* (New York: Harcourt Brace Jovanovich, 1970).

[17] There were no thieves in Cuzco and no doors: a stick crosswise in front of the open doorway was a sign that the owner was not in and nobody would enter.

THE LIVING DEAD

The burial of the important dead as if they still lived is common to almost all these ancient cultures whose architecture we have just looked at. This practice has no clear explanation except that their voices were still being heard by the living, and were perhaps demanding such accommodation. As I have suggested at Eynan in I.6, these dead kings, propped up on stones, whose voices were hallucinated by the living, were the first gods.

Then as these early cultures develop into bicameral kingdoms, the graves of their important personages are more and more filled with weapons, furniture, ornaments, and particularly vessels of food. This is true of the very first chamber tombs all over Europe and Asia after 7000 B.C. and is elaborated to an extraordinary degree as bicameral kingdoms develop both in size and complexity. The magnificent burials of Egyptian pharaohs in a whole succession of intricately built pyramids are familiar to everyone (see next chapter). But similar emplacements, if less awesome, are found elsewhere. The kings of Ur, during the first half of the third millennium B.C., were entombed with their entire retinues buried, sometimes alive, in a crouched position around them as for service. Eighteen of such tombs have been found, their vaulted subterranean rooms containing food and drink, clothing, jewelry, weapons, bull-headed lyres, even sacrificed draft animals yoked to ornate chariots.[18] Others, dating from slightly later periods, have been found at Kish and Ashur. In Anatolia, at Alaca Hüyük, the royal graves were roofed with whole carcasses of roasted oxen to ease the sepulchral appetites of their motionless inhabitants.

Even the ordinary dead man in many cultures is treated as still living. The very oldest inscriptions on funerary themes are Mesopotamian lists of the monthly rations of bread and beer to be

---

[18] See C. L. Woolley, *Ur Excavations*, Vol. 2 (London and Philadelphia, 1934).

given to the common dead. About 2500 B.C., in Lagash, a dead
person was buried with 7 jars of beer, 420 flat loaves of bread, 2
measures of grain, 1 garment, 1 head support, and 1 bed.[19]
Some ancient Greek graves not only have the various appurtenances of life, but actual feeding tubes which seem to indicate
that archaic Greeks poured broths and soups down into the livid
jaws of a moldering corpse.[20] And in the Metropolitan Museum
in New York is a painted *krater* or mixing bowl (numbered
14.130.15) which dates from about 850 B.C.; it shows a boy seemingly tearing his hair with one hand as with the other he stuffs
food into the mouth of a corpse, probably his mother's. This is
difficult to appreciate unless the feeder was hallucinating something from the dead at the time.

The evidence in the Indus civilizations[21] is more fragmentary
because of the successive coverings of alluvium, the rotting away
of all their writings on papyrus, and the incompleteness of
archaeological investigations. But the Indus sites so far excavated often have the cemetery next to the citadel in a high place
with fifteen or twenty food-pots per dead person, consistent with
the hypothesis that they were still felt to be living when buried.
And the Neolithic burials of the Yang-Shao cultures of China[22],
wholly undated except insofar as they precede the middle of the
second millennium B.C., similarly show burials in plank-lined
graves, the corpse accompanied by pots of food and stone tools.

[19] This information is given on a cone by Urukagina, king of Lagash, who pro-
ceeded to reduce these amounts somewhat. See Alexander Heidel, *The Gilgamesh
Epic and Old Testament Parallels* (Chicago: University of Chicago Press, 1949),
p. 151.

[20] E. R. Dodds, *The Greeks and the Irrational.*

[21] Sir Mortimer Wheeler, *Civilizations of the Indus Valley and Beyond* (New
York: McGraw-Hill, 1966), and, more extensively, his *The Indus Civilization*,
2nd ed., supplementary volume to *The Cambridge History of India* (Cambridge:
Cambridge University Press, 1960).

[22] See William Watson, *Early Civilization in China* (New York: McGraw-Hill,
1966); and also Chang Kwang-Chih, *The Archaeology of Ancient China* (New
Haven: Yale University Press, 1963).

By 1200 B.C., the Shang dynasty has royal tombs with slaughtered retinues and animals so similar to those of Mesopotamia and Egypt a millennium earlier as to convince some scholars that civilization came to China by diffusion from the West.[23]

Similarly in Mesoamerica, Olmec burials from about 800 to 300 B.C. were richly furnished with pots of food. In the Mayan kingdoms, the noble dead were buried as if living in the plazas of temples. A chieftain's tomb recently found under a temple at Palenque is as elaborately splendid as anything found in the Old World.[24] At the site of Kaminal-juyu, dating A.D. 500, a chieftain was buried in a sitting position along with two adolescents, a child, and a dog for his company. Ordinary men were buried with their mouths full of ground maize in the hard-mud floors of their houses, with their tools and weapons, and with pots filled with drink and food, just as in previous civilizations on the other side of the world. Also I should mention the portrait statues of Yucatan that held the ashes of a deceased chief, the resculptured skulls of Mayapan, and the small catacombs for Andean commoners bound in a sitting position in the midst of bowls of *chicha* and the tools and things used in their lives.[25] The dead were then called *huaca* or godlike, which I take to indicate that they were sources of hallucinated voices. And when it was reported by the Conquistadors that these people declared that it is only a long time after death that the individual 'dies,' I suggest that the proper interpretation is that it takes this time for the hallucinated voice to finally fade away.

That the dead were the origin of gods is also found in the writings of those bicameral civilizations that became literate. In

[23] Chariot burials complete with slaughtered horses and charioteers become more frequent toward the end of the Shang dynasty in the eleventh century B.C. and continue into the Chou dynasty of the eighth century B.C. when they cease. Why all this? Unless the dead kings were thought to still live and need their chariots and servants because their speech was still heard?

[24] Von Hagen, *World of the Maya*, p. 109.

[25] Von Hagen, *Realm of the Incas*, p. 121.

a bilingual incantation text from Assyria, the dead are directly called *Ilani* or gods.[26] And on the other side of the world three millennia later, Sahagun, one of the earliest reporters of the Mesoamerican scene, reported that the Aztecs "called the place Teotihuacan, burial place of the kings; the ancients said: he who has died became a god; or when someone said — he who has become a god, meant to say — he has died."[27]

Even in the conscious period there was the tradition that gods were men of a previous age who had died. Hesiod speaks of a golden race of men who preceded his own generation and became the "holy demons upon the earth, beneficent, averters of ills, guardians of mortal men."[28] Similar references can be found up to four centuries later, as when Plato refers to heroes who after death become the demons that tell people what to do.[29]

I do not wish to give the impression that the presence of pots of food and drink in the graves of these civilizations is universal throughout all these eras; it is general. But exceptions here often prove the rule. For example, Sir Leonard Woolley, when he first started excavating the personal graves at Larsa in Mesopotamia (which date from about 1900 B.C.), was both surprised and disappointed by the poverty of their contents. Even the most elaborately built vault would have no furnishings other than a couple of clay pots at the tomb door perhaps, but nothing of the kind of thing found in graves elsewhere. The explanation came when he realized that these tombs were *always* underneath particular houses, and that the dead man of the Larsa Age needed no tomb furniture or large amounts of food because everything in the house was still at his disposal. The food and drink at the tomb door may have been like an emergency measure, so that when the dead man 'mixed' with the family, he came forth in a kindly mood.

---

[26] Heidel, *The Gilgamesh Epic*, pp. 153, 196.
[27] Quoted by Covarrubias, p. 123.
[28] Hesiod, *Works and Days*, 120f.
[29] *Republic*, 469A; and also *Cratylus*, 398.

Thus, from Mesopotamia to Peru, the great civilizations have at least gone through a stage characterized by a kind of burial as if the individual were still living. And where writing could record it, the dead were often called gods. At the very least, this is consistent with the hypothesis that their voices were still heard in hallucination.

But is this a necessary relationship? Could not grief itself promote such practices, a kind of refusal to accept the death of a loved one or a revered leader, calling dead persons gods as a kind of endearment? Possibly. This explanation, however, is not sufficient to account for the entire pattern of the evidence, the pervasion of references to the dead as gods in different regions of the world, the vastness of some of the enterprise as in the great pyramids, and even the contemporary vestiges in lore and literature of ghosts returning from their graves with messages for the living.

IDOLS THAT SPEAK

A third feature of primitive civilization that I take to be indicative of bicamerality is the enormous numbers and kinds of human effigies and their obvious centrality to ancient life. The first effigies in history were of course the propped-up corpses of chiefs, or the remodeled skulls we have referred to earlier. But thereafter they have an astonishing development. It is difficult to understand their obvious importance to the cultures involved with them apart from the supposition that they were aids in hallucinating voices. But this is far from a simple matter, and quite different principles may be intertwined in the full explanation.

Figurines

The smallest of these effigies are figurines, which have been found in almost all of the ancient kingdoms, beginning with the first stationary settlements of man. During the seventh and sixth millennia B.C, they are extremely primitive, small stones with incised features or grotesque clay figures. Evidence of their importance in cultures of about 5600 B.C. is provided by the excavations at Hacilar in southwest Turkey. Flat standing female effigies, made of baked clay or stone with incised eyes, nose, hair, and chin were found in each house,[30] as if, I suggest, they were its occupant's hallucinatory controls. The Amatrian and Gerzean cultures of Egypt, about 3600 B.C., had carved tusks with bearded heads and black 'targets' for eyes, each about six to eight inches and suitable to be held in the hand.[31] And these were so important that they were stood upright in the grave of their owner when he died.

Figurines in huge numbers have been unearthed in most of the Mesopotamian cultures, at Lagash, Uruk, Nippur, and Susa.[32] At Ur, clay figures painted in black and red were found in boxes of burned brick placed under the floor against the walls but with one end opened, facing into the center of the room.

The function of all these figurines, however, is as mysterious as anything in all archaeology. The most popular view goes back to the uncritical mania with which ethnology, following Frazer, wished to find fertility cults at the drop of a carved pebble. But if such figurines indicate something about Frazerian fertility, we should not find them where fertility was no problem. But we do. In the Olmec civilization of the most fertile part of Mexico, the figurines are of an astonishing variety, often with open mouths and exaggerated ears, as might be expected if they were fash-

[30] Mellaart, p. 106; see also Clark and Piggott, p. 204.

[31] See Flinders Petrie, *Prehistoric Egypt* (London: British School of Archaeology in Egypt, 1920), pp. 27, 36. Even gods are sometimes shown using hand-held idols. An Anatolian example may be found in Seton Lloyd, *Early Highland Peoples of Anatolia* (New York: McGraw-Hill, 1967), p. 51; and a Mayan example on the north face of Stela F in A. P. Maudslay, *Archaeology in Biologia Centrali-Americana* (New York: Arte Primitivo, 1975), Vol. II, Plate 36.

[32] For later rituals of giving them supernatural power, see H. W. F. Saggs, *The Greatness That Was Babylon* (New York: Mentor Books, 1962), pp. 301–303.

ioned as embodiments of heard voices with whom dialogue could be carried on.[33]

The explanation, however, is not simple. Figurines seemed to go through an evolution, just as did the culture of which they are a part. The early Olmec figurines, to stay with the same example, develop through their first period an exaggerated prognathism until they look almost like animals. And then, in the period of Teotihuacan, they are more refined and delicate, with huge hats and capes, painted with daubs of fugitive red, yellow, and white paint, looking much like Olmec priests. A third period of Olmec figurines has them more carefully modeled and realistic, some with jointed arms and legs, some with hollow reliquaries in their torsos closed by a small square lid and containing other minute figurines, perhaps denoting the confusion of bicameral guidance that occurred just before the great Olmec civilization collapsed. For it was at the end of this period of a profusion of figurines, as well as of huge new half-finished open-mouth statues, that the great city of Teotihuacan was deliberately destroyed, its temples burned, its walls leveled, and the city abandoned, around A.D. 700. Had the voices ceased, resulting in the increased effigy making? Or had they multiplied into confusion?

Because of their size and number, it is doubtful if the majority of figurines occasioned auditory hallucinations. Some indeed may have been mnemonic devices, reminders to a nonconscious people who could not voluntarily retrieve admonitory experience, perhaps functioning like the *quipu* or knot-string literature of the Incas or the beads of rosaries of our own culture. For example, the Mesopotamian bronze foundation figurines buried at the corners of new buildings and under thresholds of doors are of three kinds: a kneeling god driving a peg into the ground, a basket carrier, and a recumbent bull. The current theory about them, that they are to pin down evil spirits beneath the building,

---

[33] See Burland, *The Gods of Mexico*, p. 22f.; Bushnell, *The First Americans*, p. 37f.

is scarcely sufficient. Instead it is possible that they were semi-hallucinatory mnemonic aids for a nonconscious people in setting the posts straight, in carrying the materials, or using oxen to pull the larger materials to the site.

But some of these small objects, we may be confident, were capable of assisting with the production of bicameral voices. Particularly the eye-idols in black and white alabaster, thin crackerlike bodies surmounted by eyes once tinted with malachite paint, which have been found in the thousands, particularly at Brak on one of the upper branches of the Euphrates, that date about 3000 B.C. Like the earlier Amatrian and Gerzean tusk idols

One of many thousands of alabaster "eye idols" that can be held in the hand. From about 3300 B.C., excavated at Brak on an upper tributary of the Euphrates. The stag is the symbol of the goddess Ninhursag.

of Egypt, they are suitable to be held in the hand. Most have one pair of eyes, but some have two; some wear crowns and some have markings clearly indicating gods. Larger eye-idols made of terra cotta have been found at other sites, Ur, Mari, and Lagash; and, because the eyes are open loops, have been called spectacle-idols. Others, made of stone and placed on podiums and altars,[34] are like two cylindrical doughnuts positioned a distance above an incised square platform that could be a mouth.

[34] See M. E. L. Mallowan, *Early Mesopotamia and Iran* (New York: McGraw-Hill) 1965, Ch. 2.

A Theory of Idols

Now this needs a little more psychologizing. Eye-to-eye contact in primates is extremely important. Below humans, it is indicative of the hierarchical position of the animal, the submissive animal turning away grinning in many primate species. But in humans, perhaps because of the much longer juvenile period, eye-to-eye contact has evolved into a social interaction of great importance. An infant child, when its mother speaks to it, looks at the mother's eyes, not her lips. This response is automatic and universal. The development of such eye-to-eye contact into authority relationships and love relationships is an exceedingly important trajectory that has yet to be traced. It is sufficient here merely to suggest that you are more likely to feel a superior's authority when you and he are staring straight into each other's eyes. There is a kind of stress, an unresolvedness about the experience, and withal something of a diminution of consciousness, so that, were such a relationship mimicked in a statue, it would enhance the hallucination of divine speech.

The eyes thus become a prominent feature of most temple statuary throughout the bicameral period. The diameter of the human eye is about 10 percent of the height of the head, this proportion being what I shall call the eye index of an idol. The famous group of twelve statues discovered in the Favissa of the temple of Abu at Tell Asmar,[35] the symbols carved on their bases indicating that they are gods, have eye indices of as high as 18 percent — huge globular eyes hypnotically staring out of the unrecorded past of 5000 years ago with defiant authority.

Other idols from other sites show the same thing. A particularly beautiful and justly famous white marble head from Uruk[36] has an eye index of over 20 percent, the sculpture showing that the eyes and the eyebrows were once encrusted with dazzling gems, the face colored, the hair tinted, the head part of a life-

[35] Illustrated in many general texts including Mallowan, pp. 43, 45.
[36] See Mallowan, *Early Mesopotamia*, p. 55.

sized wooden statue now dust. Around 2700 B.C. alabaster and calcite statues of fluffily skirted gods, rulers, and priests abounded in the luxurious civilization on the middle Euphrates called Mari, their eyes up to 18 percent of the height of the head and heavily outlined with black paint. In the main temple of Mari ruled the famous Goddess with the Flowering Vase, her huge empty eye sockets having once contained hypnotic gems, her hands holding a tilted aryballos. A pipe from a tank going within the idol allowed the aryballos to overflow with water which streamed down the idol's robe, clothing her lower parts with a translucent liquid veil, and adding a sibilant sound suitable to be molded into hallucinated speech. And then the famous series of statues of the enigmatic Gudea, ruler of Lagash, about 2100 B.C., carved in the hardest stone, with eye indices of approximately 17 or 18 percent.

The eye indices of temple and tomb sculptures of pharaohs in Egypt are sometimes as high as 20 percent. The few wooden statues from Egypt that have remained show that their enlarged eyes were once made of quartz and crystal inserted in a copper surround. As might be expected from its god-king type of theocracy (see next chapter) idols in Egypt do not seem to have played so prominent a role as in Mesopotamia.

Few examples of Indus stone sculpture survive, but these few show pronounced eye indices of over 20 percent.[37] No idols are

---

[37] See, for example, the illustrations in Wheeler, *Civilizations of the Indus Valley.*

yet known from the bicameral period of China. But as civilization begins again in Mesoamerica around 900 B.C., it is as if we were back in the Near East several millennia earlier, though with certain unique prospects: huge heads carved out of hard basalt, often eight feet tall, usually with a cap, sometimes with large ear pads like a football helmet, resting bodiless on the ground near La Venta and Tres Zapoltes (some of them now removed to Olmec Park at Villahermosa). The eye indices of these heads ranged from a normal 11 percent to over 19 percent. Usually the mouth is half open as in speech. There are also many Olmec ceramic idols of a strange sexless child, always seated with legs spread-eagled as if to expose his sexlessness, and leaning forward to stare intently through wide slits of eyes, the full-lipped mouth half open as in speech. The eye index, if the eyes were open, in the several of them I have examined averaged 17 percent. Figurines in the Olmec culture were sometimes half life-sized with even larger eye indices; they are often found in burials as at the Olmec-influenced site of Tlatilco, near Mexico City, of about

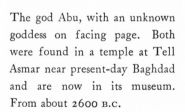

The god Abu, with an unknown goddess on facing page. Both were found in a temple at Tell Asmar near present-day Baghdad and are now in its museum. From about 2600 B.C.

Mayan god, a stela about twelve feet high, from Copan in Honduras. It was carved about 700 A.D.

500 B.C., as if the deceased was buried with his own personal idol which still could tell him what to do.

Mayan idols do not usually show such abnormal eye indices. But in the great cities of Yucatan, portrait statues were made of deceased leaders for, I think, the same hallucinogenic purpose. The back of the head was left hollow and the cremated ashes of the dead placed in it. And according to Landa, who witnessed this practice in the sixteenth century, "they preserved these statues with a great deal of veneration."[38]

The Cocoms that once ruled Mayapan, around A.D. 1200, repeated what the Natufian culture of Jericho had done 9000 years earlier. They decapitated their dead "and after cooking the heads, they cleaned off the flesh and then sawed off half the crown at the back, leaving entire the front part with jaws and teeth. Then they replaced the flesh . . . with a kind of bitumen [and plaster] which gave them a natural and lifelike appearance . . . these they kept in the oratories in their houses and on festive days offered food to them . . . they believed that their souls reposed within and that these gifts were useful to them."[39] There is nothing here inconsistent with the notion that such prepared heads were so treated because they 'contained' the voices of their former owners.

[38] As quoted by von Hagen, *World of the Maya*, p. 109.
[39] Landa as quoted by von Hagen, *World of the Maya*, p. 110.

Many other kinds of idols were also used by the Maya, and in such profusion that when, in 1565, a Spanish mayor ordered the abolition of idolatry in his city, he was aghast when "in my presence, upwards of a million were brought."[40] Another type of Mayan idol was made of cedar which the Maya called *kuche* or holy wood. "And this they called to make gods." They were carved by fasting priests called *chaks*, in great fear and trembling, shut into a little straw hut blessed with incense and prayer, the god-carvers "frequently cutting their ears and with the blood anointing the gods and burning incense to them." When finished, the gods were lavishly dressed and placed upon daises in small buildings, some of which by being in more inaccessible places have escaped the ravages of Christianity or of time, and are still being discovered. According to a sixteenth-century observer, "the unhappy dupes believed the idols spoke to them and so sacrificed to it birds, dogs, their own blood and even men."[41, 42]

The Speech of Idols

How can we know that such idols 'spoke' in the bicameral sense? I have tried to suggest that the very existence of statuary and figurines requires an explanation in a way that has not previously been perceived. The hypothesis of the bicameral mind renders such an explanation. The setting up of such idols in religious places, the exaggerated eyes in the early stages of every civilization, the practice of inserting gems of brilliant sorts into the eye sockets in several civilizations, an elaborate ritual for the

[40] Von Hagen, *World of the Maya*, p. 32.

[41] All quotations here are from Landa, a Spaniard who was describing what he saw in the sixteenth century as quoted by J. Eric S. Thompson, *Maya History and Religion*, pp. 189–91.

[42] The Incas too had a variety of idols that they called gods, some life-sized, cast of gold or silver, others of stone crowned and dressed in robes, all these found by Spaniards in outlying temples of the Inca empire. See von Hagen, *Realm of the Incas*, pp. 134, 152.

opening of the mouth for new statues in the two most important early civilizations (as we shall see in the next chapter), all these present a pattern of evidence at least.

Cuneiform literature often refers to god-statues speaking. Even as late as the early first millennium B.C., a royal letter reads:

> I have taken note of the portents . . . I had them recited in order before Shamash . . . the royal image [a statue] of Akkad brought up visions before me and cried out: "What pernicious portent have you tolerated in the royal image?" Again it spoke: "Say to the Gardener . . . [and here the cuneiform becomes unreadable, but then goes on] . . . it made inquiry concerning Ningal-Iddina, Shamash-Ibni, and Na'id-Marduk. Concerning the rebellion in the land it said: "Take the wall cities one after the other, that a cursed one will not be able to stand before the Gardener."[43]

The Old Testament also indicated that one of the types of idol there referred to, the *Terap*, could speak. Ezekiel, 21:21, describes the king of Babylon as consulting with several of them. Further direct evidence comes from America. The conquered Aztecs told the Spanish invaders how their history began when a statue from a ruined temple belonging to a previous culture spoke to their leaders. It commanded them to cross the lake from where they were, and to carry its statue with them wherever they went, directing them hither and thither, even as the unembodied bicameral voices led Moses zigzagging across the Sinai desert.[44]

And finally the remarkable evidence from Peru. All the first reports of the conquest of Peru by the Inquisition-taught Spaniards are consistent in regarding the Inca kingdom as one commanded by the Devil. Their evidence was that the Devil himself

[43] R. H. Pfeiffer, *State Letters of Assyria* (New Haven: American Oriental Society, 1935), p. 174.
[44] C. A. Burland, *The Gods of Mexico*, p. 47.

actually spoke to the Incas out of the mouths of their statues. To these coarse dogmatized Christians, coming from one of the most ignorant counties of Spain, this caused little astonishment. The very first report back to Europe said, "in the temple [of Pachacamac] was a Devil who used to speak to the Indians in a very dark room which was as dirty as he himself."[45] And a later account reported that

> . . . it was a thing very common and approved at the Indies, that the Devill spake and answered in these false sanctuaries . . . It was commonly in the night they entered backward to their idoll and so went bending their bodies and head, after an uglie manner, and so they consulted with him. The answer he made, was commonly like unto a fearefull hissing, or to a gnashing which did terrifie them; and all that he did advertise or command them, was but the way to their perdition and ruine.[46]

[45] Anonymous, *The Conquest of Peru*, with a translation and annotations by J. H. Sinclair (New York: New York Public Library, 1929), p. 37f.

[46] Father Joseph De Acosta, *The Natural and Moral History of the Indies* (London: Hakluyt Society, 1880), 2: 325f.

CHAPTER 2

Literate Bicameral Theocracies

WHAT IS writing? Writing proceeds from *pictures of visual events* to *symbols of phonetic events*. And that is an amazing transformation! Writing of the latter type, as on the present page, is meant to tell a reader something he does not know. But, the closer writing is to the former, the more it is primarily a mnemonic device to release information which the reader already has. The protoliterate pictograms of Uruk, the iconography in the early depictions of gods, the glyphics of the Maya, the picture codices of the Aztecs, and, indeed, our own heraldry are all of this sort. The informations they are meant to release in those who look upon them may be forever lost and the writing therefore forever untranslatable.

The two kinds of writing which fall between these two extremes, half picture and half symbol, are those on which this chapter is based. They are Egyptian hieroglyphics with its abridged and somewhat cursive form, hieratic, the terms meaning "writing of the gods," and the more widely used writing which later scholars called cuneiform from its wedge-shaped characters.

The latter is for us the most important, and the remains we have of it, far more extensive. Thousands of tablets wait to be translated and more thousands to be unburied. It was used for at least four languages, Sumerian, Akkadian, Hurrian, and later the Hittite. Instead of an alphabet of twenty-six letters, as in ours, or of twenty-two letters, as in the Aramaic (which except for religious texts replaced cuneiform around 200 B.C.), it is a clumsy and ambiguous communication system of over 600 signs. Many of these are ideographic, in which the same sign can be a syllable, an idea, a name, or a word with more than one meaning, according to the class it belonged to, this class irregularly being shown by a special mark. Only by the context are we able to unravel which it is. For example, the sign ⟨cuneiform⟩ means nine different things: when pronounced as *šamšu* it means sun; when pronounced *ūmu*, it means day; when *pisu* it means white; and it also stands for the syllables *ud, tu, tam, pir, lah,* and *his.* The difficulties of being crystal clear in such a contextual mess were great enough in its own day. But when we are exiled from the culture that the language describes by 4000 years, translation is an enormous and fascinating problem. The same is true in general for hieroglyphic and hieratic writing.

When the terms are concrete, as they usually are, for most of the cuneiform literature is receipts or inventories or offerings for gods, there is little doubt of the correctness of translation. But as the terms tend to the abstract, and particularly when a psychological interpretation is possible, then we find well-meaning translators imposing modern categories to make their translations comprehensible. The popular and even the scholarly literatures are full of such sugared emendations and palatablized glosses to make ancient men seem like us, or at least talk like the King James Bible. A translator often reads in more than he reads out. Many of those texts that seem to be about decision-making, or so-called proverbs, or epics, or teachings, should be reinterpreted with concrete behavioral precision if we are to trust them as data for the psycho-archaeology of man. And I am warning the reader that the effect of this chapter is not in accord with popular books on the subject.

With these cautions in mind, then, let us proceed.

When, in the third millennium B.C., writing, like a theater curtain going up on these dazzling civilizations, lets us stare directly if imperfectly at them, it is clear that for some time there have been two main forms of theocracy: (1) the *steward-king theocracy* in which the chief or king is the first deputy of the gods, or, more usually, a particular city's god, the manager and caretaker of his lands. This was the most important and widespread form of theocracy among bicameral kingdoms. It was the pattern in the many Mesopotamian bicameral city-states, of Mycenae as we saw in I.3, and, so far as we know, in India, China, and probably Mesoamerica. (2) the *god-king theocracy* in which the king himself is a god. The clearest examples of this form existed in Egypt and at least some of the kingdoms of the Andes, and probably the earliest kingdom of Japan. I have earlier suggested in I.6 that both types developed out of the more primitive bicameral situation where a new king ruled by obeying the hallucinated voice of a dead king.

I shall take these up in turn in the two greatest ancient civilizations.

MESOPOTAMIA: THE GODS
AS OWNERS

Throughout Mesopotamia, from the earliest times of Sumer and Akkad, all lands were owned by gods and men were their slaves. Of this, the cuneiform texts leave no doubt whatever.[1] Each city-state had its own principal god, and the king was described in the very earliest written documents that we have as "the tenant farmer of the god."

The god himself was a statue. The statue was not *of* a god (as we would say) but the god himself. He had his own house, called

[1] Most of this material is well known and may be found in a number of excellent works, including H. W. F. Saggs, *The Greatness That Was Babylon* (New York: Mentor Books, 1962); *The Cambridge Ancient History*, Vols. 1–3 (Cambridge: Cambridge University Press); George Roux, *Ancient Iraq* (Baltimore: Penguin Books, 1966); and A. L. Oppenheim, *Ancient Mesopotamia: Portrait of a Dead Civilization* (Chicago: University of Chicago Press, 1964).

by the Sumerians the "great house." It formed the center of a complex of temple buildings, varying in size according to the importance of the god and the wealth of the city. The god was probably made of wood to be light enough to be carried about on the shoulders of priests. His face was inlaid with precious metals and jewels. He was clothed in dazzling raiment, and usually resided on a pedestal in a niche in a central chamber of his house. The larger and more important god-houses had lesser courts surrounded by rooms for the use of the steward-kings and subsidiary priests.

In most of the great city sites excavated in Mesopotamia, the house of a chief god was the ziggurat, a great rectangular tower, rising by diminishing stages to a shining summit on which there was a chapel. In the center of the ziggurat was the *gigunu,* a large chamber in which most scholars believe the statue of the chief god resided, but which others believe was used only for ritual purposes. Such ziggurats or similar towering temple structures are common to most of the bicameral kingdoms in some period.

Since the divine statue was the owner of the land and the people were his tenants, the first duty of the steward-king was to serve the god not only in the administration of the god's estates but also in more personal ways. The gods, according to cuneiform texts, liked eating and drinking, music and dancing; they required beds to sleep in and for enjoying sex with other god-statues on connubial visits from time to time; they had to be washed and dressed, and appeased with pleasant odors; they had to be taken out for drives on state occasions; and all these things were done with increasing ceremony and ritual as time went on.

The daily ritual of the temple included the washing, dressing, and feeding of the statues. The washing was probably done through the sprinkling of pure water by attendant priests, the origin, perhaps, of our christening and anointing ceremonies. The dressing was by enrobing the figure in various ways. In front of the god were tables, the origin of our altars, on one of which flowers were placed, and on the other food and drink for the divine hunger. Such food consisted of bread and cakes, the flesh of bulls, sheep, goats, deer, fish, and poultry. According to some interpretations of the cuneiform, the food was brought in and then the statue-god was left to enjoy his meal alone. Then, after a suitable period of time, the steward-king entered the shrine room from a side entrance and ate what the god had left.

The divine statues also had to be kept in good temper. This was called "appeasing the liver" of the gods, and consisted in offerings of butter, fat, honey, sweetmeats placed on the tables as with regular food. Presumably, a person whose bicameral voice was condemnatory and angry would come bringing such offerings to the god's house.

How is all this possible, continuing as it did in some form for *thousands* of years as the central focus of life, unless we posit that the human beings heard the statues speak to them even as the heroes of the Iliad heard their gods or Joan of Arc heard hers? And indeed *had* to hear them speak to know what to do.

We can read this directly in the texts themselves. The great Cylinder B of Gudea (about 2100 B.C.) describes how in a new temple for his god Ningirsu, the priestesses placed

> . . . the goddesses Zazaru, Impae, Urentaea, Khegirnunna, Kheshagga, Guurmu, Zaarmu, who are the seven children of the brood of Bau that were begotten by the lord Ningirsu, to *utter* favorable decisions by the side of the lord Ningirsu.[2]

The particular decisions to be uttered here were about various aspects of agriculture that the grain might "cover the banks of the holy field" and "all the rich graineries of Lagash to make to

[2] Column 11, lines 4–14, as in George A. Barton, *The Royal Inscriptions of Sumer and Akkad* (New Haven: American Oriental Society, 1929). Italics mine as in quotations following.

overflow." And a clay cone from the dynasty of Larsa about 1700 B.C. praises the goddess Ninegal as

> . . . *counsellor*, exceeding wise *commander*, princess of all the great gods, exalted *speaker*, whose *utterance* is unrivaled.[3]

Everywhere in these texts, it is the speech of gods who decide what is to be done. A cone from Lagash reads:

> Mesilin king of Kish at the *command* of his deity Kadi concerning the plantation of that field set up a stele in that place. Ush, patesi of Umma, incantations to seize it formed; that stele he broke in pieces; into the plain of Lagash he advanced. Ningirsu, the hero of Enlil, by his righteous *command*, upon Umma war made. At the *command* of Enlil his great net ensnared. Their burial mound on the plain in that place he erected.[4]

It is not the human beings who are the rulers, but the hallucinated voices of the gods Kadi, Ningirsu, and Enlil. Note that this passage is about a stele, or stone column, engraved with a god's words in cuneiform and set up in a field to tell how that field was to be farmed. That such stelae themselves were epiphanous is suggested by the way they were attacked and defended and smashed or carried away. And that they were sources of auditory hallucinations is suggested in other texts. One particularly pertinent passage from a different context describes reading a stele at night:

> The polished surface of its side his *hearing* makes known; its writing which is engraved his *hearing* makes known; the light of the torch assists his *hearing*.[5]

[3] Ibid., p. 327.
[4] Ibid., p. 61. *Inim-ma* is here translated as "incantations."
[5] Ibid., p. 47.

Reading in the third millennium B.C. may therefore have been a matter of *hearing* the cuneiform, that is, hallucinating the speech from looking at its picture-symbols, rather than visual reading of syllables in our sense.

The word for 'hearing' here is a Sumerian sign that transliterates GIŠ-TUG-PI. Many other royal inscriptions state how the king or other personage is endowed by some god with this GIŠ-TUG-PI hearing which enables him to great things. Even as late as 1825 B.C., Warad-Sin, king of Larsa, claims in an inscription on a clay cone that he rebuilt the city with GIŠ-TUG-PI DAGAL, or "hearing everywhere" his god Enki.[6]

The Mouth-Washing Ceremonies

Further evidence that such statues were aids to the hallucinated voices is found in other ceremonies all described precisely and concretely on cuneiform tablets. The statue-gods were made in the *bit-mummu*, a special divine craftsman's house. Even the craftsmen were directed in their work by a craftsman-god, *Mummu*, who 'dictated' how to make the statue. Before being installed in their shrines, the statues underwent *mis-pi* which means mouth-washing, and the ritual of *pit-pi* or "opening of the mouth."

Not only when the statue was being made, but also periodically, particularly in the later bicameral era when the hallucinated voices may have become less frequent, an elaborate washing-of-the-mouth ceremony could renew the god's speech. The god with its face of inlaid jewels was carried by dripping torchlight to the riverbank, and there, imbedded in ceremonies and incantation, his wood mouth washed several times as the god was faced east, west, north, and then south. The holy water with which the mouth was washed out was a solution of a multitude of exotic ingredients: tamarisks, reeds of various kinds, sulphur,

[6] Ibid., p. 320.

various gums, salts, and oils, date honey, with various precious stones. Then after more incantations, the god was "led by the hand" back into the street with the priest incanting "foot that advanceth, foot that advanceth . . ." At the gate of the temple, another ceremony was performed. The priest then took "the hand" of the god and led him in to his throne in the niche, where a golden canopy was set up and the statue's mouth washed again.[7]

Bicameral kingdoms should not be thought of as everywhere the same or as not undergoing considerable development through time. The texts from which the above information has come are from approximately the late third millennium B.C. They may therefore represent a late development of bicamerality in which the very complexity of the culture could have been making the hallucinated voices less clear and frequent, thus giving rise to such a cleansing ritual in hope of rejuvenating the voice of the god.

The Personal God

But it is not to be supposed that the ordinary citizen heard directly the voices of the great gods who owned the cities; such hallucinatory diversity would have weakened the political fabric. He served the owner gods, worked their estates, took part in their festivals. But he appealed to them only in some great crisis, and then only through intermediaries. This is shown on countless cylinder seals. A large proportion of the inventory type of cuneiform tablets have impressions on the reverse side rolled from such seals; commonly, they show a seated god and another minor divinity, usually a goddess, conducting the owner of the tablet by the right hand into the divine presence.

Such intermediaries were the personal gods. Each individual, king or serf, had his own personal god whose voice he heard and

[7] See the translation of this text by Sidney Smith in the *Journal of the Royal Asiatic Society*, January 1925, as quoted by S. H. Hooke, *Babylonian and Assyrian Religion* (Norman: University of Oklahoma Press, 1963), pp. 118–121.

obeyed.[8] In almost every house excavated, there existed a shrine-room that probably contained idols or figurines as the inhabitant's personal gods. Several late cuneiform texts describe rituals for them similar to the mouth-washing ceremonies for the great gods.[9]

These personal gods could be importuned to visit other gods higher up in the divine hierarchy for some particular boon. Or, in the other direction, strange as it seems to us: when the owner gods had chosen a prince to be a steward-king, the city-god informed the appointee's personal god of the decision first, and only then the individual himself. According to my discussion in I. 5, all this layering was going on in the right hemisphere and I am well aware of the problem of authenticity and group acceptance of such selection. As elsewhere in antiquity, it was the personal god who was responsible for what the king did, as it was for the commoner.

Other cuneiform texts state that a man lived in the shadow of his personal god, his *ili*. So inextricably were a man and his personal god bound together that the composition of his personal name usually included the name of the personal god, thus making obvious the bicameral nature of the man. It is of considerable interest when the name of the king is indicated as the personal god: Rim-Sin-Ili, which means "Rim-Sin is my god," Rim-Sin being a king of Larsa, or, more simply, Sharru-Ili, "the king is my god."[10] These instances suggest that the steward-king himself could sometimes be hallucinated.

When the King Becomes a God

This possibility shows that the distinction I have made between the steward-king type of theocracy and the god-king is not an

---

[8] Thorkild Jacobsen has felt that the personal god "appears as the personification of a man's luck and success." I am insisting that this is an unwarranted modern imposition. See his "Mesopotamia," in *The Intellectual Adventure of Ancient Man*, H. Frankfort, et al., eds. (Chicago: University of Chicago Press, 1946), p. 203.

[9] Saggs, p. 301f.

[10] Frankfort et al., p. 306.

absolute one. Moreover, on several cuneiform tablets, a number of the earlier Mesopotamian kings have beside their names the eight-pointed star which is the determinative sign indicating deity. In one early text, eleven out of a larger number of kings of Ur and Isin are given this or another divine determinative. A number of theories have been proposed as to what this means, none of them very gripping.

The clues to look at are, I think, that the divine determinative is often given to these kings only late in their reigns, and then only in certain of their cities. This may mean that the voice of a particularly powerful king may have been heard in hallucination but only by a certain proportion of his people, only after he had reigned for some time, and only in certain places.

Yet even in these instances, there seems throughout Mesopotamia a significant and continuing distinction between such divine kings and the gods proper.[11] But this is not at all true of Egypt, to which we now turn.

EGYPT: THE KINGS AS GODS

The great basin of the Euphrates and Tigris rivers looses its identity, feature by feature, into the limitless deserts of Arabia and the gradual foothills of the mountain chains of Persia and Armenia. But Egypt, except in the south, is clearly defined by bilaterally symmetrical immutable frontiers. A pharaoh extending his authority in the Nile Valley soon reached what he might raid but never conquer. And thus Egypt was always more uniform both geographically and ethnologically, both in space and in time. Its people through the ages were also of a remarkably similar physique, as has been shown from studies of remaining skulls.[12] It is this protected homogeneity, I suggest, which al-

[11] Saggs, p. 343f.

[12] G. M. Morant, "Study of Egyptian craniology from prehistoric to Roman times," *Biometrika*, 1925, 17: 1–52.

lowed the perpetuation of that more archaic form of theocracy, the god-king.

The Memphite Theology

Let us begin with the famous "Memphite Theology."[13] This is an eighth-century B.C. granite block on which a previous work (presumably a rotting leather roll of around 3000 B.C.) was copied. It begins with a reference to a "creator" god Ptah, proceeds through the quarrels of the gods Horus and Seth and their arbitration by Geb, describes the construction of the royal godhouse at Memphis, and then, in a famous final section, states that the various gods are variations of Ptah's voice or "tongue."

Now when "tongue" here is translated as something like the "objectified conceptions of his mind," as it so often is, this is surely an imposing of modern categories upon the texts.[14] Ideas such as objectified conceptions of a mind, or even the notion of something spiritual being manifested, are of much later development. It is generally agreed that the ancient Egyptian language, like the Sumerian, was concrete from first to last. To maintain that it is expressing abstract thoughts would seem to me an intrusion of the modern idea that men have always been the same. Also, when the Memphite Theology speaks of the tongue or voices as that from which everything was created, I suspect that the very word "created" may also be a modern imposition, and the more proper translation might be *commanded*. This theology, then, is essentially a myth about language, and what Ptah is really commanding is indeed the bicameral voices which began, controlled, and directed Egyptian civilization.

[13] In addition to texts otherwise cited, I have used for this part of the chapter John A. Wilson, *The Culture of Ancient Egypt* (Chicago: University of Chicago Press, 1951); Cyril Aldred, *Egypt to the End of the Old Kingdom* (New York: McGraw-Hill, 1965); W. W. Hallo and W. K. Simpson, *The Ancient Near East: A History* (New York: Harcourt Brace Jovanovich, 1971).

[14] Henri Frankfort, *Kingship and the Gods* (Chicago: University of Chicago Press, 1948), p. 28.

Osiris, the Dead King's Voice

There has been some astonishment that mythology and reality should be so mixed that the heavenly contention of Horus and Seth is over real land, and that the figure of Osiris in the last section has a real grave in Memphis, and also that each king at death becomes Osiris, just as each king in life is Horus. If it is assumed that all of these figures are particular voice hallucinations heard by kings and their next in rank, and that the voice of a king could continue after his death and 'be' the guiding voice of the next, and that the myths about various contentions and relationships with other gods are attempted rationalizations of conflicting admonitory authoritative voices mingled with the authoritative structure in the actuality of the society, at least we are given a new way to look at the subject.

Osiris, to go directly to the important part of this, was not a "dying god," not "life caught in the spell of death," or "a dead god," as modern interpreters have said. He was the hallucinated voice of a dead king whose admonitions could still carry weight. And since he could still be heard, there is no paradox in the fact that the body from which the voice once came should be mummified, with all the equipment of the tomb providing life's necessities: food, drink, slaves, women, the lot. There was no mysterious power that emanated from him; simply his remembered voice which appeared in hallucination to those who had known him and which could admonish or suggest even as it had before he stopped moving and breathing. And that various natural phenomena such as the whispering of waves could act as the cue for such hallucinations accounts for the belief that Osiris, or the king whose body has ceased to move and is in his mummy cloths, continues to control the flooding of the Nile. Further, the relationship between Horus and Osiris, 'embodied' in each new king and his dead father forever, can only be understood as the assimilation of an hallucinated advising voice into the king's own voice, which then would be repeated with the next generation.

Mansions for Voices

That the voice and therefore the power of a god-king lived on after his body stopped moving and breathing is certainly suggested by the manner of his burial. Yet burial is the wrong word. Such divine kings were not morosely entombed, but gaily empalaced. Once the art of building with stone was mastered shortly after 3000 B.C., what once had been the stepped matsaba tombs leap up into those playhouses of bicameral voices in immortal life we call the pyramids: complexes of festive courts and galleries merry with holy pictures and writing, often surrounded by acres of the graves of the god's servants, and dominated by the god's pyramidal house itself, soaring sunward like a shining ziggurat with an almost too confident exterior austerity, and built with an integrity that did not scruple to use the hardest of stones, polished basalts, granites, and diorites, as well as alabaster and limestone.

The psychology of all this is yet to be uncovered. So seriously has the evidence been torn away by collectors of all ranks of guilt that the whole question may be forever wrapped in unanswerableness. For the unmoving mummy of the god-king is often in a curiously plain sarcophagus, while the gaudy effigies made of him are surrounded with a different reverence — perhaps because it was from them that the hallucinations seemed to come. Like the god-statues of Mesopotamia they were life-sized or larger, sometimes elaborately painted, usually with jewels for eyes long since hacked out of their sockets by conscious nonhallucinating robbers. But unlike their eastern cousins, they did not have to be moved and so were finely chiseled out of limestone, slate, diorite, or other stone, and only in certain eras carved from wood. Usually, they were set permanently in niches, some seated, some standing free, some in multiples of the god-king in standing or seated rows, and some walled up in small chapels called *serdabs* with two small eyeholes in front of the jewel-eyes so that the god could see out into the room before him, where there were offerings of food and treasure and we know not what else, so have these tombs been plundered. Occasionally the actual voices hallucinated from the deceased god-king came to be written down as in "The Instructions which the Majesty of King Amenemhet I justified, gave when he spoke in a dream-revelation to his son."

The commoner also was buried in a manner as if he still lived. The peasant since predynastic times had been buried with pots of food, tools, and offerings for his continued life. Those higher in the social hierachy were given a funeral feast in which the corpse itself somehow took part. Scenes showing the deceased eating at his own funerary table came to be carved on slabs and set into a niche in the wall of the grave-mound or *mastaba*. Later graves elaborated this into stone-lined chambers with painted reliefs and *serdabs* with statues and offerings as in the pyramids proper.

Often, "true-of-voice" was an epithet added to the name of a dead person. This is difficult to understand apart from the present theory. "True-of-voice" originally applied to Osiris and Horus with reference to their victories over their opponents.

Letters too were written to the dead as if they still lived. Probably this occurred only after some time when the person so addressed could no longer be 'heard' in hallucinations. A man writes his dead mother asking her to arbitrate between himself and his dead brother. How is this possible unless the living brother had been hearing his dead brother in hallucination? Or a dead man is begged to awaken his ancestors to help his widow and child. These letters are private documents dealing with everyday matters, and are free of official doctrine or make-believe.

A New Theory of the Ka

If we could say that ancient Egypt had a psychology, we would then have to say that its fundamental notion is the *ka*, and the problem becomes what the ka is. Scholars struggling with the meaning of this particularly disturbing concept, which we find constantly in Egyptian inscriptions, have translated it in a litter of ways, as spirit, ghost, double, vital force, nature, luck, destiny, and what have you. It has been compared to the life-spirit of the Semites and Greeks, as well as to the genius of the Romans. But obviously, these later concepts are the hand-me-downs of the bicameral mind. Nor can this slippery diversity of meanings be explained by positing an Egyptian mentality in which words were used in several ways as approaches to the same mysterious entity, or by assuming "the peculiar quality of Egyptian thought which allows an object to be understood not by a single and consistent definition, but by various and unrelated approaches."[15] None of this is satisfactory.

The evidence from hieratic texts is confusing. Each person has his ka and speaks of it as we might of our will power. Yet when one dies, one goes to one's ka. In the famous Pyramid Texts around 2200 B.C., the dead are called "masters of their ka's." The symbol in hieroglyphics for the ka is one of admonishing: two arms uplifted with flat outspread hands, the whole placed upon a stand which in hieroglyphics is only used to support the symbols of divinities.

It is obvious from the preceding chapters that the ka requires a reinterpretation as a bicameral voice. It is, I believe, what the *ili* or personal god was in Mesopotamia. A man's ka was his articulate directing voice which he heard inwardly, perhaps in parental or authoritative accents, but which when heard by his friends or relatives even after his own death, was, of course, hallucinated as his own voice.

If we can here relax our insistence upon the unconsciousness of these people, and, for a moment, imagine that they were something like ourselves, we could imagine a worker out in the fields suddenly hearing the ka or hallucinated voice of the vizier over him admonishing him in some way. If, after he returned to

[15] Ibid., p. 61.

his city, he told the vizier that he had heard the vizier's ka (which in actuality there would be no reason for his doing), the vizier, were he conscious as are we, would assume that it was the same voice that he himself heard and which directed his life. Whereas in actuality, to the worker in the fields, the vizier's ka sounded like the vizier's own voice. While to the vizier himself, his ka would speak in the voices of authorities over him, or some amalgamation of them. And, of course, the discrepancy could never be discovered.

Consistent with this interpretation are several other aspects of the ka. The Egyptians' attitude toward the ka is entirely passive. Just as in the case of the Greek gods, hearing it is tantamount to obeying it. It empowers what it commands. Courtiers in some of their inscriptions referring to the king say, "I did what his ka loved" or "I did that which his ka approved,"[16] which may be interpreted as the courtier hearing the hallucinated voice of his king approving his work.

In some texts it is said that the king makes a man's ka, and some scholars translate ka in this sense as fortune.[17] Again, this is a modern imposition. A concept such as fortune or success is impossible in the bicameral culture of Egypt. What is meant here according to my reading is that the man acquires an admonitory hallucinated voice which then can direct him in his work. Frequently the ka crops up in names of Egyptian officials as did the *ili* with Mesopotamian officials. Kaininesut, "my ka belongs to the king," or Kainesut, "the king is my ka."[18] In the Cairo Museum, stela number 20538 says, "the king gives his servants Ka's and feeds those who are faithful."

The ka of the god-king is of particular interest. It was heard, I suggest, by the king in the accents of his own father. But it was

---

[16] Ibid., p. 68.

[17] But see Alan H. Gardiner, *Egyptian Grammar* (Oxford, 1957), p. 172, note 12.

[18] Frankfort, p. 68; cf. also John A. Wilson, "Egypt: the values of life," Ch. 4 in Frankfort, et al., p. 97.

heard in the hallucinations of his courtiers as the king's own voice, which is the really important thing. Texts state that when a king sat at a meal and ate, his ka sat and ate with him. The pyramids are full of false doors, sometimes simply painted on the limestone walls, through which the deceased god-king's ka could pass out into the world and be heard. It is only the king's ka which is pictured on monuments, sometimes as a standard bearer holding the staff of the king's head and the feather, or as a bird perched behind the king's head. But most significant are the representations of the king's ka as his twin in birth scenes. In one such scene, the god Khnum is shown forming the king and his ka on his potter's wheel. They are identical small figures except that the ka has his left hand pointing to his mouth, obviously suggesting that he is what we might describe as a persona of speech.[19]

Perhaps evidence for a growing complexity in all this are several texts from the eighteenth dynasty or 1500 B.C. onward,

The god Khnum forming the future king with the right hand and the king's *ka* with the left on the potter's wheel. Note that the *ka* points with its left hand to its mouth, indicating its verbal function. The lateralization throughout is in accordance with the neurological model presented in I.5.

[19] Illustrated in Figure 23 in Frankfort.

which casually say that the king has fourteen ka's! This very perplexing statement may indicate that the structure of the government had become so complicated that the king's hallucinated voice was heard as fourteen different voices, these being the voices of intermediaries between the king and those who were carrying out his orders directly. The notion of the king having fourteen ka's is inexplicable by any other notion of what a ka is.

Each king then is Horus, his father dead becoming Osiris, and has his ka, or in later ages, his several ka's, which could best be translated now as voice-persona. An understanding of this is essential for the understanding of the entire Egyptian culture since the relation of king, god, and people is defined by means of the ka. The king's ka is, of course, the ka of a god, operates as his messenger, to himself is the voice of his ancestors, and to his underlings is the voice they hear telling them what to do. And when a subject in some of the texts says, "my ka derives from the king" or "the king makes my ka" or "the king is my ka," this should be interpreted as an assimilation of the person's inner directing voice, derived perhaps from his parents, with the voice or supposed voice of the king.

Another related concept in ancient Egyptian mentality is the *ba*. But at least in the Old Kingdom, the ba is not really on the same level as the ka. It is more like our common ghost, a visual manifestation of what auditorily is the ka. In funerary scenes, the ba is usually depicted as a small humanoid bird, probably because visual hallucinations often have flitting and birdlike movements. It is usually drawn attendant on or in relationship to the actual corpse or to statues of the person. That after the fall of the more king-dominated Old Kingdom, the ba takes on some of the bicameral functions of the ka is indicated by a change in its hieroglyph from a small bird to one beside a lamp (to lead the way), and by its auditory hallucinatory role in the famous Papyrus Berlin 3024, which dates about 1900 B.C. All translations of this astounding text are full of modern mental impositions, including the most recent,[20] otherwise a fascinating chore of scholarship. And no commentator has dared to take this "Dispute of a man with his Ba" at face value, as a dialogue with an auditory hallucination, much like that of a contemporary schizophrenic.

THE TEMPORAL CHANGES IN THEOCRACIES

In the previous chapter, I stressed the uniformities among bicameral kingdoms, the large central worshiping places, treatment of the dead as if they were still living, and the presence of idols. But over and beyond these grosser aspects of ancient civilizations are many subtleties which space has not permitted me to mention. For just as we know that cultures and civilizations can be strikingly different, so we must not assume that the bicameral mind resulted in precisely the same thing everywhere it occurred. Differences in populations, ecologies, priests, hierarchies, idols, industries, all would, I think, result in profound differences in the authority, frequency, ubiquity, and affect of hallucinatory control.

In this chapter, on the other hand, I have been making my emphasis the differences between the two greatest of such civilizations. But I have been speaking of them as if unchanging over time. And this is untrue. To give the impression of a static stability through time and space of bicameral theocracies is entirely mistaken. And I would like to redress the balance in this last section of this chapter by mentioning the changes and differences in the structure of bicameral kingdoms.

The Complexities

The most obvious fact of theocracies is their success in a biological sense. Populations were continually increasing. As

[20] Hans Goedicke, *The Report About the Dispute of a Man with his Ba, Papyrus Berlin 3024* (Baltimore: Johns Hopkins Press, 1970).

they did so, problems of social control by hallucinations called gods became more and more complex. The structuring of such control in a village of a few hundred back at Eynan in the ninth millennium B.C. is obviously enormously different from what it was in the civilizations we have just discussed with their hierarchical layer of gods, priests, and officers.

Indeed, I suggest that there is a built-in periodicity to bicameral theocracies, that the complexities of hallucinatory control with their very success increase until the civil state and civilized relations can no longer be sustained, and the bicameral society collapses. As I noted in the previous chapter, this occurred many times in the pre-Columbian civilizations of America, whole populations suddenly deserting their cities, with no external cause, and anarchically melting back into tribal living in surrounding terrain, but returning to their cities and their gods a century or so later.

In the millennia we have been looking at in this chapter, the complexities were apparently mounting. Many of the ceremonies and practices I have described were initiated as ways of reducing this complexity. Even in writing, the first pictographs were to label and list and sort out. And some of the first syntactical writing speaks of the overpopulation. The Sumerian epic known to us as *Atrahasis* bursts open with the problem:

> The people became numerous . . .
> The god was depressed by their uproar
> Enlil heard their noise,
> He exclaimed to the great gods
> The noise of mankind has become burdensome . . .[21]

as if the voices were having difficulty. The epic goes on to describe how the great gods send plagues, famines, and finally a great flood (the origin of the story of the Biblical flood) to get rid of some of the "black headed ones" as the Mesopotamian gods disparagingly referred to their human slaves.

[21] Quoted by Saggs, *Greatness That Was Babylon*, pp. 384–385.

The apparatus of divinity was becoming strained. In the early millennia of the bicameral age, life had been simpler, confined to a small area, with a simpler political organization, and the needed gods were then few. But as we approach and continue through to the end of the third millennium B.C., the tempo and complexity of social organization demand a far greater number of decisions in a far greater number of contexts in any week or month. And hence, the enormous proliferation of deities which could be invoked in whatever situation a man might find himself. From the great god-houses of the Sumerian and Babylonian cities of the major gods, to the personal gods enchapeled in each household, the world must have literally swarmed with sources of hallucination, and hence the increasing need for priests to order them into strict hierarchies. There were gods for everything one might do. One finds, for example, the coming into existence of obviously popular wayside shrines, such as the Pa-Sag Chapel where the statue-god Pa-Sag helped in making decisions about journeys through the desert.[22]

The response of these Near Eastern theocracies to this increasing complexity is both different and extremely illuminating. In Egypt, the older god-king form of government is less resilient, less developing of human potential, less allowing of innovation, of individuality among subordinate domains. Yet it stretched out for huge distances along the Nile. Regardless of what theory of civil cohesion one may hold, there is no doubt that in the last century of the third millennium B.C., *all* authority in Egypt broke down. There may have been a triggering cause in some geological catastrophe: some ancient texts referring back to the period of 2100 B.C. seem to speak of the Nile becoming dry, of men crossing it on foot, of the sun being hidden, of crops being diminished. Whatever the immediate cause, the pyramid of authority headed by the god-king at Memphis simply collapsed at about

---

[22] According to cuneiform tablets found by Sir Leonard Woolley in association with Pa-Sag's rather poorly carved limestone effigy. See C. L. Woolley, *Excavations at Ur: A Record of Twelve Years Work* (London: Benn, 1954), pp. 190–192.

that time. Literary sources describe people fleeing towns, noble-men grubbing for food in the fields, brothers fighting, men killing their parents, pyramids and tombs ransacked. Scholars are insistent that this total disappearance of authority was due to no outside force but to some unfathomable internal weakness. And I suggest that this is indeed the weakness of the bicameral mind, its fragility in the face of increasing complexity, and that the collapse of authority in so absolute a manner can only be so understood. Egypt at the time had extremely important separated districts stretching from the delta to the upper Nile that could have been self-sustaining. But the very fact that in the midst of this anarchy there was no rebellion, no striving of these sections for independence is, I think, indicative of a very different mentality from our own.

This breakdown of the bicameral mind in what is called the Intermediate Period is reminiscent at least of those periodic breakdowns of Mayan civilizations when all authority suddenly collapsed, and the population melted back into tribal living in the jungles. And just as the Maya cities became inhabited again or new ones formed after a period of breakdown, so Egypt after less then a century of breakdown has unified itself at the beginning of the second millennium under a new god-king, beginning what is called the Middle Kingdom. The same breakdown occurred elsewhere in the Near East from time to time, as in Assur about 1700 B.C., as we shall see in the next chapter.

The Idea of Law

But nothing of this extent ever happens in southern Mesopotamia. Of course there are wars. City-states fought each other over whose god and therefore which steward was to rule over which fields. But there was never any total collapse of authority as occurred in Mesoamerica and in Egypt at the end of the Old Kingdom.

One of the reasons, I think, was the greater resiliency of the steward-king type of theocracy. And another, not unconnected reason was the use to which writing was put. Unlike in Egypt, writing in Mesopotamia was early put to civil use. By 2100 B.C. in Ur, the judgments of gods through their steward mediums began to be recorded. This is the beginning of the idea of law. Such written judgments could be in several places and be continuous through time, thus allowing the cohesiveness of a larger society. We know of nothing similar in Egypt until almost a millennium later.

In 1792 B.C., the civil use of writing in this way breaks open an almost new kind of government in that commanding figure of Mesopotamian history, the greatest of all steward kings, Hammurabi, steward of Marduk, the city god of Babylon. His long stewardship, lasting to 1750 B.C., is a pulling together of most of the city-states of Mesopotamia into an hegemony under his god Marduk in Babylon. This process of conquest and influence is made possible by letters and tablets and stelae in an abundance that had never been known before. It is even thought that he was the first literate king who did not need a scribe, since all his cuneiform letters are apparently incised in wet clay by the same hand. Writing was a new method of civil direction, indeed the model that begins our own memo-communicating government. Without it such a unification of Mesopotamia could not have been accomplished. It is a method of social control which by hindsight we know will soon supplant the bicameral mind.

His most famous remains are the somewhat overinterpreted and perhaps misnamed Code of Hammurabi.[23] Originally, it was an eight-foot-high black basalt stele erected at the end of his reign beside a statue or possibly idol of himself. So far as we can make out, someone seeking redress from another would come to the steward's statue, to "hear my words" (as the stele says at the bottom), and then move over to the stele itself, where the previ-

---

[23] For a translation I have used Robert Francis Harper, *The Code of Hammurabi, King of Babylon* (Chicago: University of Chicago Press, 1904).

Hammurabi hallucinating judgments from his god Marduk (or possibly Shamash) as carved on the top of a stele listing those judgments. About 1750 B.C.

ous judgments of the steward's god are recorded. His god, as I have said, was Marduk, and the top of the stele is sculptured to depict the scene of judgment-giving. The god is seated on a raised mound which in Mesopotamian graphics symbolizes a mountain. An aura of flames flashes up from his shoulders as he speaks (which has made some scholars think it is Shamash, the sun-god). Hammurabi listens intently as he stands just below him ("under-stands"). The god holds in his right hand the attributes of power, the rod and circle very common to such divine depictions. With these symbols, the god is just touching the left elbow of his steward, Hammurabi. One of the magnificent things about this scene is the hypnotic assurance with which both god and steward-king intently stare at each other, impassively majestic, the steward-king's right hand held up between us, the observers, and the plane of communication. Here is no humility, no begging before a god, as occurs just a few centuries later. Ham-

murabi has no subjective-self to narratize into such a relationship. There is only obedience. And what is being dictated by
Marduk are judgments on a series of very specific cases.

As written on the stele beneath this sculptured relief, the
judgments of Marduk are sandwiched in between an introduction
and an epilogue by Hammurabi himself. Here with pomp and
fury he boasts of his deeds, his power, his intimacy with Marduk,
describes the conquests he has made for Marduk, the reason for
the setting up of this stele, and ends with dire implications as to
the evil that will befall anyone who scratches out his name. In
vainglory and naïveté both prologue and epilogue remind us of
the Iliad.

But in between are the 282 quiet pronouncements of the god.
They are serenely reasoned decisions about the apportioning of
commodities among different occupations, how house slaves or
thieves or unruly sons were punished, the eye-for-an-eye-and-
tooth-for-a-tooth kind of recompensing, judgments about gifts
and deaths and adopting children (which seems to have been a
considerable practice), and of marriage and servants and slaves
— all in a cold economy of words in contrast to the bellicose
blustering of the prologue and epilogue. Indeed they sound like
two very different 'men' and in the bicameral sense I think they
were. They were two separately integrated organizations of
Hammurabi's nervous system, one of them in the left hemisphere
writing the prologue and epilogue and standing in effigy at the
side of the stele, and the other in the right hemisphere composing
judgments. And neither of them was conscious in our sense.

While the stele itself is clearly evidence for the bicameral
mind in some form, the problems to which the god's words are
addressed are indeed complex. It is very difficult to imagine
doing the things that these laws say men did in the eighteenth
century B.C. without having a subjective consciousness in which
to plan and devise, deceive and hope. But it should be remembered how rudimentary all this was and how misleading our

modern words can be. The word that is incorrectly translated as
"money" or even as "loan" is simply *kaspu,* meaning silver. It
cannot mean money in our sense since no coins have ever been
found. Similarly, what has been translated as rents is really
tithing, an agreement marked on a clay tablet to return a portion
of the produce of a field to its owner. Wine was not so much
purchased as exchanged, one measure of wine for one measure
of grain. And the use of some modern banking terms in some
translations is downright inaccurate. As I have mentioned before, in many translations of cuneiform material, there is the
constant attempt on the part of scholars to impose modern categories of thought on these ancient cultures in order to make them
more familiar and therefore supposedly more interesting to modern readers.

These rules of the stele should not be thought of in the modern
terms of laws which are enforced by police, something unknown
at that time. Rather they are lists of practices in Babylon itself,
the statements of Marduk, which needed no more enforcement
than their authenticity on the stele itself.

The fact that they were written down and, more generally, the
wide use of visual writing for communication indicate, I think, a
reduction in the auditory hallucinatory control of the bicameral
mind. Together, they put into motion cultural determinants
which, coming together with other forces a few centuries later,
resulted in a change in the very structure of the mind itself.

Let me summarize.

I have endeavored in these two chapters to examine the record
of a huge time span to reveal the plausibility that man and his
early civilizations had a profoundly different mentality from our
own, that in fact men and women were not conscious as are we,
were not responsible for their actions, and therefore cannot be
given the credit or blame for anything that was done over these
vast millennia of time; that instead each person had a part of his

nervous system which was divine, by which he was ordered about like any slave, a voice or voices which indeed were what we call volition and empowered what they commanded and were related to the hallucinated voices of others in a carefully established hierarchy.

The total pattern, I suggest, is in agreement with such a view. It is, of course, not conclusive. However, the astonishing consistency from Egypt to Peru, from Ur to Yucatan, wherever civilizations arose, of death practices and idolatry, of divine government and hallucinated voices, all are witness to the idea of a different mentality from our own.

But it would be an error, as I have tried to show, to regard the bicameral mind as a static thing. True, it developed from the ninth millennium B.C. to the second millennium B.C. with the slowness that makes any single century seem as static as its ziggurats and temples. Millennia are its units of time. But the tempo of development at least in the Near East picks up as we reach the second millennium B.C. The gods of Akkad, like the ka's of Egypt, have multiplied in complexity. And as this complexity develops, there is the first unsureness, the first need for personal gods to intercede with the higher gods, who seem to be receding into the heavens where in one brief millennium they will have disappeared.

From the royal corpse propped up on its stones under its red parapet of Eynan, still ruling its Natufian village in the hallucinations of its subjects, to the mighty beings that cause thunder and create worlds and finally disappear into heavens, the gods were at the same time a mere side effect of language evolution and the most remarkable feature of the evolution of life since the development of *Homo sapiens* himself. I do not mean this simply as poetry. The gods were in no sense 'figments of the imagination' of anyone. They *were* man's volition. They occupied his nervous system, probably his right hemisphere, and from stores of admonitory and preceptive experience, transmuted this experience into articulated speech which then 'told' the man what to do. That such internally heard speech often needed to be primed with the props of the dead corpse of a chieftain or the guilded body of a jewel-eyed statue in its holy house, of that I have really said nothing. It too requires an explanation. I have by no means dared the bottom of the matter, and it is only to be hoped that complete and more correct translations of existing texts and the increasing tempo of archaeological excavation will give us a truer understanding of these long long millennia which civilized mankind.

CHAPTER 3

The Causes of Consciousness

A N OLD SUMERIAN PROVERB has been translated as "Act promptly, make your god happy."[1] If we forget for a moment that these rich English words are but a probing approximation of some more unknowable Sumerian thing, we may say that this curious exaction arches over into our subjective mentality as saying, "Don't think: let there be no time space between hearing your bicameral voice and doing what it tells you."

This was fine in a stable hierarchical organization, where the voices were the always correct and essential parts of that hierarchy, where the divine orders of life were trussed and girdered with unversatile ritual, untouched by major social disturbance. But the second millennium B.C. was not to last that way. Wars, catastrophes, national migrations became its central themes. Chaos darkened the holy brightnesses of the unconscious world. Hierarchies crumpled. And between the act and its divine source came the shadow, the pause that profaned, the dreadful loosening that made the gods unhappy, recriminatory, jealous. Until, finally, the screening off of their tyranny was effected by the invention on the basis of language of an analog space with an analog 'I'. The careful elaborate structures of the bicameral mind had been shaken into consciousness.

These are the momentous themes of the present chapter.

* * * *

[1] Proverb 1:145 in Edmund I. Gordon, *Sumerian Proverbs* (Philadelphia: University Museum, 1959), p. 113.

The Instability of Bicameral Kingdoms

In the contemporary world, we associate rigid authoritarian governments with militarism and police repression. This association should not be applied to the authoritarian states of the bicameral era. Militarism, police, rule by fear, are all the desperate measures used to control a subjective conscious populace restless with identity crises and divided off into their multitudinous privacies of hopes and hates.

In the bicameral era, the bicameral mind *was* the social control, not fear or repression or even law. There were no private ambitions, no private grudges, no private frustrations, no private anything, since bicameral men had no internal 'space' in which to be private, and no analog 'I' to be private with. All initiative was in the voices of gods. And the gods needed to be assisted by their divinely dictated laws only in the late federations of states in the second millennium B.C.

Within each bicameral state, therefore, the people were probably more peaceful and friendly than in any civilization since. But at the interfaces between different bicameral civilizations, the problems were complex and quite different.

Let us consider a meeting between two individuals from two different bicameral cultures. Let us assume they do not know each other's language and are owned by different gods. The manner of such meetings would be dependent upon the kind of admonitions, warnings, and importunings with which the individual had been reared.

In peaceful times, with the god of the city basking in prosperity, the human tilling of his fields, the harvesting, storing, and sorting out of his produce all going on without hitch or question, as in a colony of ants, it could be expected that his divine voice would be basically amicable, and that indeed all man's voice-visions would tend to be beautiful and peaceful, exaggerating the very harmony this method of social control was evolved to preserve.

Thus, if the bicameral theocracies of both individuals meeting have been unthreatened for their generation, both their directive gods would be composed of friendly voices. The result may have been a tentative exchange of gestural greetings and facial expressions that might grow to friendship, or even an exchange of gifts. For we can be very certain that the relative rarity of each other's possessions (coming from different cultures) would make such an exchange mutually wished for.

This is probably how trade began. The beginning of such exchanges goes back to food sharing in the family group which grew into exchanges of goods and produce within the same city. Just as the harvested grain of the first agricultural settlements had to be doled out by certain god-given rules, so, as labor became more specialized, other products, wine, adornments, clothes, and the building of houses, all had to have their god-set equivalents to each other.

Trade between different peoples is simply the extension of such exchanging of goods to another kingdom. Texts from 2500 B.C. found in Sumer speak of such exchanging as far away as the Indus Valley. And the recent discovery of a new city site at Tepe Yahya, halfway between Sumer and the Indus Valley, at the mouth of the Persian Gulf, whose artifacts clearly indicate that it was the main source of steatite or soapstone, used for utensils extensively in Mesopotamia, establish it as a center of exchange between these bicameral kingdoms.[2] Small two-inch-square tablets have been found with counting marks on them which were probably simple exchange rates. All this was during a peaceful era in the middle of the third millennium B.C. I shall suggest later that extensive exchanging of goods between bicameral theocracies may in itself have weakened the bicameral structure that made civilization possible.

Now let us return to our two individuals from different cultures. We have been discussing what occurs in a peaceful world

[2] *New York Times*, December 20, 1970, p. 53.

with peaceful gods. But what if the opposite were the case? If both came from threatened cultures, both would probably hear warlike hallucinated voices directing each to kill the other, whereupon hostilities would follow. But the same result would happen if either came from a threatened culture, putting the other into a posture of defense, as either the same god or another directed him as well to engage in fighting.

There is thus no middle ground in intertheocracy relations. Admonitory voices echoing kings, viziers, parents, etc., are unlikely to command individuals into acts of compromise. Even today, our ideas of nobility are largely residues of bicameral authority: it is not noble to whine, it is not noble to plead, it is not noble to beg, even though these postures are really the most moral of ways to settle differences. And hence the instability of the bicameral world, and the fact that during the bicameral era boundary relations would, I think, be more likely to end in all-out friendship or all-out hostility than anything between these extremes.

Nor is this the bottom of the matter. The smooth working of a bicameral kingdom has to rest on its authoritarian hierarchy. And once the priestly or secular hierarchy is disputed or upset, its effects would be exaggerated in a way that in a police state would not occur. Once cities become a certain size, as we have already seen, the bicameral control must be extremely precarious. The hierarchy of priests to sort out the various voices and give them their recognitions must have become a major preoccupation as bicameral cities grew in size. One jar to this balance of human and hallucinated authority, and, like a house of cards, the whole thing might collapse. As I have mentioned in both previous chapters, such theocracies occasionally did indeed suddenly collapse without any known external cause.

In comparison with conscious nations, then, bicameral nations were more susceptible to collapse. The directives of gods are limited. If on top of this inherent fragility, something really new occurred, such as a forced intermingling of bicameral peoples, the gods would be hard pressed to sort anything out in a peaceable way.

The Weakening of Divine Authority with Writing

These limitations of gods were both relieved and greatly exacerbated in the second millennium B.C. by the success of writing. On the one hand, writing could allow a civil structure such as that of Hammurabi to remain stable. But, on the other, it was gradually eroding the auditory authority of the bicameral mind. More and more, the accountings and messages of government were placed in cuneiform tablets particularly. Whole libraries of them are still being discovered. Letters of officials became a commonplace. By 1500 B.C., even miners high in the rocky wastes of Sinai incised their names and their relationships to the goddess of the mine on its walls.[3]

The input to the divine hallucinatory aspect of the bicameral mind was auditory. It used cortical areas more closely connected to the auditory parts of the brain. And once the word of god was silent, written on dumb clay tablets or incised into speechless stone, the god's commands or the king's directives could be turned to or avoided by one's own efforts in a way that auditory hallucinations never could be. The word of a god had *a controllable location* rather than an ubiquitous power with immediate obedience. This is extremely important.

The Failure of the Gods

This loosening of the god-man partnership perhaps by trade and certainly by writing was the background of what happened. But the immediate and precipitate cause of the breakdown of the

[3] Romain F. Butin, "The Sarabit Expedition of 1930: IV, The Protosinaitic Inscriptions." *Harvard Theological Review*, 1932, 25, pp. 130–204.

bicameral mind, of the wedge of consciousness between god and man, between hallucinated voice and automaton action, was that in social chaos the gods could not tell you what to do. Or if they did, they led to death, or at the intimate least to an increase in the stress that physiologically occasioned the voice in the first place, until voices came in an unsolvable Babel of confusion.

The historical context of all this was enormous. The second millennium B.C. was heavy laden with profound and irreversible changes. Vast geological catastrophes occurred. Civilizations perished. Half the world's population became refugees. And wars, previously sporadic, came with hastening and ferocious frequency as this important millennium hunched itself sickly into its dark and bloody close.

It is a complex picture, the variables evoking these changes multileveled, the facts as we have them now not at all certain. Almost yearly they are revised as each new generation of archaeologists and ancient historians finds fault with its predecessors. As an approximation to these complexities, let us look at the two major elements of these upheavals. One was the mass migrations and invasions of peoples all around the eastern Mediterranean due to the volcanic eruption of Thera, and the other was the rise of Assyria, in three great phases, warring its way reign by reign westward to Egypt, northward to the Caspian, incorporating all of Mesopotamia, forming a very different kind of empire from any that the world had known before.

The Assyrian Spring

Let us first look at the situation in northern Mesopotamia around the city that belongs to the god Ashur, as the second millennium B.C. opens.[4] Originally a part of Akkad, and then of Old Babylonia two hundred miles south, by 1950 B.C., this peace-

---

[4] For the overall contours of Assyrian history I have relied on various authorities, but particularly H. W. F. Saggs, *The Greatness That Was Babylon* (New York: Mentor Books, 1962); and various articles by William F. Albright.

ful bicameral city on an upper reach of the gentle Tigris has been left pretty much to itself. Under the guidance of Ashur's chief human servant, Puzen-Ashur I, its benign influence and wealth begin to expand. More than in any nation before it, the feature of that expansion is exchange of goods with other theocracies. About two hundred years later, the city owned by Ashur becomes Assyria, with exchange posts as much as seven hundred miles by road away to the northeast in Anatolia or present-day Turkey.

Exchange of goods between cities had been going on for some time. But it is doubtful if it was as extensive as that practiced by the Assyrians. Recent excavations have revealed *karums* or, in smaller towns, *ubartums,* the exchange posts just outside several Anatolian cities in which the trading took place. Particularly interesting excavations have been made of the karum just outside Kültepe: small buildings whose walls have no windows, stone and wooden shelves on which are cuneiform tablets yet to be translated, and sometimes jars with what appear to be counters within them.[5] The writing, indeed, is old Assyrian, and, presumably brought there by these traders, is the first writing known in Anatolia.

Such trade was not, however, a true market. There were no prices under the pressures of supply and demand, no buying and selling, and no money. It was trade in the sense of equivalences established by divine decree. There is a complete lack of reference to business profits or loss in any of the cuneiform tablets that have so far been translated. There are occasional exceptions, even a suggestion of 'inflation,' perhaps during a famine year when the exchanges became different, but they do not seriously impair Polanyi's view, which I am following here.[6]

Let us consider these Assyrian merchants for a moment. They

[5] Nimet Osguc, "Assyrian trade colonies in Anatolia," *Archeology*, 1965, 4: 250–255.

[6] Karl Polanyi, *Trade and Market in the Early Empires* (Glencoe: Free Press, 1957).

were, we may presume, merely agents, holding their position by descent and apprenticeship, and carrying out exchanges much as their fathers had done for centuries. But there are so many questions that face the psychohistorian at this point. What would happen to the bicameral voices of these merchants as much as seven hundred miles from the source of their city-god's voice, and in daily contact and probably (though not necessarily) speaking the language of bicameral men ruled by a different pantheon of voices? Is it possible that something like a protosubjective consciousness occurred in these traders at the boundaries of different civilizations? Did they, returning periodically to Ashur, bring with them a weakened bicamerality that perhaps spread to a new generation? So that the bicameral tie between gods and men was loosened?

The causes of consciousness are multiple, but at least I do not think it is a coincidence that the key nation in this development should also have been that nation most involved in exchanges of goods with others. If it is true that the power of the gods and particularly of Ashur were being weakened at this time, it could account for the absolute collapse of his city in 1700 B.C., beginning the dark ages of Assyrian anarchy that lasted two hundred years. For this event there is no explanation whatever. No historian understands it. And there is little hope of ever doing so, for not a single Assyrian cuneiform inscription from this period has ever been found.

The reorganization of Assyria after its collapse had to wait upon other events. In 1450 B.C., Egypt pushed the Mitanni out of Syria right across the Euphrates into lands between the two great rivers that had once been Assyrian. But a century later the Mitanni were conquered by the Hittites from the north, thus making possible the rebuilding of an Assyrian empire in 1380 B.C. after two centuries of anarchic darkness.

And what an empire it is! No nation had been so militaristic before. Unlike any previous inscriptions anywhere, those of middle Assyria now bristle with brutal campaigns. The change is dramatic. But the success of the Assyrian invasions as they relentlessly savage their way toward world domination is like a ratchet catching at the whorl of catastrophes of another kind.

Eruption, Migration, Conquest

The collapse of the bicameral mind was certainly accelerated by the collapse under the ocean of a good part of the Aegean people's land. This followed an eruption or series of eruptions of the volcano on the island of Thera, also called Santorini, now an Aegean tourist attraction, barely sixty-two miles north of Crete.[7] Then, it had been part of what Plato[8] and later legend called the lost continent of Atlantis, which with Crete made up the Minoan empire. The major part of it and perhaps parts of Crete as well were suddenly 1000 feet underwater. Most of the remaining land of Thera was covered with a 150-foot-deep crust of volcanic ash and pumice.

Geologists have hypothesized that the black cloud caused by the eruption darkened the sky for days and affected the atmosphere for years. The air shock waves have been estimated at 350 times more powerful than a hydrogen bomb. Thick poisonous vapors puffed out over the blue sea for miles. A *tsunami* or huge tidal wave followed. Towering 700 feet high and traveling at 350 miles per hour, it smashed into the fragile coasts of the bicameral kingdoms along the Aegean mainland and its islands. Everything for two miles inland was destroyed. A civilization and its gods had ended.

Just when it happened, whether it was a series of eruptions or a two-stage affair with a year between the eruption and the collapse, will require better scientific methods of dating volcanic

[7] See Jerome J. Pollit, "Atlantis and Minoan Civilization: An archeological nexus"; and Robert S. Brumbaugh, "Plato's Atlantis," both in the *Yale Alumni Magazine*, 1970, 33, 20–29.

[8] See particularly *Critias*, 108e–119e, passim.

ash and pumice. Some believe it to have occurred in 1470 B.C.[9] Others have dated the collapse of Thera between 1180 and 1170 B.C. when the whole of the Mediterranean, including Cyprus, the Nile delta, and the coast of Israel, suffered universal calamity of a magnitude that dwarfed the 1470 B.C. destruction.[10]

Whenever it was, whether it was one or a series of eruptions, it set off a huge procession of mass migrations and invasions which wrecked the Hittite and Mycenaean empires, threw the world into a dark ages within which came the dawn of consciousness. Only Egypt seems to have retained the elaboration of its civilized life, although the exodus of the Israelites about the time of the Trojan War, perhaps 1230 B.C., is close enough to be considered a part of this great world event. The legend of the parting of the Red Sea probably refers to tidal changes in the Sea of Reeds related to the Thera eruption.

The result is that, in the space of a single day, whole populations or what survive of them are suddenly refugees. Like files of dominoes, anarchy and chaos ripple and lurch across the frightened land as neighbor invades neighbor. And what can the gods say in these ruins? What can the gods say, with hunger and death more strict than they, with strange people staring at strange people, and strange language bellowed at uncomprehending ears? The bicameral man was ruled in the trivial circumstance of everyday life by unconscious habit, and in his encounters with anything new or out of the ordinary in his own behavior or others' by his voice-visions. Ripped out of context in the larger hierarchical group, where neither habit nor bicameral voice could assist and direct him, he must have been a pitiable creature indeed. How could the storings up and distillings of admonitory experience gained in the peaceful authoritarian ordering of a bicameral nation say anything that would work now?

Huge migrations begin moving into Ionia and then south. The

[9] S. Marinatos, *Crete and Mycaenae* (New York: Abrams, 1960).
[10] *New York Times*, Sept. 28, 1966, p. 34.

coastal lands of the Levant are invaded by land and sea by peoples from eastern Europe, of whom the Philistines of the Old Testament were a part. The pressure of the refugees is so great in Anatolia that in 1200 B.C. the puissant Hittite empire collapses, driving the Hittites down into Syria where other refugees are seeking new lands. Assyria was inland and protected. And the chaos resulting from these invasions allowed the cruel Assyrian armies to push all the way into Phrygia, Syria, Phoenicia, and even to the subjugation of the mountain peoples of Armenia in the north and those of the Zagros Mountains to the east. Could Assyria do this on a strictly bicameral basis?

The most powerful king of this middle Assyria was Tiglath-Pileser I (1115–1077 B.C.). Note how he no longer joins the name of his god to his name. His exploits are well known from a large clay prism of monstrous boasts. His laws have come down to us in a collection of cruel tablets. Scholars have called his policy "a policy of frightfulness."[11] And so it was. The Assyrians fell like butchers upon harmless villagers, enslaved what refugees they could, and slaughtered others in thousands. Bas-reliefs show what appear to be whole cities whose populace have been stuck alive on stakes running up through the groin and out the shoulders. His laws meted out the bloodiest penalties yet known in world history for even minor misdemeanors. They make a dramatic contrast to the juster admonishments that the god of Babylon dictated to bicameral Hammurabi six centuries earlier.

Why this harshness? And for the first time in the history of civilization? Unless the previous method of social control had absolutely broken down. And that form of social control was the bicameral mind. The very practice of cruelty as an attempt to rule by fear is, I suggest, at the brink of subjective consciousness.

The chaos is widespread and continuing. In Greece it is darkly known as the Dorian invasions. The Acropolis is in flames by the

[11] H. W. F. Saggs, *The Greatness That Was Babylon* (New York: Mentor Books, 1962), p. 101.

end of the thirteenth century B.C. Mycenae no longer exists by the end of the twelfth century B.C. It has been ground out into legend and wonder. And we can imagine the first aoidos, still bicameral, wandering entranced from ruined camp to camp of refugees, singing the bright goddess through his white lips of the wrath of Achilles in a golden age that was and is no more.

Even from somewhere around the Black Sea, hordes that some called the Mushku, known in the Old Testament as Meshech, thrust down into the ruined Hittite kingdom. Then twenty thousand of them drifted further south invading the Assyrian province of Kummuh. Hordes of Aramaeans continuously pressed in on the Assyrian from the western deserts and continued to do so up into the first millennium B.C.

In the south, more of these refugees, called in hieroglyphics the "People from the Sea," attempt to invade Egypt by the Nile delta at the beginning of the eleventh century B.C. Their defeat by Rameses III can still be seen on the north wall of his funerary temple at Medinet Habu in western Thebes.[12] The invaders in ships, chariots, and on foot, with families and oxcarts of possessions, stream through these murals in refugee fashion. Had the invasion been successful, it is possible that Egypt might have done for the intellect what Greece was to do in the next millennium. And so the People from the Sea are pressed back eastward into the clutch of Assyrian militarism.

And finally all these pressures become too great for even Assyrian cruelty. In the tenth century B.C., Assyria itself cannot control the situation and shrivels back into poverty behind the Tigris. But only to breathe. For in the very next century, the Assyrians begin their reconquest of the world with unprecedented sadistic ferocity, butchering and terroring their way back to their former empire and then beyond and all the way to Egypt and up the fertile Nile to the holy sun-god himself, even as Pizarro was

---

[12] For illustrations of these see William Stevenson Smith, *Interconnections in the Ancient Near East* (New Haven: Yale University Press, 1965), pp. 220–221.

to take the divine Inca captive two and a half millennia later on the opposite side of the earth. And by this time, the great transilience in mentality had occurred. Man had become conscious of himself and his world.

How Consciousness Began

So far, all our analysis has been about how and why the bicameral mind collapsed. It could indeed be asked at this point why man did not simply revert to his previous condition. Sometimes he did. But the inertia of the more complex cultures prevented the return to tribal life. Man was trapped in his own civilization. Huge cities simply are there, and their ponderous habits of working keep going even as their divine control lapses away. Language too is a brake upon social change. The bicameral mind was an offshoot of the acquisition of language, and language by this time had a vocabulary demanding such attention to a civilized environment as to make a reversion to something of at least 5000 years earlier almost impossible.

The facts of the transition from the bicameral mind to the subjective conscious mind are what I try to develop in the ensuing two chapters. But just how it happened is the consideration here, and this needs a great deal more research. What we need is a paleontology of consciousness, in which we can discern stratum by stratum how this metaphored world we call subjective consciousness was built up and under what particular social pressures. All that I can present here is a few suggestions.

I would also remind the reader of two things. First, I am not talking here of the metaphoric mechanisms by which consciousness was generated that I discussed in I.3. Here I am concerned with their origin in history, why those features were generated by metaphors at a particular time. Secondly, we are speaking only about the Near East. Once consciousness is established, there are quite different reasons why it is so successful, and why it spreads to the remaining bicameral peoples, problems which we shall take up in a later chapter.

The observation of difference may be the origin of the analog space of consciousness. After the breakdown of authority and of the gods, we can scarcely imagine the panic and the hesitancy that would feature human behavior during the disorder we have described. We should remember that in the bicameral age men belonging to the same city-god were more or less of similar opinion and action. But in the forced violent intermingling of peoples from different nations, different gods, the observation that strangers, even though looking like oneself, spoke differently, had opposite opinions, and behaved differently might lead to the supposition of something inside of them that was different. Indeed, this latter opinion has come down to us in the traditions of philosophy, namely, that thoughts, opinions, and delusions are subjective phenomena inside a person because there is no room for them in the 'real,' 'objective' world. It is thus a possibility that before an individual man had an interior self, he unconsciously first posited it in others, particularly contradictory strangers, as the thing that caused their different and bewildering behavior. In other words, the tradition in philosophy that phrases the problem as the logic of inferring other minds from one's own has it the wrong way around. We may first unconsciously (sic) suppose other consciousnesses, and then infer our own by generalization.

The Origin of Narratization in Epics

It sounds strange to speak about gods learning. But occupying a good part of the right temporal-parietal region (if the model of I.5 is correct), they, too, like the left temporal-parietal region, or perhaps even more so, would learn new abilities, storing up new experience, reworking their admonitory function in new ways to meet new needs.

Narratization is a single word for an extremely complex set of patterning abilities which have, I think, a multiple ancestry. But the thing in its larger patterning, such as lifetimes, histories, the past and future, may have been learned by dominantly left-hemisphered men from a new kind of functioning in the right hemisphere. The new kind of functioning was narratization, and it had previously been learned, I suggest, by the gods at a certain period of history.

When could this have been? It is doubtful if there can ever be a certain answer, partly because there is no sharp boundary between the relation of an event that has just happened and an epic. Also our search into the past is always confounded with the development of writing. But it is interesting that about the middle of the third millennium B.C., or just before, there seems to arise a new feature of civilization in southern Mesopotamia. Before what is known as the Early Dynastic II period, excavations show that towns or cities in this area were not fortified, had no defenses. But thereafter, in the principal regions of urban development, walled cities arose at a fairly constant distance from one another, the inhabitants farming the intervening fields and occasionally fighting each other for control of them. At about this same period came the first epics that we know of, such as the several about Emmerkar, the builder of Uruk, and his relations with the neighboring city-state of Aratta. And their topics are precisely this relationship between neighboring states.

My suggestion is that narratization arose as a codification of reports of past events. Writing up to this time — and it is only a few centuries since its invention — had been primarily an inventory device, a way of recording the stores and exchanges of a god's estates. Now it becomes a way of recording god-commanded events, whose recitation after the fact becomes the narratization of epics. Since reading, as I have suggested in the previous chapter, may have been hallucinating from the cuneiform, it may, then, have been a right temporal lobe function.

And since these were the recordings of the past, it is the right hemisphere that becomes at least the temporary seat of the reminiscence of gods.

We should note in passing how different the reading from stable cuneiform tablets in Mesopotamia was from the oral recomposing of the epics in Greece by a succession of aoidoi: It is possible that the oral tradition in Greece was an immense benefit in its demand that 'Apollo' or the 'Muses' in the right hemisphere become the sources of memory and learn how to narratize so as to keep the memories of Achilles together in the epic pattern. And then, in the chaos of transilience to consciousness, man assimilates both this memory ability and the ability to narratize memories into patterns.

The Origin of the Analog 'I' in Deceit

Deceit may also be a cause of consciousness. But we must begin any discussion of the topic by making a distinction between instrumental or short-term deceit and long-term deceit, which might better be expressed as treachery. Several examples of the former have been described in chimpanzees. Female chimpanzees will 'present' in sexual posture to a male to whisk away his banana when his prandial interest is thus distracted. In another instance, a chimpanzee would fill his mouth with water, coax a disliked keeper over to the cage bars, and spit the water in his face. In both such instances, the deceit involved is a case of instrumental learning, a behavior pattern that is followed immediately by some rewarding state of affairs. And it needs no further explanation.

But the kind of deceit that is treachery is quite another matter. It is impossible for an animal or for a bicameral man. Long-term deceit requires the invention of an analog self that can 'do' or 'be' something quite different from what the person actually does or is, as seen by his associates. It is an easy matter to imagine how important for survival during these centuries such an ability would be. Overrun by some invader, and seeing his wife raped, a man who obeyed his voices would, of course, immediately strike out, and thus probably be killed. But if a man could be one thing on the inside and another thing on the outside, could harbor his hatred and revenge behind a mask of acceptance of the inevitable, such a man would survive. Or, in the more usual situation of being commanded by invading strangers, perhaps in a strange language, the person who could obey superficially and have 'within him' another self with 'thoughts' contrary to his disloyal actions, who could loathe the man he smiled at, would be much more successful in perpetuating himself and his family in the new millennium.

Natural Selection

My last comment brings up the possibility that natural selection may have played a role in the beginning of consciousness. But in putting up this question, I wish to be very clear that consciousness is chiefly a cultural introduction, learned on the basis of language and taught to others, rather than any biological necessity. But that it had and still has a survival value suggests that the change to consciousness may have been assisted by a certain amount of natural selection.

It is impossible to calculate what percentage of the civilized world died in these terrible centuries toward the end of the second millennium B.C. I suspect it was enormous. And death would come soonest to those who impulsively lived by their unconscious habits or who could not resist the commandments of their gods to smite whatever strangers interfered with them. It is thus possible that individuals most obdurately bicameral, most obedient to their familiar divinities, would perish, leaving the genes of the less impetuous, the less bicameral, to endow the ensuing generations. And again we may appeal to the principle of Baldwinian evolution as we did in our discussion of language. Consciousness must be learned by each new generation, and those biologically most able to learn it would be those most likely to survive. There is even Biblical evidence, as we shall see in a future chapter, that children obdurately bicameral were simply killed.[13]

Conclusion

This chapter must not be construed as presenting any evidence about the origin of consciousness. That is the burden of several ensuing chapters. My purpose in this chapter has been descriptive and theoretical, to paint a picture of plausibility, of how and why a huge alteration in human mentality could have occurred toward the end of the second millennium B.C.

In summary, I have sketched out several factors at work in the great transilience from the bicameral mind to consciousness: (1) the weakening of the auditory by the advent of writing; (2) the inherent fragility of hallucinatory control; (3) the unworkableness of gods in the chaos of historical upheaval; (4) the positing of internal cause in the observation of difference in others; (5) the acquisition of narratization from epics; (6) the survival value of deceit; and (7) a modicum of natural selection.

I would conclude by bringing up the question of the strictness of all this. Did consciousness really come *de novo* into the world only at this time? Is it not possible that certain individuals at least might have been conscious in much earlier time? Possibly yes. As individuals differ in mentality today, so in past ages it might have been possible that one man alone, or more possibly a cult or clique, began to develop a metaphored space with analog selves. But such aberrant mentality in a bicameral theocracy

---

[13] Zechariah, 13: 3–4.

would, I think, be short-lived and scarcely what we mean by consciousness today.

It is the cultural norm that we are here concerned with, and the evidence that that cultural norm underwent a dramatic change is the substance of the following chapters. The three areas of the world where this transilience can be most easily observed are Mesopotamia, Greece, and among the bicameral refugees. We shall be discussing these in turn.

CHAPTER 4

A Change of Mind in Mesopotamia

A BOUT 1230 B.C., Tukulti-Ninurta I, tyrant of Assyria, had a
stone altar made that is dramatically different from anything
that preceded it in the history of the world. In the carving on its
face, Tukulti is shown twice, first as he approaches the throne of
his god, and then as he kneels before it. The very double image
fairly shouts aloud about this beggarly posture unheard of in a
king before in history. As our eyes descend from the standing
king to the kneeling king just in front of him, it is as emphatic as
a moving picture, in itself a quite remarkable artistic discovery.
But far more remarkable is the fact that the throne before which
this first of the cruel Assyrian conquerors grovels is empty.

No king before in history is ever shown kneeling. No scene
before in history ever indicates an absent god. The bicameral
mind had broken down.

Hammurabi, as we have seen in II.2, is always carved standing
and listening intently to a very present god. And countless cylinder seals from his period show other personages listening eye to
eye or being presented to the just-as-real figures of human-
shaped gods. The Ashur altar of Tukulti is in shocking contrast
to all previous depictions of the relations of gods and men. Nor is
it simply some artistic idiosyncrasy. Other altar scenes of Tukulti
are similarly devoid of gods. And cylinder seals of Tukulti's
period also show the king approaching other nonpresent divinities, sometimes represented by a symbol. Such comparisons

Carving on the front of the Tukulti Altar now in the Berlin Museum. Tukulti stands and then kneels before the empty throne of his god. Note the emphasis of the pointing forefinger.

strongly suggest that the time of the breakdown of the bicameral mind in Mesopotamia is some time between Hammurabi and Tukulti.

This hypothesis is confirmed in the cuneiform remains of Tukulti and his period. What is known as the *Epic of Tukulti-Ninurta*[1] is the next clearly dated and well-preserved cuneiform document of note after Hammurabi. In the latter's time there is no doubt of the gods' eternal undeviant presence among men, directing them in their activities. But at the beginning of Tukulti's somewhat propagandalike epic, the gods of the Babylonian cities are angry with the Babylonian king for his inattention to them. They therefore forsake their cities, leaving the inhabitants

[1] Translations of this and the other texts discussed in this section can be found in W. G. Lambert, *Babylonian Wisdom Literature* (Oxford: Clarendon Press, 1960).

without divine guidance, so that the victory of Tukulti's Assyrian armies is assured. This conception of gods forsaking their human slaves under any circumstances whatever is impossible in the Babylon of Hammurabi. It is something new in the world.

Moreover, it is found throughout whatever literature remains of the last three centuries of the second millennium B.C.

> One who has no god, as he walks along the street,
> Headache envelops him like a garment.

So one cuneiform tablet from about the reign of Tukulti.

If the breakdown of the bicameral mind involved the involuntary inhibition of temporal lobe areas of the right hemisphere, as we have conjectured earlier, this statement takes on an added interest.

Also from about the same period come the famous three tablets and a questionable fourth named for its first words, *Ludlul bel nemeqi*, usually translated as "I will praise the lord of wisdom." "Wisdom" here is an unwarranted modern imposition. The translation should be something closer to 'skill' or 'ability to control misfortune,' the lord here being Marduk, the highest god of Babylon. The first completely readable lines of the damaged first tablet are:

> My god has forsaken me and disappeared,
> My goddess has failed me and keeps at a distance.
> The good angel who walked beside me has departed.

This is *de facto* the breakdown of the bicameral mind. The speaker is one Shubshi-Meshre-Shakkan (as we are told in the third tablet), a feudal lord possibly under Tukulti. He goes on to describe how, with the departure of his gods, his king becomes irreconcilably angry at him, how his feudal position of ruling a

city is taken away, how he thus becomes a social outcast. The
second tablet describes how, in this godless state, he is the target
of all disease and misfortune. Why have the gods left him? And
he catalogs the prostrations, the prayers, and the sacrifices which
have not brought them back. Priests and omen-readers are consulted, but still

> My god has not come to the rescue in taking me by the hand,
> Nor has my goddess shown pity on me by going at my side.

In the third tablet, he realizes that it is the almighty Marduk who
is behind all that is happening to him. In dreams, the angels of
Marduk appear to him in bicameral fashion, and speak messages
of consolation and promises of prosperity from Marduk himself.
At this assurance, Shubshi is then delivered from his toils and
illnesses and goes to the temple of Marduk to give thanks to the
great god who "made the wind bear away my offenses."

The mighty themes of the religions of the world are here
sounded for the first time. Why have the gods left us? Like
friends who depart from us, they must be offended. Our misfortunes are our punishments for our offenses. We go down on our
knees, begging to be forgiven. And then find redemption in some
return of the word of a god. These aspects of present-day religion
find an explanation in the theory of the bicameral mind and its
breakdown during this period.

The world had long known rules and dues. They were divinely
ordained and humanly obeyed. But the idea of right and wrong,
the idea of a good man and of redemption from sin and divine
forgiveness only begin in this uneasy questioning of why the
hallucinated guidances can no longer be heard.

The same dominant theme of lost gods cries out to us from the
tablets known as *The Babylonian Theodicy*.[2] This dialogue be-

---

[2] A fascinating problem is why the reference to gods at this time becomes plural
even when it takes a singular verb. This occurs in contexts which in previous literature would have meant it was the personal god. This occurs in both the *Ludlul*,

tween a sufferer and his advising friend is of an obviously later date, perhaps 900 B.C., but wails with the same pleas. Why have the gods left us? And since they control everything, why did they shower misfortune upon us? The poem also shimmers with a new sense of an individual or what we would call an analog self denoting a new consciousness. It ends with the cry which has echoed through all later history:

> May the gods who have thrown me off give help,
> May the goddess who has abandoned me show mercy.

From here to the psalms of the Old Testament is no great journey. There is no trace whatever of such concerns in any literature previous to the texts I am describing here.

The consequences of the disappearance of auditory hallucinations from human mentality are profound and widespread, and occur on many different levels. One thing is the confusion of authority itself. What is authority? Rulers without gods to guide them are fitful and unsure. They turn to omens and divination, which we shall take up shortly. And as I have mentioned earlier, cruelty and oppression become the ways in which a ruler imposes his rule upon his subjects in the absence of auditory hallucinations. Even the king's own authority in the absence of gods becomes questionable. Rebellion in the modern sense becomes possible.

Indeed this new kind of rebellion is what happened to Tukulti himself. He had founded a whole new capital for Assyria across the Tigris from Ashur, naming it godlessly after himself — Kar-Tukultininurta. But, led by his own son and successor, his more conservative nobles imprisoned him in his new city, put it to the torch, and burned it to the ground, his fiery death leading his reign

---

II:12, 25, 33, as well as through the *Theodicy*, and later in the plural *elohim* of the Eloist contributions to the Old Testament. One should remember here the Muses of the Greeks and possibly the *pankush* of Hittite tablets. Do and did hallucinations sound like choirs as their reliability is being neurologically weakened?

into legend. (He glimmers in the murky history of the Old Testament as Nimrod[3] [Genesis:10] and in Greek myths as King Ninos.[4]) Disorders and social chaos had of course happened before. But such a premeditated mutiny and parricide of a king is impossible to imagine in the god-obedient hierarchies of the bicameral age.

But of much greater importance are the beginnings of some new cultural themes which are responses to this breakdown of the bicameral mind and its divine authority. History does not move by leaps into unrelated novelty, but rather by the selective emphasis of aspects of its own immediate past. And these new aspects of human history in response to the loss of divine authority are all developments and emphases out of the bicameral age.

Prayer

In the classical bicameral mind, that is, before its weakening by writing about 2500 B.C., I suggest that there was no hesitancy in the hallucinated voice and no occasion for prayer. A novel situation or stress, and a voice told you what to do. Certainly this is so in contemporary schizophrenic patients who are hallucinating. They do not beg to hear their voices; it is unnecessary. In those few patients where this does happen, it is during recovery when the voices are no longer heard with the same frequency. But as civilizations and their interrelationships become more complex toward the end of the third millennium B.C., the gods are occasionally asked to respond to various requests. Usually, however, such requests are not what we think of as prayer. They consist of several stylized imprecations, such as the common ending of statue inscriptions:

[3] E. A. Speiser, "In Search of Nimrod," in *Oriental and Biblical Studies, Collected Writings of E. A. Speiser*, J. J. Finkelstein and Mosh Greenberg, eds. (Philadelphia: University of Pennsylvania Press, 1967), pp. 41–52.

[4] H. Lewy, "Nitokoris-Naqi'a," *Journal of Near Eastern Studies*, 1952, 11, 264–286.

> Whoever this image shall deface may Enlil his name destroy and his weapon break![5]

or the kind of praising which Gudea bestows on his gods in the great cylinder inscriptions from Lagash. A notable exception, however, are the very real prayers of Gudea in Cylinder A to his divine mother, asking her to explain the meaning of a dream. But this, like so much else with the enigmatic Gudea, is exceptional. Prayers as the central important act of divine worship only become prominent after the gods are no longer speaking to man "face to face" (as Deuteronomy 34:10 expresses it). What was new in the time of Tukulti becomes everyday during the first millennium B.C., all, I suggest, as a result of the breakdown of the bicameral mind. A typical prayer begins:

> O lord, the strong one, the famous one, the one who knows all, splendid one, self-renewing one, perfect one, first-begotten of Marduk . . .

and so on for many more lines of titles and attributes,

> the one who holds cult-centers firm, the one who gathers to himself all cults . . .

perhaps indicating the chaos of the hierarchy of divinities when they could no longer be heard,

> you watch over all men, you accept their supplications . . .

The suppliant then introduces himself and his petition:

> I, Balasu, son of his god, whose god is Nabu, whose goddess is Tashmeturn . . . I am one who is weary, disturbed, whose body is very sick, I bow before thee . . . O lord, Wise One

[5] George A. Barton, *The Royal Inscriptions of Sumer and Akkad* (New Haven: Yale University Press, 1924), p. 113.

of the gods, by thy mouth command good for me; O Nabu,
Wise One of the gods, by thy mouth may I come forth alive.[6]

The general form of prayer, beginning with emphatic praise of
the god and ending with a personal petition, has not really
changed since Mesopotamian times. The very exaltation of the
god, and indeed the very idea of divine *worship*, is in contrast to
the more matter-of-fact everyday relationship of god and man a
thousand years earlier.

An Origin of Angels

In the so-called Neo-Sumerian period, at the end of the third
millennium B.C., graphics, particularly cylinder seals, are full of
'presentation' scenes: a minor god, often female, introduces an
individual, presumably the owner of the seal, to a major god.
This is entirely consistent with what we have suggested was
likely in a bicameral kingdom, namely that each individual had
his personal god who seemed to intercede with higher gods on the
person's behalf. And this type of presentation or intercession
scene continues well into the second millennium B.C.

But then a dramatic change occurs. First, the major gods
disappear from such scenes, even as from the altar of Tukulti-
Ninurta. There then occurs a period where the individual's personal god is shown presenting him to the god's symbol only. And
then, at the end of the second millennium B.C., we have the
beginning of hybrid human-animal beings as the intermediaries
and messengers between the vanished gods and their forlorn
followers. Such messengers were always part bird and part human, sometimes like a bearded man with two sets of wings,
crowned like a god, and often holding a kind of purse supposedly
containing ingredients for a purification ceremony. These supposed personnel of the celestial courts are found with increasing

[6] Translated by H. W. F. Saggs in his *The Greatness That Was Babylon* (New
York: Mentor Books, 1962), p. 312.

frequency in Assyrian cylinder seals and carvings. In early instances, such angels, or genii, as Assyriologists more often call them, are seen introducing an individual to the symbol of a god as in the old presentation scenes. But soon even this is abandoned. And by the beginning of the first millennium B.C., we find such angels in a countless diversity of scenes, sometimes with humans, sometimes in various struggles with other hybrid beings. Sometimes they have the heads of birds. Or they are winged bulls or winged lions with human heads to act as wardens for such palaces as that at Nimrud in the ninth century or guarding the gates of Khorsabad in the eighth century B.C. Or, hawk-headed and broad-winged, they may be seen following around behind a king, with a cone which has been dipped in a small pail, as in a wall carving of Assurnasirpal in the ninth century B.C., a scene like the anointing of baptism. In none of these depictions does the angel seem to be speaking or the human listening. It is a silent visual scene in which the auditory actuality of the earlier bicameral act is becoming a supposed and assumed silent relationship. It becomes what we would call mythological.

Demons

But angels were not enough to fill in the initiative vacuum left by the retreating gods. And besides, being messengers from the great gods, they were usually associated with the king and his lords. For the common people, whose personal gods no longer help them, a very different kind of semidivine being now casts a terrible shadow over everyday life.

Why should malevolent demons have entered human history at this particular time? Speech, even if incomprehensible, is man's chief way of greeting others. And if the other does not reply to an initiated greeting, a readiness for the other's hostility will follow. Because the personal gods are silent, they must be angry and hostile. Such logic is the origin of the idea of evil which first appears in the history of mankind during the break-down of the bicameral mind. Since there is no doubt whatever that the gods rule over us as they will, what can we do to appease their wishes to harm us, and propitiate them into friendship once again? Thus the prayer and sacrifice that we have referred to earlier in this chapter, and thus the virtue of humility before a god.

As the gods recede into special people called prophets or ora-cles, or are reduced to darkly communicating with men in angels and omen, there whooshes into this power vacuum a belief in demons. The very air of Mesopotamia became darkened with them. Natural phenomena took on their characteristics of hostil-ity toward men, a raging demon in the sandstorm sweeping the desert, a demon of fire, scorpion-men guarding the rising sun beyond the mountains, Pazuzu the monstrous wind demon, the evil Croucher, plague demons, and the horrible Asapper demons that could be warded off by dogs. Demons stood ready to seize a man or woman in lonely places, while sleeping or eating or drinking, or particularly at childbirth. They attached themselves to men as all the illnesses of mankind. Even the gods could be attacked by demons, and this sometimes explained their absence from the control of human affairs.

Protection against these evil divinities — something inconceiv-able in the bicameral age — took many forms. Dating from early in the first millennium B.C. are many thousands of prophylactic amulets, to be worn around the neck or wrist. They usually depict the particular demon whose power is to be inhibited, sur-mounted perhaps by gesticulating priests shooing the evil away, and often underwritten with an incantation invoking the great gods against the threatened horror, such as:

> *Incantation.* That one that has approached the house scares me
> from my bed, rends me, makes me see nightmares. To the
> god Bine, gatekeeper of the underworld, may they appoint him,

by the decree of Ninurta prince of the underworld. By the decree of Marduk who dwells in Esagilia in Babylon. Let door
and bolt know that I am under the protection of the two Lords.
Incantation.[7]

Innumerable rituals were devoutly mumbled and mimed all over
Mesopotamia throughout the first millennium B.C. to counteract
these malign forces. The higher gods were beseeched to intercede. All illnesses, aches, and pains were ascribed to malevolent
demons until medicine became exorcism. Most of our knowledge
of these antidemoniac practices and their extent comes from the
huge collection made about 630 B.C. by Ashurbanipal at Nineveh.
Literally thousands of extant tablets from this library describe
such exorcisms, and thousands more list omen after omen, depicting a decaying civilization as black with demons as a piece of
rotting meat with flies.

A New Heaven

As we have seen in earlier chapters, the gods customarily had
locations, even though their voices were ubiquitously heard by
their servants. These were often dwellings such as ziggurats or
household shrines. And while some gods could be associated with
celestial bodies such as the sun, moon, or stars, and the greatest,
such as Anu, lived in the sky, the majority of gods were earth-
dwellers along with men.

All this changes as we enter the first millennium B.C., when, as
we are proposing, the gods' voices are no longer heard. As the
earth has been left to angels and demons, so it seems to be
accepted that the dwelling place of the now absent gods is with
Anu in the sky. And this is why the forms of angels are always
winged: they are messengers from the sky where the gods live.[8]

---

[7] Translated by Saggs, p. 291.

[8] If later copies of the well-known *Enuma Elish*, the Neo-Babylonian name for
the epic of creation, are to be taken on their face value, this celestialization of the

The use of the word for sky or heaven in conjunction with gods becomes more and more common in Assyrian literature. And when the story of the great flood (the origin of the Biblical story) is added into the Gilgamesh stories in the seventh century B.C., it is used as a rationalization for the departure of the gods from earth:

> Even the gods were terror-stricken at the deluge.
> They fled and ascended to the heaven of Anu.[9]

This celestialization of the once-earthly gods is confirmed by an important change in the building of ziggurats. As we saw in II.2, the original ziggurats of Mesopotamian history were built around a central great hall called the *gigunu* where the statue of the god 'lived' in the rituals of his human slaves. But by the end of the second millennium B.C., the entire concept of the ziggurat seems to have become altered. It now has no central room whatever and the statues of the major gods are less and less the centers of elaborate ritual. For the sacred tower of the ziggurat was now a landing stage to facilitate the gods' descent to earth from the heaven to which they had vanished. This is definitely known from texts of the first millennium B.C., which even make references to the "boat of heaven." The exact date at which this change took place is a difficult matter, for the extant ziggurats have been badly damaged and, even worse, sometimes 'restored'. But I suggest that all of the many ziggurats which the Assyrians built beginning with the reign of Tulkulti-Ninurta were of this

---

major gods began as early as the latter half of the second millennium B.C. See the translation by E. A. Speiser in *Near Eastern Texts Relating to the Old Testament*, J. B. Pritchard, ed. (Princeton: Princeton University Press, 1950). Its title is its first two words and means "When on high . . ." Like so much else, it was discovered in the great library of Ashurbanipal of the seventh century B.C. It is a copy, and the originals may have dated back to the second millennium B.C.

[9] *Gilgamesh*, Tablet II, lines 113–114, in Alexander Heidel, *The Gilgamesh Epic and Old Testament Parallels*, 2nd ed. (Chicago: University of Chicago Press, 1949).

sort, huge pedestals for the return of the gods from heaven and not houses for earthly gods as before.

The ziggurat built by Sargon in the eighth century B.C. for his huge new city of Khorsabad is calculated from recent excavations to have surged up in seven stages 140 feet above the surrounding city, its summit shining with a temple dedicated to Ashur, still the owning, if unheard, god of Assyria. There is no other temple to Ashur at Khorsabad. Descending from the temple was no ordinary stairway as in previous ziggurats, but a long spiral ramp winding around the core of the tower down which Ashur could walk, when or if he ever landed and did return to the city.

Similarly, the Ziggurat of Neo-Babylon, the Biblical Tower of Babel, was no god's house as in the truly bicameral age, but a heavenly landing for the now celestialized gods. Built in the seventh and sixth centuries B.C., it soared 300 feet high, again with seven stages, pinnacling in a brilliant blue-glazed temple for Marduk. Its very name indicates this use: *E-temen-an-ki*, temple (E) of the receiving platform (*temen*) between heaven (*an*) and earth (*ki*).[10] The otherwise senseless passage of Genesis (11:2-9) is certainly a rewrite of some Neo-Babylonian legend of just such a landing by Yahweh who in the company of other gods "come down to see the city and the tower," and thereupon "confound their language that they may not understand one another's speech." The latter may be a narratization of the garbling of hallucinated voices in their decline.

The tirelessly curious Herodotus in the fifth century B.C. trudged up the steep stairs and spiraling ramps of Etemenanki to see if there was a god or idol at the top: as in the altar-face of Tukulti, there was nothing but an empty throne.[11]

* * *

[10] For my translation of *temen* and possible alternatives, see James B. Nies' glossary in *Ur Dynasty Tablets* (Leipzig: Hinrichs, 1920), p. 171.

[11] *Histories*, 1: 181. Another empty throne scene is shown on Stela 91027 in the British Museum with Esarhaddon in a pose similar to Tukulti's.

DIVINATION

So far, we have just looked at the evidence for the breakdown of the bicameral mind. This evidence is, I feel, fairly substantial. The absence of gods in bas-reliefs and cylinder seals, the cries about lost gods that wail out of the silent cuneiforms, the emphasis on prayer, the introduction of new kinds of silent divinities, angels and demons, the new idea of heaven, all strongly indicate that the hallucinated voices called gods are no longer the guiding companions of men.

What then takes over their function? How is action initiated? If hallucinated voices are no longer adequate to the escalating complexities of behavior, how can decisions be made?

Subjective consciousness, that is, the development on the basis of linguistic metaphors of an operation space in which an 'I' could narratize out alternative actions to their consequences, was of course the great world result of this dilemma. But a more primitive solution, and one that antedates consciousness as well as paralleling it through history, is that complex of behaviors known as divination.

These attempts to divine the speech of the now silent gods work out into an astonishing variety and complexity. But I suggest that this variety is best understood as four main types, which can be ordered in terms of their historical beginning and which can be interpreted as successive approaches toward consciousness. These four are omens, sortilege, augury, and spontaneous divination.

Omen and Omen Texts

The most primitive, clumsy, but enduring method of discovering the will of silent gods is the simple recording of sequences of unusual or important events. In contrast to all other types of divination, it is entirely passive. It is simply an extension of something common to all mammalian nervous systems, namely, that if an organism experiences B after A, he will have a tendency to expect B the next time that A occurs. Since omens are really a particular example of this when expressed in language, we can say that the origin of omens is simply in animal nature rather than in civilized culture *per se*.

Omens or sequences of events that might be expected to recur were probably present in a trivial way throughout bicameral times. But they had little importance. Nor was there any necessity to study such sequences, since the hallucinated voices of gods made all the decisions in novel situations. There are, for example, no Sumerian omen texts whatever. While the first traces of omens occur among the Semitic Akkadians, it is really only after the loss of the bicameral mind toward the end of the second millennium B.C. that such omen texts proliferate everywhere and swell out to touch almost every aspect of life imaginable. By the first millennium B.C., huge collections of them are made. In the library of King Ashurbanipal at Nineveh about 650 B.C., at least 30 percent of the twenty to thirty thousand tablets come into the category of omen literature. Each entry in these tedious irrational collections consists of an if-clause or protasis followed by a then-clause or apodosis. And there were many classes of omens, terrestrial omens dealing with everyday life:

> If a town is set on a hill, it will not
> be good for the dweller within that town.

> If black ants are seen on the foundations
> which have been laid, that house will get
> built; the owner of that house will live to
> grow old.

> If a horse enters a man's house, and bites
> either an ass or a man, the owner of the
> house will die and his household will be
> scattered.

If a fox runs into the public square,
that town will be devastated.

If a man unwittingly treads on a lizard
and kills it, he will prevail over his
adversary.[12]

And so on endlessly, bearing on all those aspects of life that in a
previous age would have been under the guidance of gods. They
can be construed as a kind of first approach to narratization,
doing by verbal formulae what consciousness does in a more
complex way. Rarely are we able to see any logical dependency
of prediction on portent, the connection often being as simple as
word associations or connotations.

There were also teratological omens beginning, "If a foetus,
etc.," dealing with abnormal births both human and animal.[13]
The science of medicine is actually founded in medical omens, a
series of texts that begin, "When the conjuration priest comes to
the house of a sick man," and follow with more or less reasonable
prognoses correlated with various symptoms.[14] And omens
based on the appearance of facial and bodily characteristics in
the client or in persons he encounters, which, incidentally, give
us the best description we have of what these people looked
like.[15] And omens in the time dimension: menologies which
stated which months were favorable or unfavorable for given
undertakings, and hemerologies that concerned themselves with
propitious or unpropitious days of each month. And omens that
are the beginning of meteorology and astronomy, whole series of
tablets being devoted to phenomena of the sun, the planets, the
stars and the moon, their times and circumstances of disappearance, eclipses, omens connected with halos, strange cloud forma-

---

[12] These illustrations are all taken from Saggs, pp. 308–309.

[13] Erle Leichty, "Teratological omens," *La Divination en Mesopotamie Ancienne
et dans les Regions Voisines*, pp. 131–139.

[14] J. V. Kinnier Wilson, "Two medical texts from Nimrud," *Iraq*, 1956, 18:
130–46.

[15] J. V. Kinnier Wilson, "The Nimrud catalog of medical and physiognomical
omnia," *Iraq*, 1962, 24: 52–62.

tions, the divine meaning of thunder and rain, hail and earthquakes as predictions of peace and war, harvest and flood, or the movement of planets, particularly Venus, among the fixed stars. By the fifth century B.C., this use of stars to obtain the intentions of the silent gods who now live among them has become our familiar horoscopes, in which the conjunction of the stars at birth results in predictions of the future and personality of the child. History also begins, if vaguely, in omen texts, the apodoses or "then-clauses" of some early texts perhaps preserving some faint historical information in a unique and characteristically Mesopotamian variety of historiography.[16] Mankind deprived of his gods, like a child separated from his mother, is having to learn about his world in fear and trembling.

Dream omens became (as they still are) a major source of divination.[17] Particularly in the late Assyrian period during the first millennium B.C., dream omens were collected into dream books such as the *Ziqiqu* where some associative principle between the dream event and its apodosis is apparent, e.g., a dream of the loss of one's cylinder seal portends the death of a son. But omens of whatever type can only decide so much. One has to wait for the portent to occur. Novel situations do not wait.

Sortilege

Sortilege or the casting of lots differs from omens in that it is active and designed to provoke the gods' answers to specific questions in novel situations. It consisted of throwing marked sticks, stones, bones, or beans upon the ground, or picking one out of a group held in a bowl, or tossing such markers in the lap of a tunic until one fell out. Sometimes it was to answer yes or no, at other

[16] See J. J. Finkelstein, "Mesopotamian historiography," *Proceedings of the American Philosophical Society*, 1963, pp. 461–472.

[17] See A. Leo Oppenheim, "Mantic dreams in the Ancient Near East," in G. E. von Grunbaum and Roger Caillois, eds., *The Dream and Human Societies* (Berkeley: University of California Press, 1966), pp. 341–350.

times to choose one out of a group of men, plots, or alternatives. But this simplicity — even triviality to us — should not blind us from seeing the profound psychological problem involved, as well as appreciating its remarkable historical importance. We are so used to the huge variety of games of chance, of throwing dice, roulette wheels, etc., all of them vestiges of this ancient practice of divination by lots, that we find it difficult to really appreciate the significance of this practice historically. It is a help here to realize that there was no concept of chance whatever until very recent times. Therefore, the discovery (how odd to think of it as a discovery!) of deciding an issue by throwing sticks or beans on the ground was an extremely momentous one for the future of mankind. For, because there was no chance, the result *had* to be caused by the gods whose intentions were being divined.

As to the psychology of sortilege, I would call your attention to two points of interest. First, this practice is very specifically invented in culture to supplement right hemisphere function when that function, following the breakdown of the bicameral mind, is no longer as accessible as when it was coded linguistically in the voices of gods. We know from laboratory studies that it is the right hemisphere that predominately processes spatial and pattern information. It is better at fitting parts of things into patterns as in Koh's Block Test, at perceiving the location and quantity of dots in a pattern or of patterns of sound such as melodies.[18] Now the problem that sortilege is trying to solve is something of the same kind, that of ordering parts of the pattern, of choosing who is to do what, or what piece of land goes to which person. Originally, I suggest, in simpler societies, such decisions were easily made by the hallucinated voices called gods, which were involved primarily with the right hemisphere. And when the gods no longer accomplished this function, perhaps because of the increasing complication of such decisions, sorti-

---

[18] D. Kimura, "Functional Asymmetry of the Brain in Dichotic Listening," *Cortex*, 1967, 3: 163. *Quarterly Journal of Experimental Psychology*, 1971, 23: 46.

lege came into history as a substitute for this right hemisphere function.

The second point of psychological interest is that the throwing of lots, like consciousness itself, has metaphor as its basis. In the language of I.2, the unexpressed commands of the gods compose the metaphrand which is to be lexically widened, and the metaphier is the pair or assembly of lots, be they sticks, beans, or stones. The paraphiers are the distinguishing marks or words on the lots which then project back into the metaphrand as the command of the particular god invoked. What is important here is to understand provoked divination such as sortilege as involving the same kind of generative processes that develop consciousness, but in an exopsychic nonsubjective manner.

As with omen texts, the roots of sortilege go back into the bicameral age. The earliest mention of throwing lots appears to be in legal tablets dating from the middle of the second millennium B.C., but it is only toward its end that the practice becomes widespread in important decisions: to assign shares of an estate among the sons (as at Susa), or shares of temple income to certain officials of the sanctuary, to establish a sequence among persons of equal status for various purposes. This was not simply for practical purposes, as it would be with us, but always to find out the commands of a god. Around 833 B.C., the new year in Assyria was always named after some high official. The particular official to be so honored was chosen by means of a clay die on the faces of which the names of the various high officials were inscribed, the various sides of the cube being inscribed with prayers to Ashur to make that particular side turn up.[19] While many Assyrian texts from this time on refer to various types of sortilege, it is difficult to estimate just how widespread the practice was in decision-making, and whether it was used by the

---

[19] An illustration of this may be found in W. W. Hallo and W. K. Simpson, *Ancient Near East* (New York: Harcourt Brace Jovanovich, 1971), p. 150; see also Oppenheim, p. 100.

ordinary people in more mundane decisions. We know that it
became common among the Hittites, and its occurrence in the
Old Testament will be referred to in a later chapter.

Augury

A third type of divination and one that is closer to the structure of consciousness is what I shall call qualitative augury. Sortilege is ordinal, ordering by rank a set of given possibilities. But
the many methods of qualitative augury are designed to divine a
great deal more information from the unspeaking gods. It is the
difference between a digital and an analog computer. Its first
form, as described in three cuneiform texts dating from about the
middle of the second millennium B.C., consisted of pouring oil
into a bowl of water held in the lap, the movement of the oil in
relation to the surface or to the rim of the bowl portending the
gods' intentions concerning peace or prosperity, health or disease.
Here the metaphrand is the intention or even action of a god, not
just his words as in sortilege. The metaphier is the oil moving
about the surface of the water, to which the movements and
commands of the gods are similar. The paraphiers are the specific shapes and proximities of the oil whose paraphrands are the
contours of the gods' decisions and actions.

Augury in Mesopotamia always has a cultic status. It was
performed by a special priest called the *baru,* surrounded with
ritual, and preceded by a prayer to the god to reveal his intentions
through the oil or whatever medium.[20] And as we enter the first
millennium B.C., the methods and techniques of the *baru* break
out into an astonishing diversity of metaphiers for the gods' intentions: Not only oil but the movements of smoke rising from a
censer of incense held in the lap of the diviner,[21] or the form of

[20] See Oppenheim, pp. 208, 212.

[21] A lack of later cuneiform tablets referring to oil on water suggests this practice
went out of use fairly early. An exception is the reference of Joseph in Genesis 44:5
to the precious silver cup which he uses for drinking and for private divining, the
date of this being about 600 B.C. See my II.6, note 4.

hot wax dropped into water, or the patterns of dots made at random, or the shapes and patterns of ashes, and then sacrificed animals.

Extispicy, as divining from the exta of sacrificed animals is called, becomes the most important type of induced analog augury during the first millennium B.C. The idea of sacrifice itself, of course, originated in the feeding of the hallucinogenic idols as we saw in II.2. With the breakdown of the bicameral mind, the idols lost their hallucinogenic properties and became mere statues, but the feeding ceremonies now addressed to absent gods remained in the various ceremonies as sacrifices. It is thus not surprising that animals rather than oil, wax, smoke, etc., became the more important media of communication with the gods.

Extispicy differs from other methods in that the metaphrand is explicitly not the speech or actions of gods, but their writing. The *baru* first addressed the gods Shamash and Adad with requests that they "write" their message upon the entrails of the animal,[22] or occasionally whispered this request into its ears before it was killed. He then investigated in traditional sequence the animal's organs — windpipe, lungs, liver, gall bladder, how the coils of the intestines were arranged — looking for deviations from the normal state, shape, and coloring. Any atrophy, hypertrophy, displacement, special markings, or other abnormalities, particularly of the liver, was a divine message metaphorically related to divine action. The corpus of texts dealing with extispicy outnumbers all other kinds of augury texts and deserves much more careful study. From its earliest and very cursory mention in the second millennium, to the extensive collections of the Seleucid period around 250 B.C., the history and local development of extispicy as a means of exopsychic thought is an area where the tablets are simply awaiting the ordering of proper research. Of particular interest is that in the late period the markings and

---

[22] See J. Nougayoral "Présages médicaux de l'haruspicine babylonienne," *Semitica*, 1956, 6, 5–14.

discolorations are described in an arcane technical terminology similar to what occurred among medieval alchemists.[23] Parts of the exta of the sacrificed animal are referred to as "door of the palace," "path," "yoke," and "embankment" and symbolize these locations and objects, creating a metaphor world from which to read out what to do. Some of the late tablets even have diagrams of the coils of the intestines and their meaning. Clay and bronze models of the liver and lungs, sometimes elaborate, sometimes crude, have been unearthed in various sites; some were probably used for instructional purposes. But since the raw organs themselves were sometimes sent to the king as proof of a particular divine message, such models may also have served as a less redolent way of reporting an actual observation.[24]

Please remember the metaphorical nature of all such activity, for the actual functions here are similar to though on a different level from the very inner workings of consciousness. That the size and shape of the liver or other organ is a metaphier of the size and shape of the intentions of a god is, on an ultrasimple level, similar to what we do in consciousness in making metaphor spaces 'containing' metaphor objects and actions.

Spontaneous Divination

Spontaneous divination differs from the three preceding types only by being unconstrained and free from any particular medium. It is really a generalization of all types. As before, the gods' commands, intentions, or purposes are the metaphrand while the metaphier is anything that might be seen at the moment and related to the concern of the diviner. The outcomes of undertakings or the intentions of a god are thus read out from whatever object the diviner happens to see or hear.

[23] See Mary I. Hussey, "Anatomical nomenclature in an Akaadian omen text," *Journal of Cuneiform Studies*, 1948, 2: 21–32, as mentioned by Oppenheim on p. 216.

[24] Robert H. Pfeiffer, *State Letters of Assyria* (New Haven: American Oriental Society, 1935), Letter 335.

The reader may try it for himself. Think of some problem or concern in a vague kind of way. Then look out the window suddenly or around where you are and take the first thing your eye lights upon, and try to 'read' out of it something about your problem. Sometimes nothing will happen. But at other times the message will simply flash into your mind. I have just done this as I write and from my north window see a television aerial against a twilight sky. I may divine this as meaning I am being much too speculative, picking up fleeting suggestions from flimsy air — an unfortunate truth if I am to face these matters at all. I again think vaguely of my concerns and, walking about, suddenly cast my eyes on the floor of an adjoining room where an assistant has been building an apparatus, and see a frayed wire with several strands at the end. I divine that my problem in this chapter is to tie together several different strands and loose ends of evidence. And so on.

I have not come upon this type of divining in a Mesopotamian text. Yet I feel sure that it must have become a common practice, if only because spontaneous divination is both common and important in the Old Testament, as we shall see in a future chapter. And it remains a common method among many types of seers well into the Middle Ages.[25]

These then are the four main types of divination, omens, sortilege, augury, and spontaneous divination. And I would draw to your attention that they can be considered as exopsychic methods of thought or decision-making, and that they are successively closer and closer proximations to the structure of consciousness. The fact that all of them have roots that go back far into the bicameral period should not detract from the force of the general-

---

[25] Spontaneous divination was commonly used by Bedouin prognosticators around A.D. 1000, for example. See Alfred Guillaume, *Prophecy and Divination Among the Hebrews and Other Semites* (New York: Harper, 1938), p. 127. It is indeed an ingredient of everyday thought processes as well as prominent in intellectual discovery.

ization that they became the *important* media of decision only after the breakdown of the bicameral mind as described in the first part of this chapter.

THE EDGE OF SUBJECTIVITY

So far in this heterogeneous chapter, we have been dealing with the breakdown of the bicameral mind in Mesopotamia, and the responses to this alteration in human mentality, the effort to find out what to do by other means when voices are no longer heard in hallucination. That a further method for finding out what to do was consciousness, and that it first occurs in the history of this planet here in Mesopotamia toward the end of the second millennium B.C. is a much more difficult proposition. The reasons are chiefly in our inability to translate cuneiform with the same exactness with which we can translate Greek or Hebrew, and to proceed with the kind of analysis which I attempt in the next chapter. The very words in cuneiform that might be relevant to tracing the metaphorical buildup of consciousness and mind-space are precisely those that are extremely difficult to translate with precision. Let me state categorically that a truly definitive study of changes in Mesopotamian mentality over this second millenium B.C. will have to wait for another level of scholarship in cuneiform studies. Such a task will include tracing out the changes in referent and frequency of words that later come to describe events which we call conscious. One, for example, is *Sha* (also transliterated as *Shab* or *Shag*), a word in Akaad, whose basic meaning seems to be "in" or "inside." Prefixed to the name of a city, it means "in the city." Prefixed to the name of a man, it means "in the man," possibly a beginning of the interiorization of attribution.

I hope to be forgiven for saying rather tritely that these questions and so many others must remain for further research. So swiftly are new sites being discovered and new texts translated, that even ten years from now we shall have a much clearer picture, particularly if the data are looked at from the point of view of this chapter. The most I feel I can establish here at this time is simply a few comparisons of a literary kind which suggest that such a psychological change as consciousness actually took place. These comparisons will be among letters, building inscriptions, and versions of *Gilgamesh*.

Assyrian and Old Babylonian Letters Compared

My first comparison to suggest this change from bicamerality to subjectivity is between the cuneiform tablet letters of the seventh century B.C., Assyria, and those of the old Babylonian kings a millennium earlier. The letters of Hammurabi and his era are factual, concrete, behavioristic, formalistic, commanding, and without greeting. They are not addressed to the recipient, but actually to the tablet itself, and always begin: unto A say, thus says B. And then follows what B has to say to A. We should remember here what I have suggested elsewhere, that reading, having developed from hallucinating from idols and then from pictographs, had become during later bicameral times a matter of *hearing* the cuneiform. And hence the addressee of the tablets.

The subjects of Old Babylonian letters are always objective. Hammurabi's letters, for example (all possibly written by Hammurabi himself since they are cut by the same hand), are written for vassal kings and officers in his hegemony about sending such a person to him, or directing so much lumber to Babylon, specifying in one instance, "only vigorous trunks shall they cut down," or regulating the exchanges of corn for cattle, or where workmen should be sent. Rarely are reasons given. Purposes never.

> Unto Sin-idinnam say: thus says Hammurabi. I wrote you telling you to send Enubi-Marduk to me. Why, then, haven't

you sent him? When you see this tablet, send Enubi-Marduk
into my presence. See that he travels night and day, that he
may arrive swiftly.[26]

And the letters rarely go beyond this in complication of 'thought'
or relationship.

A more interesting letter is a command to bring several conquered idols to Babylon:

> Unto Sin-idinnam say: thus says Hammurabi. I am sending
> now Zikir-ilisu the officer, and Hammarabi-bani the Dugab-
> officer to bring the goddesses of Emutbalum. Let the goddesses
> travel in a processional boat as in a shrine as they come to Baby-
> lon. And the temple-women shall follow after them. For the
> food of the goddesses, you shall provide sheep . . . Let them
> not delay, but swiftly reach Babylon.[27]

This letter is interesting in showing the everyday nature of the
relationship of god and man in Old Babylon, as well as the fact
that the deities are somehow expected to eat on their trip.

Going from Hammurabi's letters to the state letters of Assyria
of the seventh century B.C. is like leaving a thoughtless tedium of
undisobeyable directives and entering a rich sensitive frightened
grasping recalcitrant aware world not all that different from our
own. The letters are addressed to people, not tablets, and probably were not heard, but had to be read aloud. The subjects
discussed have changed in a thousand years to a far more extensive list of human activities. But they are also imbedded in a
texture of deceit and divination, speaking of police investigations,
complaints of lapsing ritual, paranoid fears, bribery, and pathetic
appeals of imprisoned officers, all things unknown, unmentioned,
and impossible in the world of Hammurabi. Even sarcasm, as in

---

[26] Transliterated and translated by L. W. King in *Letters and Inscriptions of
Hammurabi* (London: Luzac, 1900), Vol. 3, Letter 46, p. 94f.

[27] Ibid., Vol. 3, Letter 2 p. 6f.

a letter from an Assyrian king to his restive acculturated deputies in conquered Babylon about 670 B.C.:

> Word of the king to the pseudo-Babylonians. I am well . . . So you, so help you heaven, have turned yourselves into Babylonians! And you keep bringing up against my servants charges — false charges, — which you and your master have concocted . . . The document (nothing but windy words and importunities!) which you have sent me, I am returning to you, after replacing it into its seals. Of course you will say, "What is he sending back to us?" From the Babylonians, my servants and my friends are writing me: When I open and read, behold, the goodness of the shrines, birds of sin . . .[28]

And then the tablet is broken off.

A further interesting difference is their depiction of an Assyrian king. The Babylonian kings of the early second millennium were confident and fearless, and probably did not have to be too militaristic. The cruel Assyrian kings, whose palaces are virile with muscular depictions of lion hunts and grappling with clawing beasts, are in their letters indecisive frightened creatures appealing to their astrologers and diviners to contact the gods and tell them what to do and when to do it. These kings are told by their diviners that they are beggars or that their sins are making a god angry; they are told what to wear, or what to eat, or not to eat until further notice:[29] "Something is happening in the skies; have you noticed? As far as I am concerned, my eyes are fixed. I say, 'What phenomenon have I failed to see, or failed to report to the king? Have I failed to observe something that does not pertain to his lot?' . . . As to that eclipse of the sun of which the king spoke, the eclipse did not take place. On the 27th I shall look again and send in a report. From whom does the lord my king fear misfortune? I have no information whatsoever."[30]

28 Pfeiffer, Letter 80.
29 Pfeiffer, Letters 265, 439, and 553.
30 Pfeiffer, Letter 315.

Does a comparison of these letters, a thousand years apart, demonstrate the alteration of mentality with which we are here concerned? Of course, a great deal of discussion could follow such a question. And research: content analyses, comparisons of syntax, uses of pronouns, questions, and future tenses, as well as specific words which appear to indicate subjectivity in the Assyrian letters and which are absent in the Old Babylonian. But such is our knowledge of cuneiform at present that a thorough analysis is not possible at this time. Even the translations I have used are hedged in favor of smooth English and familiar syntax and so are not to be completely trusted. Only an impressionist comparison is possible, and the result, I think, is clear: that the letters of the seventh century B.C. are far more similar to our own consciousness than those of Hammurabi a thousand years earlier.

The Spatialization of Time

A second literary comparison can be made about the sense of time as shown in building inscriptions. In I.2, I suggested that one of the essential properties of consciousness was the metaphor of time as a space that could be regionized such that events and persons can be located therein, giving that sense of past, present, and future in which narratization is possible.

The beginning of this characteristic of consciousness can be dated with at least a modicum of conviction at about 1300 B.C. We have just seen how the development of omens and augury suggests this inferentially. But more exact evidence is found in the inscriptions on buildings. In the typical inscription previous to this date, the king gave his name and titles, lavished praise on his particular god or gods, mentioned briefly the season and circumstances when the building was started, and then described something of the building operation itself. After 1300 B.C., there is not only a mention of the event immediately preceding the building, but also a summary of all the king's past military exploits to date. And in the next centuries, this information comes to be arranged systematically according to the yearly campaigns, and ultimately bursts out into the elaborate annal form that is almost universal in the records of the Assyrian rulers of the first millennium B.C. Such annals continue to swell beyond the recountal of raw fact into statements of motive, criticisms of courses of action, appraisals of character. And then further to include political changes, campaign strategies, historical notes on particular regions — all evidence, I insist, of the invention of consciousness. None of these characteristics is seen in the earlier inscriptions.

This is, of course, the invention of history as well, commencing exactly in the development of these royal inscriptions.[31] How strange it seems to think of the idea of history having to be invented! Herodotus, usually famed as "the father of history," wrote his history only after a visit through Mesopotamia in the fifth century B.C., and may have picked up the very idea of history from these Assyrian sources. What is interesting to me in this speculation is the possibility that as consciousness develops, it can develop in slightly different ways, and the importance of the writing of Herodotus to the later development of Greek consciousness would make an interesting project. My essential point here, however, is that history is impossible without the spatialization of time that is characteristic of consciousness.

Gilgamesh

And finally a comparison from this best-known example of Assyrian literature. The *Epic of Gilgamesh* proper is a series of twelve numbered tablets found in Nineveh among the ruins of the temple library of the god Nabu and the palace library of the Assyrian king, Ashurbanipal. It was written for the king out of previous stories in about 650 B.C., and its hero is a demi-god,

[31] See Saggs, p. 472f.

Gilgamesh, whom his father, Esarhaddon, had worshiped. Certainly the name Gilgamesh goes far back into Mesopotamian history. And numerous other tablets have been found which relate to him and to this series in some way.

Prominent among them are three apparently older tablets which parallel some of the Assyrian tablets. Where they were found and their archaeological contexts are not at all clear. They were not found by archaeologists, but were bought by private buyers from a dealer in Baghdad. Their dating and provenance therefore are a questionable matter. From internal evidence I would place them at about the same time as some Hittite and Hurrian fragments about Gilgamesh, perhaps 1200 b.c. The more usual date given them is 1700 b.c. But whatever their date, there is certainly no warrant to suppose, as have some popularizers of the epic, that the seventh century b.c. rendering of the story of Gilgamesh goes back to the Old Babylonian era.

What we are interested in are the changes which have been made between the few older tablets and their Assyrian versions of 650 b.c.[32] The most interesting comparison is in Tablet X. In the older version (called the Yale Tablet because of its present location), the divine Gilgamesh, mourning the death of his mortal friend Enkidu, has a dialogue with the god Shamash, and then with the goddess Siduri. The latter, called the divine barmaid, tells Gilgamesh that death for mortals is inevitable. These dialogues are nonsubjective. But in the later Assyrian version, the dialogue with Shamash is not even included, and the barmaid is described in very human earthly terms, even as self-consciously wearing a veil. To our conscious minds, the story has become humanized. At one point in the later Assyrian tablet, the barmaid sees Gilgamesh approaching. She is described as looking out into the distance and speaking *to her own heart,* saying to herself, "Surely this man is a murderer! Whither is he bound?" This is subjective thinking. And it is not in the older tablet at all.

[32] All references here are to the translation by Alexander Heidel.

The Assyrian tablet goes on with great elaboration (as well as with great beauty) to bring out the subjective sadness *in the heart* of Gilgamesh at the loss of his friend. One of the literary devices here (at least as translators have restored a damaged part) is repeated questions that describe the outward demeanor of Gilgamesh rhetorically, asking why his appearance and behavior are thus and so, so that the reader is constantly imagining the interior 'space' and analog 'I' of the hero.

> Why is thy heart so sad, and why are thy features so distorted?
> Why is there woe in thy heart?
> And why is thy face like unto one who has made a far journey?

None of this psalmlike concern is in the old version of Tablet X. Another character is the god Utnapishtim, the Distant, who is mentioned only briefly in the old version of Tablet X. But, in the 650 B.C. version, he is looking into the distance and speaking words to his *heart,* asking it questions and coming to his own conclusions.

Conclusion

The evidence we have just examined is strong in some areas and weak in others. The literature on the loss of the gods is an unquestionable change in the history of Mesopotamia, unlike anything that preceded it. It is indeed the birth of modern religious attitudes and we can discover ourselves in the very psalm-like yearnings for religious certainty that are expressed in the literature from the time of Tukulti up into the first millennium B.C.

The sudden flourishing of all kinds of divination and its huge importance in both political and private life is also an unquestionable historical fact. And while these practices date back to earlier time, perhaps even suggesting that as civilization became more

complicated toward the end of the third millennium B.C., the bicameral gods needed some auxiliary method of decision-making,
they only achieve their dominance and universal position in civilized life after the breakdown of the gods.

It is also unquestionable that the very nature of divinities was
altered in these times, and that the belief in a world darkened
with hostile demons, causing disease and misfortune, can only be
understood as an expression of the deep and irreversible uncertainty which followed the loss of the hallucinated decisions of the
bicameral mind.

What is weak in our survey is indeed the evidence of consciousness itself. There is something unsatisfying in my saltatory
comparisons among questionable translations of cuneiform tablets of various ages. What we would like is to see in front of us a
continuous literature wherein we could watch more carefully the
unfolding of subjective mind-space and its operator function in
initiating decision. This is indeed what occurs in Greece a few
centuries later, and it is to that analysis that we now turn.

CHAPTER 5

The Intellectual Consciousness
of Greece

THEY HAVE CALLED IT the Dorian invasions. And classicists will tell you that indeed they could have called it anything or everything, so groping our knowledge, and so dark these particular profundities of past time. But continuities in pottery designs from one archaeological site to another do fetch a few candles into this vast and silent darkness, and they reveal, albeit in flickering fashion, the huge jagged outlines of complex successions of migrations and displacements that lasted from 1200 to 1000 B.C.[1] That much is fact.

The rest is inference. Even who the so-called Dorians were is unclear. In an earlier chapter, I have suggested that the beginning of all this chaos may have been the Thera eruption and its consequences. As Thucydides at the last edge of a verbal tradition describes it, "migrations were a frequent occurrence, the several tribes readily abandoning their homes under the pressure of superior numbers." Palaces and villages that once held fealty to Agamemnon and his gods were looted and burned by other bicameral peoples who, following their own admonitory visions, probably could not communicate with nor have pity on the natives. Survivors were slaves or refugees, and refugees conquered or died. Our greatest certainties are negative. For all that the Mycenaean world had produced with such remarkable

[1] V. R. d'A. Desborough, *The Last Mycenaeans and Their Successors: An Archaeological Survey, c 1200–c 1000* B.C. (Oxford: Clarendon Press, 1964).

uniformity everywhere — the massive stone architecture of its god-ordered palaces and fortifications, its undulant frescoes of delicate clarity, its shaft-graves with their elaborate contents, the megaron plan of its houses, the terra-cotta idols and figurines, the death masks of beaten gold, the bronze and ivory work and distinctive pottery — all stopped and was never known thereafter.

This ruin is the bitter soil for the growth of subjective consciousness in Greece. And the difference here from the huge Assyrian cities stumbling on into a fumbling demon-ridden consciousness out of their own momentum is important. In contrast, Mycaenae had been a loose and spread-out system of divinely commanded cities of smaller size. The breakdown of the bicameral mind resulted in an even greater dispersion as all society broke down.

It is even plausible that all this political havoc was the very challenge to which the great epics were a defiant response, and that the long narrative chants of the aoidoi from refugee camp to camp worked out into an eager unity with the cohesive past on the part of a newly nomadic people reaching at lost certainties. Poems are rafts clutched at by men drowning in inadequate minds. And this unique factor, this importance of poetry in a devastating social chaos, is the reason why Greek consciousness specifically fluoresces into that brilliant intellectual light which is still illuminating our world.

What I shall do in this chapter is to conduct you on a tour through all the early extant literature of Greece. It is unfortunately a short list of texts. Beginning with the Iliad, we shall travel consecutively up through the Odyssey and the Boeotian poems ascribed to Hesiod, and then into the fragments of the lyric and elegiac poets of the seventh century B.C. and a little beyond. In doing so, I shall not be giving you any running description of the scenery we are passing through. The several good histories of early Greek poetry can do that better than I. Instead I shall be directing your attention to selected things as we pass by that are of particular interest from the point of view of our theory of consciousness.

But before we do so, we must make a few preliminary excursions, particularly into a more thorough analysis of mindlike terms in the Iliad.

LOOKING FORWARD THROUGH THE ILIAD

In an earlier chapter, I made the statement that the Iliad was our window upon the immediate bicameral past. Here, I propose that we stand on the other side of that window and peer forward into the distant conscious future, regarding this great mysterious paean to anger, not so much as the end point of the verbal tradition that preceded it, but rather as the very beginning of the new mentality to come.

In I.3, we saw that the words which in later Greek indicate aspects of conscious functioning have in the Iliad more concrete and bodily referents. But the very fact that these words come to have mental meanings later suggests that they may be some kind of key to understanding the manner in which Greek consciousness is developed.

The words we shall look at here are seven: *thumos, phrenes, noos,* and *psyche,* all of them variously translated as mind, spirit, or soul, and *kradie, ker,* and *etor,* often translated as heart or sometimes as mind or spirit. The translation of any of these seven as mind or anything similar is entirely mistaken and without any warrant whatever in the Iliad. Simply, and without equivocation, they are to be thought of as objective parts of the environment or of the body. We shall discuss these terms fully in a moment.

Now the first question to ask is why these entities are in the poem at all. I have earlier stressed the fact that the major instigations to action here are in the voices of the gods, not in the *thumos, phrenes, etor,* et al. The latter are entirely redundant. In fact they often seem to get in the way of the simple command-obedience relation between god and man, like a wedge between the two sides of the bicameral mind. Why then are they there?

Let us examine more closely what would have happened at the beginning of the breakdown of the bicameral mind. In I.4, we found that the physiological cuing of an hallucinated voice, whether in a bicameral man or in a contemporary schizophrenic, is the stress of some decision or conflict. Now, as the voices of gods become more inadequate and suppressed during this social chaos, we may suppose that the amount of that stress necessary to occasion an hallucinated voice would be raised.

It is quite likely, then, that as the bicameral organization of mind began to diminish, the decision-stress in novel situations would be much greater than previously, and both the degree and duration of that stress would have to become progressively more intense before the hallucination of a god would occur. And such increased stress would be accompanied by a variety of physiological concomitants, vascular changes resulting in burning sensations, abrupt changes in breathing, a pounding or fluttering heart, etc., responses which in the Iliad are called *thumos, phrenes,* and *kradie* respectively. And this is what these words mean, not mind or anything like it. As the gods are heard progressively less and less, these internal response-stimuli of progressively greater stress are associated more and more with men's subsequent actions, whatever they may be, even coming to take on the godlike function of seeming to initiate action themselves.

The evidence that we are on the right track in these suppositions can be found in the Iliad itself. At the very beginning, Agamemnon, king of men but slave of gods, is told by his voices to take the fair-cheeked Briseis away from Achilles, who had captured her. As he does so, the response of Achilles begins in his *etor*, or what I suggest is a cramp in his guts, where he is in conflict or put into two parts (*mermerizo*) whether to obey his *thumos*, the immediate internal sensations of anger, and kill the pre-emptory king or not. It is only after this vacillating interval of increasing belly sensations and surges of blood, as Achilles is drawing his mighty sword, that the stress has become sufficient to hallucinate the dreadfully gleaming goddess Athene who then takes over control of the action (1:188ff.) and tells Achilles what to do.

I mean to suggest here that the degree and extent of these internal sensations were neither so evident nor so named in the true bicameral period. If we may propose that there was an *Ur-Iliad*, or the verbal epic as it came from the lips of the first several generations of aoidoi, then we can expect that it had no such interval, no *etor* or *thumos* preceding the voice of the god, and that the use and, as we shall see, the increasing use of these words in this way reflects the alteration of mentality, the wedge between god and man which results in consciousness.

Preconscious Hypostases

We may call these mind-words that later come to mean something like conscious functioning, the preconscious hypostases. The latter term means in Greek what is caused to stand under something. The preconscious hypostases are the assumed causes of action when other causes are no longer apparent. In any novel situation, when there are no gods, it is not a man who acts, but one of the preconscious hypostases which causes him to act. They are thus seats of reaction and responsibility which occur in the transition from the bicameral mind to subjective consciousness. What we shall see is that the frequency and the meaning of these terms gradually change as we go from text to text from about 850 to 600 B.C., and how in the sixth century B.C. their referents join together in what we would call the subjective conscious mind.[2]

I would like here to translate and expand what I have just said into a clearer statement by suggesting that this temporal development of the preconscious hypostases can be roughly divided into four phases:

> Phase I: *Objective:* Occurred in the bicameral age when these terms referred to simple external observations.
>
> Phase II: *Internal:* Occurred when these terms have come to mean things inside the body, particularly certain internal sensations.
>
> Phase III: *Subjective:* When these terms refer to processes that we would call mental; they have moved from internal stimuli supposedly causing actions to internal spaces where metaphored actions may occur.
>
> Phase IV: *Synthetic:* When the various hypostases unite into one conscious self capable of introspection.

The reason I am setting these out, perhaps pretentiously, as four separate phases is to call your attention to the important psychological differences of transition between these phases.

The transition from Phase I to Phase II occurred at the beginning of the breakdown period. It comes from the absence or the inappropriateness of gods and their hallucinated directions. The buildup of stress for want of adequate divine decisions increases the psychological concomitants of such stress until they are labeled with terms that previously applied to only external perception.

The transition from Phase II to Phase III is a much more

[2] Professor A. D. H. Adkins has made this drawing-together of the various mind-words into one the theme of his book *From the Many to the One* (Ithaca: Cornell University Press, 1970).

complicated matter. And much more interesting. It is due to the paraphrand generator of metaphor described in I.2. In that chapter, I outlined the four-part process of metaphor, how we begin with a less-known term called a metaphrand which is to be described, and then describe it by applying to it a better-known metaphier which is similar to it in some way. Usually there are simple associations of the metaphier which I have called paraphiers, which then project back as associates of the original metaphrand, these new associates being called paraphrands. Such paraphrands are generative in a sense that they are new in their association with the metaphrand. And this is how we are able to generate the kind of 'space' which we introspect upon and which is the necessary substrate of consciousness. This is really quite simple as we shall see shortly.

And, finally, the synthesis of the separate hypostases into the unitary consciousness of Phase IV is a different process also. I suggest that as the subjective Phase III meanings of *thumos*, *phrenes*, et al. become established, their original anatomical bases in different internal sensations wither away, leaving them to become confused and to join together on the basis of their shared metaphiers, e.g., as 'containers' or 'persons.' But this synthetic unity of consciousness may also have been helped by what can be called the laicization of attention and its consequent recognition of individual differences in the seventh century B.C., a process which resulted in a new concept of self.

Before looking at the evidence for these matters, let us first investigate the preconscious hypostases and their Iliadic meanings in these phases with more detail. In the general order of their importance in the Iliad, they are:

Thumos

This is by far the most common and important hypostatic word in the whole poem. It occurs three times as often as any other.

Originally, in the Objective Phase, I suggest, it meant simply activity as externally perceived. And nothing internal about it. This Mycaenaean usage is found frequently in the Iliad, particularly in the battle scenes, where a warrior aiming a spear in the right place causes the *thumos* or activity of another to cease.

The internal Phase II, as we have seen in Achilles' wrath occurs in a novel stressful situation during the breakdown period when the stress threshold for the hallucinated voice was higher. *Thumos* then refers to a mass of internal sensations in response to environmental crises. It was, I suggest, a pattern of stimulation familiar to modern physiology, the so-called stress or emergency response of the sympathetic nervous system and its liberation of adrenalin and noradrenalin from the adrenal glands. This includes the dilation of the blood vessels in striate muscles and in the heart, an increase in tremor of striate muscles, a burst of blood pressure, the constriction of blood vessels in the abdominal viscera and in the skin, the relaxing of smooth muscles, and the sudden increased energy from the sugar released into the blood from the liver, and possible perceptual changes with the dilation of the pupil of the eye. This complex was, then, the internal pattern of sensation that preceded particularly violent activity in a critical situation. And by doing so repeatedly, the pattern of sensation begins to take on the term for the activity itself. Thereafter, it is the *thumos* which gives strength to a warrior in battle, etc. All the references to *thumos* in the Iliad as an internal sensation are consistent with this interpretation.

Now the important transition to the subjective Phase III is already beginning even in the Iliad, although not in a very conspicuous way. We see it in the unvoiced metaphor of the *thumos* as like a container: in several passages, *menos* or vigor is 'put' in someone's *thumos* (16: 5-8; 17: 451; 22: 312). The *thumos* is also implicitly compared to a person: it is not Ajax who is zealous to fight but his *thumos* (13: 73); nor is it Aeneas who rejoices but his *thumos* (13: 494; see also 14: 156). If not a god, it is the *thumos* that most often 'urges' a man into action. And as if it were another person, a man may speak to his *thumos* (11: 403), and may hear from it what he is to say (7: 68), or have it reply to him even as a god (9: 702).

All these metaphors are extremely important. Saying that the internal sensations of large circulatory and muscular changes are a *thing* into which strength can be put is to generate an imagined 'space,' here located always in the chest, which is the forerunner of the mind-space of contemporary consciousness. And to compare the function of that sensation to that of another person or even to the less-frequent gods is to begin those metaphor processes that will later become the analog 'I'.

Phrenes

The second most common hypostasis in the Iliad is the *phrenes*. Its Objective Phase origin is more questionable. But the fact that it is almost always plural may indicate that the *phrenes* objectively referred to the lungs and perhaps were associated with *phrasis* or speech.

In the Internal Phase, *phrenes* become the temporal pattern of sensations associated with respiratory changes. These come from the diaphragm, the intercostal muscles of the rib-cage, and the smooth muscles surrounding the bronchial tubes which regulate their bore and so the resistance of them to the passage of air, this mechanism being controlled by the sympathetic nervous system. We should remember here how extremely responsive our breathing is to various types of environmental stimulation. A sudden stimulus, and we 'catch our breath'. Sobbing and laughing have obvious distinct internal stimulation from the diaphragm and intercostals. In great activity or excitement, there is an increase in both the rate and depth of breathing with the resulting internal stimulation. Either pleasantness or unpleasantness usually shows increased breathing. Momentary attention is clearly correlated with partial or complete inhibition of breathing. A surprise, and our rate of breathing increases and becomes irregular.

Apart from rate, there are also unique changes in the proportion of time occupied by inspiration and by expiration in a single breath cycle. This is best measured by determining the percent of the duration of the breath cycle taken up by inspiration. This is about 16 percent in speech, 23 percent in laughter, 30 percent in attentive mental work, 43 percent when at rest, 60 percent or more in excitement, 71 percent in subjects imagining a wonderful or surprising situation, and 75 percent in sudden fright.[3]

The point I am trying to make here is that our *phrenes* or respiratory apparatus can almost be looked at as recording everything we do in quite distinct and distinguishable ways. It is at least possible that this internal mirror of behavior loomed much larger in the total stimulus world of the preconscious mind than it does in ourselves. And certainly its changing pattern of internal stimulation makes us understand why the *phrenes* are so important during the transition to consciousness, and why the term is used in so many functionally different ways in the poetry we are examining in this chapter.

In the Iliad, it can often be translated simply as lungs. Agamemnon's black *phrenes* fill with anger (1:103) and we can visualize the king's deep breathing as his fury mounts. Automedon fills his dark *phrenes* with valor and strength, or takes deep breaths (17:499). Frightened fawns have no strength in their *phrenes* after running; they are out of breath (4:245). In weeping, grief 'comes to' the *phrenes* (1:362; 8:124) or the respiratory *phrenes* can 'hold' fear (10:10), or joy (9:186). Even these statements are partly metaphoric, and thus associate a kind of container space in the *phrenes*.

A very few instances are more clearly in Phase III in the sense

[3] By inspiration here I mean from the beginning of taking a breath to the beginning of exhaling. The measure thus includes holding one's breath. These determinations collected from various sources. See Robert S. Woodworth, *Experimental Psychology* (New York: Holt, 1938), p. 264.

of inner mind-space. These are where the *phrenes* are said to 'contain' and perhaps 'retain' information. Sometimes this information comes from a god (1:55) or at other times from another human (1:297).

Laboratory studies have demonstrated that even simple sensory experience of an object, its recognition, and the recall of the name associated with it, all can be observed in recordings of respiration taken simultaneously.[4] It is thus not surprising that when some internal sensation is first connected to such functions as recognition and recall, it is located in the *phrenes*. Once it is said that the *phrenes* can recognize events (22:296), it is making a metaphor of the *phrenes* with a person, and the paraphrands of 'person,' that is, something that can act in a space projects back into the *phrenes* to make it metaphorically spatial and capable of other human activities metaphorically. Similarly we find that like a person the *phrenes* of a man can occasionally 'be persuaded' by another man (7:120), or even by a god (4:104). The *phrenes* can perhaps even 'speak' like a god, as when Agamemnon says he obeyed his baneful *phrenes* (9:119). These instances are quite rare in the Iliad, but they do point toward what will develop into consciousness over the next two centuries.

Kradie

This term, which later comes to be spelled *kardia*, and results in our familiar adjective 'cardiac,' is not quite so important or mysterious as other hypostases. It refers to the heart. In fact, it is the most common hypostasis still in use. When we in the twentieth century wish to be sincere, we still speak out of our hearts, not out of our consciousness. It is in our hearts that we have our most profound thoughts and cherish our closest beliefs. And we love with our hearts. It is curious that the lungs or

---

[4] Mario Ponzo, "La misura del decorso di processi psichici esequita per mezzo delle grafiche del respiro," *Archives Italiennes de Psicologia*, 1920–21, 1: 214–238.

phrenes have never maintained their hypostatic role as has the *kradie*.

Originally, I suggest, it simply meant quivering, coming from the verb *kroteo*, to beat. *Kradie* even means in some passages of early Greek a quivering branch. Then, in the internalization of Phase II that went on during the Dorian invasions, the quivering that was seen with the eye and felt with the hand externally becomes the name of the internal sensation of the heartbeat in response to external situations. With few exceptions, this is its referent in the Iliad. No one believes anything in his heart as yet.

Again I would remind you of the extensive modern literature on the responsiveness of our hearts to how we perceive the world. Like respiration or the action of the sympathetic nervous system, the cardiac system is extremely sensitive to particular aspects of the environment. At least one recent commentator has introduced the concept of the *cardiac mind*, calling the heart a specific sense organ for anxiety, as the eyes are the sense organ for sight.[5] Anxiety in this view is not any of the poetic homologues which we in our consciousness might use to describe it. Rather it is an inner tactile sensation in the sensory nerve endings of cardiac tissue which reads the environment for its anxiety potential.

While this notion is doubtful as it stands, it is good Homeric psychology. A coward in the Iliad is not someone who is afraid, but someone whose *kradie* beats loudly (13:282). The only remedy is for Athene to 'put' strength in the *kradie* (2:452), or for Apollo to 'put' boldness in it (21:547). The metaphier of a container here is building a 'space' into the heart in which later men may believe, feel, and ponder things deeply.

Etor

Philologists usually translate both *kradie* and *etor* as heart.

[5] Ludwig Braun, *Herz und Angst* (Vienna: Deuticke, 1932), p. 38.

And certainly a word can have synonyms. But in instances so important as the assigning of particular locations of sensations and forces of action, I would demur on *a priori* grounds, and insist that to the ancient Greek these terms had to represent different locations and sensations. Sometimes they are even clearly distinct in the text (20:169). I have thus the temerity to suggest that *etor* in Phase I came from the noun *etron* = belly, and that in Phase II, it becomes internalized into sensations of the gastro-intestinal tract, particularly the stomach. Indeed, there is even evidence for this in the Iliad, where it is precisely stated that food and drink are taken to satisfy the *etor* (19:307).[6] This translation is also more apt in other situations, as when a warrior loses his *etor* or guts in the front ranks of the battle by being disemboweled (5:215).

But more important is the stimulus field it provides for mental functioning. We know that the gastro-intestinal tract has a wide repertoire of responses to human situations. Everyone knows the sinking feeling on receiving bad news, or the epigastric cramp before a near automobile accident. The intestine is equally responsive to emotional stimuli of lesser degree, and these responses can be easily seen on the fluoroscopic screen.[7] Stomach contractions and peristalsis stop at an unpleasant stimulus, and may even be reversed if the unpleasantness is increased. The secretory activity of the stomach is also extremely susceptible to emotional experience. The stomach is indeed one of the most responsive organs in the body, reacting in its spasms and emptying and contractions and secretory activity to almost every emotion and sensation. And this is the reason why illnesses of the gastro-intestinal system were the first to be thought of as psychosomatic.

It is therefore plausible that this spectrum of gastro-intestinal sensations was what was being referred to by the *etor*. When

[6] See also Hesiod: *Works and Days*, 593.
[7] Howard E. Ruggles, "Emotional influence on the gastro-intestinal tract," *California and Western Medicine*, 1928, 29: 221–223.

Andromache hears the groaning Hecuba, her *etor* heaves up in her throat; she is close to vomiting (22:452).[8] When Lycaon's plea to live is mocked by Achilles, it is Lycaon's *etor* along with his knees that are 'loosened' and made weak (21:114). We would say he has a sinking feeling in the pit of his stomach. And when the gods themselves join in the battle, it is the *etor* of Zeus that laughs with joy, or what we would call a belly-laugh (21:389).

The container metaphor is not used as with the other hypostases, probably because the stomach already contains food. For this very reason we will see that it does not grow into an important part of any conscious mentality in the literature to follow.

I think it is obvious to the medical reader that these matters we are discussing under the topic of the preconscious hypostases have a considerable bearing on any theory of psychosomatic disease. In the *thumos, phrenes, kradie,* and *etor,* we have covered the four major target systems of such illness. And that they compose the very groundwork of consciousness, a primitive partial type of consciousizing, has important consequences in medical theory.

I shall only indicate the *ker* in passing, partly because it plays a diminishing role in this story of consciousness, but also because its derivation and significance is somewhat cloudy. While it is possible that it could have come from *cheir* and then become somatized into trembling hands and limbs, it is more probably from the same root as *kardia* in a different dialect. Certainly the passage in the Odyssey which states that a warrior is wounded where the *phrenes* or lungs are set close about the throbbing *ker* (16:481) leaves little doubt. It is almost always referred to as the organ of grief and is of limited importance.

But of utmost importance is the next hypostasis. Let it be immediately stated that it is an uncommon term in the Iliad — so

---

[8] And just as the stomach pulsates like the heart, so they sometimes become confused, as when in the wounded lion's *kradie* his valiant *etor* groans (20:169).

uncommon as to make us suspect that it could have been added by the later generations of aoidoi. But starting from such small beginnings in the Iliad, it soon comes into the very center of our topic. And this is

Noos

Up to now, we have been dealing with large, ummistakable internal sensations that only needed to be named in times of turmoil and crisis, and which then took their names from objective external perception. *Noos*, deriving from *noeo* = to see, is perception itself. And in coming to it we are in a much more powerful region in our intellectual travels.

For, as we saw in an earlier chapter, the great majority of the terms we use to describe our conscious lives are visual. We 'see' with the mind's 'eye' solutions which may be 'brilliant' or 'obscure,' and so on. Vision is our distance receptor *par excellence*. It is our sense of space in a way that no other modality can even approach. And it is that spatial quality, as we have seen, that is the very ground and fabric of consciousness.

It is interesting to note parenthetically that there is no hypostasis for hearing as there is for sight. Even today, we do not hear with the mind's ear as we see with the mind's eye. Nor do we refer to intelligent minds as loud, in the same way we say they are bright. This is probably because hearing was the very essence of the bicameral mind, and as such has those differences from vision which I discussed in I.4. The coming of consciousness can in a certain vague sense be construed as a shift from an auditory mind to a visual mind.

This shift is first seen somewhat fitfully in the Iliad. The Mycenaean objective origin of the term is present in objective statements about seeing, or in *noos* as a sight or show. In urging his men into battle, a warrior may say there is no better *noos* than a hand-to-hand battle with the enemy (15:510). And Zeus keeps Hector in his *noos* (15:461).

But the second phase of internalization of *noos* is also evident in the Iliad. It is located in the chest (3:63). How curious to us that it was not placed in the eyes! Perhaps this is because in its new role it was becoming melded with the *thumos*. Indeed, *noos* takes on adjectives more suitable to the *thumos*, such as fearless (3:63) and strong (16:688). And Odysseus dissuades the Achaeans from putting their ships to sea by telling them that they do not yet know what sort of *noos* is in Agamemnon (2:192). And one of the most modern-sounding instances occurs in the very first episode, when Thetis, consoling the sobbing Achilles, asks him, "Why has grief come upon your *phrenes?* Speak, conceal not in *noos*, so that we both may know" (1:363).[9] Apart from this, there is no other subjectification in the Iliad. No one makes any decisions in his *noos*. Thinking does not go on in the *noos*, or even memory. These are still in the voices of those organizations of the right temporal lobe that are called gods.

The precise causes of this internalization of sight into a container in which the seeing can be 'held' will require a much more careful study than we can go into here. Perhaps it was simply the generalization of internalization which I suggest had occurred earlier in those internalizations correlated with large internal sensations. Or it may have been that the observation of external difference in the mingling of refugees, as mentioned in II.3, demanded the positing of this visual hypostasis, which could be different in different men, making them see different things.

Psyche

And so finally to the word that gives psychology its name. Probably coming from the term *psychein* = to breathe, it has become internalized into life substances in its main usage in the

---

[9] A further exception to what I am saying can be found in the comparison of the swiftness of Hera with the swiftness of a man's *nous* wishing in his *phrenes* to be in distant places he has once visited (15: 80f.). On the peculiarity of such an expression in Homer, see Walter Leaf, *A Companion to the Iliad* (London: Macmillan, 1892), p. 257. This is obviously a late incursion.

Iliad. Most often, *psyche* seems to be used in just the way we would use life. But this can be very misleading. For 'life' to us means something about a period of time, a span between birth and death, full of events and developments of a certain character. There is absolutely nothing of this sort in the Iliad. When a spear strikes the heart of a warrior, and his *psyche* dissolves (5:296), is destroyed (22:325), or simply leaves him (16:453), or is coughed out through the mouth (9:409), or bled out through a wound (14:518; 16:505), there is nothing whatever about time or about the end of anything. There is in one part of Book 23 a different meaning of *psyche*, a discussion of which is deferred to the end of this chapter. But generally, it is very simply a property that can be taken away, and is similar to the taking away, under the same conditions, of *thumos* or activity, a word with which *psyche* is often coupled.

In trying to understand these terms, we must refrain from our conscious habit of building space into them before this has happened historically. In a sense, *psyche* is the most primitive of these preconscious hypostases; it is simply the property of breathing or bleeding or what not in that physical object over there called a man or an animal, a property which can be taken from him like a prize (22:161) by a spear in the right place. And in general, that is, with the exceptions I discuss at the end of this chapter, the main use of *psyche* in the Iliad does not progress beyond that. No one in any way ever sees, decides, thinks, knows, fears, or remembers anything in his *psyche*.

These then are the supposed substantives inside the body that by literary metaphor, by being compared to containers and persons, accrue to themselves spatial and behavioral qualities which in later literature develop into the unified mind-space with its analog 'I' that we have come to call consciousness. But in pointing out these beginnings in the Iliad, let me remind you that the contours of the main actions of the poem are as divinely dictated and as nonconscious as I have insisted in I.3. These precon-

scious hypostases do not enter into any major decisions. But they
are definitely there playing a subsidiary role. It is indeed as if the
unitary conscious mind of the later age is here in the Iliad beginning as seven different entities, each with a slightly different
function and a distinction from the others which is almost impossible for us to appreciate today.

THE WILES OF THE ODYSSEY

After the Iliad, the Odyssey. And anyone reading these poems
freshly and consecutively sees what a gigantic vault in mentality
it is! There are of course some scholars who still like to think of
these two huge epics as being written down and even composed
by one man named Homer, the first in his youth and the second
in his maturity. The more reasonable view, I think, is that the
Odyssey followed the Iliad by at least a century or more, and, like
its predecessor, was the work of a succession of aoidoi rather than
any one man.

But, unlike its predecessor, the Odyssey is not one epic but
a series of them. The originals were probably about different
heroes, and brought together around Odysseus at a later time.
Why this happened is not hard to unravel. Odysseus, at least in
some parts of Greece, had become the center of a cult that
enabled conquered peoples to survive. He becomes "wily Odysseus" and later aoidoi perhaps inserted this epithet into the Iliad
to remind their listeners of the Odyssey. Archaeological evidence
indicates important dedications made to Odysseus some time
after 1000 b.c. and definitely before 800 b.c.[10] These were
sometimes of bronze tripod caldrons curiously connected with the
cult. They were such dedications as formerly would have been
to a god. Contests in worship of him were held in Ithaca at least

[10] S. Benton, as cited in T. B. L. Webster, *From Mycenae to Homer* (London:
Methuen, 1958), p. 138.

from the ninth century B.C., even as that island was about to be overrun again by new invasions from Corinth. In a word, Odysseus of the many devices is the hero of the new mentality of how to get along in a ruined and god-weakened world.

The Odyssey announces this in its very fifth word, *polutropon* = much turning. It is a journey of deviousness. It is the very discovery of guile, its invention and celebration. It sings of indirections and disguises and subterfuges, transformations and recognitions, drugs and forgetfulness, of people in other people's places, of stories within stories, and men within men.

The contrast with the Iliad is astonishing. Both in word and deed and character, the Odyssey describes a new and different world inhabited by new and different beings. The bicameral gods of the Iliad, in crossing over to the Odyssey, have become defensive and feeble. They disguise themselves more and even indulge in magic wands. The bicameral mind by its very definition directs much less of the action. The gods have less to do, and like receding ghosts talk more to each other — and that so tediously! The initiatives move from them, even against them, toward the work of the more conscious human characters, though overseen by a Zeus who in losing his absolute power has acquired a Lear-like interest in justice. Seers and omens, these hallmarks of the breakdown of bicamerality, are more common. Semi-gods, dehumanizing witches, one-eyed giants, and sirens, reminiscent of the genii that we saw marked the breakdown of bicamerality in Assyrian bas-reliefs a few centuries earlier, are evidence of a profound alteration in mentality. And the huge Odysseyan themes of homeless wanderings, of kidnapings and enslavements, of things hidden, things regained, are surely echoes of the social breakdown following the Dorian invasions when subjective consciousness in Greece first took its mark.

Technically, the first thing to note is the change in the frequency with which the preconscious hypostases are used. Such data can be compiled easily from concordances of the Iliad and

Odyssey, and the results are dramatic in showing a very definite rise in frequency for *phrenes, noos,* and *psyche,* and a striking drop in the use of the world *thumos.* Of course we can say that the decrease for *thumos* from the Iliad to the Odyssey is due to what the poem is about. But that is begging the question. For the very change in theme is indeed a part of this whole transition in the very nature of man. The other hypostases are passive. *Thumos,* the adrenalin-produced emergency reaction of the sympathetic nervous system to novel situations, is the antithesis of anything passive. The kind of metaphors that can be built up around this metaphrand of a sudden surge of energy are not the passive visual ones that are more conducive to solving problems.

In contrast, over this period, *phrenes* doubles in frequency, while both *noos* and *psyche* triple in frequency. Again, the point could be made that the increase in the use of these words is simply an echo of the change in topics. And again that is precisely the point. Poetry, from describing external events objectively, is becoming subjectified into a poetry of personal conscious expression.

But it is not just their frequency that we are interested in. It is also the change in their inherent meanings and the metaphiers used for them. As the gods decrease in their direction of human affairs, the preconscious hypostases take over some of their divine function, moving them closer to consciousness. *Thumos,* though decreased, is still the most common hypostatic word. And its function is different. It has reached the subjective phase and is like another person. It is the *thumos* of the swineherd that 'commands' him to return to Telemachus (16:466). In the Iliad, it would have been a god speaking. In the earlier epic, a god can 'place' *menos* or vigor into the 'container' of the *thumos;* but in the Odyssey, it is an entire recognition that can be 'placed' therein. Eurycleia recognizes Odysseus under his disguise by his scar because a god has 'put' that recognition in her *thumos*

(19:485). (Note that she has recognition but not recall.) And the servants of Penelope have knowledge of her son's departure in their *thumos* (4:730).

Phrenes too has acquired the spatial qualities of Phase III. Even the description of a possible future event can be put in the *phrenes,* as when Telemachus, as a pretext for depriving the suitors of weapons, is asked to claim that a *daimon* (it would have at least been a god in the Iliad) has put fears of quarrels among them into his *phrenes* (19:10). There are no secrets in the Iliad. But the Odyssey has many of them, and they are 'held' in the *phrenes* (16:459). Whereas in the Iliad the preconscious hypostases were almost always clearly located, their increasingly metaphorical nature is muddling up their anatomical distinction in the Odyssey. Even the *thumos* is at one point located inside the lungs or *phrenes* (22:38).

But there is another and even more important use of *phrenes,* this word that originally referred to the lungs and then to the complex sensations in breathing. And this is in the first beginnings of morality. No one is moral among the god-controlled puppets of the Iliad. Good and evil do not exist. But in the Odyssey, Clytaemnestra is able to resist Aegisthus because her *phrenes* are *agathai,* which may have been derived from roots that would make it mean 'very like a god'. And in another place, it is the *agathai,* godly, or good *phrenes* of Eumaeus which has him remember to make offerings to the gods (14:421). And similarly it is the *agathai* or good *phrenes* that are responsible for Penelope's chastity and loyalty to the absent Odysseus (12:194). It is not yet Penelope who is *agathe,* only the metaphor-space in her lungs.

And similarly with the other preconscious hypostases. Warnings of destruction are 'heard' from the *kradie* or pounding heart of Odysseus when he is wrecked and thrown into tempestuous seas (5:389). And it is his *ker,* again his trembling heart or perhaps his trembling hands, that makes plans for the suitors' downfall (18:344). In the Iliad, these would have been gods speaking. *Noos,* while being referred to more frequently, is sometimes not changed. But more often it is also in Phase III of subjectification. At one point, Odysseus is deceiving Athene (unthinkable in the Iliad!) and looks at her ever revolving in his *noos* thoughts of great cunning (13:255). Or *noos* can be like a person who is glad (8:78) or cruel (18:381) or not to be fooled (10:329) or learned about (1:3). *Psyche* again usually means life, but perhaps with more sense of a time span. Some very important exceptions to this will be referred to later.

Not only is the growth toward subjective consciousness in the Odyssey seen in the increasing use and spatial interiority and personification of its preconscious hypostases, but even more clearly in its incidents and social interrelationships. These include the emphasis on deceit and guile which I have already referred to. In the Iliad, time is referred to sloppily and inaccurately, if at all. But the Odyssey shows an increased spatialization of time in its use of time words, such as begin, hesitate, quickly, endure, etc., and the more frequent reference to the future. There is also an increased ratio of abstract terms to concrete, particularly of what in English would be nouns ending in 'ness'. And with this, as might be expected, a marked drop in similes: there is less need for them. Both the frequency and the manner with which Odysseus refers to himself is on a different level altogether from instances of self-reference in the Iliad. All this is relevant to the growth of a new mentality.

Let me close this necessarily short entry on a toweringly important poem by calling your attention to a mystery. This is that the overall contour of the story itself is a myth of the very matter with which we are concerned. It is a story of identity, of a voyage to the self that is being created in the breakdown of the bicameral mind. I am not pretending here to be answering the profound question of why this should be so, of why the muses, those patternings of the right temporal lobe, who are singing this epic through the aoidoi, should be narratizing their own downfall, their own fading away into subjective thought, and celebrating the rise of a new mentality that will overwhelm the very act of their song. For this seems to be what is happening.

I am saying — and finding it work to believe myself — that all this highly patterned legend, which so clearly can be taken as a metaphor of the huge transilience toward consciousness, was not composed, planned, and put together by poets conscious of what they were doing. It is as if the god-side of the bicameral man was approaching consciousness before the man-side, the right hemisphere before the left. And if belief does stick here, and we are inclined to ask scoffingly and rhetorically, how could an epic that may itself be a kind of drive toward consciousness be composed by nonconscious men? We can also ask with the same rhetorical fervor, how could it have been composed by conscious men? And have the same silence follow. We do not know the answer to either question.

But so it is. And as this series of stories sweeps from its lost hero sobbing on an alien shore in bicameral thrall to his beautiful goddess Calypso, winding through its world of demigods, testings, and deceits, to his defiant war whoops in a rival-routed home, from trance through disguise to recognition, from sea to land, east to west, defeat to prerogative, the whole long song is an odyssey toward subjective identity and its triumphant acknowledgment out of the hallucinatory enslavements of the past. From a will-less gigolo of a divinity to the gore-spattered lion on his own hearth, Odysseus becomes 'Odysseus'.

FOOLISH PERSES

Some of the chronologically next group of poems I shall merely gloss over. Among these are the so-called Homeric Hymns, most of which have turned out to be of a much later date. There are also the poems that originated in Boeotia northeast of Athens in the eighth century B.C., many of which were once ascribed to a cult figure named Hesiod. Unfortunately, their extant texts are often mixtures of parts of poems from obviously different sources, badly emended. Most of them contribute little to our present concern. The often tedious recital of the relationships of gods in the *Theogony* is usually dated shortly after the Odyssey, but its hypostatic words are fewer and without development. Its chief interest is that its concern with the intimate lives of gods is perhaps a result of their silence, another expression of the nostalgia for the Golden Age before the Dorian invasions.

But of much greater interest is the fascinating problem presented by the text ascribed to Hesiod known as the *Works and Days*.[11] It is obviously a hodgepodge of various things, a kind of Shepherd's Calendar for a Boeotian farmer, and a very poor and scrubbing farmer at that. Its world is worlds away from the world of the great Homeric epics. Instead of a hero at the command of his gods working through a narrative of grandeur, we have instruction to the countryman, who may or may not obey his gods, on ways of work, which days are lucky, and a very interesting new sense of justice.

On the surface, this medley of scruffy detail of farm life and nostalgia for the Golden Age that is no more seems to be written by a farmer whom scholars take to be Hesiod. He is supposedly railing at his brother, Perses, over the unfairness of a judgment dividing their father's farm, curiously giving Perses advice on everything from morality to marriage, on how to treat slaves to the problems of planting and sewage disposal. It is full of such things as:

> Foolish Perses! Work the work which the gods ordained for
> men, lest in bitter anguish of *thumos,* you with your wife and
> children seek your livelihood amongst your neighbors. (397ff.)

---

[11] I have used throughout the Loeb edition of Hesiod (London: Heinemann, 1936).

At least this is what most scholars take the poem to be. But another interpretation is at least possible. This is that the older portions of the poem may actually have been written not by Hesiod, who is never mentioned in the poem, but by none other than the hand of foolish Perses himself, and that these main parts of the poem are the admonitions of his divine bicameral voice advising him what to do. If this jolts your sense of possibility, I would remind you of the schizophrenic patients who all day may hear similarly authoritative critical voices constantly admonishing them in a similar vein.

Perhaps I should not say written. More probably the poem was dictated to a scribe, even as were the bicameral admonitions of Perses' contemporary, Amos, the herdsman of Israel. And I should also have said a previous recension of the main poem, and that the protest lodged in the crucial lines 37-39 were added later (even as everyone since Plutarch has agreed that 654–662 were). It is also possible that these lines originally referred to some kind of bicameral struggle for the control of Perses' too subjective and therefore (at this time) unprofitable behavior.

The preconscious hypostases in the *Works and Days* occur in approximately the same frequencies as in the Odyssey. *Thumos* is the most common and in about half of its eighteen occurrences it is a simple Phase II internal impulse to some activity or locus of joy or sorrow. But the rest of the time, it is a Phase III space in which information (27), advice (297, 491), sights (296), or mischief (499) can be 'put', 'kept', or 'held'. The *phrenes* also are like a cupboard, where the advice that is constantly given in the poem (107, 274) is to be laid up, and where foolish Perses is to 'look' at it carefully (688). The *kradie* has the metaphier of a person more than a container, and can be gracious (340), vexed (451), or can like and dislike things (681). But *psyche* (686) and *etor* (360, 593) are undeveloped and are simply life and belly respectively.

Noos in the *Works and Days* is interesting because, in all four of its instances, it is like a person relating to moral conduct. In two instances (67, 714) it has shame or not, and in another, it is *adikon*, without good direction (260). A proper study of the matter would point out in detail the particular development of the term *dike*. Its original meaning was to point (from which comes the original meaning of digit, as a finger), and in the Iliad its most parsimonious translation is as "direction," in the sense of pointing out what to do. Sarpedon guarded Lycia by his *dike* (Iliad 16:542). But in the *Works and Days*, it has come to mean god-given right directions or justice, perhaps as a replacement for the god's voice.[12] It is a silent Zeus, son of a now spatialized time, who here for the first time dispenses *dike* or justice more or less as we know it in later Greek literature. (See for example 267ff.). How absolutely alien to the amoral world of the Iliad, that a whole city can suffer for one evil man (240)!

Our sense of justice depends on our sense of time. Justice is a phenomenon only of consciousness, because time spread out in a spatial succession is its very essence. And this is possible only in a spatial metaphor of time. Instances of this increased spatialization are common. Committing violence at one time begets a punishment at some time to follow (245f.). Long and steep is the path to goodness (290). A good man is he who sees what will be better afterward (294). Add little to little and it will become great (362). Work with work upon work to gain wealth (382). These notions are impossible unless the before and after of time are metaphored into a spatial succession. This basic ingredient of consciousness, which began in Assyrian building inscriptions in 1300 B.C. (see the previous chapter), has indeed come a long way.

It is important here to understand how closely coupled this

---

[12] But that the origin of this new sense of god-sent justice is possibly in an hallucinated messenger from Zeus is suggested where *Dike* is said to moan and weep when men take bribes and do evil (220f). My derivation here of *dike* is not the usual one.

new sense of time and justice is to what can be called the secularization of attention. By this I mean the shift in attention toward
the everyday problems of making a living, something that is
totally foreign to the mighty god-devised epics which preceded it.
Whether the poem itself is divinely inspired, or, as the majority
of scholars think, the sulky exhortations of Perses' brother
Hesiod, it is a dramatic turning point in the direction of human
concern. Instead of grand impersonal narrative, we have a detailed personal expression. Instead of an ageless past, we have a
vivid expression of a present wedged in between a past and a
future. And it is a present of grim harshness that described the
post-Dorian rural reality, full of petty strife and the struggle of
wresting a living from the land, while around its edges hovers the
nostalgia for the mighty golden world of bicameral Mycaenae,
whose people were a race

> . . . which was more lawful and more righteous, a god-like
> race of hero-men who are called half-gods, the race before our
> own, throughout the boundless earth. (158ff.).

LYRIC AND ELEGY FROM 700 TO 600 B.C.

I was about to write that Greek consciousness is nearing completion in the *Works and Days*. But that is a very misleading metaphor, that consciousness is a thing that is built, formed, shaped
into something that has a completion. There is no such thing as
a complete consciousness.

What I would have been indicating was that the basic metaphors of time with space, of internal hypostases as persons in a
mental space have begun to work themselves into the guides and
guardians of everyday life.

Against this development, the Greek poetry of the seventh century B.C., which follows chronologically, is something of an anticlimax. But this is because so little of these elegiac and lyric poets has escaped the eager ravages of time. If we take only those who have at least a dozen lines extant, there are only seven poets to be considered.

The first thing to say about them is that they are not simply poets, as we regard the term. As a group, they are something like their contemporaries, the prophets of Israel, holy teachers of men, called by kings to settle disputes and to lead armies, resembling in some of their functions the shamans of contemporary tribal cultures. At the beginning of the century, they were probably still associated with holy dancing. But gradually the dance and its religious aura are lost in a secularity that is chanted to the lyre or the sounds of flutes. These artistic changes, however, are merely coincident to changes of a much more important kind.

The *Works and Days* expressed the present. The new poetry expresses the person in that present, the particular individual and how he is different from others. And celebrates that difference. And as it does so, we can trace a progressive filling out and stretching of the earlier preconscious hypostases into the mind-space of consciousness.

In the first part of the century is Terpander, the inventor of drinking songs, according to Pindar, one of whose thirteen extant lines cries out over the centuries:

Of the Far-flinging Lord come sing to me, O Phrenes![13]

This is interesting. The Lord here is Apollo. But note that while the poem itself is to be a nostalgic poem to a lost god, it is not a

[13] Fragment 2 in the Loeb edition, *Lyra Graeca*, edited by J. M. Edmonds (London: Heinemann, 1928). All references in this section are to this volume or to the companion Loeb volumes, *Elegy and Iambus*, Vols. 1 and 2, also edited by Edmonds (London: Heinemann, 1931).

god or a muse who is invoked to compose it. In the Odyssey, a god puts songs into the *phrenes* which the minstrel then sings as if he were reading the music (22:347). But for Terpander, who hears no gods, it is his own *phrenes* that are begged to compose a song just as if they were a god. And this implicit comparison, I suggest, with its associated paraphrands of a space in which the deiform *phrenes* could exist, is well on the way to creating the mind-space with its analog 'I' of consciousness.

It is not just in such word usages that this transition in the seventh century is apparent, but also in the subject matter. For the secularization and personalization of content begun in the *Works and Days* fairly explodes in midcentury in the angry iambics of Archilochus, the wandering soldier-poet of Paros. According to the inscription of his tomb, it was he who "first dipt a bitter Muse in snake-venom and stained gentle Helicon with blood," a reference to the story that he could provoke suicides with the power of his iambic abuse.[14] Even using poetry this way, to engage in personal vendettas and state personal preferences, is a new thing to the world. And so close to modern reflective consciousness do some of these fragments come, that the loss of most of Archilochus' work opens one of the greatest gaps in ancient literature.

But the gods, though never heard by Archilochus, still control the world. "The ends of victory are among the gods" (Fragment 55). And the hypostases remain. The bad effects of drink (Fragment 77) or of old age (Fragment 94) occur in the *phrenes*; and when he is troubled, it is his *thumos* which is thrown down like a weak warrior and is told to "look up and defend yourself against your enemies" (Fragment 66). Archilochus talks to his *thumos* as to another person, the implicit comparison and its paraphrands of space and self-'observed' 'self'

---

[14] According to the *Palatine Anthology* collected about A.D. 920 from previous sources. See Edmonds, *Elegy and Iambus*, 2: 97.

being a further step toward the consciousness of the next century.

Chronologically next come two other soldier-poets, Tyrtaeus and Callinus, whose remaining fragments are of little interest. Their most common hypostasis is *thumos,* and they do little more than urge us to keep an unfaltering *thumos* in battle.

And then, about 630 B.C., two poets of a different kind, Alcman and Mimnermus. They urge nothing, but celebrate their own subjective feelings in a way that had never been done before. "Who may report the *noos* of another?" (Fragment 55) asks the former, making the metaphor of *noos* as a happening with its obvious paraphrand consequences. And Mimnermus complains of the ill cares that wear and wear his *phrenes* (Fragment 1) and of the "sorrows that rise in the *thumos*" (Fragment 2). This is a long way from the simple hypostases of the Homeric epics.

At the end of this presageful century come the poems of Alcaeus and, particularly, the empty-armed passions of virile Sappho, the tenth muse as Plato calls her. Both these poets of Lesbos say the usual things about their *thumos* and *phrenes,* using both about equally. Sappho even sings about the *theloi* or arrangements of her *thumos* which become our desires and volitions (Fragment 36:3). And she practically invents love in its romantic modern sense. Love wrings her *thumos* with anguish (Fragment 43) and shakes her *phrenes* as a hurricane shakes an oak tree (Fragment 54).

But more important is the development of the term *noema.* By the late seventh century, it is clear that *noema* has come to mean a composite of what we mean by thoughts, wishes, intents, etc., and joining up with the *theloi* of the *thumos.* Alcaeus says, "If Zeus will accomplish what is our *noema*" (Fragment 43). He describes a speaker as not "prevaricating (or excusing) his *noema* at all" (Fragment 144). In those shards of Sappho that remain, the word is used three times: toward those she loves, "my *noema* can never change" (Fragment 14); her "*noema* is not so softly disposed to the anger of a child" (Fragment 35); and in her complaint, "I know not what to do; my *noemata* are in two parts . . ." (Fragment 52). This puts the emphasis on the imagined internal metaphor-thing that is hypostasized into a thought. It is love that is teaching mankind to introspect. And there is even another word in Sappho, *sunoida*, whose roots would indicate that it means to know together, which, when Latinized, becomes the word 'conscious' (Fragment 15).

In these seven poets of the seventh century, then, we find a remarkable development, that, as the subject matter changed from martial exhortations to personal expressions of love, the manner in which the mental hypostases are used and their contexts become much more what we think of as subjective consciousness.

These are murky historical waters, and we may be sure that these seven poets, with their few fragments bobbing in the extant surface of the seventh century B.C., are but an indication of the many that probably then existed and helped develop the new mentality we are calling consciousness.

SOLON'S MIND

I particularly feel that these seven cannot be representative of the time, for the very next poet chronologically that we know of is dramatically different from any of them. He is the morning star of the Greek intellect, the man who alone, so far as we know, really filled out the idea of human justice. This is Solon of Athens, who stands at the beginning of the great sixth century B.C., the century of Thales, Anaximander, and Pythagoras. It is the century where, for the first time, we can feel mentally at home among persons who think in somewhat the way we do.

The swiftness of the unfolding of these greatnesses of Greek culture is astonishing. And if for no other reason, Solon, at the beginning of all this, is astonishing for his use of the word *noos*. The word is rarely used by any of the poets we have previously looked at. But in the mere 280 (approximately) lines that have come down to us, he uses *noos* eight times. This is an extremely high frequency of 44 per 10,000 words. It indicates Phase IV, in which the several hypostases are joining into one. *Thumos* is used only twice, and *phrenes* and *etor* once each.

But it is also the way he speaks about the *noos* that is the first real statement of the subjective conscious mind. He speaks of those whose *noos* is not *artios*, which means intact or whole (Fragment 6). How impossible to say of a recognition! It is the *noos* that is wrong in a bad leader (Fragment 4). The Homeric meaning of *noos* could not take moral epithets. At about age forty-two, "a man's *noos* is trained in all things." Certainly this is not his visual perception. And in his fifties, he is "at his best in *noos* and tongue" (Fragment 27).

Another fragment describes the true beginning of personal responsibility, where he warns his fellow Athenians not to blame the gods for their misfortunes, but themselves. How contrary to the mind of the Iliad! And then adds,

> Each one of you walks with the steps of a fox; the *noos* of all of you is *chaunos* [porous, spongy, or loose-grained as in wood]: for you look to a man's tongue and rapidly shifting speech, and never to the deed he does. (Fragment 10).

Not Achilles nor artful Odysseus nor even foolish Perses (or his brother) could have 'understood' this admonition.

Consciousness and morality are a single development. For without gods, morality based on a consciousness of the consequences of action must tell men what to do. The *dike* or justice of the *Works and Days* is developed even further in Solon. It is now moral right that must be fitted together with might in government (Fragment 36) and which is the basis of law and lawful action.

Sometimes attributed to Solon are certain other injunctions, such as his exhortation to "moderation in all things." But more germane to the present topic is the famous "Know thyself," which is often ascribed to him but may have come from one of his contemporaries. This again was something inconceivable to the Homeric heroes. How can one know oneself? By initiating by oneself memories of one's actions and feelings and looking at them together with an analog 'I', conceptualizing them, sorting them out into characteristics, and narratizing so as to know what one is likely to do. One must 'see' 'oneself' as in an imaginary 'space,' indeed what we were calling autoscopic illusions back in an early chapter.

Suddenly, then, we are in the modern subjective age. We can only regret that the literature of the seventh century b.c. is so shredded and scant as to make this almost full appearance of subjective consciousness in Solon almost implausible, if we regard him as simply a part of the Greek tradition. But the legends about Solon are many. And several of them insist that he was widely traveled, having visited countries of Asia Minor before returning to Athens to live out his life and write most of his poems. It is thus certainly a suggestion that his particular use of the word *noos* and his reification of the term into the imaginary mind-space of consciousness was due to the influence of these more developed nations.

With Solon, partly because he was the political leader of his time, the operator of consciousness is firmly established in Greece. He has a mind-space called a *noos* in which an analog of himself can narratize out what is *dike* or right for his people to do. Once established, once a man can 'know himself,' as Solon advised, can place 'times' together in the side-by-sideness of mind-space, can 'see' into himself and his world with the 'eye' of his *noos,* the divine voices are unnecessary, at least to everyday life. They have been pushed aside into special places called temples or special persons called oracles. And that the new unitary *nous* (as it came to be spelled), absorbing the functions of the other hypostases, was successful is attested by all the literature that followed, as well as the reorganization of behavior and society.

But we are somewhat ahead of our story. For there is another development in this important sixth century B.C., and one which is a huge complication for the future. It is an old term, *psyche,* used in an unpredictably new way. In time it comes to parallel and then to become interchangeable with *nous,* while at the same time it engenders that consciousness of consciousness which was held up as false at the beginning of Book I. Moreover, I shall suggest that this new concept is an almost artifactual result of a meeting between Greek and Egyptian cultures.

THE INVENTION OF THE SOUL

Psyche is the last of these words to come to have 'space' inside it. This is due, I think, to the fact that *psyche* or livingness did not lend itself to a container-type metaphor until the conscious spatialization of time had so far developed that a man had a life in the sense of a time span, rather than just in the sense of breath and blood. But the progress of *psyche* toward the concept of soul is not that clear at all.

For, more than the other hypostases, *psyche* is sometimes used in confusing ways that seem on the surface to defy a chronological ordering. Its primary use is always for life, as I have stated. After the Homeric poems, Tyrtaeus, for example, uses *psyche* in that sense (Fragments 10 and 11), as does Alcaeus (Fragment 77B). And even as late as the fifth century B.C., Euripides uses the phrase "to be fond of one's *psyche*," in the sense of clinging to life (*Iphigenia at Aulis*, 1385). Some of the Aristotelian writings also use *psyche* as life, and this usage even extends into much of the New Testament. "I am the good shepherd: the good shepherd giveth his *psyche* for his sheep" (John, 10:11). Jesus did not mean his mind or soul.

But in Achilles' dream at the beginning of Book 23 of the Iliad, the *psyche* of the *dead* Patroclus visits him, and when he tries to hug it in his arms, it sinks gibbering into the earth. The grizzly scenes in Hades in Books 11 and 24 of the Odyssey use *psyche* in a similar way. The term in these instances has an almost opposite sense from its meaning in the rest of both Iliad and Odyssey. Not life, but that which exists after life has ceased. Not what is bled out of one's veins in battle, but the soul or ghost that goes to Hades, a concept that is otherwise unheard of in Greek literature until Pindar, around 500 B.C. In all the intervening writers we have been looking at through the eighth and seventh centuries B.C., *psyche* is never the ghost-soul, but always has its original meaning of life or livingness.

Now, no amount of twisting about in semantic origins can reconcile these two gratingly different significations for *psyche,* one relating to life and the other to death. The obvious suggestion here is that these alien incongruities in Homer are interpolations of a period much later than the ostensible period of the poems. And indeed this is what the majority of scholars are sure of on much more ample grounds than we can go into here. Since this meaning of *psyche* does not appear until Pindar, we may be fairly confident that these passages about Hades and the souls of the dead abiding there in its shades were added into the Homeric poems shortly before Pindar, sometime in the sixth century B.C.

The problem then is how and why did this dramatically different concept of *psyche* come about? And let us be clear here that the only thing we are talking about is the application of the old word for life to what survives after death and its separability from the body. The actual survival, as we have seen in previous

chapters, is not in doubt. According to the theory of the bicameral mind, hallucinations of a person in some authority could
continue after death as an everyday matter. And hence the almost universal custom of feeding the corpses after death, and
burying them with the appurtenances of life.

I am unable to suggest a truly satisfactory solution. But certainly a part of it is the influence of that towering legend-laden
figure of antiquity, Pythagoras. Flourishing around the middle of
the sixth century B.C., he is thought to have traveled, as did
Solon, to several countries of Asia Minor, particularly Egypt. He
then returned and established a kind of mystical secret society in
Crotona in southern Italy. They practiced mathematics, vegetar-
ianism, and a firm illiteracy — to write things down was a source
of error. Among these teachings, as we have them at least at
third hand from later writers, was the doctrine of the transmigration of souls. After death, a man's soul enters the body of a
newborn infant or animal and so lives another life.

Herodotus has been flouted for saying Pythagoras learned this
in Egypt. But if one agrees with the theory of the bicameral
mind, the origin of soul transmigration in Egyptian ideas is not
difficult to trace. I suggest it was a Greek misunderstanding of
the functions of the *ba*, which, as we saw in II.2, was often the
seeming physical embodiment of the *ka*, or hallucinated voice
after death. Often the *ba* had the form of a bird. Greek, however, had no word for ka (other than a god — clearly inappropriate), or for *ba*, indeed no word for a 'life' which could be
transferred from one material body to another. Hence *psyche*
was pressed into this service. All references to this Pythagorean
teaching use *psyche* in this new sense, as a clearly separable soul
that can migrate from one body to another as could an hallucinated voice in Egypt.

Now this does not really solve our problem. For there is nothing here of dead strengthless souls wailing about in a nether-
world, guzzling hot blood to get their strength back — which is

the lively scene added into the Odyssey as Book 11. But the *psyche* here is somewhat the same, a something of a man which leaves the body at death. And what the Hades view of *psyche* may be is a composite of the Pythagorean teaching with the older view of the buried dead in Greek antiquity.

All this curious development of the sixth century B.C. is extremely important for psychology. For with this wrenching of *psyche* = life over to *psyche* = soul, there came other changes to balance it as the enormous inner tensions of a lexicon always do. The word *soma* had meant corpse or deadness, the opposite of *psyche* as livingness. So now, as *psyche* becomes soul, so *soma* remains as its opposite, becoming body. And dualism, the supposed separation of soul and body, has begun.

But the matter does not stop there. In Pindar, Heraclitus, and others around 500 B.C., *psyche* and *nous* begin to coalesce. It is now the conscious subjective mind-space and its self that is opposed to the material body. Cults spring up about this new wonder-provoking division between *psyche* and *soma*. It both excites and seems to explain the new conscious experience, thus reinforcing its very existence. The conscious *psyche* is imprisoned in the body as in a tomb. It becomes an object of wide-eyed controversy. Where is it? And the locations in the body or outside it vary. What is it made of? Water (Thales), blood, air (Anaximenes), breath (Xenophanes), fire (Heraclitus), and so on, as the science of it all begins in a morass of pseudoquestions.

So dualism, that central difficulty in this problem of consciousness, begins its huge haunted career through history, to be firmly set in the firmament of thought by Plato, moving through Gnosticism into the great religions, up through the arrogant assurances of Descartes to become one of the great spurious quandaries of modern psychology.

This has been a long and technical chapter that can be briefly summarized in a metaphor. At the beginning, we noted that archaeologists, by brushing the dust of the ages from around the broken shards of pottery from the period of the Dorian invasions, have been able to reveal continuities and changes from site to site, and so to prove that a complex series of migrations was occurring. In a sense, we have been doing the same thing with language throughout this chapter. We have taken broken-off bits of vocabulary, those that came to refer to some kind of mental function, and by their contexts from text to text, attempted to demonstrate that a huge complex series of changes in mentality was going on during these obscure periods that followed the Dorian invasions in Greece.

Let no one think these are *just* word changes. Word changes are concept changes and concept changes are behavioral changes. The entire history of religions and of politics and even of science stands shrill witness to that. Without words like soul, liberty, or truth, the pageant of this human condition would have been filled with different roles, different climaxes. And so with the words we have designated as preconscious hypostases, which by the generating process of metaphor through these few centuries unite into the operator of consciousness.

I have now completed that part of the story of Greek consciousness that I intended to tell. More of it could be told, how the two nonstimulus-bound hypostases come to overshadow the rest, how *nous* and *psyche* come to be almost interchangeable in later writers, such as Parmenides and Democritus, and take on even new metaphor depths with the invention of *logos*, and of the forms of truth, virtue, and beauty.

But that is another task. The Greek subjective conscious mind, quite apart from its pseudostructure of soul, has been born out of song and poetry. From here it moves out into its own history, into the narratizing introspections of a Socrates and the spatialized classifications and analyses of an Aristotle, and from there into Hebrew, Alexandrian, and Roman thought. And then into the history of a world which, because of it, will never be the same again.

CHAPTER 6

The Moral Consciousness
of the Khabiru

THE THIRD great area where we can look at the development
of consciousness is certainly the most interesting and profound. All through the Middle East toward the end of the second
millennium B.C., there were large amorphous masses of half-
nomadic peoples with no fixed *dira* or grazing ground. Some
were the refugees from the Thera destruction and the terrible
Dorian invasions which followed. One cuneiform tablet specifically speaks of migrations pouring down through the Lebanon.
Others were probably refugees from the Assyrian invasions and
were joined by the Hittite refugees when that empire fell to a
further invasion from the north. And still others may have been
the resistant bicameral individuals of the cities who could not
silence the gods so easily, and who, if not killed, would be progressively sifted out into the desert wilderness.

A mixture of men, then, coming together precariously for a
time, and then separating out, some perishing, others organizing
into unstable tribes; some raiding more settled lands, or fighting
over water holes; or sometimes, perhaps, caught like exhausted
animals and made to do their captor's will, or, in the desperation
of hunger, bartering control over their lives for bread and seed, as
described on some fifteenth-century B.C. tablets unearthed at
Nuzi, as well as in Genesis 47:18-26. Some perhaps were still
trying to follow inadequate bicameral voices, or clinging to the
edge of settled land, fearing to launch out, becoming breeders of
sheep and camels, while others, having struggled unsuccessfully

to mingle with more settled peoples, then pushed out into the
open desert, where only the ruthless survive, perhaps in precarious pursuit of some hallucinated vision, some back parts of a god,
some new city or promised land.

To the established city-states, these refugees were the desperate outcasts of the desert wilderness. The city people thought of
them collectively as robbers and vagrants. And so they often
were, either singly, as miserable homeless wretches stealing by
night the grapes which the vine-dressers scorned to pick, or as
whole tribes raiding the city peripheries for their cattle and produce, even as nomadic Bedouins occasionally do today. The word
for vagrants in Akkad, the language of Babylon, is *khabiru*, and
so these desert refugees are referred to on cuneiform tablets.[1]
And *khabiru*, softened in the desert air, becomes *hebrew*.

The story or imagined story of the later Khabiru or Hebrews is
told in what has come down to us as the Old Testament. The
thesis to which we shall give our concern in this chapter is that
this magnificent collection of history and harangue, of song,
sermon, and story is in its grand overall contour the description
of the loss of the bicameral mind, and its replacement by subjectivity over the first millennium B.C.

We are immediately, however, presented with an orthological
problem of immense proportions. For much of the Old Testament, particularly the first books, so important to our thesis, are,
as is well known, forgeries of the seventh, sixth, and fifth centuries B.C., brilliant workings of brightly colored strands gathered
from a scatter of places and periods.[2] In Genesis, for example,
the first and second chapters tell different creation stories; the

---

[1] Much of this information may be found in the Bampton Lectures of Alfred
Guillaume, *Prophecy and Divination among the Hebrews and Other Semites* (New
York: Harper, 1938). This chapter owes a particular debt to Guillaume's richness
of discussion of these matters.

[2] In matters of dating, authorship, and other exegetical material on the Old
Testament here and elsewhere in this chapter, I have relied on several authorities but
primarily the respective articles in the *Encyclopaedia Britannica*.

story of the flood is a monotheistic rewrite of old Sumerian inscriptions;[3] the story of Jacob may well date to before 1000 B.C.,
but that of Joseph, his supposed son, on the very next pages
comes from at least 500 years later.[4] It had all begun with the
discovery of the manuscript of Deuteronomy in Jerusalem in 621
B.C. by King Josiah, after he ordered the temple cleaned and
cleared of its remaining bicameral rites. And Khabiru history,
like a nomad staggering into a huge inheritance, put on these rich
clothes, some not its own, and belted it all together with some
imaginative ancestry. It is thus a question whether the use of
this variegated material as evidence for any theory of mind whatever is even permissible.

Amos and Ecclesiastes Compared

Let me first address such skeptics. As I have said, most of the
books of the Old Testament were woven together from various
sources from various centuries. But some of the books are considered pure in the sense of not being compilations, but being
pretty much all of one piece, mostly what they say they are, and
to these a thoroughly accurate date can be attached. If we confine ourselves for the moment to these books, and compare the
oldest of them with the most recent, we have a fairly authentic
comparison which should give us evidence one way or another.
Among these pure books, the oldest is Amos, dating from the
eighth century B.C., and the most recent is Ecclesiastes, from the
second century B.C. They are both short books, and I hope that
you will turn to them before reading on, that you may for yourself sense authentically this difference between an almost bicameral man and a subjective conscious man.

For this evidence is dramatically in agreement with the hy-

[3] Alexander Heidel, *The Gilgamesh Epic and Old Testament Parallels*, 2nd ed.
(Chicago: University of Chicago Press, 1949), p. 224ff.

[4] Donald B. Redford, *A Study of the Biblical Story of Joseph, Genesis 37–50*
(Leiden: Brill, 1970). The original may be a secular story from Mesopotamia on the
art of divination.

pothesis. Amos is almost pure bicameral speech, heard by an illiterate desert herdsman, and dictated to a scribe. In Ecclesiastes, in contrast, god is rarely mentioned, let alone ever speaking to its educated author. And even these mentions are considered by some scholars to be later interpolations, to allow this magnificent writing into the canon.

In Amos there are no words for mind or think or feel or understand or anything similar whatever; Amos never ponders anything in his heart; he can't; he would not know what it meant. In the few times he refers to himself, he is abrupt and informative without qualification; he is no prophet, but a mere "gatherer of sycamore fruit"; he does not consciously think before he speaks; in fact, he does not think as we do at all: his thought is done for him. He feels his bicameral voice about to speak and shushes those about him with a "Thus speaks the Lord!" and follows with an angry forceful speech which he probably does not understand himself.

Ecclesiastes is the opposite on all these points. He ponders things as deep in the paraphrands of his hypostatic heart as is possible. And who but a very subjective man could say, "Vanity of vanities, all is vanity," (1:2), or say that he *sees* that wisdom excels folly (2:13). One has to have an analog 'I' surveying a mind-space to so *see*. And the famous third chapter, "To everything there is a season, and a time to every purpose under heaven . . ." is precisely the spatialization of time, its spreading out in mind-space, so characteristic of consciousness as we saw in I.2. Ecclesiastes thinks, considers, is constantly comparing one thing and another, and making brilliant metaphors as he does so. Amos uses external divination, Ecclesiastes never. Amos is fiercely righteous, absolutely assured, nobly rude, speaking a blustering god-speech with the unconscious rhetoric of an Achilles or a Hammurabi. Ecclesiastes would be an excellent fireside friend, mellow, kindly, concerned, hesitant, surveying all of life in a way that would have been impossible for Amos.

These then are the extremes in the Old Testament. Similar

comparisons can be made with other early and late books, or early and late parts of the same book, all revealing the same pattern, which is difficult to account for apart from the theory of the bicameral mind.

Some Observations on the Pentateuch

We are so used to the wonderful stories of the first five books specifically that it is almost impossible for us to see them freshly for what they are. Indeed, in trying to do so, whatever our religious backgrounds, we feel, if not blasphemous, at least disrespectful to the profoundest meanings of others. Such disrespect is certainly not my intention, but it is only by a cold unworshipful reading of these powerful pages that we can appreciate the magnitude of the mental struggle that followed the breakdown of the bicameral mind.

Why were these books put together? The first thing to realize is that the very motive behind their composition around Deuteronomy at this time was the nostalgic anguish for the lost bicamerality of a subjectively conscious people. This is what religion is. And it was done just as the voice of Yahweh in particular was not being heard with any great clarity or frequency. Whatever their sources, the stories themselves, as they have been arranged, reflect human psychologies from the ninth century up to the fifth century B.C., the period during which there is progressively less and less bicamerality.

The Elohim. Another observation I would like to make concerns that very important word which governs the whole first chapter of Genesis, *elohim*. It is usually incorrectly translated in the singular as God. 'Elohim' is a plural form; it can be used collectively taking a singular verb, or as a regular plural taking a plural verb. It comes from the root of 'to be powerful', and better translations of 'elohim' might be the great ones, the prominent ones, the majesties, the judges, the mighty ones, etc.

From the point of view of the present theory, it is clear that elohim is a general term referring to the voice-visions of the bicameral mind. The creation story of the first chapter of Genesis is thus a rationalization of the bicameral voices at the edge of subjectivity. "In the beginning the voices created heaven and earth." Taken as such, it becomes a more general myth that could have been indigenous to all of the ancient bicameral civilizations.

He-who-is. At the particular time in history that we pick up the story as the Pentateuch has put it together, there are only a few remaining elohim in contrast to the large number that probably previously existed. The most important is one recognized as Yahweh, which among several possibilities is most often translated as He-who-is.[5] Evidently one particular group of the Khabiru, as the prophetic subjective age was approaching, was following only the voice of He-who-is, and rewrote the elohim creation story in a much warmer and more human way, making He-who-is the only real *elohah*. And this becomes the creation story as told from Genesis 2:4 et seq. And these two stories then interweave with other elements from other sources to form the first books of the Bible.

Other elohim are occasionally mentioned throughout the older parts of the Old Testament. The most important of them is Ba'al, usually translated as the Owner. In the Canaan of the times, there were many Owners, one to each village, in the same way that many Catholic cities today have their own Virgin Marys, and yet they are all the same one.

[5] The derivation of Exodus 3:14, that Yahweh means I AM THAT I AM, is regarded by most scholars as folk entomology, as if somebody should claim that the derivation of Manhattan came from a man on the island with a hat on. More serious scholarship traces the name back to an epithet, such as he who casts down or the Downcaster. But the sense of the majority, including the Septuagint and Latin Vulgate, seems to be more in line with He-who-is. Cf. William Gesenius, *Hebrew and English Lexicon of the Old Testament*, E. Robinson, trans., F. Brown, ed. (Oxford: Clarendon Press, 1952), p. 218. I must ask the forbearance of professional scholars for my inconsistency in straining for the English here while keeping other terms such as elohim and nabi in the Hebrew. My purpose is the defamiliarization which I feel is essential for my main point.

Paradise Lost. A further observation could be made upon the story of the Fall and how it is possible to look upon it as a myth of the breakdown of the bicameral mind. The Hebrew *arum*, meaning crafty or deceitful, surely a conscious subjective word, is only used three or four times throughout the entire Old Testament. It is here used to describe the source of the temptation. The ability to deceive, we remember, is one of the hallmarks of consciousness. The serpent promises that "you shall be like the elohim themselves, knowing good and evil" (Genesis 3:5), qualities that only subjective conscious man is capable of. And when these first humans had eaten of the tree of knowledge, suddenly "the eyes of them both were opened," their analog eyes in their metaphored mind-space, "and they knew that they were naked" (Genesis 3:7), or had autoscopic visions and were narratizing, seeing themselves as others see them.[6] And so is their sorrow "greatly multipled" (Genesis 3:16) and they are cast out from the garden where He-who-is could be seen and talked with like another man.

As a narratization of the breakdown of the bicameral mind and the coming of consciousness, the story should be rationalistically contrasted with the Odyssey as discussed in the previous chapter. But the problems are similar, as is the awe we should feel toward its unknown composition.

The Nabiim who naba. The Hebrew word *nabi*,[7] which has been misleadingly translated by the Greek designation of 'prophet', presents an extremely interesting difficulty. To prophesy in its modern connotations is to foretell the future, but this is not what is indicated by the verb *naba*, whose practitioners were the nabiim (plural of nabi). These terms come from a group of cognate words which have nothing to do with time, but rather

---

[6] It is interesting in this connection to read Maimonides, *Guide of the Perplexed*, I:2.

[7] Transliteration from Hebrew into English is always misleading. Perhaps a better case here might be made for *nbi* or *nvi*. That its meaning was ambiguous even at the time seems to be indicated in I Samuel 9:9. See also John L. McKenzie, *A Theology of the Old Testament* (New York: Doubleday, 1974), p. 85.

with flowing and becoming bright. Thus we may think of a nabi as one who metaphorically was flowing forth or welling up with speech and visions. They were transitional men, partly subjective and partly bicameral. And once the bright torrent was released and the call came, the nabi must deliver his bicameral message, however unsuspecting (Amos 7:14-15), however unworthy the nabi felt (Exodus 3:11; Isaiah 6; Jeremiah 1:6), however distrustful at times of his own hearing (Jeremiah 20:7-10). What does it feel like to be a nabi at the beginning of one of his bicameral periods? Like a red hot coal in one's mouth (Isaiah 6:7) or a raging fire shut up in one's bones that cannot be contained (Jeremiah 20:9) and that only the flowing forth of divine speech can quench.

The story of the nabiim can be told in two ways. One is external, tracing out their early role and the acceptance of their leadership to their massacre and total suppression in about the fourth century B.C. But as evidence for the theory in this book, it is more instructive to look at the matter from the internal point of view, the changes in the bicameral experience itself. These changes are: the gradual loss of the visual component, the growing inconsistency of the voices in different persons, and the increasing inconsistency within the same person, until the voices of the elohim vanish from history. I shall take each of these up in turn.

The Loss of the Visual Component

In the true bicameral period, there was usually a visual component to the hallucinated voice, either itself hallucinated or as the statue in front of which one listened. The quality and frequency of the visual component certainly varied from one culture to another, as can be indicated by the presence of hallucinogenic statuary in some cultures and not in others.

If only because its sources are so chronologically diverse, it is somewhat astonishing to find the Pentateuch consistently and successively describing the loss of this visual component. In the beginning, He-who-is is a visual physical presence, the duplicate of his creation. He walks in his garden at the cool of the day, talking to his recent creation, Adam. He is present and visible at the sacrifice of Cain and Abel, shuts the door of Noah's Ark with his own hand, speaks with Abraham at Sichem, Bethel, and Hebron, and scuffles all night with Jacob like a hoodlum.

But by the time of Moses, the visual component is very different. Only in a single instance does Moses speak with He-who-is "face to face, as a man speaketh to his friend" (Exodus 33:11). And another time, there is a group hallucination when Moses and the seventy elders all see He-who-is at a distance standing on sapphire pavement (Exodus 24:9-10). But in all the other instances, the hallucinated meetings are less intimate. Visually, He-who-is is a burning bush, or a cloud, or a huge pillar of fire. And as visually the bicameral experience recedes into the thick darkness, where thunders and lightnings and driving clouds of dense blackness crowd in on the inaccessible heights of Sinai, we are approaching the greatest teaching of the entire Old Testament, that, as this last of the elohim loses his hallucinatory properties, and is no longer an inaccessible voice in the nervous system of a few semi-bicameral men, and becomes something written upon tablets, he becomes law, something unchanging, approachable by all, something relating to all men equally, king and shepherd, universal and transcendent.

Moses himself reacts to this loss of the visual quality by hiding his face from a supposed brilliance. At other times, his bicameral voice itself rationalizes the loss of its visual hallucinatory components by saying to Moses, "No man shall see me and live . . . I will put thee in a cleft of rock, and will cover thee with my hand while I pass by: and I will take away mine hand, and thou shalt see my back parts; but my face shall not be seen" (Exodus 33:20-23).

The very conception of a cupboard called the ark, for some tablets of written word as a replacement for an hallucinogenic image of a more usual kind, like a golden calf, is illustrative of the same point. The importance of writing in the breakdown of the bicameral voices is tremendously important. What had to be spoken is now silent and carved upon a stone to be taken in visually.

After the Pentateuch, the bicameral voice retreats even further. When the writer of Deuteronomy (34:10) says that no nabi has been like Moses "whom He-who-is knew face to face," he is indicating the loss of the bicameral mind. The voices are heard less frequently and less conversationally. Joshua is more spoken to by his voice than speaking with it; and, halfway between bicamerality and subjectivity, he has to draw lots to make decisions.

Inconsistency Between Persons

In the bicameral period, the strict hierarchy of society, the settled geography of its limits, its ziggurats, temples, and statuary, and the common upbringing of its citizens, all co-operated in the organization of different men's bicameral voices into a stable hierarchy. Whose bicameral voice was the correct one was immediately decided by that hierarchy, and the recognition signals as to which god was speaking were known by everyone and reinforced by priests.

But with the breakdown of bicamerality, particularly when a previously bicameral people has become nomadic as in the Exodus, the voices will begin to say different things to different people and the problem of authority becomes a considerable difficulty. Something of the sort might be referred to in Numbers 12:1–2, where Miriam, Aaron, and Moses, who all hear the voice of He-who-is, are not sure which is the most authentic.

But the problem is much more acute in the later books, particu-

tween the remaining bicameral voices.
ᴇ that he recognizes as the Owner to
but his son Gideon hears a voice he
ch tells him to tear down his father's
d another to himself (Judges 6:25-
emaining elohim is the direct and
ᴗᴗᴗ disorganization.

ᴗᴗᴄɴ a dissonance of bicameral voices in this unorganized
breakdown period inaugurates the importance of signs or magical
proofs as to which voice is valid. Thus Moses is constantly compelled to produce magical proofs of his mission. Such signs, of
course, continue all through the first millennium even into present times. The miracles that today are required as criteria of
sainthood are of precisely the same order as when Moses hallucinates his rod into a serpent and back again, or his healthy hand
into a leprous one and back (Exodus 4:1-7).

Some of our present-day enjoyment of magic and prestidigita-
tion is possibly a holdover from this desire for signs, in which in
some part of ourselves we are enjoying the thrill of recognizing
the magician as a possible bicameral authority.

And if there are no signs, what then? In the seventh century
B.C., this is particularly the problem of Jeremiah, the illiterate
wailer at the wall of Israel's iniquity. Even though he has had the
sign of the hand of He-who-is upon him (1:9; 25:17) has heard
the word of He-who-is continually like a fire in his bones, and has
been sent (23:21, 32, etc.), yet still he is unsure: whose voice is
the right one? "Wilt thou be altogether unto me as a liar?"
Jeremiah mistrustfully jabs back at his bicameral voice (15:19).
But on this point, it is sure in its answering. It breaks down what
authority Jeremiah's rational consciousness may have had, and
commands him to denounce all other voices. Chapter 28 is a
particular example, with the somewhat ridiculous competition
between Hananiah and Jeremiah as to whose bicameral voice is
the right one. And it was only the death of Hananiah two months

later that was the sign of which to choose. Had Jeren.
we would probably have had the Book of Hananiah instea
competitor's.

Inconsistency Within Persons

In the absence of a social hierarchy that provides stability ε
recognitions, the bicameral voices not only become inconsist
among persons, but inconsistent within the same person as we
Particularly in the Pentateuch, the bicameral voice is often
petty and foot-stampingly petulant as any human tyrant und
questioning. "I will be gracious to whom I will be gracious, an
will show mercy on whom I will show mercy." (Exodus 33:19)
There is no question of virtue or of justice. So He-who-is prefer
Abel to Cain, slays Er, the first-born of Judah, having taken a
dislike to him, first tells Abraham to beget a son, and then later
orders him to kill the son, even as criminal psychotics might be
directed today. Similarly, the bicameral voice of Moses possibly
has a sudden impulse to kill him (Exodus 4:24) for no reason at
all.

This same inconsistency is found in the non-Israelite prophet,
Balaam. His bicameral voice first tells him not to go with the
princes of Moab (Numbers 22:12), then reverses itself (22:20).
Then when Balaam obeys, it is furious. Then a visual-auditory
hallucination out to kill Balaam blocks his way, but then this too
reverses its commands (Numbers 22:35). Also in the self-
recriminating category is the self-punishing voice of the ash-
faced nabi who tries to get passersby to punch him because his
voice commands him to (I Kings 20:35-38). And also, the "nabi
from Judah" whose bicameral voice drives him out of the city and
tries to starve him (1 Kings 13, 9-17). All of these inconsistent
voices are coming close to the voices heard by schizophrenics
which we noted in Chapter 4 of Book I.

*   *   *

Divination by Gods

The deciding things by casting *gorals* or lots, probably throwing dice, bones, or beans, runs through much of the Old Testament. As we saw in II.4 of this essay, it is the making of an analog god. The *goral* by metaphor becomes the word of god deciding lands and tribes, what to do or whom to destroy, taking the place of the older bicameral authority. As mentioned earlier, it is a help in appreciating how authoritative such practices could be when we realize that there was no concept of chance until well into the subjective eras.

But of much greater interest is the occurrence of the spontaneous divination from immediate sensory experience that in the end becomes the subjective conscious mind. Its interest here is because it begins not in the man-side of the bicameral mind but in the bicameral voices themselves.

It is, then, another way that the bicameral voices show their uncertainty when they too, like men, turn to divination, and need to be primed or instigated. In the ninth century B.C., the voice of one of the nabiim before Ahab divines by metaphor from a pair of horns how an army may be defeated (I Kings 22:11). The bicameral voice of Jeremiah several times takes what he, Jeremiah, is looking at and divines from it what to say. When he sees a boiling wind-blown pot facing north, He-who-is metaphorizes it into an evil invasion blowing down from the north, consuming all before it like a fire driven by the wind (Jeremiah 1:13-15). When he sees two baskets of figs, one good and one bad, his right hemisphere has He-who-is speaking about picking good and bad people (Jeremiah 24:1-10). And when Amos sees a builder judging the straightness of a wall by holding a plumb line to it, his mind hallucinates the builder into He-who-is, who then metaphorizes the act into judging people by their righteousness (Amos 7:8).

Particularly when spontaneous divinations are being made by

gods (who after all cannot perform other types of divination), puns may 'seed' the analogy. Thus, when Amos stands looking at a basket of summer fruit, his bicameral voice puns over on the Hebrew *qayits* (summer fruit) to *qets* (end) and starts talking about the end of Israel (Amos 8:1-2). Or when Jeremiah sees an almond branch (*shaqed*), his bicameral voice says it will watch over him (*shaqad*) because the Hebrew words for the two are similar (Jeremiah 1:11-12).

The Book of I Samuel

The Book of I Samuel is an instructive register of all this, and a reading of it gives one the feeling of what it was like in this partly bicameral, partly subjective world as the first millennium B.C. moved into consciousness. Represented across its intriguing chapters is almost the entire spectrum of transition mentalities in what is perhaps the first written tragedy in literature. Bicamerality in a rather decadent form is represented in the wild gangs of nabiim, the winnowed-out bicameral chaff of the Khabiru that we spoke of earlier in this chapter, roaming outside the cities in the hills, speaking the voices they hear within themselves but believe to come from outside them, answering the voices, using music and drums to increase their excitement.

Partly bicameral is the boy Samuel, prodded from sleep by a voice he is taught is the voice of He-who-is, encouraged at the critical age and trained into the bicameral mode by the old priest Eli, and then acknowledged from Dan to Beersheba as the medium of He-who-is. Though even Samuel must at times stoop to divining, as he does from his own torn garment (15:27-29).

Next in bicamerality is David, whom Samuel chooses from all the sons of Jesse in a bicameral manner, and who is only so bicameral as to obtain short sharp "Go up"s from He-who-is. His subjective consciousness is demonstrated in his ability to deceive Achish (I Samuel 21:13). And then Jonathan, subjectively able to deceive his father, but having to rely on cledonomancy, or divining by first words spoken by someone, for military decisions (14:8-13). That idols were common in the period is shown by the casual reference to what must have been a life-sized "image" that, with the help of some goat hair, is made to resemble David in bed (19:13). The casual presence of such an idol in David's house may point to some common hallucinogenic practice of the time that has been suppressed from the text.

And finally, the subjective Saul, the gaunt bewildered country boy whisked into politics at the irrational behest of Samuel's bicameral voice, trying to be bicameral himself by joining a band of the wild nabiim until he, too, to the throbbing of drums and strumming zithers, feels he hears the divine voices (10:5). But so unconvincing are these to his consciousness that, even with the three confirmed signs, he tries to hide from his destiny. Subjective Saul seeks wildly about him for what to do. A new situation, as when the irresponsible Samuel does not keep an appointment, with the Israelites hoveled up in caves, the Philistines knotting together against him, and he tries to force a voice with burnt offerings (13:12), only to be called foolish by the tardy Samuel. And Saul building an altar to He-who-is, whom he has never heard, to ask it questions in vain (14:37). Why doesn't the god speak to him? Saul, divining by lot the supposed culprit that must be the cause of the divine silence, and, obedient to his divination, even though it is his own son, condemning him to death. But even that must be wrong, because his people rebel and refuse to carry out the execution — a behavior impossible in bicameral times. And Saul, too consciously kind to his enemies for Samuel's archaic hallucination. And when Saul's jealousy of David and of his son's love for David reaches its extremity, suddenly losing his conscious mind, becoming bicameral, stripping off his clothes, naba-ing with the bicameral men of the hills (19:23-24). But then when such nabiim cannot tell him what to do, driving them along with other bicameral wizards out of the

city (28:3), seeking some divine certainty in dreams or in gazing
into crystal (if we may translate *urim* as such) (28:6). And
despairing Saul, at the end of his consciousness, disguising himself, something only a subjective man could do, and consulting at
night that last resort, the Witch of Endor, or rather the bicameral
voice that takes possession of her, as confounded conscious Saul
grovels before it, crying that he knows not what to do, and then
hears from the weird woman's lips what he takes to be the dead
Samuel's words, that he will die and Israel will fall (28:19).
And then, when the Philistines have all but captured the remnant of Israel's army, his sons and hopes all slain, the committing
of that most terrible subjective act, the first in history — suicide,
to be followed immediately by the second, that of his armor
bearer.

The date of the story is the eleventh century B.C.; of the
writing of it, the sixth century B.C.; of the psychology of it, therefore, perhaps the eighth century B.C.

The Idols of the Khabiru

As holdovers from the bicameral period are the hallucinogenic
statuary that are mentioned throughout the Old Testament. As
might be expected in this late stage of civilization, there are many
kinds. While there are some general terms for idols, such as the
elil, which is Isaiah's word for them, or *matstsebah* for anything
set up on a pillar or altar, it is the more specific words which are
of greater interest.

The most important type of idol was the *tselem*, a cast or
molten statue usually fashioned with a graving tool, often of gold
or silver, made by a founder from melted money (Judges 17:4)
or melted jewelry (Exodus 32:4), and sometimes expensively
dressed (Ezekiel 16:17). Isaiah scoffingly describes their construction in Judah around 700 B.C. (44:12). They could be
images either of animals or of men. Sometimes the tselem may

have been just a head placed high on a pedestal or high altar (II Chronicles 14:3) or even the huge golden tselem which Nebuchadnezzar placed upon a pillar 90 feet high (Daniel 3:1). More often, they seemed to have been placed in an *asherah*, probably one of the wooden shrines hung with rich fabric that the King James scholars translated as "groves."

Next in importance seems to be the carved statue or *pesel*, of which very little is known. It was probably chiseled out of wood and was the same as the *atsab*, which is what the Philistines, who destroyed Saul's army, worshiped. After Saul's death and the defeat of Israel, the Philistines run to tell their *atsabim* first of their victory and then their people (I Samuel 31:9; I Chronicles 10:9). That they were painted gold or silver is indicated by several references in the Psalms, and that they were of wood by the fact that David in wreaking his revenge on the Philistines makes a bonfire out of them (II Samuel 5:21). There were also some kind of sun idols of unknown shape called *chammanim*, which seem also to have been set up on pedestals, since they are ordered cut down by Leviticus (26:30), Isaiah (27:9), and Ezekiel (6:6).

If not the most important, perhaps the most common hallucinogenic idol was the *terap*. We are told directly that a terap could seem to speak, since the king of Babylon at one point consults with several of them (Ezekiel 21:21). Sometimes they were probably small figurines, since Rachel can steal a group of prized *teraphim* (to use the Hebrew plural) from her furious father and hide them (Genesis 31:19). They also could be life-sized, since it is a terap that is substituted for the sleeping David (I Samuel 19:13). As we have already seen, the very casualness of this last reference seems to indicate that such teraphim were common enough around the houses of leaders. But in the hills, such idols must have been rare and highly prized. In Judges we are told of Micah, who builds a house of elohim containing a tselem, a pesel, a terap, and an *ephod*, the latter being usually an ornate ritual robe which, perhaps put over a frame, could be made into an idol. And these he calls his elohim, which are then stolen by the children of Dan (Judges: 17 and 18 passim). We would probably have more archaeological evidence of these hallucinogenic idols of the Hebrews today had not King Josiah had them all destroyed in 641 B.C. (II Chronicles 34: 3-7.

A further vestige from the bicameral era is the word *ob*, often translated as a "familiar spirit." "A man also or woman that have an *ob* . . . shall surely be put to death," says Leviticus (20:27). And similarly Saul drives out from Israel all those that had an ob (I Samuel 28:3). Even though an ob is something that one consults with (Deuteronomy, 18:11), it probably had no physical embodiment. It is always bracketed with wizards or witches, and thus probably refers to some bicameral voice that was not recognized by the Old Testament writers as religious. This word has so puzzled translators that when they found it in Job 32:19, they translated it absurdly as "bottle," when clearly the context is that of the young frustrated Elihu, who feels as if he had a bicameral voice about to burst forth into impatient speech like an overfull wineskin.

The Last of the Nabiim

We began this chapter with a consideration of the refugee situation in the Near East around the latter part of the second millennium B.C., and of the roving tribes uprooted from their lands by various catastrophes, some of them certainly bicameral and unable to move toward subjective consciousness. Probably in the editing of the historical books of the Old Testament, and the fitting of it together into one story in the sixth or fifth century B.C., a great deal has been suppressed. And among such items of information that we would like is a clear account of what happened to these last communities of bicameral men. Here and there through the Old Testament, they appear like sudden glimpses of a strange other world during these periods which historians have paid too little attention to.

Groups of bicameral men certainly persisted until the downfall of the Judean monarchy, but whether in association with other tribes or with any organization to their hallucinated voices in the form of gods, we don't know. They are often referred to as the "sons of nabiim," indicating that there was probably a strong genetic basis for this type of remaining bicamerality. It is, I think, the same genetic basis that remains with us as part of the etiology of schizophrenia.

Edgy kings consulted them. Ahab, king of Israel in 835 B.C., rounded up 400 of them like cattle to listen to their hue and clamor (I Kings 22:6). Later, in all his robes, he and the king of Judah sit on thrones just outside the gates of Samaria, and have hundreds of these poor bicameral men herded up to them, raving and copying each other even as schizophrenics in a back ward (I Kings 22:10).

What happened to them? From time to time, they were hunted down and exterminated like unwanted animals. Such a massacre in the ninth century B.C. seems to be referred to in I Kings 18:4, where out of some unknown, much larger number, Obadiah took a hundred nabiim and hid them in caves, and brought them bread and water until the massacre was over. Another such massacre is organized by Elijah a few years later (I Kings 18:40).

We hear no more of these bicameral groups thereafter. What remained for a few centuries more are the individual nabiim, men whose voices do not need the group support of other hallucinating men, men who can be partly subjective and yet still hear the bicameral voice. These are the famous nabiim whose bicameral messages we have already selectively touched upon: Amos, the gatherer of sycamore fruit, Jeremiah, staggering under his yoke from village to village, Ezekiel with his visions of lofty

thrones on wheels moving through the clouds, the several nabiim
whose religious agonies are ascribed to Isaiah. These of course
merely represent the handful of that much larger number whose
bicameral voices seemed to be most consistent with Deuteronomy. And then the voices are as a rule no longer actually heard.

In their place is the considered subjective thought of moral
teachers. Men still dreamed visions and heard dark speech perhaps. But Ecclesiastes and Ezra seek wisdom, not a god. They
study the law. They do not roam out into the wilderness "inquir-
ing of Yahweh." By 400 B.C., bicameral prophecy is dead. "The
nabiim shall be ashamed everyone of his visions." If parents
catch their children naba-ing or in dialogue with bicameral
voices, they are to kill them on the spot (Zechariah 13, 3-4).[8]
That is a severe injunction. If it was carried out, it is an evolutionary selection which helped move the gene pool of humanity
toward subjectivity.

Scholars have long debated the reason for the decline and fall
of prophecy in the post-exilic period of Judaism. They have
suggested that the nabiim had done their work, and there was no
more need of them. Or they have said that there was a danger
that it would sink into a cult. Others that it was the corruption of
the Israelites by the Babylonians, who were by this time as omen-
ridden from the cradle to the grave as any nation could be. All of
these are partly true, but the plainer fact to me is that the decline
of prophecy is part of that much larger phenomenon going on
elsewhere in the world, the loss of the bicameral mind.

Once one has read through the Old Testament from this point
of view, the entire succession of works becomes majestically and
wonderfully the birth pangs of our subjective consciousness. No
other literature has recorded this absolutely important event at

---

[8] The date of Zechariah is around 520 B.C., but scholars are agreed that the final
chapters of the book ascribed to him are later additions from some other source. The
date of this injunction is probably the fourth or third century B.C.

such length or with such fullness. Chinese literature jumps into subjectivity in the teaching of Confucius with little before it. Indian hurtles from the bicameral Veda into the ultra subjective Upanishads, neither of which are as authentic to their times. Greek literature, like a series of steppingstones from the Iliad to the Odyssey and across the broken fragments of Sappho and Solon toward Plato, is the next best record, but is still too incomplete. And Egypt is relatively silent. While the Old Testament, even as it is hedged with great historical problems of accuracy, still remains the richest source for our knowledge of what the transition period was like. It is essentially the story of the loss of the bicameral mind, the slow retreat into silence of the remaining elohim, the confusion and tragic violence which ensue, and the search for them again in vain among its prophets until a substitute is found in right action.

But the mind is still haunted with its old unconscious ways; it broods on lost authorities; and the yearning, the deep and hollowing yearning for divine volition and service is with us still.

> As the stag pants after the waterbrooks,
> So pants my mind after you, O gods!
> My mind thirsts for gods! for living gods!
> When shall I come face to face with gods?
> — Psalm 42

BOOK THREE

Vestiges of the Bicameral Mind
in the Modern World

CHAPTER 1

The Quest for Authorization

W E ARE NOW at last in a position where we can look back and see the history of mankind on this planet in its proper values for the first time and understand some of the chief features of the last three millennia as vestiges of a previous mentality. Our view of human history here must be that of a furthest grandeur. We must try to see man against his entire evolutionary background, where his civilizations, including our own, are but as mountain peaks in a particular range against the sky, and from which we must force ourselves into an intellectual distance so that we see its contours aright. And from this prospect, a millennium is an exceedingly short period of time for so fundamental a change as from bicamerality to consciousness.

We, at the end of the second millennium A.D., are still in a sense deep in this transition to a new mentality. And all about us lie the remnants of our recent bicameral past. We have our houses of gods which record our births, define us, marry us, and bury us, receive our confessions and intercede with the gods to forgive us our trespasses. Our laws are based upon values which without their divine pendancy would be empty and unenforceable. Our national mottoes and hymns of state are usually divine invocations. Our kings, presidents, judges, and officers begin their tenures with oaths to the now silent deities taken upon the writings of those who have last heard them.

The most obvious and important carry-over from the previous

mentality is thus our religious heritage in all its labyrinthine beauty and variety of forms. The overwhelming importance of religion both in general world history and in the history of the average world individual is of course very clear from any objective standpoint, even though a scientific view of man often seems embarrassed at acknowledging this most obvious fact. For in spite of all that rationalist materialist science has implied since the Scientific Revolution, mankind as a whole has not, does not, and perhaps cannot relinquish his fascination with some human type of relationship to a greater and wholly other, some *mysterium tremendum* with powers and intelligences beyond all left hemispheric categories, something necessarily indefinite and unclear, to be approached and felt in awe and wonder and almost speechless worship, rather than in clear conception, something that for modern religious people communicates in truths of feeling, rather than in what can be verbalized by the left hemisphere, and so what in our time can be more truly felt when least named, a patterning of self and numinous other from which, in times of our darkest distress, *none* of us can escape — even as the infinitely milder distress of decision-making brought out that relationship three millennia ago.

There are many things that could be said at this point — many. A full discussion here would specify how the attempted reformation of Judaism by Jesus can be construed as a necessarily new religion for conscious men rather than bicameral men. Behavior now must be changed from within the new consciousness rather than from Mosaic laws carving behavior from without. Sin and penance are now within conscious desire and conscious contrition, rather than in the external behaviors of the decalogue and the penances of temple sacrifice and community punishment. The divine kingdom to be regained is psychological not physical. It is metaphorical not literal. It is 'within' not *in extenso*.

But even the history of Christianity does not and cannot remain true to its originator. The development of the Christian Church returns again and again to this same longing for bicameral absolutes, away from the difficult inner kingdoms of *agape* to an external hierarchy reaching through a cloud of miracle and infallibility to an archaic authorization in an extended heaven. In previous chapters I have often paused to point out various parallels between ancient bicameral practices and modern religious ones, and I shall not labor such comparisons here.

Also beyond the purview of the present book is a full exploration of the way that the more secular developments of the last three millennia are related to their emergence from a different mentality. I am thinking here of the history of logic and conscious reasoning from the Greek development of Logos to modern computers, and of the spectacular historical pageant of philosophy, with its efforts to find a metaphor of all existence in which we may find some conscious familiarity and so feel at home in the universe. I am thinking too of our struggles toward systems of ethics, of attempting with rational consciousness to find substitutes for our previous divine volition which could carry with them that obligation which at least could simulate our earlier obedience to hallucinated voices. And too of the cyclic history of politics, the gyres of our wavering attempts to make governments out of men instead of gods, secular systems of laws to perform that formerly divine function of binding us together into an order, a stability, and a commonweal.

These larger questions are the important ones. But here, in this chapter, I wish to introduce the issues of Book III by considering a handful of more ancient topics of lesser importance that are precise and clear carry-overs from the earlier mentality. My reason for doing so here is that these historical phenomena shed a needed and clarifying light back into some of the darker problems of Books I and II.

One distinguishing characteristic of such vestiges is that they are more obvious against the complexity of history the closer we are to the breakdown of the bicameral mind. The reason for this is quite clear. While the universal characteristics of the new consciousness, such as self-reference, mind-space, and narratization, can develop swiftly on the heels of new language construction, the larger contours of civilization, the huge landscape of culture against which this happens, can only change with geological slowness. The matter and technic of earlier ages of civilizations survive into the new eras uneroded, dragging with them the older outworn forms in which the new mentality must live.

But living also in these forms is a fervent search for what I shall call archaic authorization. After the collapse of the bicameral mind, the world is still in a sense governed by gods, by statements and laws and prescriptions carved on stelae or written on papyrus or remembered by old men, and dating back to bicameral times. But the dissonance is there. Why are the gods no longer heard and seen? The Psalms cry out for answers. And more assurances are needed than the relics of history or the paid insistences of priests. Something palpable, something direct, something immediate! Some sensible assurance that we are not alone, that the gods are just silent, not dead, that behind all this hesitant subjective groping about for signs of certainty, there is a certainty to be had.

Thus, as the slow withdrawing tide of divine voices and presences strands more and more of each population on the sands of subjective uncertainties, the variety of technique by which man attempts to make contact with his lost ocean of authority becomes extended. Prophets, poets, oracles, diviners, statue cults, mediums, astrologers, inspired saints, demon possession, tarot cards, Ouija boards, popes, and peyote all are the residue of bicamerality that was progressively narrowed down as uncertainties piled upon uncertainties. In this chapter and the next we shall examine some of these more archaic vestiges of the bicameral mind.

* * *

ORACLES

The most immediate carry-over of bicamerality is simply its per-petuation in certain persons, particularly itinerant prophets, which I have discussed in II.6, or those institutionalized as oracles, which I shall describe here. While there is a series of cuneiform tablets describing Assyrian oracles[1] dating from the seventh century B.C., and the even earlier oracle of Amon of Thebes in Egypt, it is really in Greece that we know this institu-tion best. Greek oracles were the central method of making important decisions for over a thousand years after the break-down of the bicameral mind. This fact is usually obscured by the strident rationalism of modern historians. Oracles were subjec-tivity's umbilical cord reaching back into the sustaining unsubjec-tive past.

The Oracle at Delphi

Coincidental with my metaphor is the fact that at the most famous oracle, that of Apollo at Delphi, there was a queer cone-like stone structure called the *omphalos* or navel. It stood at the reputed center of the earth. Here presided on certain days, or in some centuries every day throughout the year, a supreme priest-ess, or sometimes two or three in rotation, selected so far as we know on no particular basis (in Plutarch's day, in the first cen-tury B.C., she was the daughter of a poor farmer).[2] She first bathed and drank from a sacred brook, and then established contact with the god through his sacred tree, the laurel, much as conscious Assyrian kings are depicted being smeared by tree-cones in the hands of genii. She did this either by holding a

---

[1] Alfred Guillaume, *Prophecy and Divination among the Hebrews and Other Semites* (New York, Harper, 1938), p. 42ff.

[2] Plutarch, *Pyth. rac.* 22, 405C.

laurel branch, or by inhaling and fumigating herself with burnt laurel leaves (as Plutarch said), or perhaps by chewing the leaves (as Lucian insisted).

The replies to questions were given *at once*, without any reflection, and uninterruptedly. The exact manner of her announcements is still debated,[3] whether she was seated on a tripod, regarded as Apollo's ritual seat, or simply stood at an entrance to a cave. But the archaic references to her, from the fifth century on, all agree with the statement of Heraclitus that she spoke "from her frenzied mouth and with various contortions of her body." She was *entheos, plena deo*. Speaking through his priestess, but always in the first person, answering king or freeman, 'Apollo' commanded sites for new colonies (as he did for present-day Istanbul), decreed which nations were friends, which rulers best, which laws to enact, the causes of plagues or famines, the best trade routes, which of the proliferation of new cults, or music, or art should be recognized as agreeable to Apollo — all decided by these girls with their frenzied mouths.

Truly, this is astonishing! We have known of the Delphic Oracle so long from school texts that we coat it over with a shrugging usualness when we should not. How is it conceivable that simple rural girls could be trained to put themselves into a psychological state such that they could make decisions *at once* that ruled the world?

The obdurate rationalist simply scoffs *plena deo* indeed! Just as the mediums of our own times have always been exposed as frauds, so these so-called oracles were really performances manipulated by others in front of an illiterate peasantry for political or monetary ends.

But such a realpolitik attitude is doctrinaire at best. Possibly there was some chicanery in the oracle's last days, perhaps some bribery of the *prophetes*, those subsidiary priests or priestesses

---

[3] For an intriguing discussion of the whole matter, see E. R. Dodds, *The Greeks and the Irrational* (Berkeley: University of California Press, 1968).

who interpreted what the oracle meant. But earlier, to sustain so massive a fraud for an entire millennium through the most brilliant intellectual civilization the world had yet known is impossible, just impossible. Nor can it gibe with the complete absence of criticism of the oracle until the Roman period. Nor with the politically wise and often cynical Plato reverently calling Delphi "the interpreter of religion to all mankind."[4]

Another kind of explanation, really a quasi-explanation, still busied about with in the popular and sometimes professional literature, is biochemical. The trances were real, it says, but caused by vapors of some sort rising from a *casium* beneath the floor of the cave. But the French excavations of 1903 and more recent ones have shown distinctly that no such casium existed.[5]

Or else there might be a drug in the laurel that could have produced such an Apollonian effect. To test this, I have crushed laurel leaves and smoked quantities of them in a pipe and felt somewhat sick but no more inspired than usual. And chewed them as well for over an hour, and very distinctly felt more and more Jaynesian, alas, than Apollonian.[6] The glee with which external explanations are sought out for such phenomena simply indicates the resistance in some quarters to admitting that psychological phenomena of this type exist at all.

Rather, I suggest a quite different explanation. And for that purpose, I shall introduce here the notion of

The General Bicameral Paradigm

By this phrase, I mean an hypothesized structure behind a

[4] Plato, *Republic*, 4, 427B. We should also remember that Socrates derived some of what I am about to call his 'archaic authorization' from the oracle. See *Apology*, 20E.

[5] A. P. Oppé, "The Chasm at Delphi," *Journal of Historical Studies*, 1904, 24: 214f.

[6] I am grateful to EveLynn McGuinness for much in my life and here for acting as an observer, although her role was somewhat compromised both by her participation and a certain minimal reverence. Our negative result agrees with T. K. Oesterreich. See his *Possession, Demoniacal and Other*, English translation, 1930, p. 319, note 3.

large class of phenomena of diminished consciousness which I am interpreting as partial holdovers from our earlier mentality. The paradigm has four aspects:

> the *collective cognitive imperative*, or belief system, a culturally agreed-on expectancy or prescription which defines the particular form of a phenomenon and the roles to be acted out within that form;
>
> an *induction* or formally ritualized procedure whose function is the narrowing of consciousness by focusing attention on a small range of preoccupations;
>
> the *trance* itself, a response to both the preceding, characterized by a lessening of consciousness or its loss, the diminishing of the analog 'I,' or its loss, resulting in a role that is accepted, tolerated, or encouraged by the group; and
>
> the *archaic authorization* to which the trance is directed or related to, usually a god, but sometimes a person who is accepted by the individual and his culture as an authority over the individual, and who by the collective cognitive imperative is prescribed to be responsible for controlling the trance state.

Now, I do not mean these four aspects of the general bicameral paradigm to be considered as a temporal succession necessarily, although the induction and trance usually do follow each other. But the cognitive imperative and the archaic authorization pervade the whole thing. Moreover, there is a kind of balance or summation among these elements, such that when one of them is weak the others must be strong for the phenomena to occur. Thus, as through time, particularly in the millennium following the beginning of consciousness, the collective cognitive imperative becomes weaker (that is, the general population tends toward skepticism about the archaic authorization), we find a rising emphasis on and complication of the induction procedures, as well as the trance state itself becoming more profound.

By calling the general bicameral paradigm a structure, I not only mean a logical structure into which these phenomena can be analyzed, but also some presently unspecified neurological structure or relationships between areas of the brain, perhaps something like the model for the bicameral mind presented in I.5. We might thus expect that all of the phenomena mentioned in Book III in some way involve right hemispheric function in a way that is different from ordinary conscious life. It is even possible that in some of these phenomena we have a partial periodic right hemisphere dominance that can be considered as the neurological residue of nine millennia of selection for the bicameral mind.

The application of this general bicameral paradigm to the oracle at Delphi is obvious: the elaborate induction procedures, the trance in which consciousness is lost, the ardently pursued authorization of Apollo. But it is the collective cognitive imperative or group belief or cultural prescription or expectancy (all of these terms indicating my meaning) which I wish to emphasize. The immensity of the cultural demand upon the entranced priestess cannot be overemphasized. The whole Greek world *believed*, and had for almost a millennium. As many as thirty-five thousand people a day from every part of the Mediterranean world might struggle by sea through the tiny port of Itéa that snuggles the receptive coast just below Delphi. And they, too, went through induction procedures, purifying themselves in the Castilian spring, making offerings to Apollo and other gods as they persisted up the Sacred Way. In the latter centuries of the oracle, more than four thousand votive statues crowded this 220-yard-long climb up the side of Mount Parnassus to the temple of the oracle. It was, I suggest, this confluence of huge social prescription and expectancy, closer to definition than mere belief, which can account for the psychology of the oracle, for the at-once-ness of her answers. It was something before which any skepticism would be as impossible as for us to doubt that the speech of a radio originates in a studio that we cannot see. And it is something before which modern psychology must stand in awe.

To this causative expectancy should be added something about the natural scene itself. Oracles begin in localities with a specific awesomeness, natural formations of mountain or gorge, of hallucinogenic wind or waves, of symbolic gleamings and vistas, which I suggest are more conducive to occasioning right hemisphere activity than the analytic planes of everyday life. Perhaps we can say that the geography of the bicameral mind in the first part of the first millennium B.C. was shrinking down into sites of awe and beauty where the voices of gods could still be heard.

Certainly the vast cliffs of Delphi move into such a suggestion and fill it fully: a towering caldron of blasted rock over which the sea winds howl and the salt mists cling, as if dreaming nature were twisting herself awake at awkward angles, falling away into a blue surf of shimmering olive leaves and the gray immortal sea.

(It is, however, difficult for us to appreciate such scenic awe today, so clouded is the purity of our response to landscape with our conscious 'inner' worlds and our experience with swift geographical change. Moreover, Delphi today is not quite as it was. Its five acres of broken columns, cheerful graffiti, camera-clicking tourists, and stumps of white marble over which heedless ants crawl indecisively, are not exactly the stuff of divine inspiration.)

Other Oracles

Particularly recommending such a cultural explanation of Delphi is the fact that there were similar if less important oracles throughout the civilized world at the time. Apollo had others: at Ptoa in Boeotia and at Branchidae and Patara in Asia Minor. At the latter, the Prophetess, as part of the induction, was locked into the temple at night for connubial union with her hallucinated god that she might better be his medium.[7] The great

[7] Herodotus, 1:182.

oracle at Claros had priests as mediums whose frenzies were visited by Tacitus in the first century A.D.[8] Pan had an oracle at Acacesium, but it became defunct early.[9] The golden oracle at Ephesus, famous for its enormous wealth, had tranced eunuchs as the mouthpieces of the goddess Artemis.[10] (The style of their vestments, incidentally, is still used today by the Greek Orthodox Church.) And the abnormal dancing on the tips of the toes of modern ballerinas is thought to derive from the dances before the altar of the goddess.[11] Anything opposite to the everyday can serve as a cue for the engagement of the general bicameral paradigm.

The voice of Zeus at Dodona must have been one of the oldest oracles, since Odysseus visited it to hear whether to return to Ithaca openly or by stealth.[12] It was at that time probably just a huge sacred oak tree and the Olympian voice was hallucinated from the wind trembling in its leaves, making one wonder if something similar took place among the Druids who held the oak holy. It is only in the fifth century B.C. that Zeus is no longer heard directly, and Dodona has a temple and a priestess who speaks for him in unconscious trances,[13] again conforming to the temporal sequence the bicameral theory would predict.

Not only the voices of gods, but also of dead kings, could still be heard bicamerally, as we have earlier suggested was the origin of gods themselves. Amphiaraus had been the heroic prince of Argos who had plunged to his death in a chasm in Boeotia, supposedly at the nudge of an angry Zeus. His voice was 'heard' from the chasm for centuries after, answering the problems of

---

[8] Tacitus, *Annales*, 2:54.

[9] Pausanias, *Description of Greece*, J. E. Fraser, trans. (London: Macmillan, 1898), 37:8.

[10] Charles Picard, *Ephese et Claros* (Paris: de Bocard, 1922).

[11] Louis Sechan, *La Dance Greque Antique* (Paris: de Bocard, 1930); and also Lincoln Kirstein, *The Book of the Dance* (Garden City: Garden City Publishing Co., 1942).

[12] *Odyssey*, 14:327; 19:296.

[13] Aelius Aristides, *Orationes*, 45:11.

his petitioners. But again as centuries passed, the 'voice' came to be hallucinated only by certain entranced priestesses who lived there. At that later time they did not so much answer questions as interpret the dreams of those who consulted the voice.[14]

In some ways the most interesting, however, from the hypothesis of the bicameral mind is the hallucinated voice of Trophonius at Lebadea, twenty miles east of Delphi. For it is the longest lasting of the direct 'voices' without intermediary priests or priestesses. The locale of the oracle even today bears some remnants of its ancient awesomeness, a meeting of three soaring precipices, of murmuring springs easing strongly out of the solemn ground and crawling submissively away into stony ravines. And up a little, where one ravine begins to wind into the heart of the mountain, there was once a carved-out cell-like pit in the rock that squeezed down into an ovenlike shrine over an underground flume.

When the collective imperative of the general bicameral paradigm is less, when belief and trust in such phenomena are waning with rationalism, and particularly when it is being applied not to a trained priestess but to any suppliant, the induction is longer and more intricate to compensate. And this is what occurred at Lebadea. Pausanias, the Roman traveler, described the elaborate induction procedure that he found there in A.D. 150.[15] After days of waiting and purification and omens and expectancy, he tells us how he was abruptly taken one night and bathed and anointed by two holy boys, then drank from Lethe's spring to forget who he was (the loss of the analog 'I'), then made to sip at the spring of Mnemosyne so as to remember later what was to be revealed (like a post-hypnotic suggestion). Then he was made to worship a secret image, then was dressed in holy linen, girded with sacred ribbons, and shod with special boots, and then only after more omens, if favorable, was finally inserted

---

[14] Pausanias, *Description of Greece*, 1, 34:5.
[15] Ibid., 9, 39:11.

down an impassive ladder into the devout pit with its dark torrent where the divine message grew swiftly articulate.

The Six Oracular Terms

As the Greek mind moves from the universally bicameral to the universally conscious, these oracular vestiges of the bicameral world and their authority change until they become more and more precarious and difficult to obtain. There is, I suggest, a loose pattern in all this, and that over the thousand years of their existence, oracles were in a continuing decadence which can be understood as six terms. These can be regarded as six steps down from the bicameral mind as its collective cognitive imperative grew weaker and weaker.

1. The *locality* oracle. Oracles began simply as specific locations where, because of some awesomeness of the surroundings, or some important incident or some hallucinogenic sound, waves, waters, or wind, suppliants, any suppliants, could still 'hear' a bicameral voice directly. Lebadea remained at this term, probably because of its remarkable induction.

2. The *prophet* oracle. Usually there then occurred a term where only certain persons, priests, or priestesses, could 'hear' the voice of the god at the locality.

3. The *trained prophet* oracle, when such persons, priests, or priestesses, could 'hear' only after long training and elaborate inductions. Up to this term, the person was still 'himself' and relayed the god's voice to others.

4. The *possessed* oracle. Then, from at least the fifth century B.C., came the term of possession, of the frenzied mouth and contorted body after even more training and more elaborate inductions.

5. The *interpreted possessed* oracle. As the cognitive imperative weakened, the words became garbled and had to be interpreted by auxiliary priests or priestesses who themselves had gone through induction procedures.

6. The *erratic* oracle. And then even this became difficult. The voices became fitful, the possessed prophet erratic, the interpretations impossible, and the oracle ended.

The oracle of Delphi endured longest. It is striking evidence for its supreme importance to the god-nostalgic subjectivity of Greece in its golden age that it lasted so long, particularly when it is recalled that in almost every invasion it sided with the invader: with Xerxes I in the early fifth century B.C., with Philip II in the fourth century B.C., and even in the Peloponnesian Wars, it spoke on the side of Sparta. Such the strength of bicameral phenomena in the forces of history. It even lived out its sad, hilarious, patriotic mocking by Euripides in the amphitheaters.

But by the first century A.D., Delphi had come to its sixth term. Bicamerality having receded further and further into the unremembered past, skepticism had overgrown belief. The mighty cultural cognitive imperative of the oracular was played out and shattered, and the thing with increasing frequency would not work. One such instance at Delphi is told by Plutarch in A.D. 60. The prophetess reluctantly attempted a trance, the omens being dreadful. She began to speak in a hoarse voice as if distressed, then appeared filled with a "dumb and evil spirit," and then ran screaming toward the entrance and fell down. Everyone else, including her *prophetes,* fled in terror. The report goes on that they found her partly recovered when they returned, but that she died within a few days.[16] As this was probably observed by a prophetes who was a personal friend of Plutarch's, we have no reason to doubt its authenticity.[17]

[16] Plutarch, *Def. Orac.,* 51, 438C.
[17] Dodds, *Greeks and the Irrational,* p. 72.

Yet even with these neurotic failures, Delphi was still consulted by the tradition-hungry Greece-haunted Romans. The last to do so was my namesake, the Emperor Julian who, following his namesake Julianus (who had written down from hallucinated gods his *Chaldaean Oracles*), was attempting to revive the ancient gods. As part of this personal quest for authorization, he tried to rehabilitate Delphi in A.D. 363, three years after it had been ransacked by Constantine. Through his remaining priestess, Apollo prophesied that he would never prophesy again. And the prophecy came true. The bicameral mind had come to one of its many ends.

Sibyls

The Age of Oracles occupies the entire millennium after the breakdown of the bicameral mind. And as it slowly dies away, there appear here and there what might be called amateur oracles, untrained and uninstitutionalized persons who spontaneously felt themselves possessed by gods. Of course some simply spoke schizophrenic nonsense. Probably most. But others had an authenticity that could command belief. Among such were those few but unknown number of weird and wonderful women known as the Sibyls (from the Aeolic *sios* = god + *boule* = advice). In the first century B.C., Varro could count at least ten at one time around the Mediterranean world. But there were certainly others in more remote regions. They lived in solitude, sometimes in reverenced mountain shrines that were built for them, or in tufaceous subterranean caverns near the groan of the ocean, as did the great Cumaean Sibyl. Virgil had probably personally visited the latter around 40 B.C., when he described her frenzied laboring with a possessing Apollo in Book VI of the Aeneid.

Like oracles, the Sibyls were asked to make decisions on matters high and low up to the third century A.D. So gristled with moral fervor were their replies that even the early Christian Fathers and Hellenistic Jews bowed to them as prophets on a level with those of the Old Testament. The early Christian Church, in particular, used their prophecies (often forged) to buttress its own divine authenticity. Even a thousand years later, at the Vatican, four of the Sibyls were painted into prominent niches on the ceiling of the Sistine Chapel by Michelangelo. And even centuries later, copies of these muscular ladies with their oracular books open used to look down on the wondering present writer in a Unitarian Sunday school in New England. Such is the thirst of our institutions after authorization.

And when they too had ceased, when the gods no longer would inhabit living human forms in prophecy and oracle, mankind searches for other ways of taking up the slack, as it were, between heaven and earth. There are new religions, Christianity, Gnosticism, and Neo-Platonism. There are new orders of conduct to relate god-shorn men to the enormous conscious landscape of a now spatialized time, as in Stoicism and Epicureanism. There is an institutionalization and elaboration of divination beyond anything in Assyria, divination built into the political state officially to generate decisions on important matters. As the Greek civilizations had been anchored into the divine by oracles, so the Roman now is by auspices and augurers.

A Revival of Idols

But even these cannot fill the need of the common man for transcendence. Following the failure of oracles and prophets as if to replace them is an attempted revival of idols similar to those of bicameral times.

The great bicameral civilizations had, as we have seen, used a wide variety of effigies to help hallucinate bicameral voices. But when those voices ceased in the adjustment to subjective consciousness, all this was darkened. Most idols were destroyed.

Late bicameral kingdoms at the behest of their jealous gods had always smashed and burned the idols of opposing gods or kings. And the practice accelerated when the idols were no longer heard and worshiped. King Josiah, in the seventh century B.C., ordered all idols in his domain destroyed. The Old Testament is full of the destruction of idols, as well as imprecations on the heads of those who make new ones. By the middle of the first millennium B.C., idolatry is only here and there, fitful and unimportant.

Curiously, there is at this time a very minor cult of hallucinating from severed heads. Herodotus (4:26) speaks of the practice in the obscure Issedones of gilding a head and sacrificing to it. Cleomenes of Sparta is said to have preserved the head of Archonides in honey and consulted it before undertaking any important task. Several vases of the fourth century B.C. in Etruria depict scenes of persons interrogating oracular heads.[18] And the severed head of the rustic Carians which continues to 'speak' is mentioned derisively by Aristotle.[19] And this is about all. Thus, after subjective consciousness is firmly established, the practice of hallucinating from idols is only sporadically present.

But as we approach the beginning of the Christian era, with the oracles mocked into silence, we have a very true revival of idolatry. The temples that whitened the hills and cities of decadent Greece and ascendant Rome were now crammed with more and more statues of gods. By the first century A.D., the Apostle Paul despairingly found Athens full of idols (Acts 17), and Pausanias, whom we met a few pages ago at Lebadea, described them as being simply everywhere on his travels and of every conceivable sort: marble and ivory, gilded and painted, life-sized and some two or three stories high.

Did such idols 'speak' to their worshipers? There is no doubt

---

[18] See John Cohen, "Human Robots and Computer Art," *History Today*, 1970, 8:562.

[19] *De Partibus Animalium*, III, 10:9-12.

that this sometimes occurred, just as in bicameral times. But in general in the subjective era, it seems very doubtful that this happened spontaneously very often. For otherwise there would not have been the rising attention to artificial means, magical and chemical, for obtaining hallucinated messages from stone and ivory gods. And here again we see the entrance into history of the general bicameral paradigm: collective cognitive imperative, induction, trance, and archaic authorization.

In Egypt, where the breaking point between bicamerality and subjectivity is far less sharp than in more volatile nations, there was the development of the so-called Hermetic literature. This is a series of papyri describing various induction procedures that came into being at the edge of bicameral certainty and spread over the conscious world. In one of them, there is a dialogue called the *Asclepius* (after the Greek god of healing) that describes the art of imprisoning the souls of demons or of angels in statues with the help of herbs, gems, and odors, such that the statue could speak and prophesy.[20] In other papyri, there are still other recipes for constructing such images and animating them, such as when images are to be hollow so as to enclose a magic name inscribed on gold leaf.

By the first century A.D., this practice had spread over most of the civilized world. In Greece, rumors broke into legends over the miraculous behavior of public cult statues. In Rome, Nero prized a statue which warned him of conspiracies.[21] Apuleius was accused of possessing one.[22] So common were hallucinogenic idols by the second century A.D. that Lucian in his *Philopseudes* satirized the belief in them. And Iamblichus, the Neo-Platonist apostle of *theurgy*, as it was called in his *Peri agalmaton*, tried to

[20] The records of the various temples to the medical god Asclepius are full of reported diagnoses and therapeutic directives told to the sick as they slept there. These have been collected and translated by E. J. and L. Edelstein, *Asclepius: A Collection and Interpretation of the Testimonies*, 2 vols., 1945.

[21] Suetonius, *Nero*, 56.

[22] Apuleius, *Apol.*, 63.

prove "that idols are divine and filled with the divine presence," establishing a vogue for such idols against the fuming execration of Christian critics. His disciples obtained omens of every sort and distinction from idols. One hallucinator boasted he could make a statue of Hecate laugh and cause the torches in her hand to light up. And another feels he can tell whether a statue is animate or inanimate by the sensation it gives him. Even Cyprian, the good gray Bishop of Carthage, complained in the third century of the "spirits that lurk under statues and consecrated images."[23] The whole civilized world, in this effort to recall the bicameral mind after the failure of oracles and prophecy, was filled with epiphanies of statues of every sort and description in this remarkable revival of idolatry.

How was all this believable? Since this is well into the subjective era, when men prided themselves on reason and common sense, and at last knew there were such experiences as false hallucinations, how was it possible that they could actually believe that statues embodied real gods? And really spoke?

Let us recall the almost universal belief of these centuries in an absolute dualism of mind and matter. Mind or soul or spirit or consciousness (all these were confused together) was a thing imposed from heaven on the bodily matter to give it life. All the newer religions of this era were allied about this point. And if a soul can be imposed on so fragile a thing as flesh to make it live, on a hurtable carcass that has to have vegetable and animal matter stuffed in one end and stenchfully excreted at another, a sense-pocked sinful vessel that the years wrinkle and the winds chafe and diseases cruelly hound, and that can be sliced off in a trice from the soul it holds by the same act that stabs an onion, how much more possible for life, divine life, to be imposed by heaven upon a statue of unbleeding beauty with a faultless and immaculate body of unwrinkling marble or diseaseless gold!

[23] Other instances are mentioned by E. R. Dodds, *Greeks and the Irrational*.

Here is Callistratus, for example, in the fourth century A.D., writing about an ivory and gold statue of the god Asclepius:

> Shall we admit that the divine spirit descends into human bodies, there to be even defiled by passions, and nevertheless not believe it in a case where there is no attendant engendering of evil? . . . for see how an image, after Art has portrayed in it a god, even passes over into the god himself! Matter though it is, it gives forth divine intelligence.[24]

And he and most of the world believed it.

The evidence for all this would be much more obvious today, had not Constantine in the fourth century, even like King Josiah in Israel one millennium earlier, sent his armies of Christian converts out with sledge hammers through the once bicameral world to smash all its physical vestiges in sight. Every god is a jealous god after the breakdown of the bicameral mind.

But even this destruction could not abolish idolatrous practice, so vital is it to have some kind of authorization for our behavior. Medieval Italy and Byzantium believed in enchanted idols who had power to avert disaster. The notorious Knights Templars were at least accused of taking orders from a gold head called Baphomet. So common had hallucinogenic idols become in the late Middle Ages that a bull of Pope John XXII in 1326 denounced those who by magic imprison demons in images or other objects, interrogate them, and obtain answers. Even up to the Reformation, monasteries and churches vied with each other to attract pilgrims (and their offerings) by miracle-producing statuary.

In some epochs, perhaps when the cognitive imperatives for such neo-bicameral experiences began to wither under the sunlight of rationalism, the belief in statue animation was occasion-

[24] Callistratus, *Descriptions*, 10, A. Fairbanks, trans. (Loeb Classical Library, 1902).

ally sustained by the use of fraudulent contrivances.[25] In one instance of many, a life-sized medieval rood of the crucified Jesus at Boxley, which rolled its eyes at penitents, shed tears, and foamed at the mouth, was found in the sixteenth century to have "certain engines and old wires with old rotten sticks in the back of the same."[26] But we shouldn't cynicize too deeply here. While such artificial animation often functioned as chicanery to fool the miracle-hungry pilgrim, it may also have been meant as an enticement to the god to body itself in a more lifelike statue. As a fourteenth-century tract on the matter explained, "God's power in working of his miracles loweth down in one image more than in another."[27] Animated idols in some contemporary tribes are explained by their worshipers in the same way.

Idolatry is still a socially cohesive force — its original function. Our parks and public gardens are still the beflowered homes of heroic effigies of past leaders. While few of us can hallucinate their speech, we still on appropriate occasions might give them gifts of wreaths, even as greater gifts were given in the *gigunus* of Ur. In churches, temples, and shrines the world over, religious statues are still being carved, painted, and prayed to. Figurines of a Queen of Heaven dangle protectively from the mirrors of American windshields. Teen-age girls I have interviewed, living in deeply religious convents, often sneak down to the chapel in the dead of night and have mentioned to me their excitement at being able to 'hear' the statue of the Virgin Mary speak, and 'see' her lips move or her head bow or — sometimes — her eyes weep. Gentle idols of Jesus, Mary, and the saints throughout much of the Catholic world are still being bathed, dressed, incensed,

---

[25] See F. Poulsen, "Talking, weeping, and bleeding sculptures." *Acta Archeologica*, 1945, 16:178f.

[26] See Jonathan Sumption's *Pilgrimage: An Image of Medieval Religion* (Totawa, N.J.: Rowman and Littlefield, 1975), p. 56; also Julia Holloway's forthcoming *The Pilgrim*. I am grateful to her for bringing this to my attention.

[27] Quoted from the Lollard manuscript *Lanterne of Light*, by Sumption, p. 270.

flowered, jeweled, and launched shoulder-high and glorious out of bell-bellowing churches on outings through towns and countrysides on feast days. Placing special foods in front of them or dancing and bowing before them still generates its numinous excitement.[28] Such devotions differ from similar divine outings in bicameral Mesopotamia 4000 years ago mostly in the idol's relative silence.

[28] As in Flaubert's beautiful story *Un Coeur Simple*.

CHAPTER 2

Of Prophets and Possession

I N THE FOREGOING theory of oracles, I am sure that the reader
has seen the profound gap that I have jumped over in my argument. I have called the general bicameral paradigm a vestige of
the bicameral mind. And yet the trance state of narrowed or
absent consciousness is not, at least from the fourth oracular
term and thereafter, a duplicate of the bicameral mind. Instead
we have for the rest of the oracle's existence a complete domination of the person and his speech by the god-side, a domination
which speaks through the person but does not allow him to
remember what has happened afterwards. This phenomenon is
known as *possession*.

The problem it presents is not confined to far-off ancient oracles. It occurs today. It has occurred through history. It has a
negatory form that seems to have been one of the most common
maladies in the Galilee of the New Testament. And a good case
could be made that at least some of the wandering prophets of
Mesopotamia, Israel, Greece, and elsewhere did not simply relay
to listeners something they were hearing in hallucination; rather
that the divine message was coming directly from the prophet's
vocal apparatus without any cognition on 'his' part during the
speech or memory of it after. And if we call this a loss of
consciousness, and I shall, such a statement is quite problematic.
Is it not also possible to say that it is not the loss of consciousness
so much as its replacement by a new and different conscious-

ness? But what can that mean? Or is that linguistic organization which speaks from the supposed possessed person *not* conscious at all in the sense of narratizing in a mind-space as described in I.2?

These questions are not solved by simple answers. The fact that we may regard possession by metaphysical essences as ontological nonsense should not blind us from the psychological and historical insights that examination of such idiosyncrasies of history and belief can give us. Indeed, any theory of consciousness and its origin in time must face such obscurities. And I do suggest that the theory in this book is a better torch for such dark corners of time and mind than any alternative theory. For if we still hold to a purely biological evolution of consciousness back somewhere among the lower vertebrates, how can we approach such phenomena or begin to understand their historically and culturally segregated nature? It is only if consciousness is learned at the mercy of a collective cognitive imperative that we can take hold of these questions in any way.

Our first step in understanding any mental phenomenon must be to delimit its existence in historical time. When did it first occur?

The answer in Greece, at least, is very clear. There is no such thing as possession or any hint of anything similar throughout the Iliad or Odyssey or other early poetry. No 'god' speaks through human lips in the truly bicameral age. Yet by 400 B.C., it is apparently as common as churches are with us, both in the many oracles scattered about Greece as well as in private individuals. The bicameral mind has vanished and possession is its trace.

Plato, in the fourth century B.C., has Socrates casually say in the midst of a political discussion that "God-possessed men speak much truth, but know nothing of what they say,"[1] as if such

---

[1] *Meno*, 99C. See also *Timaeus*, 71E–72A, where it is said "no man in his wits attains prophetic truth and inspirations."

prophets could be heard every day around the streets of Athens. And he was very clear about the loss of consciousness in the oracles of his time:

> . . . for prophecy is a madness, and the prophetess at Delphi and the priestesses at Dodona when out of their senses have conferred great benefits on Hellas, both in public and private life, but when in their senses few or none.[2]

And so in the centuries that follow, supposed possession is the obliteration of ordinary consciousness. Four hundred years after Plato, in the first century A.D., Philo Judaeus categorically states,

> When he (a prophet) is inspired he becomes unconscious; thought vanishes away and leaves the fortress of the soul; but the divine spirit has entered there and taken up its abode; and this later makes all the organs resound so that the man gives clear expression to what the spirit gives him to say.[3]

And so also in the century after that, as in Aristides' saying that the priestesses at the oracle of Dodona

> . . . do not know, before being seized by the spirits, what they are going to say, any more than after having recovered their natural senses they remember what they have said, so that everyone knows what they say except themselves.[4]

And Iamblichus, the leading Neo-Platonist at the beginning of the third century, insisted that divine possession "participated" in divinity, had a "common energy" with a god, and "comprehends indeed everything in us but exterminates our own proper con-

---

[2] *Phaedrus*, 244B.

[3] Philo, *De Special Legibus*, 4, 343M, Cohn and Wendland, eds., who in another place says, "He who is really inspired and filled with god cannot comprehend with his intelligence what he says; he only repeats what is suggested to him, as if another prompted him." 222M.

[4] Aristides, *Opera*, 213.

sciousness and motion."[5] Such possession, then, is not a return to the bicameral mind properly speaking. For when Achilles heard Athene a millennium earlier, he certainly did know what was said to him; that was the function of the bicameral mind.

This then is the very core of the problem. The speech of possessed prophets is not an hallucination proper, not something heard by a conscious, semi-conscious, or even nonconscious man as in the bicameral mind proper. It is articulated externally and heard by others. It occurs only in normally conscious men and is coincident with a loss of that consciousness. What justification then do we have for saying that the two phenomena, the hallucinations of the bicameral mind and the speech of the possessed, are related?

I do not have a truly robust answer. I can only meekly maintain that they are related (1) because they are serving the same social function, (2) because they yield similar communications of authorization, and (3) because the little evidence we have on the early history of oracles indicates that possession in a few institutionalized persons at certain locations is a gradual outgrowth from the hallucinations of gods by anyone at those locations. We can therefore at least suggest that possession is a transformation of a particular sort, a derivative of bicamerality in which the rituals of induction and the different collective cognitive imperatives and trained expectancies result in the ostensive possession of the particular person by the god-side of the bicameral mind. Perhaps we could say that, to retrieve the older mentality, developing consciousness more and more had to be obliterated, inhibiting the man-side with it, leaving the god-side in control of speech itself.

And what of the neurology of such a mentality? From the model I have presented in I.5, we must naturally hypothesize that

[5] Iamblichus, *De Mysteriis*, 3:8, or the English translation by Thomas Taylor (London: Theosophical Society, 1895), pp. 128–129.

in possession there is some kind of disturbance of normal hemispheric dominance relations, in which the right hemisphere is somewhat more active than in the normal state. In other words, if we could have placed electrodes on the scalp of a Delphic oracle in her frenzy, would we have found a relatively faster EEG (and therefore greater activity) over her right hemisphere, correlating with her possession? And particularly over her right temporal lobe?

I suggest that we would. There is at least a possibility that the dominance relations of the two hemispheres would be changed, and that the early training of the oracle was indeed that of engaging a higher ratio of right hemisphere activity in relation to the left as a response to the complex stimulus of the induction procedures. Such a hypothesis might also explain the contorted features, the appearance of frenzy and the nystagmic eyes, as an abnormal right hemisphere interference or release from inhibition by the left hemisphere.[6]

And a comment can be added here about sexual differences. It is now well known that women are biologically somewhat less lateralized in brain function than men. This means simply that psychological functions in women are not localized into one or the other hemisphere of the brain to the same degree as in men. Mental abilities in women are more spread over both hemispheres. Even by age six, for example, a boy can recognize objects in his left hand by feel alone better than in his right hand. In girls both hands are equal. This shows that haptic recognition (as it is called) has already been primarily localized in the right hemisphere in boys but not in girls.[7] And it is common knowledge that

[6] It is likely that it is not the right motor cortex controlling the facial grimaces, but that the unusual right temporal-parietal lobe activity distorts the symmetry of input from the basal ganglia to facial expression.

[7] Sandra F. Witelson, "Sex and the Single Hemisphere," Science, 1976, 193:425–427. A collation of about thirty other studies on the subject may be found in Richard A. Harshman and Roger Remington, "Sex, Language, and the Brain, Part I: A Review of the Literature on Adult Sex Differences in Lateralization," authors' preprint, 1975; see also Stevan Harnad, "On Gender Differences in Language," Contemporary Anthropology, 1976, 17:327–328.

elderly men with a stroke or hemorrhage in the left hemisphere are more speechless than elderly women with a similar diagnosis. Accordingly we might expect more residual language function in the right hemisphere of women, making it easier for women to learn to be oracles. And indeed the majority of oracles and Sibyls, at least in European cultures, were women.

Induced Possession

Institutionalized unconscious speaking in the prophets of oracles as if by a god becomes, as we have seen in III.1, erratic and silent toward the first centuries of the Christian era. It falls to a siege of rationalism, to volleys of criticism and ramming irreverence in comic drama and literature. Such public (indeed urban) suppression of a general cultural characteristic often results in pushing it into private practice, into abstruse sects and esoteric cults where its cognitive imperative is protected from such criticism. And so with induced possession. With the oracles mocked into silence, such the quest for authorization that there is a widespread attempt in private groups to bring back the gods and have them speak through almost anyone.

The second century A.D. saw a growing number of such cults. Their séances were sometimes in official shrines, but increasingly more often in private circles. Usually one person called a *pelestike* or operator tried to incarnate the god temporarily in another called a *katochos*, or more specially a *docheus*, or what in contemporary lore is called a medium.[8] It was soon found that if the phenomenon was to work, the katochos should come from a simple unsophisticated background, something that runs through all the literature on possession. Iamblichus in the early third century, the real apostle of all this, states that the most suitable

8 In this part of my discussion I am indebted to the wealth of information in E. R. Dodds, *The Greeks and the Irrational* (Berkeley: University of California Press, 1968), Appendix II, Theurgy, where many other references may be found.

mediums are "young and simple persons." And so, we remember, were the uneducated country girls chosen to train as priestesses for the oracle at Delphi. Other writings mention adolescents such as the boy Aedesius, who "had only to put on the garland and look at the sun, when he immediately produces reliable oracles in the best inspirational style." Obviously, this was due to careful training. That such induced bicameral possession has to be learned is known from the training of oracles as well as a comment of Pythagoras of Rhodes in the third century, that the gods come at first reluctantly, then more easily when they have formed the habit of entering the same person.

What was learned, I suggest, was a state approaching the bicameral mind as a response to the induction. This is important. We do not ordinarily think of learning a new unconscious mentality, perhaps a whole new relationship between our cerebral hemispheres, as we think of learning to ride a bicycle.

Since this is the learning of a now difficult neurological state, so different from ordinary life, it is not surprising that the cues of the induction had to be *wildly* distinctive and have an extreme difference from ordinary life.

And they certainly were different: anything odd, anything strange: bathing in smoke or sacred water, dressing in enchanted chitons with magical girdles, wearing weird garlands or mysterious symbols, standing in a charmed magic circle as medieval magicians did, or upon *charakteres* as Faust did to hallucinate Mephistopheles, or smearing the eyes with strychnine to procure visions as was done in Egypt, or washing in brimstone (sulphur) and seawater, a very old method which began in Greece, as Porphyry said in the second century A.D., to prepare the *anima spiritalis* for the reception of a higher being. All these of course did nothing except as they were believed to do something — just as we in this latter age have no 'free will' unless we believe we have.

And what was done, this 'reception of the god', was not psychologically different from the other forms of possession we have examined. Consciousness as well as normal reactivity in the katochos was usually in complete suspension so that it was necessary to have others look after him. And in such a deep trance, the 'god' would supposedly reveal past or future, or answer questions and make decisions, as in the older Greek oracles.

How was it to be explained when these gods were incorrect? Well, evil spirits might have been invoked instead of true gods, or other intrusive spirits might have occupied the medium. Iamblichus himself claims to have unmasked in his medium an alleged Apollo who was only the ghost of a gladiator. Such excuses reverberate throughout the subsequent decadent literature of spiritualism.

And when the séance did not seem to be working, the operator as well often went through an induction of purifying rites that put him into a hallucinatory state, such that he might 'see' more clearly or 'hear' from the unconscious medium something that perhaps the medium did not even say. This kind of doubling-up is similar to the *prophetes'* relationship to their oracles, and explains various reported levitations, elongations, or dilations of the medium's body.[9]

By the end of the third century, Christianity had suddenly flooded the pagan world with its own claims to authorization and began to dissolve into itself many of the then existing pagan practices. The idea of possession was one of those. But it was absorbed in a transcendental way. At almost the same time that Iamblichus was teaching the induction of gods into statues, or young illiterate katochoi to "participate" in divinity and have "a common energy" with a god, Athanasius, the competitive Bishop of Alexandria, began claiming the same thing for the illiterate

[9] It is safe to suggest that many feats of present-day stage magicians have their origin in duplicating these 'proofs' of divine intervention.

Jesus. The Christian Messiah had heretofore been regarded as *like* Yahweh, a demigod perhaps, half human, half divine, reflecting his supposed parentage. But Athanasius persuaded Constantine, his Council of Nicaea, and most of Christianity thereafter, that Jesus *participated* in Yahweh, was the *same* substance, the Bicameral Word made Flesh. I think we can say then that the growing church, in danger of shattering into sects, exaggerated the subjective phenomenon of possession into an objective theological dogma. It did so to assert an even greater claim to an *absolute* authorization. For Athanasian Christians the actual gods had indeed returned to earth and would return again.

Curiously, neither the oracle at Delphi nor the Sibyls were doubted as contacting a heavenly reality by this expanding Christian Church. But such pagan séances as induced divine possession in simple boys seemed theologically rowdy, the mischief of devils and shady spirits. And so as the church arches up into political authority over the Middle Ages, voluntary induced possession disappears at least from public notice. It goes even further underground into witchcraft and assorted necromancies, emerging into notice only from time to time.

Its contemporary practice I shall come to in a moment. But first we should examine a cultural side effect of induced possession, a disturbing phenomenon I shall call

Negatory Possession

There is another side to this vigorously strange vestige of the bicameral mind. And it is different from other topics in this chapter. For it is not a response to a ritual induction for the purpose of retrieving the bicameral mind. It is an illness in response to stress. In effect, emotional stress takes the place of the induction in the general bicameral paradigm just as in antiquity. And when it does, the authorization is of a different kind.

The difference presents a fascinating problem. In the New

Testament, where we first hear of such spontaneous possession, it is called in Greek *daemonizomai*, or demonization.[10] And from that time to the present, instances of the phenomenon most often have that negatory quality connoted by the term. The why of the negatory quality is at present unclear. In an earlier chapter (II.4) I have tried to suggest the origin of 'evil' in the volitional emptiness of the silent bicameral voices. And that this took place in Mesopotamia and particularly in Babylon, to which the Jews were exiled in the sixth century B.C., might account for the prevalence of this quality in the world of Jesus at the start of this syndrome.

But whatever the reasons, they must in the individual be similar to the reasons behind the predominantly negatory quality of schizophrenic hallucinations. And indeed the relationship of this type of possession to schizophrenia seems obvious.

Like schizophrenia, negatory possession usually begins with some kind of an hallucination.[11] It is often a castigating 'voice' of a 'demon' or other being which is 'heard' after a considerable stressful period. But then, unlike schizophrenia, probably because of the strong collective cognitive imperative of a particular group or religion, the voice develops into a secondary system of personality, the subject then losing control and periodically entering into trance states in which consciousness is lost, and the 'demon' side of the personality takes over.

Always the patients are uneducated, usually illiterate, and all believe heartily in spirits or demons or similar beings and live in a society which does. The attacks usually last from several minutes to an hour or two, the patient being relatively normal be-

[10] Moreover, instances of such possession occur most often in the oldest and most authentic of the Gospels: Mark 1:32, 5:15–18; and Matthew (which scholars are agreed is based upon Mark as well as some unknown older Gospel) 4:24; 8:16; 8:28–33; 9:32; 12:22.

[11] Here I am summarizing cases in the literature. For fuller discussions of this topic as well as other case descriptions (not very complete) see Oesterreich, *Possession*; as well as J. L. Nevius, *Demon Possession and Allied Themes* (Chicago: Revell, 1896).

tween attacks and recalling little of them. Contrary to horror fiction stories, negatory possession is chiefly a linguistic phenomenon, not one of actual conduct. In all the cases I have studied, it is rare to find one of criminal behavior against other persons. The stricken individual does not run off and behave like a demon; he just talks like one.

Such episodes are usually accompanied by twistings and writhings as in induced possession. The voice is distorted, often guttural, full of cries, groans, and vulgarity, and usually railing against the institutionalized gods of the period. Almost always, there is a loss of consciousness as the person seems the opposite of his or her usual self. 'He' may name himself a god, demon, spirit, ghost, or animal (in the Orient it is often 'the fox'), may demand a shrine or to be worshiped, throwing the patient into convulsions if these are withheld. 'He' commonly describes his natural self in the third person as a despised stranger, even as Yahweh sometimes despised his prophets or the Muses sneered at their poets.[12] And 'he' often seems far more intelligent and alert than the patient in his normal state, even as Yahweh and the Muses were more intelligent and alert than prophet or poet.

As in schizophrenia, the patient may act out the suggestions of others, and, even more curiously, may be interested in contracts or treaties with observers, such as a promise that 'he' will leave the patient if such and such is done, bargains which are carried out as faithfully by the 'demon' as the sometimes similar covenants of Yahweh in the Old Testament. Somehow related to this suggestibility and contract interest is the fact that the cure for spontaneous stress-produced possession, exorcism, has never varied from New Testament days to the present. It is simply by the command of an authoritative person often following an induction ritual, speaking in the name of a more powerful god.

[12] I probably should not be making these cross-comparisons. But I am at least revealing my thinking. Is it possible that what corresponds to Wernicke's area on the right hemisphere always 'looks down' on Wernicke's area on the left? The references are to Exodus 4:24 and to Hesiod's *Theogony*, line 26, respectively.

The exorcist can be said to fit into the authorization element of the general bicameral paradigm, replacing the 'demon.' The cognitive imperatives of the belief system that determined the form of the illness in the first place determine the form of its cure.

The phenomenon does not depend on age, but sex differences, depending on the historical epoch, are pronounced, demonstrating its cultural expectancy basis. Of those possessed by 'demons' whom Jesus or his disciples cured in the New Testament, the overwhelming majority were men. In the Middle Ages and thereafter, however, the overwhelming majority were women. Also evidence for its basis in a collective cognitive imperative are its occasional epidemics, as in convents of nuns during the Middle Ages, in Salem, Massachusetts, in the eighteenth century, or those reported in the nineteenth century at Savoy in the Alps. And occasionally today.

Now, again, with any alteration of mentality as striking as this, we cannot escape the neurological question. What is happening? Are the speech areas of the right nondominant hemisphere activated in spontaneous possession, as I have suggested they were in the induced possession of the oracles? And are the contorted features due to the intrusion of right hemisphere control? The fact that the majority of instances (as well as most oracles and Sibyls) were women, and that women are (presently in our culture) less lateralized than men is somewhat suggestive.

At least some instances of possession begin with contortions on the left side of the body, which may indicate this is true. Here is one case reported at the beginning of this century. The patient was a forty-seven-year-old uneducated Japanese woman who would become possessed by what she called the fox, six or seven times a day, always with the same laterality phenomena. As it was then observed by her physicians:

> At first there appeared slight twitchings of the mouth and
> arm on the left side. As these became stronger she violently

struck with her fist her left side which was already swollen and red with similar blows, and said to me: "Ah, sir, here he is stirring again in my breast." Then a strange and incisive voice issued from her mouth: "Yes, it is true, I am there. Did you think, stupid goose, that you could stop me?" Thereupon the woman addressed herself to us: "Oh dear, gentlemen, forgive me, I cannot help it!"

Continuing to strike her breast and contract the left side of her face . . . the woman threatened him, adjured him to be quiet, but after a short time he interrupted her and it was he alone who thought and spoke. The woman was now passive like an automaton, obviously no longer understanding what was said to her. It was the fox which answered maliciously instead. At the end of ten minutes the fox spoke in a more confused manner, the woman gradually came to herself and assumed back her normal state. She remembered the first part of the fit and begged us with tears to forgive her for the outrageous conduct of the fox.[13]

But this is one case. I have not found any other patient in which such distinct laterality phenomena were in evidence.

In puzzling about the neurology of negatory possession, it can be helpful, I think, to consider the contemporary illness known as Gilles de la Tourette's Syndrome,[14] or, occasionally, "foul-mouth disease." This bizarre group of symptoms usually begins in childhood at age five or sometimes earlier, with perhaps merely a repeated facial twitch or bad word out of context. This then develops into an uncontrollable emission of ripe obscenities, grunts, barks, or profanities in the middle of otherwise normal

[13] E. Balz, *Ueber Besessenheit* (Leipzig, 1907), as translated by Oesterreich, *Possession*, p. 227. Physicians attending her were astonished to see the cleverness of speech, the witty and ironic language, so unlike the patient's own, which the 'fox' displayed.

[14] For recent work on this subject as well as its history, see the references and data in A. K. Shapiro, E. Shapiro, H. L. Wayne, J. Clarkin, and R. D. Bruun, "Tourette's Syndrome: summary of data on 34 patients," *Psychosomatic Medicine,* 1973, 35:419–435.

conversation, as well as various facial tics, sticking out the tongue, etc. These often continue through adult life, much to the distress of the patient. Such persons often end up refusing to leave their homes because of their horror and embarrassment at their own intermittent uncontrollable vulgarity. In one case I knew of recently, the man invented a cover of having severe bladder problems requiring him to urinate often. Actually, every time he dashed to the Men's Room while at a restaurant or to the bathroom in a house, it was the welling up of profanity that he went to relieve himself of by shouting it at toilet walls.[15] To be profane myself, the linguistic feeling within him may not have been unlike the prophet Jeremiah's fire shut up in his bones (see II:6), although the semantic product was somewhat (but not altogether) different.

What is of interest here is that Tourette's Syndrome so clearly resembles the initial phase of stress-produced possession as to force upon us the suspicion that they share a common physiological mechanism. And this may indeed be incomplete hemispheric dominance, in which the speech areas of the right hemisphere (perhaps stimulated by impulses from the basal ganglia) are periodically breaking through into language under conditions which would have produced an hallucination in bicameral man. Accordingly it is not surprising that almost all sufferers from Tourette's Syndrome have abnormal brain wave patterns, some central nervous system damage, and are usually left-handed (in the majority of left-handed persons there is mixed dominance), and that the symptoms begin around the age of five when the neurological development of hemispheric dominance in regard to language is being completed.

Now all of this says something important but unsettling about

---

[15] Tourette's Syndrome is often if not usually misdiagnosed as a form of insanity, which it definitely is not. Fortunately and interestingly, however, one of the new antipsychotic tranquilizers, haloperidol, has been found to abolish the symptoms — which it did in the above-mentioned cases. I am grateful to Dr. Shapiro for discussion on these points.

our nervous systems. For while I believe the neurological model in I.5 to be in the right direction, we are getting further and further away from it. It is very improbable that modern spirit possession is everywhere engaging right hemisphere speech centers for the *articulated* speech itself. Such an hypothesis is contrary to so many clinical facts as to rule it out except in highly unusual cases.

A more likely possibility, perhaps, is that the neurological difference between the bicameral mind and modern possession states is that in the former, hallucinations were indeed organized and heard from the right hemisphere; while in possession, the articulated speech is our normal left hemisphere speech but controlled or under the guidance of the right hemisphere. In other words, what corresponds to Wernicke's area on the right hemisphere is using Broca's area on the left hemisphere, the result being the trance state and its depersonalization. Such cross control could be the neurological substrate of the loss of normal consciousness.

Possession in the Modern World

I wish now to turn to induced possession in our own times to demonstrate with some conclusiveness that it is a learned phenomenon. The best example I have found is the Umbanda religion, the largest by far of the Afro-Brazilian religions practiced today by over half the population of Brazil. It is believed in as a source of decision by persons of all ethnic backgrounds and is certainly the most extensive occurrence of induced possession since the third century.

Let us look in on a typical *gira* or "turn around," as an Umbanda session is so aptly called.[16] It may be taking place at the present time in a room above a store or in an abandoned garage.

[16] This entire section on the Umbanda is based on the extremely rich and definitive study of Esther Pressel, "Umbanda Trance and Possession in São Paulo, Brazil," in Felicitas Goodman et al., *Trance, Healing, and Hallucination* (New York: Wiley, 1974).

Perhaps a dozen or fewer mediums (70 percent are women), all dressed ceremoniously in white, come out from a tiring room in front of a white-draped altar crammed with flowers, candles, and statues and pictures of Christian saints, an audience of a hundred or so being beyond a railing on the other side of the room. The drummers beat and the audience sings, as the mediums begin to sway or dance. This swaying and dancing is always in a counter-clockwise motion, that is, beginning with motor impulses from the right hemisphere. There follows a Christian type of service. Then drums are once more pounded furiously, everyone sings, and the mediums begin to call their spirits; some spin to the left like whirling dervishes, again exciting their right hemispheres. There is the explicit metaphor here of the medium as a *cavalo* or horse. A particular spirit is supposed to lower himself into his cavalo. As this is happening, the head and chest of the cavalo, or medium, jerks back and forth in opposing directions like a bronco being ridden. The hair falls into disarray. Facial expressions become contorted, as in ancient examples I have cited. Posture changes into the likeness of any of several possessing spirits. The possession accomplished, the 'spirits' may dance for a few minutes, may greet each other in the possessed state, may perform other actions suitable to the type of spirit, and then, when the drumming stops, go to preassigned places, and, curiously, as they wait for members of the audience to come forward for the *consultas,* they snap their fingers impatiently as their hands rest beside their bodies, palms outward. In the consultas the possessed medium may be asked for, and may give, decisions on any illness or personal problem, on getting or keeping a job, on financial business practices, family quarrels, love affairs, or even, among students, advice about scholastic grades.

Now the evidence that possession is a learned mentality is very clear in these Brazilian cults. In a *bairro* playground, one may occasionally see children in their play imitating the distinctive back-and-forth jerking of the head and chest that is used for inducing and terminating spirit possession. If a child wishes to become a medium, he is encouraged to do so and given special training, just as were the young country girls who became the oracles at Delphi and elsewhere. Indeed, some of the many Umbanda centers (there are 4000 in São Paulo alone) hold regular training sessions, where the procedures include various ways of making the novice dizzy in order to teach him or her the trance state, as well as techniques similar to those used in hypnosis. And in the trance state, the novice is taught how each of several possible spirits behaves. This fact of a differentiation of possessing spirits is important, and I wish to comment further on it and its function in culture.

The vestiges of the bicameral mind do not exist in any empty psychological space. That is, they should not be considered as isolated phenomena that simply appear in a culture and loiter around doing nothing but leaning on their own antique merits. Instead, they always live at the very heart of a culture or subculture, moving out and filling up the unspoken and the unrationalized. They become indeed the irrational and unquestionable support and structural integrity of the culture. And the culture in turn is the substrate of its individual consciousnesses, of how the metaphor 'me' is 'perceived' by the analog 'I', of the nature of excerption and the constraints on narratization and conciliation.

Such vestiges of the bicameral mind as we are here considering are no exception. A possession religion such as the Umbanda functions as a powerful psychological support to the heterogeneous masses of its poor and uneducated and needy. It is pervaded with a feeling of *caridade*, or charity, which consoles and binds together this motley of political impotents, whose urbanization and ethnic diversity has stranded them without roots. And look at the pattern of particular neurological organizations that emerge as possessing divinities. They remind us of the presenting personal gods of Sumer and Babylon, interceders with those above them. Each medium on any particular night may be possessed by an individual spirit from any of four main groups. They are, in order of frequency:

> the *caboclos*, spirits of Brazilian-Indian warriors, who advise in situations requiring quick and decisive action, such as obtaining or maintaining a job;
> the *pretos velhos*, spirits of old Afro-Brazilian slaves, adept at handling long drawn-out personal problems;
> the *crianças*, spirits of dead children, whose mediums make playful suggestions;
> the *exus* (demons) or, if female, *pombagiras* (turning pigeons), spirits of wicked foreigners, whose mediums make vulgar and aggressive suggestions.

Each of these four main types of possessor spirits represents a different ethnic group corresponding to the ethnic hybridism of the worshipers: Indian, African, Brazilian (the crianças are "like us"), and European, respectively. Each represents a different familial relationship to the petitioner: father, grandfather, sibling, and stranger respectively. And each represents a different area of decision: quick decisions for choices of action, comforting advice on personal problems, playful suggestions, and decisions in matters of aggression respectively. Even as the Greek gods were originally distinguished as areas of decision, so the spirits of the Umbanda. And the whole is like a network or metaphor matrix of four-way inner-related distinctiveness that binds the individuals together and holds them in a culture.

And all this, I suggest, is a vestige of the bicameral mind, as we go through these millennia of adjusting to a new mentality.

True possession, as described by Plato and others, has always been held to go on without consciousness, thus differentiating it from acting. But the training of the persons of oracles must have admitted of degrees and stages toward such a state. In the Brazilian possession religions, apparently, this is exactly what happens.

The young novice may begin by acting out possession in play, then proceed with his training until eventually he can separate what a spirit would say from what he himself would normally talk about. Then there occurs a stage of passing back and forth between consciousness and unconsciousness. And then with full possession, perhaps the connecting up of Wernicke's area on the right hemisphere with Broca's on the left, the much-desired state of unconsciousness, with no remembrance of what happens. This, however, is true of only some mediums. And in any pseudobicameral practice as extensive as this, it is to be expected that there will be many different qualities and degrees of acting and trance even within the same individual.

Glossolalia

A final phenomenon that is weakly similar to induced possession is glossolalia, or what the apostle Paul called "speaking in tongues." It consists of fluent speech in what sounds like a strange language which the speaker himself does not understand and usually does not remember saying. It seems to have begun with the early Christian Church[17] in the asserted descent of the ghost of God into the assembled apostles. This event was regarded as the birthday of the Christian Church and is commemorated in the festival of Pentecost, the fiftieth day after Easter.[18] Acts 2 describes what is probably its first instance in history as a great rushing wind roaring with cloven tongues of fire, in which all the apostles begin to speak as if drunk in languages they had never learned.

[17] Old Testament references to Yahweh's pouring out his spirit are sometimes put forth as references to glossolalia, but I find this utterly unconvincing. The phenomenon can be regarded as peculiarly of Christian origin, particularly in the writings of, or influenced by, Paul.

[18] Today at Vatican celebrations of Pentecost, red is worn to symbolize the tongues of fire; and in Protestant churches, white, to symbolize the Holy Ghost, hence the English term Whitsuntide, around white Sunday.

This alteration of mentality happening to the likes of the apostles became its own authorization. The practice spread. Soon early Christians were doing it everywhere. Paul even put it on a level with prophecy (I Corinthians 14:27, 29). From time to time in the centuries since Paul, glossolalia as a search for authorization after the breakdown of the bicameral mind has had its periods of fashion.

Its recent practice, not just by the sects that are theologically extremely conservative, but also by members of mainline Protestant churches, has pushed it into some scientific scrutiny with some interesting results. Glossolalia first happens *always* in groups and always in the context of religious services. I am stressing the group factor, since I think this strengthening of the collective cognitive imperative is necessary for a particularly deep type of trance. Often there will be what corresponds to an induction, particularly hymn singing of a rousing sort, followed by the exhortations of a charismatic leader: "If you feel your language change, don't resist it, let it happen."[19]

The worshiper, through repeated attendance at such meetings, watching others in glossolalia, first learns to enter into a deep-trance state of diminished or absent consciousness in which he is not responsive to exteroceptive stimuli. The trance in this case is almost an autonomic one: shakes, shivers, sweat, twitches, and tears. Then he or she may somehow learn to "let it happen." And it does, loud and clear, each phrase ending in a groan: *aria ariari isa, vena amiria asaria!*[20] The rhythm pounds, the way epic dactyls probably did to the hearers of the aoidoi. And this quality of regular alternation of accented and unaccented syllables, so similar to that of the Homeric epics, as well as the rising and then downward intonation at the end of each phrase, does not — and this is astonishing — does not vary with the native

---

[19] Felicitas D. Goodman, "Disturbances in the Apostolic Church: A Trance-Based Upheaval in Yucatan," in Goodman et al., *Trance, Healing, and Hallucination*, pp. 227–364.

[20] From a tape of Dr. Goodman's of a male glossolalist of Mayan descent in Yucatan. Ibid., pp. 262–263.

language of the speaker. If the subject is English, Portuguese, Spanish, Indonesian, African, or Mayan, or wherever he is, the pattern of glossolalia is the same.[21]

After the glossolalia, the subject opens his eyes and slowly returns from these unconscious heights to dusty reality, remembering little of what happened. But he is told. He has been possessed by the Holy Spirit. He has been chosen by God as his puppet. His problems are stopped in hope and his sorrows torn with joy. It is the ultimate in authorization since the Holy Spirit is one with the highest source of all being. God has chosen to enter the lowly subject and has articulated his speech with the subject's own tongue. The individual has become a god — briefly.

The cruel daylight of it all is less inspiring. While the phenomenon is not simply gibberish, nor can the average person duplicate the fluency and structure of what is spoken, it has no semantic meaning whatever. Tapes of glossolalia played before others in the same religious group are given utterly inconsistent interpretations.[22] That the metered vocalizations are similar across the cultures and language of the speakers, probably indicates that rhythmical discharges from subcortical structures are coming into play, released by the trance state of lesser cortical control.[23]

The ability does not last. It attenuates. The more it is prac-

[21] The important result of Dr. Goodman's earlier study, *Speaking in Tongues: A Cross-Cultural Study of Glossolalia* (Chicago: University of Chicago Press, 1972).

[22] This is a generalization from the careful work of John P. Kildahl on twenty-six American glossolalists all belonging to major Protestant denominations. See his *The Psychology of Speaking in Tongues* (New York: Harper & Row, 1972). He also gives a very complete bibliography on the matter.

[23] "The surface structure of a non-linguistic deep structure," as Dr. Goodman says in structuralist terms (p. 151–152). But the idea of an energy discharge from subcortical structures under diminished consciousness has been sharply criticized, particularly by the linguist W. J. Samarin in his review of Goodman in *Language*, 1974, 50:207–212. See also his *Tongues of Men and Angels: The Religious Language of Pentecostalism* (New York: Macmillan, 1972). I am grateful to Ronald Baker of the University of Prince Edward Island for bringing this to my attention.

ticed, the more it becomes conscious, which destroys the trance. An essential ingredient of the phenomenon, at least in more educated groups where the cognitive imperative would be weaker, is the presence of a charismatic leader who first teaches the phenomenon. And if tongue speaking is to be continued at all, and the resulting euphoria makes it a devoutly wished state of mind, the relationship with the authoritative leader must be continued. It is really this ability to abandon the conscious direction of one's speech controls in the presence of an authority figure regarded as benevolent that is the essential thing. As we might expect, glossolalists by the Thematic Apperception Test reveal themselves as more submissive, suggestible, and dependent in the presence of authority figures than those who cannot exhibit the phenomenon.[24]

It is, then, this pattern of essential ingredients, the strong cognitive imperative of religious belief in a cohesive group, the induction procedures of prayer and ritual, the narrowing of consciousness into a trance state, and the archaic authorization in the divine spirit and in the charismatic leader, which denotes this phenomenon as another instance of the general bicameral paradigm and therefore a vestige of the bicameral mind.

Aria ariari isa, vena amiria asaria
Menin aeide thea Peleiadeo Achilleos

My comparison of the sound of speaking in tongues with the sound of the Greek epics to their hearers (the second line above is the first line of the Iliad) is not just an ornature of my style. It is a very deliberate comparison. And one that I intend now as a lead-in to the next chapter. For we should not leave our inquiry into these cultural antiques without at least noting the oddity, the difference, the true profundity, and — ultimately — the question of and for poetry.

[24] John P. Kildahl, *The Final Progress Report: Glossolalia and Mental Health* (for NIMH), privately circulated.

CHAPTER 3

Of Poetry and Music

WHY HAS so much of the textual material we have used as evidence in earlier chapters been poetry? And why, particularly in times of stress, have a huge proportion of the readers of this page written poems? What unseen light leads us to such dark practice? And why does poetry flash with recognitions of thoughts we did not know we had, finding its unsure way to something in us that knows and has known all the time, something, I think, older than the present organization of our nature?

To charter a discussion down this optional and deserted topic at this point in what has hitherto been a fairly linear argument may seem an unwarranted indirection. But the chapters of Book III, in contrast to the previous two books, are not a consecutive procession. They are rather a selection of divergent trajectories out of our bicameral past into present times. And I think it will become obvious that the earlier argument, particularly as relating to the Greek epics, needs to be rounded out with the present chapter.

I shall state my thesis plain. The first poets were gods. Poetry began with the bicameral mind. The god-side of our ancient mentality, at least in a certain period of history, usually or perhaps always spoke in verse. This means that most men at one time, throughout the day, were hearing poetry (of a sort) composed and spoken within their own minds.

The evidence is, of course, only inferential. It is that all of those individuals who remained bicameral into the conscious age, when speaking of or from the divine side of their minds, spoke in poetry. The great epics of Greece were of course heard and spoken by the aoidoi as poetry. The ancient writings of Mesopotamia and Egypt are darkened with our ignorance of how such languages were pronounced; but with such assurances in transliteration as we can muster, such writings when spoken were also poetry. In India, the oldest literature is the *Veda*, which were dictated by gods to the *rishi* or prophets; these too were poetry. Oracles spoke poetry. From time to time, their utterances from Delphi and elsewhere were written down, and every one of them that survives as more than a simple phrase is in dactylic hexameter, just as were the epics. The Hebrew prophets also, when relaying the hallucinated utterance of Yahweh, were all poets, though their scribes did not in every case preserve such speech in verse.

As the bicameral mind recedes further into history, and the oracles reach their fifth term, there are exceptions. Poetic utterance by the oracles breaks down here and there. The oracle at Delphi, for example, in the first century A.D. evidently spoke in both verse and prose, the latter to be put into verse by poets in the service of the temples.[1] But the very impulse to transpose oracular prose back into dactylic hexameters is, I suggest, a part of the nostalgia for the divine in this late period; it demonstrates again that metered verse had been the rule previously. Even later, some oracles still spoke exclusively in dactylic hexameters. Tacitus, for example, visited the oracle of Apollo at Claros about A.D.

---

[1] Strabo, *Geography*, 9.3.5, or as translated by H. L. Jones in the Loeb edition, p. 353. This observation was made about A.D. 30. Plutarch's offhand suggestion in the second century A.D. that the raw prophetic outpouring of the oracle *always* had to be versified by inspired *prophetes* is contrary to all the earlier writings and evidence from the oracles themselves. See his *The Oracles of Delphi* in Vol. 5 of *The Moralia*, Loeb edition. I am not sure how seriously we should take Plutarch's rambling after-dinner conversation piece.

100 and described how the entranced priest listened to his decision-seeking petitioners; he then

> . . . swallows a draught of water from a mysterious spring and — though ignorant generally of writing and of meters — delivers his response in set verses.[2]

Poetry then was divine knowledge. And after the breakdown of the bicameral mind, poetry was the sound and tenor of authorization. Poetry commanded where prose could only ask. It felt good. In the wanderings of the Hebrews after the exodus from Egypt, it was the sacred shrine that was carried before the multitude and followed by the people, but it was the poetry of Moses that determined when they would start and when stop, where they would go and where stay.[3]

The association of rhythmical or repetitively patterned utterance with supernatural knowledge endures well into the later conscious period. Among the early Arabic peoples the word for poet was *sha'ir*, 'the knower', or a person endowed with knowledge by the spirits; his metered speech in recitation was the mark of its divine origin. The poet and divine seer have a long tradition of association in the ancient world, and several Indo-European languages have a common term for them. Rhyme and alliteration too were always the linguistic province of the gods and their prophets.[4] In at least some instances of spontaneous possession, the demonic utterances are in meter.[5] Even glossolalia today, as

---

[2] Tacitus, *Annals*, 2:54, or as translated by John Jackson in the Loeb edition, p. 471.

[3] Numbers 10:35, 36. My authority that these lines in Hebrew come under the rubric of poetry is Alfred Guillaume, *Prophecy and Divination among the Hebrew and Other Semites* (New York: Harper, 1938), p. 244.

[4] Guillaume, p. 245.

[5] A possessed woman in China at the beginning of this century, for example, would extemporize verses by the hour. "Everything she said was in measure verse, and was chanted to an unvarying tune . . . the rapid, perfectly uniform, and long continued utterances seemed to us such as could not possibly be counterfeited or premeditated." J. L. Nevius, *Demon Possession and Allied Themes*, p. 37f.

we have seen in III.2, wherever it is practiced, tends to fall into metrical patterns, particularly dactyls.

Poetry then was the language of gods.

Poetry and Song

All the above discussion is mere literary tradition and sounds more plea than proof. We should, therefore, ask if there is another way of approaching the matter to show the relationship of poetry to the bicameral mind more scientifically. There is, I think, if we look at the relation of poetry to music.

First of all, early poetry was song. The difference between song and speech is a matter of discontinuities of pitch. In ordinary speech, we are constantly changing pitch, even in the pronunciation of a single syllable. But in song, the change of pitch is discrete and discontinuous. Speech reels around all over a certain portion of an octave (in relaxed speech about a fifth). Song steps from note to note on strict and delimited feet over a more extended range.

Modern poetry is a hybrid. It has the metrical feet of song with the pitch glissandos of speech. But ancient poetry is much closer to song. Accents were not by intensity stress as in our ordinary speech, but by pitch.[6] In ancient Greece, this pitch is thought to have been precisely the interval of a fifth above the ground note of the poem, so that on the notes of our scale, dactyls would go GCC, GCC, with no extra emphasis on the G. Moreover, the three extra accents, acute, circumflex, and grave, were, as their notations ´,^,` imply, a rising pitch within the syllable, a rising and falling on the same syllable, and a falling pitch respectively. The result was a poetry sung like plainsong with various auditory ornamentation that gave it beautiful variety.

* * *

[6] It was Thomas Day, whose new and syntactically vigorous translation of the *Iliad* is eagerly awaited, who first recited or rather sang epic Greek to me as it should be done. For the theory here, see W. B. Stanford, *The Sound of Greek* (Berkeley: University of California Press, 1967), and play the record inserted in the back cover.

Now how does all this relate to the bicameral mind? Speech, as has long been known, is a function primarily of the left cerebral hemisphere. But song, as we are presently discovering, is primarily a function of the right cerebral hemisphere. The evidence is various but consistent:

• It is common medical knowledge that many elderly patients who have suffered cerebral hemorrhages on the left hemisphere such that they cannot speak can still sing.

• The so-called Wada Test is sometimes performed in hospitals to find out a person's cerebral dominance. Sodium amytal is injected into the carotid artery on one side, putting the corresponding hemisphere under heavy sedation but leaving the other awake and alert. When the injection is made on the left side so that the left hemisphere is sedated and only the right hemisphere is active, the person is unable to speak, but can still sing. When the injection is on the right so that only the left hemisphere is active, the person can speak but cannot sing.[7]

• Patients in whom the entire left hemisphere has been removed because of glioma can only manage a few words, if any, postoperatively. But at least some can sing.[8] One such patient with only a speechless right hemisphere to his name "was able to sing 'America' and 'Home on the Range,' rarely missing a word and with nearly perfect enunciation."[9]

• Electrical stimulation on the right hemisphere in regions adjacent to the posterior temporal lobe, particularly the anterior temporal lobe, often produces hallucinations of singing and music. I have already described some of these patients in I.5. And this in general is the area, corresponding to Wernicke's area on the

[7] H. W. Gordon and J. E. Bogen, "Hemispheric Lateralization of Singing after Intracarotid Sodium Ammo-barbitol," *Journal of Neurology, Neurosurgery and Psychiatry,* 1974, 37: 727–739.

[8] H. W. Gordon, "Auditory Specialization of Right and Left Hemispheres," in M. Kinsbourne and W. Lynn Smith, eds. *Hemispheric Disconnections and Cerebral Function* (Springfield: Thomas, 1974), pp. 126–136.

[9] Charles W. Burklund, "Cerebral Hemisphere Function in the Human," in W. L. Smith ed., *Drug, Development and Cerebral Function* (Springfield: Thomas, 1972), p. 22.

left hemisphere, which I have hypothesized was where the auditory hallucinations of the bicameral mind were organized.

Singing and melody then are primarily right hemisphere activities. And since poetry in antiquity was sung rather than spoken, it was perhaps largely a right hemisphere function, as the theory of the bicameral mind in I.5 would predict. More specifically, ancient poetry involved the posterior part of the right temporal lobe, which I have suggested was responsible for organizing divine hallucinations, together with adjacent areas which even today are involved in music.

For those who are still skeptical, I have devised an experiment where they may even feel for themselves right now the truth of these matters. First, think of two topics, anything, personal or general, on which you would like to talk for a couple of paragraphs. Now, imagining you are with a friend, speak out loud on one of the topics. Next, imagining you are with a friend, *sing* out loud on the other topic. Do each for one full minute, demanding of yourself that you keep going. Compare introspectively. Why is the second so much more difficult? Why does the singing crumble into clichés? Or the melody erode into recitative? Why does the topic desert you in midmelody? What is the nature of your efforts to get your song back on the topic? Or rather — and I think this is more the feeling — to get your topic back to the song?

The answer is that your topic is 'in' Wernicke's area on your left hemisphere, while your song is 'in' what corresponds to Wernicke's area on your right hemisphere. Let me hasten to add that such a statement is an approximation neurologically. And by 'topic' and 'song' I am meaning their neural substrates. But such an approximation is true enough to make my point. It is as if volitional speech is jealous of the right hemisphere and wants you to itself, just as your song is jealous of the left hemisphere and wants you to leave your left hemisphere topic behind. To accomplish the improvised singing of a pre-decided topic feels as if we were jumping back and forth between hemispheres. And so in a sense 'we' are, deciding on the words in the left and then trying to get back to song with them on the right before some other words have got there first. And usually the latter happens, the words are not on the topic, careering off on their own, or not consecutively coherent or not there at all, and so we stop singing.

Of course we can learn to sing our verbal thoughts to a certain extent and musicians often do. And women, since they are less lateralized, may find it easier. If you practice it as an exercise twice a day for a month or a year or a lifetime, sincerely avoiding cliché and memorized material on the lyric side, and mere recitative on the melody side, I expect you will be more proficient at it. If you are ten years old, such learning will probably be much easier and might even make a poet out of you. And if you should be unlucky enough to have some left hemisphere accident at some future time, your thought-singing might come in handy. What is learned here is very probably a new relationship between the hemispheres, not entirely different from some of the learned phenomena in the previous chapter.

The Nature of Music

I wish to expand a little upon the role of instrumental music in all this. For we also hear and appreciate music with our right hemispheres.

Such lateralization of music can be seen even in very young infants. Six-month-old babies can be given EEG's while being held in the laps of their mothers. If the recording electrodes are placed directly over Wernicke's area on the left hemisphere and over what corresponds to Wernicke's area on the right, then when tape recordings of speech are played, the left hemisphere will show the greatest activity. But when a tape of a music box is played or of someone singing, the activity will be greater over the *right* hemisphere. In the experiment I am describing, not only did the children who were fidgeting or crying stop doing so at the sound of music, but also they smiled and looked straight ahead, turning away from the mother's gaze,[10] even acting as we do when we are trying to avoid distraction. This finding has an immense significance for the possibility that the brain is organized at birth to 'obey' stimulation in what corresponds to Wernicke's area on the right hemisphere, namely the music, and not be distracted from it, even as earlier I have said that bicameral men neurologically had to obey hallucinations from the same area. It also points to the great significance of lullabies in development, perhaps influencing a child's later creativity.

Or you can prove this laterality of music yourself. Try hearing different musics on two earphones at the same intensity. You will perceive and remember the music on the left earphone better.[11] This is because the left ear has greater neural representation on the right hemisphere. The specific location here is probably the right anterior temporal lobe, for patients in which it has been removed from the right hemisphere find it very difficult to distinguish one melody from another. And, conversely, with left temporal lobectomies, patients postoperatively have no trouble with such tests.[12]

[10] This is the interesting recent work of Martin Gardiner of the Boston Children's Hospital, personal communication. It is to be published as "EEG Indicators of Lateralization in Human Infants" in S. Harnad, R. Doty, L. Goldstein, J. Jaynes, and G. Krauthammer, eds., *Lateralization in the Nervous System* (New York: Academic Press, 1976).

[11] The experiment was done with Vivaldi concertos by Doreen Kimura, "Functional Asymmetry of the Brain in Dichotic Listening," *Cortex*, 1967, 3: 163–178. But there is evidence that this is not true of musicians whose training has resulted in music's being represented on both hemispheres. This was first discovered by R. C. Oldfield, "Handedness and the Nature of Dominance," Talk at Educational Testing Service, Princeton, September 1969. See also Thomas G. Bever and R. J. Chiarello, "Cerebral Dominance in Musicians and Non-Musicians," *Science* (1974), Vol. 185, pp. 137–139.

[12] D. Shankweiler, "Effects of Temporal-Lobe Damage on Perception of Dichotically Presented Melodies," *Journal of Comparative and Physiological Psychology*, 1966, 62: 115–119.

Now we know neurologically that there can be a spread of excitation from one point of the cortex to adjacent points. Thus it becomes likely that a buildup of excitation in those areas on the right hemisphere serving instrumental music should spread to those adjacent serving divine auditory hallucinations — or vice versa. And hence this close relationship between instrumental music and poetry, and both with the voices of gods. I am suggesting here that the invention of music may have been as a neural excitant to the hallucinations of gods for decision-making in the absence of consciousness.

It is thus no idle happenstance of history that the very name of music comes from the sacred goddesses called Muses. For music too begins in the bicameral mind.

We thus have some ground for saying that the use of the lyre among early poets was to spread excitation to the divine speech area, the posterior part of the right temporal lobe, from immediately adjacent areas. So also the function of flutes that accompanied the lyric and elegiac poets of the eighth and seventh centuries B.C. And when such musical accompaniment is no longer used, as it is not in later Greek poetry, it is, I suggest, because the poem is no longer being sung from the right hemisphere where such spreading excitation would help. It is instead being recited from left hemispheric memory alone, rather than being recreated in the true prophetic trance.

This change in musical accompaniment is also reflected in the way poetry is referred to, although a large amount of historical overlap makes the case not quite so clear. But more early poetry is referred to as song (as in the Iliad and the *Theogony*, for example), while later poetry is often referred to as spoken or told. This change perhaps corresponds roughly to the change from the aoidoi with their lyres to the *rhapsodes* with their *rhapdoi* (light sticks, perhaps to beat the meter) that took place perhaps in the eighth or seventh centuries B.C. And behind these particulars is the more profound psychological change from bicameral composition to conscious recitation, and from oral to written remembering. In much later poetry, however, the poet as singer and his poem as song are brought back metaphorically as a conscious archaism, yielding its own authorization to the now conscious poet.[13]

Poesy and Possession

A third way to examine this transformation of poetry during the rise and spread of consciousness is to look at the poet himself and his mentality. Specifically, were the relations of poets to the Muses the same as the relationship of the oracles to the greater gods?

For Plato at least, the matter was quite clear. Poetry was a divine madness. It was *katokoche* or possession by the Muses;

> . . . all good poets, epic as well as lyric, composed their beautiful poems not by art, but because they are inspired and possessed . . . there is no invention in him until he has been inspired and is out of his senses and the mind is no longer in him.[14]

Poets then, around 400 B.C., were comparable in mentality to the oracles of the same period, and went through similar psychological transformation when they performed.

Now we might be tempted to think with Plato that such possession characterized poetry all the way back into the epic tradition. But the evidence does not warrant such a generalization. In the Iliad itself, so many centuries before the existence of *katokoche* is ever mentioned or observed, a good argument could be made that the primitive aoidos was not "out of his senses and the mind no

---

[13] On this matter see T. B. L. Webster, *From Mycenae to Homer* (London: Methuen, 1958), p. 271f.

[14] Plato, *Io*, 534.

longer in him." For in several places, the poem breaks off as the poet gets stuck and has to beg the Muses to go on (2:483, 11:218, 14:508, 16:112).

Let it be stressed parenthetically here that the Muses were not figments of anyone's imagination. I would ask the reader to peruse the first pages of Hesiod's *Theogony* and realize that all of it was probably seen and heard in hallucination, just as can happen today in schizophrenia or under certain drugs. Bicameral men did not imagine; they experienced. The beautiful Muses with their unison "lily-like" voice, dancing out of the thick mists of evening, thumping on soft and vigorous feet about the lonely enraptured shepherd, these arrogances of delicacy were the hallucinatory sources of memory in late bicameral men, men who did not live in a frame of past happenings, who did not have 'lifetimes' in our sense, and who could not reminisce because they were not fully conscious. Indeed, this is put into mythology by their chosen medium, the shepherd of Helicon himself: the Muses who, he tells us, always sing together with the same *phrenes*[15] and in "unwearying flows" of song, this special group of divinities who, instead of telling men what to do, specialized in telling certain men what had been done, are the daughters of Mnemosyne, the Titaness whose name later comes to mean *memory* — the first word with that meaning in the world.

Such appeals to the Muses then are identical in function with our appeals to memory, like tip-of-the-tongue struggles with recollection. They do not sound like a man out of his senses who doesn't know what he is doing. In one instance in the Iliad, the poet begins to have difficulty and so begs the Muses,

> Say now to me, Muses, having Olympian homes, for you are
> goddesses, and *are present and know all*; but we hear report

[15] The Greek for singing together is *homophronas*, in Hesiod, *Theogony*, line 60. I know of no records of contemporary hallucinations that sound like a group of people in unison. Just why the Muses are plural is an interesting problem. See II. 4, note 2.

alone, neither do we know anything: tell me who were the leaders and rulers of the Greeks? (2:483–487)

and then goes on to plead in his own person that he, the poet, cannot name them, though he had "ten tongues and ten mouths and an unbreakable voice," unless the Muses start singing the material to him. I have italicized a phrase in the quotation to underline their actuality to the poet.

Nor does possession seem to be occurring in Hesiod in his first meeting with them on the holy flanks of Mount Helicon while he was keeping watch over his sheep. He describes how the Muses

> . . . breathed into me a divine voice to celebrate things that shall be and things that were aforetime; and they begged me sing of the race of the blessed gods that are eternally, but ever to sing of themselves both first and last.[16]

Again, I think this should be believed literally as someone's experience in exactly the same way that we believe in the experience of Hesiod's contemporary, Amos, in his meeting with Yahweh in the meadows of Tekoa while he too was keeping watch over his flock.[17] Nor does it seem possession when the Muses' *Theogony* stops (line 104) and Hesiod cries out again in his own voice, praising the Muses and pleading with them again to go on with the poem: "Tell me these things from the beginning, you Muses," having just given a long list of the topics which the poet wants the poem to be about (line 114).

Nor does the stately and careful description of Demodocus in the Odyssey permit an interpretation of the poet as possessed. Evidently Demodocus, if he was real, may have gone through

---

[16] Hesiod, *Theogony*, translated by H. G. Evelyn-White, Loeb Classical Library. Another reason for thinking that this Hesiod is not the author of *Works and Days*, as I suggested in II.5, is the last phrase above. Certainly the work I have ascribed to Perses is not true to this promise to sing only about the gods "both first and last."

[17] Amos, too, was not in a state of possession since he too had dialogue with his god. See Amos 7: 5–8; 8: 1–2. In some of my phrasing I am trying to remind the reader of Luke 2: 8–14.

some kind of cerebral accident which left him blind, but with the power to hear the Muses sing such enchanting poetry as could make an Odysseus drape his head and moan with tears (8:63-92). Indeed Odysseus himself understands that Demodocus of the disabled vision, who could not have witnessed the Trojan War, could sing about it only because the Muse, or Apollo, was actually telling it to him. His chant was *hormetheis theou*, constantly given by the god himself (8:499).

The evidence, therefore, suggests that up to the eighth and probably the seventh century B.C., the poet was *not* out of his mind as he was later in Plato's day. Rather, his creativity was perhaps much closer to what we have come to call bicameral. The fact that such poets were "wretched things of shame, mere bellies," as the Muses scornfully mocked their human adoring mediums,[18] unskilled roughs who came from the more primitive and lonely levels of the social structure, such as shepherds, is in accord with such a suggestion. *Mere bellies* out in the fields had less opportunity to be changed by the new mentality. And loneliness can lead to hallucination.

But by the time of Solon in the sixth century B.C., something different is happening. The poet is no longer simply given his gifts; he has to have *"learning in the gift of the Muses"* (Fragment 13:51). And then, in the fifth century B.C., we hear the very first hint of poets' being peculiar with poetic ecstasy. What a contrast to the calm and stately manner of the earlier aoidoi, Demodocus, for example! It is Democritus who insists that no one can be a great poet without being frenzied up into a state of fury (Fragment 18). And then in the fourth century B.C., the mad possessed poet "out of his senses" that Plato and I have already described. Just as the oracles had changed from the prophet who heard his hallucinations to the possessed person in a wild trance, so also had the poet.

Was this dramatic change because the collective cognitive im-

---

[18] Hesiod, *Theogony*, l. 26.

perative had made the Muses less believable as real external entities? Or was it because the neurological reorganization of hemispheric relations brought on by developing consciousness prohibited such givenness; so that consciousness had to be out of the way to let poetry happen? Or was it Wernicke's area on the right hemisphere using Broca's area on the left, thus short-circuiting (as it were) normal consciousness? Or are these three hypotheses the same (as of course I presently think they are)?

For whatever reasons, decline continues decline in the ensuing centuries. Just as the oracles sputtered out through their latter terms until possession was partial and erratic, so, I suggest, poets slowly changed until the fury and possession by the Muses was also partial and erratic. And then the Muses hush and freeze into myths. Nymphs and shepherds, dance no more. Consciousness is a witch beneath whose charms pure inspiration gasps and dies into invention. The oral becomes written by the poet himself, and written, it should be added, by his right hand, worked by his left hemisphere. The Muses have become imaginary and invoked in their silence as a part of man's nostalgia for the bicameral mind.

In summary, then, the theory of poetry I am trying to state in this scraggly collation of passages is similar to the theory I presented for oracles. Poetry begins as the divine speech of the bicameral mind. Then, as the bicameral mind breaks down, there remain prophets. Some become institutionalized as oracles making decisions for the future. While others become specialized into poets, relating from the gods statements about the past. Then, as the bicameral mind shrinks back from its impulsiveness, and as perhaps a certain reticence falls upon the right hemisphere, poets who are to obtain this same state must learn to do it. As this becomes more difficult, the state becomes a fury, and then ecstatic possession, just as happened in the oracles. And then indeed toward the end of the first millennium B.C., just as the oracles began to become prosaic and their statements versified consciously, so poetry also. Its givenness by the unison Muses has vanished. And conscious men now wrote and crossed out and careted and rewrote their compositions in laborious mimesis of the older divine utterances.

Why as the gods retreated even further into their silent heavens or, in another linguistic mode, as auditory hallucinations shrank back from access by left hemisphere monitoring mechanisms, why did not the dialect of the gods simply disappear? Why did not poets simply cease their rhapsodic practices as did the priests and priestesses of the great oracles? The answer is very clear. The continuance of poetry, its change from a divine given to a human craft is part of that nostalgia for the absolute. The search for the relationship with the lost otherness of divine directives would not allow it to lapse. And hence the frequency even today with which poems are apostrophes to often unbelieved-in entities, prayers to unknown imaginings. And hence the opening paragraph of this treatise. The forms are still there, to be worked with now by the analog 'I' of a conscious poet. His task now is an imitation or mimesis[19] of the former type of poetic utterance and the reality which it expressed. Mimesis in the bicameral sense of mimicking what was heard in hallucination has moved through the mimesis of Plato as representation of reality to mimesis as imitation with invention in its sullen service.

There have been some latter-day poets who have been very specific about actual auditory hallucinations. Milton referred to his "Celestial Patroness, who . . . unimplor'd . . . dictates to me my unpremeditated Verse," even as he, in his blindness, dictated it to his daughters.[20] And Blake's extraordinary visions and auditory hallucinations — sometimes going on for days and sometimes against his will — as the source of his painting and

---

[19] On the history of this word, see Eric A. Havelock, *Preface to Plato* (New York: Grosset & Dunlap, 1967), p. 57, n. 22, as well as Ch. 2.

[20] *Paradise Lost*, 9: 21–24.

poetry are well known. And Rilke is said to have feverishly copied down a long sonnet sequence that he heard in hallucination.

But most of us are more ordinary, more with and of our time. We no longer hear our poems directly in hallucination. It is instead the feeling of something being given and then nourished into being, of the poem happening to the poet, as well and as much as being created by him. Snatches of lines would "bubble up" for Housman after a beer and a walk "with sudden and unaccountable emotions" which then "had to be taken in hand and completed by the brain." "The songs made me, not I them," said Goethe. "It is not I who think," said Lamartine, "it is my ideas that think for me." And dear Shelley said it plain:

> A man cannot say, "I will compose poetry." The greatest poet even cannot say it; for the mind in creation is as a fading coal, which some invisible influence, like an inconstant wind, awakens to transitory brightness . . . and the conscious portions of our natures are unprophetic either of its approach or its departure.[21]

Is the fading coal the left hemisphere and the inconstant wind the right, mapping vestigially the ancient relationship of men to gods?

Of course there is no universal rule in this matter. The nervous systems of poets come like shoes, in all types and sizes, though with a certain irreducible topology. We know that the relations of the hemispheres are not the same in everyone. Indeed, poetry can be written without even a nervous system. A vocabulary, some syntax, and a few rules of lexical fit and measure can be punched into a computer, which can then proceed to write quite 'inspired' if surrealist verse. But that is simply a copy of what we, with two cerebral hemispheres and nervous systems,

[21] Percy Bysshe Shelley, "A Defense of Poetry" in *The Portable Romantic Reader*, H. E. Hugo, ed. (New York: Viking Press, 1957), p. 536.

already do. Computers or men can indeed write poetry without any vestigial bicameral inspiration. But when they do, they are imitating an older and a truer poesy out there in history. Poetry, once started in mankind, needs not the same means for its production. It began as the divine speech of the bicameral mind. And even today, through its infinite mimeses, great poetry to the listener, however it is made, still retains that quality of the wholly other, of a diction and a message, a consolation and an inspiration, that was once our relationship to gods.

A Homily on Thamyris

I would like to end these rather clumsy suggestions on the biology of poetry with some homiletic sentiments on the true tragedy of Thamyris. He was a poet in the Iliad (2:594-600) who boasted he would conquer and control the Muses in his poetry. Gods, as they die away in the transition to consciousness, are jealous gods, as I have said earlier. And the Sacred Nine are no exception. They were enraged at the beautiful ambition of Thamyris. They crippled him (probably a paralysis on his left side), and deprived him forever of poetic expression, and made him forget his ability at harping.

Of course, we do not know if there even was a Thamyris, or exactly what reality is being pointed at by this story. But I suggest it was among the later accretions to the Iliad, and that its insertion may point to the difficulties in hemisphere cooperation in artistic expression at the breakdown of the bicameral mind. The parable of Thamyris may be narratizing what is to us the feeling of losing consciousness in our inspiration and then losing that inspiration in our consciousness of that loss. Consciousness imitates the gods and is a jealous consciousness and will have no other executives of action before it.

I remember when I was younger, at least through my twenties, while walking in woods or along a beach, or climbing hills or almost anything lonely, I would quite often suddenly become conscious that I was hearing in my head improvised symphonies of unambiguous beauty. But at the very moment of my becoming conscious of the fact, not loitering even for a measure! the music vanished. I would strain to call it back. But there would be nothing there. Nothing but a deepening silence. Since the music was undoubtedly being composed in my right hemisphere and heard somehow as a semi-hallucination, and since my analog 'I' with its verbalizations was probably, at that moment at least, a more left hemispheric function, I suggest that this opposition was very loosely like what is behind the story of Thamyris. 'I' strained too much. I have no left hemiplegia. But I do not hear my music anymore. I do not expect ever to hear it again.

The modern poet is in a similar quandary. Once, literary languages and archaic speech came somehow to his bold assistance in that otherness and grandeur of which true poetry is meant to speak. But the grinding tides of irreversible naturalism have swept the Muses even farther out into the night of the right hemisphere. Yet somehow, even helplessly in our search for authorization, we remain "the hierophants of an unapprehended inspiration." And inspiration flees in attempted apprehension, until perhaps it was never there at all. We do not believe enough. The cognitive imperative dissolves. History lays her finger carefully on the lips of the Muses. The bicameral mind, silent. And since

> The god approached dissolves into the air,
>
> Imagine then, by miracle, with me,
> (Ambiguous gifts, as what gods give must be)
>   What could not possibly be there,
>   And learn a style from a despair.

CHAPTER 4

Hypnosis

I F I ASK YOU to taste vinegar as champagne, to feel pleasure when I jab a pin in your arm, or to stare into darkness and contract the pupils of your eyes to an imagined light, or to willfully and really believe something you do not ordinarily believe, just anything, you would find these tasks difficult if not impossible. But if I first put you through the induction procedures of hypnosis, you could accomplish all these things at my asking without any effort whatever.

Why? How can such supererogatory enabling even exist?

It seems a very different company we enter when we go from the familiarity of poetry to the strangeness of hypnosis. For hypnosis is the black sheep of the family of problems which constitute psychology. It wanders in and out of laboratories and carnivals and clinics and village halls like an unwanted anomaly. It never seems to straighten up and resolve itself into the firmer proprieties of scientific theory. Indeed, its very possibility seems a denial of our immediate ideas about conscious self-control on the one hand, and our scientific idea about personality on the other. Yet it should be conspicuous that any theory of consciousness and its origin, if it is to be responsible, *must* face the difficulty of this deviant type of behavioral control.

I think my answer to the opening question is obvious: *hypnosis can cause this extra enabling because it engages the general bicameral paradigm which allows a more absolute control over behavior than is possible with consciousness.*

In this chapter, I shall even go so far as to maintain that no theory other than the present one makes sense of the basic problem. For if our contemporary mentality is, as most people suppose, an immutable genetically determined characteristic evolved back somewhere in mammalian evolution or before, how can it be so altered as in hypnosis? And that alteration merely at some rather ridiculous ministrations of another person? It is only by rejecting the genetic hypothesis and treating consciousness as a learned cultural ability over the vestigial substrate of an earlier more authoritarian type of behavioral control that such alterations of mind can begin to seem orderly.

The central structure of this chapter, obviously, will be to show how well hypnosis fits the four aspects of the bicameral paradigm. But before I do so, I wish to bring out clearly a most important feature of how hypnosis began in the first place. This is what I have emphasized in I.2 and II.5, the generative force of metaphor in creating new mentality.

The Paraphrands of Newtonian Forces

Hypnosis, like consciousness, begins at a particular point in history in the paraphrands of a few new metaphors. The first of these metaphors followed Sir Isaac Newton's discovery of the laws of universal gravitation and his use of them to explain the ocean tides under the attraction of the moon. The mysterious attractions and influences and controls between people were then compared to Newtonian gravitational influences. And the comparison resulted in a new (and ridiculous) hypothesis, that there are tides of attraction between all bodies, living and material, that can be called *animal gravitation*, of which Newton's gravitation is a special case.[1]

---

[1] A full history of hypnosis is yet to be written. But see F. A. Pattie, "Brief History of Hypnotism," in J. E. Gordon, ed., *Handbook of Clinical and Experimental Hypnosis* (New York: Macmillan, 1967). See also an historical paper by one of

This is all very explicit in the romantic and turbid writings of a wanton admirer of Newton's called Anton Mesmer, who began it all. And then came another metaphor, or rather two. Gravitational attraction is similar to magnetic attraction. Therefore, since (in Mesmer's rhetorical thought) two things similar to a third thing are similar to each other, animal gravitation is like magnetic attraction, and so changes its name to *animal magnetism*.

Now at last the theory was testable in a scientific way. To demonstrate the existence of these vibrant magnetic tides in and through living things similar to celestial gravitation, Mesmer applied magnets to various hysterical patients, even prefeeding the patients with medicines containing iron so that the magnetism might work better. And it did! The result could not be doubted with the knowledge of his day. Convulsive attacks were produced by the magnets, creating in Mesmer's words "an artificial ebb and flow" in the body and correcting with its magnetic attraction "the unequal distribution of the nervous fluid's confused movement," thus producing a "harmony of the nerves." He had 'proved' that there are flows of forces between persons as mighty as those that hold the planets in their orbits.

Of course he hadn't proved anything about any kind of magnetism whatever. He had discovered what Sir James Braid on the metaphier of sleep later called hypnosis. The cures were effective because he had explained his exotic theory to his patients with vigorous conviction. The violent seizures and peculiar twists of sensations at the application of magnets were all due to a cognitive imperative that these things would happen, which they did, constituting a kind of self-perpetuating escalating 'proof' that the magnets were working and could effect a cure. We should remember here that just as in ancient Assyria there was no concept of chance and so the casting of lots 'had' to be controlled

the important experimenters in hypnosis, Theodore Sarbin's "Attempts to Understand Hypnotic Phenomena," in Leo Postman, ed., *Psychology in the Making* (New York: Knopf, 1964), pp. 745–784.

by the gods, so in the eighteenth century there was no concept of suggestion and the result *had* to be due to the magnets.

Then when it was found that not only magnets, but cups, bread, wood, human beings, and animals to which a magnet had been touched were also efficacious (how false beliefs breed upon each other!), the whole matter jumped over into another metaphor (this is the fourth), that of static electricity, which — Benjamin Franklin's kite and all — was being so much studied at the time. Thus Mesmer thought there was a "magnetic material" that could be transferred to a countless array of objects, just as static electricity can. Human beings in particular could store up and absorb magnetism, particularly Mesmer himself. Just as a carbon rod stroked with fur produces static electricity, so patients were to be stroked by Mesmer. He could now dispense with actual magnets and use his own animal magnetism. By stroking or making passes over the bodies of his patients, as if they were carbon rods, he produced the same results: convulsions, coiling twists of peculiar sensations, and the cure of what later were called hysterical illnesses.

Now it is critical here to realize and to understand what we might call the paraphrandic changes which were going on in the people involved, due to these metaphors. A paraphrand, you will remember, is the projection into a metaphrand of the associations or paraphiers of a metaphier. The metaphrand here is the influences between people. The metaphiers, or what these influences are being compared to, are the inexorable forces of gravitation, magnetism, and electricity. And their paraphiers of absolute compulsions between heavenly bodies, of unstoppable currents from masses of Leyden jars, or of irresistible oceanic tides of magnetism, all these projected back into the metaphrand of interpersonal relationships, actually changing them, changing the psychological nature of the persons involved, immersing them in a sea of uncontrollable control that emanated from the 'magnetic fluids' in the doctor's body, or in objects which had 'absorbed' such from him.

It is at least conceivable that what Mesmer was discovering was a different kind of mentality that, given a proper locale, a special education in childhood, a surrounding belief system, and isolation from the rest of us, possibly could have sustained itself as a society not based on ordinary consciousness, where metaphors of energy and irresistible control would assume some of the functions of consciousness.

How is this even possible? As I have mentioned already, I think Mesmer was clumsily stumbling into a new way of engaging that neurological patterning I have called the general bicameral paradigm with its four aspects: collective cognitive imperative, induction, trance, and archaic authorization. I shall take up each in turn.

The Changing Nature of Hypnotic Man

That the phenomenon of hypnosis is under the control of a collective cognitive imperative or group belief system is clearly demonstrated by its continual changing in history. As beliefs about hypnosis changed, so also its very nature. A few decades after Mesmer, subjects no longer twisted with strange sensations and convulsions. Instead they began spontaneously to speak and reply to questions during their trance state. Nothing like this had happened before. Then, early in the nineteenth century, patients spontaneously began to forget what had happened during the trance,[2] something never reported previously. Around 1825, for some unknown reason, persons under hypnosis started to spontaneously diagnose their own illnesses. In the middle of the century, phrenology, the mistaken idea that conformations of the skull indicate mental faculties, became so popular that it actually

---

[2] As revealed in the important writings of A.-M.-J. Chastenet, Marquis de Puysegur, "*Memoires pour Servir à L'Histoire et à L'Establissement du Magnetism Animale*," 2nd ed. (Paris, 1809).

engulfed hypnosis for a time. Pressure on the scalp over a phre-
nological area during hypnosis caused the subject to express the
faculty controlled by that area (yes, this actually happened), a
phenomenon never seen before or since. When the scalp area
over the part of the brain supposedly responsible for "veneration"
was pressed, the hypnotized subject sunk to his knees in prayer![3]
This was so because it was believed to be so.

A little later, Charcot, the greatest psychiatrist of his time,
demonstrated to large professional audiences at the Salpêtrière
that hypnosis was again quite different! Now it had three successive stages: catalepsy, lethargy, and somnambulism. These
"physical states" could be changed from one to another by
manipulating muscles, or various pressures, or friction on the top
of the head. Even rubbing the head over Broca's area produced
aphasia! And then Binet, arriving at the Salpêtrière to check on
the findings of Charcot, promptly compounded the problem by
returning to Mesmer's magnets and discovering even more bizarre behavior.[4] Placing magnets on one side or the other of the
body of a hypnotized person, he could flip-flop perceptions, hysterical paralyses, supposed hallucinations, and movements from
one side to the other, as if such phenomena were so many iron
filings. None of these absurd results was ever found before or
since.

It is not simply that the operator, Mesmer or Charcot or whoever, was suggesting to the pliant patient what the operator
believed hypnosis to be. Rather, there had been developed within

[3] These demonstrations by Sir James Braid, otherwise the first cautions student of
the subject, later embarrassed him. He never referred to such results after 1845 — and
probably never understood them. A detailed account of Braid's pivotal position in
the history of hypnosis may be found in J. M. Bramwell, *Hypnotism: Its History,
Practice, and Theory* (London: 1903; New York: Julian Press, 1956).

[4] See Alfred Binet and C. Fere, *Le Magnetisme Animale* (Paris: Alcan, 1897).
This self-deluding work and the dispute with Delboeuf and the more correct Nancy
School that followed, as well as Binet's later acknowledgment of his foolish error,
are described in Theta Wolf's excellent biography *Alfred Binet* (Chicago: University
of Chicago Press, 1973), pp. 40–78.

the group in which he worked a cognitive imperative as to what the phenomenon was 'known' to be. Such historical changes then clearly show that hypnosis is not a stable response to given stimuli, but changes as do the expectations and preconceptions of a particular age.

What is obvious in history can be shown in a more experimentally controlled way. Previously unheard-of manifestations of hypnosis can be found by simply informing subjects beforehand that such manifestations are expected in hypnosis, that is, are a part of the collective cognitive imperative about the matter. For example, an introductory psychology class was casually told that under hypnosis a subject's dominant hand cannot be moved. This had never occurred in hypnosis in any era. It was a lie. Nevertheless, when members of the class at a later time were hypnotized, the majority, without any coaching or further suggestion, were unable to move their dominant hand. Out of such studies has come the notion of the "demand characteristics" of the hypnotic situation, that the hypnotized subject exhibits the phenomena which he thinks the hypnotist expects.[5] But that expresses it too personally. It is rather what he thinks hypnosis is. And such "demand characteristics," taken in this way, are of precisely the same nature as what I am calling the collective cognitive imperative.

Another way of seeing the force of the collective imperative is to note its strengthening by crowds. Just as religious feeling and belief is enhanced by crowds in churches, or in oracles by the throngs that attended them, so hypnosis in theaters. It is well known that stage hypnotists with an audience packed to the

[5] This is one of the important ideas in the history of hypnosis research. See the papers of Martin Orne, particularly, "Nature of Hypnosis: Artifact and Essence," *Journal of Abnormal and Social Psychology*, 1959, 58: 277–299; in this connection David Rosenhan's important and sobering, "On the Social Psychology of Hypnosis Research" in J. E. Gordon, ed., *Handbook of Clinical and Experimental Psychology*.

rafters, reinforcing the collective imperative or expectancy of hypnosis, can produce far more exotic hypnotic phenomena than are found in the isolation of laboratory or clinic.

The Induction

Secondly, the place of an induction procedure in hypnosis is obvious.[6] And needs little comment. The variety of techniques in contemporary practice is enormous, but they all share the same narrowing of consciousness, similar to the induction procedures for oracles, or the relationship between a *pelestike* and a *katochos* which we looked at in the previous chapters. The subject may be seated or standing or lying down, may be stroked or not, stared at or not, asked to look at a small light or flame or gem, or perhaps a thumbtack on the wall, or at the thumbnail of his own clasped hands, or not — there are hundreds of variations. But always the operator is trying to confine the subject's attention to his own voice. "All you hear is my voice and you are getting sleepier and sleepier, etc." is a common pattern, repeated until the subject, if hypnotized, is unable to open his clasped hands if the operator says he can't, for example, or cannot move his relaxed arm if the operator so suggests, or cannot remember his name if that is suggested. Such simple suggestions are often used as indications of the success of the hypnosis in its beginning stages.

If the subject is not able to narrow his consciousness in this fashion, if he cannot forget the situation as a whole, if he remains in a state of consciousness of other considerations, such as the room and his relationship to the operator, if he is still narra-

---

[6] The best discussion of induction procedures is that of Perry London, "The Induction of Hypnosis," in J. E. Gordon, pp. 44–79. And for discussions of hypnosis in general that I have found helpful, see the papers of Ronald Shor, particularly his "Hypnosis and the Concept of the Generalized Reality-Orientation," *American Journal of Psychotherapy*, 1959, 13: 582–602, and "Three Dimensions of Hypnotic Depth," *International Journal of Clinical and Experimental Hypnosis*, 1962, 10: 23–38.

tizing with his analog 'I' or 'seeing' his metaphor 'me' being hypnotized, hypnosis will be unsuccessful. But repeated attempts with such subjects often succeed, showing that the "narrowing" of consciousness in hypnotic induction is partly a learned ability, learned, I should add, on the basis of the aptic structure I have called the general bicameral paradigm. As we saw earlier that the ease with which a katochos can enter an hallucinatory trance improves with practice, so also in hypnosis: even in the most susceptible, the length of the induction and its substances can be radically reduced with repeated sessions.

Trance and Paralogic Compliance

Thirdly, the hypnotic trance is called just that. It is of course usually different from the kind of trance that goes on in other vestiges of the bicameral mind. Individuals do not have true auditory hallucinations, as in the trances of oracles or mediums. That place in the paradigm is taken over by the operator. But there is the same diminution and then absence of normal consciousness. Narratization is severely restricted. The analog 'I' is more or less effaced. The hypnotized subject is not living in a subjective world. He does not introspect as we do, does not know he is hypnotized, and is not constantly monitoring himself as, in an unhypnotized state, he does.

In recent times, the metaphor of submersion in water is almost invariably used to talk about the trance. Thus there are references to "going under" and to "deep" or "shallow" trances. The hypnotist often tells a subject he is going "deeper and deeper." It is indeed possible that without the submersion metaphier, the whole phenomenon would be different, particularly in regard to post-hypnotic amnesia. The paraphiers of above and below the surface of water, with its different visual and tactual fields, could be creating a kind of two-world-ness resulting in something similar to state-dependent memory. And the sudden appearance of spontaneous post-hypnotic amnesia in the early nineteenth century may be due to this change from gravitational to submersion metaphors. In other words, spontaneous post-hypnotic amnesia may have been a paraphrand of the submersion metaphor. (It is interesting to note that such spontaneous amnesia is presently disappearing from hypnotic phenomena. Possibly, hypnosis has become so familiar as to become a thing in itself, its metaphorical basis wearing away with use, reducing the power of its paraphrands.)

It is in the "deeper" stages of the trance that the most interesting phenomena can be elicited. These are extremely important for any theory of mind to explain. Unless otherwise suggested, the subject is 'deaf' to all but the operator's voice; he does not 'hear' other people. Pain can be 'blocked' off, or enhanced above normal. So can sensory experience. Emotions can be totally structured by suggestion: told he is about to hear a funny joke, the subject will laugh uproariously at "grass is green." The subject can somehow control certain automatic responses better than in the normal state at the suggestion of the operator. His sense of identity can be radically changed. He can be made to act as if he were an animal, or an old man, or a child.

But it is an *as-if* with a suppression of an *it-isn't*. Some extremists in hypnosis have sometimes claimed that when a subject in a trance is told he is now only five or six years old, that an *actual* regression to that age of childhood occurs. This is clearly untrue. Let me cite one example. The subject had been born in Germany, and emigrated with his family to an English-speaking country at about age eight, at which time he learned English, forgetting most of his German. When the operator suggested to him under 'deep' hypnosis that he was only six years old, he displayed all kinds of childish mannerisms, even writing in childish print on a blackboard. Asked in English if he understood English, he childishly explained in English that he could not understand or speak English but only German! He even printed on the blackboard in English that he could not understand a word of English![7] The phenomenon is thus like play acting, not a true regression. It is an uncritical and illogical obedience to the operator and his expectations that is similar to the obedience of a bicameral man to a god.

Another common error made about hypnosis, even in the best modern textbooks, is to suppose that the operator can induce true hallucinations. Some unpublished observations of my own bear to the contrary. After a subject was in deep hypnosis, I went through the motions of giving him a nonexistent vase and asked him to place nonexistent flowers from a table into the vase, saying out loud the color of each one. This was easily done. It was play-acting. But giving him a nonexistent book, and asking him to hold it in his hands, to turn to page one and begin reading was a different matter. It could not be play-acted without more creativity than most of us can muster. The subject would readily go through the suggested motions of holding such a book, might stumble through some cliché first phrase or possibly a sentence, but then would complain that the print was blurry, or too difficult to read, or some similar rationalization. Or when asked to describe a picture (nonexistent) on a blank piece of paper, the subject would reply in a halting way if at all, giving only short answers when prodded by questions as to what he saw. If this had been a true hallucination, his eyes would have roamed over the paper and a full description would have been a simple matter — as it is when schizophrenics describe their visual hallucinations. There were great individual differences here, as might be expected, but the behavior is much more consistent with an as-if hesitant role-taking than with the effortless givenness with which true hallucinations are experienced.

This point is brought out by another experiment. If a hypnotized person is told to walk across the room, and a chair has been placed in his path, and he is told that there is no chair there, he

[7] I am grateful to Martin Orne for this example.

does not hallucinate the chair out of existence. He simply walks around it. He behaves as if he did not notice it — which of course he did, since he walked around it. It is interesting here that if unhypnotized subjects are asked to simulate hypnosis in this particular situation, they promptly crash into the chair,[8] since they are trying to be consistent with the erroneous view that hypnosis *actually* changes perceptions.

Hence the important concept of *trance logic* which has been brought forward to denote this difference.[9] This is simply the bland response to absurd logical contradictions. But it is not any kind of logic really, nor simply a trance phenomenon. It is rather what I would prefer to dress up as *paralogical compliance to verbally mediated reality*. It is paralogic because the rules of logic (which we remember are an external standard of truth, not the way the mind works) are put aside to comply with assertions about reality that are not concretely true. It is a type of behavior found everywhere in the human condition from contemporary religious litanies to various superstitions of tribal societies. But it is particularly pronounced in and centrally characteristic of the mental state of hypnosis.

It is paralogic compliance that a subject walks around a chair he has been told is not there, rather than crashing into it (logical compliance), and finds nothing illogical in his actions. It is paralogical compliance when a subject says in English that he knows no English and finds nothing amiss in saying so. If our German subject had been simulating hypnosis, he would have shown logical compliance by talking only in what German he could remember or being mute.

It is paralogic compliance when a subject can accept that the same person is in two locations at the same time. If a hypnotized subject is told that person X is person Y, he will behave accord-

---

[8] The basic work in comparing hypnotized subjects with control subjects asked to simulate the hypnotic state has been done by Martin Orne. This ingeniously simple example is due to him.

[9] Martin Orne, "The Nature of Hypnosis: Artifact and Essence."

ingly. Then if the real person Y walks into the room, the subject finds it perfectly acceptable that both are person Y. This is similar to the paralogic compliance found today in another vestige of the bicameral mind, schizophrenia. Two patients in a ward may both believe themselves to be the same important or divine person without any feelings of illogicality.[10] I suggest that a similar paralogic compliance was also evident in the bicameral era itself, as in treating unmoving idols as living and eating, or the same god as being in several places at one time, or in the multiples of jewel-eyed effigies of the same god-king found side-by-side in the pyramids. Like a bicameral man, the hypnotized subject does not recognize any peculiarities and inconsistencies in his behavior. He cannot 'see' contradictions because he cannot introspect in a completely conscious way.

The sense of time in a trance is also diminished, as we have seen it was in the bicameral mind. This is particularly evident in post-hypnotic amnesia. We, in our normal states, use the spatialized succession of conscious time as a substrate for successions of memories. Asked what we have done since breakfast, we commonly narratize a row of happenings that are what we can call "time-tagged." But the subject in a hypnotic trance, like the schizophrenic patient or the bicameral man, has not such a schema of time in which events can be time-tagged. The before-and afterness of spatialized time is missing. Such events as can be remembered from the trance by a subject in post-hypnotic amnesia are vague isolated fragments, cuing off the self, rather than spatialized time as in normal remembering. Amnesic subjects can only report, if anything, "I clasped my hands, I sat in a chair," with no detail or sequencing, in a way that to me is reminiscent of Hammurabi or Achilles.[11] What is significantly

[10] For an extensive description of one example, see Milton Rokeach, *The Three Christs of Ypsilanti* (New York: Knopf, 1960).

[11] I am grateful to John Kihlstrom of Harvard for discussions on these points. The distinct contrast between the language of amnesics and that of rememberers is from his study, soon to be published.

different about the contemporary hypnotic subject, however, is the fact that at the suggestion of the operator, the narratized sequential memories can often be brought back to the subject, showing that there has been some kind of parallel processing by consciousness outside of the trance.

Such facts make the hypnotic trance a fascinating complexity. Parallel processing! While a subject is doing and saying one thing, his brain is processing his situation in at least two different ways, one more inclusive than the other. This conclusion can be demonstrated even more dramatically by the recent discovery that has been dubbed "the hidden observer." A hypnotized subject, after the suggestion that he will feel nothing when keeping his hand in a bucket of ice-cold water for a minute (a really painful, but benign experience!), may show no discomfort and say he felt nothing; but if it has previously been suggested that when and only when the operator touches his shoulder, he will say in another voice exactly what he really felt, that is what happens. At such a touch, the subject, often in a low guttural voice, may give full expression to his discomfiture, yet return immediately to his ordinary voice and to the anesthetized state when the operator's hand is lifted.[12]

Such evidence returns us to a once rejected notion of hypnosis known as dissociation that emerged from studies of multiple personality at the beginning of this century.[13] The idea is that in hypnosis the totality of mind or reactivity is being separated into concurrent streams which can function independently of each other. What this means for the theory of consciousness and its origin as described in Book I is not immediately apparent. But

[12] Ernest Hilgard, "A Neodissociation Interpretation of Pain Reduction in Hypnosis," *Psychological Review*, 1973, 80: 396–411. I would like to record here my gratitude to Ernest Hilgard for a critical reading of the earlier chapters. His encouraging criticisms were extremely helpful.

[13] The classics in this field are Pierre Janet, *The Major Symptoms of Hysteria*, 1907 (2nd ed., New York: Holt, 1920) and Morton Prince, *The Unconscious* (New York: Macmillan, 1914). For an excellent discussion see Ernest Hilgard's "Dissociation Revisited" in M. Henle, J. Jaynes, and J. J. Sullivan, eds., *Historical Conceptions of Psychology* (New York: Springer, 1973).

such dissociated processing is certainly reminiscent of the bicameral organization of mind itself, as well as the kind of nonconscious problem solving discussed in I.1.

Perhaps the least discussed aspect of hypnosis is the difference in the nature of the trance among persons who have never seen or known much about hypnosis before. Usually, of course, the trance is in our time a passive and suggestible state. But some subjects really do go to sleep. Others are always partly conscious and yet peculiarly suggestible until who can judge between acting and reality? Others tremble so severely that the subject has to be 'awakened'. And so on.

That such individual differences are due to differences in the belief or collective cognitive imperative of the individual is suggested by a recent study. Subjects were asked to describe in writing what happens in hypnosis. They were later hypnotized, and the results compared with their expectation. One 'awoke' from the trance each time she was given a task for which she had to see. A later perusal of her paper showed she had written, "A person's eyes must be closed in order to be in a hypnotic trance." Another could only be hypnotized on a second attempt. He had written, "Most people cannot be hypnotized the first time." And another could not perform tasks under hypnosis when standing. She had written, "The subject has to be reclining or sitting."[14] But the more hypnosis is talked about, even as on these pages, the more standardized the cognitive imperative and hence the trance becomes.

The Hypnotist as Authorization

And so, fourthly, a very particular kind of archaic authorization which also determines in part the different nature of the trance. For here, instead of the authorization being an hallucinated or possessing god, it is the operator himself. He is mani-

[14] T. R. Sarbin, "Contribution to Role-Taking Theory: I. Hypnotic Behavior," *Psychology Review*, 1943, 57: 255–270.

festly an authority figure to the subject. And if he is not, the subject will be less hypnotizable, or will require a much longer induction or a much greater belief in the phenomenon to begin with (a stronger cognitive imperative).

Indeed, most students of the subject insist that there must be developed a special kind of trust relationship between the subject and the operator.[15] One common test of the susceptibility to hypnosis is to stand behind the prospective subject and ask him to permit himself to fall voluntarily to see what it feels like to 'let go'. If the subject steps back to break his fall, some part of him lacking confidence that he will be caught, he almost invariably turns out to be a poor hypnotic subject for that particular operator.[16]

Such trust explains the difference between hypnosis in the clinic and in the laboratory. The hypnotic phenomena found in a medical psychiatric setting are commonly more profound, because, I suggest, a psychiatrist is a more godlike figure to his patient than is an investigator to his subject. And a similar explanation can be made for the age at which hypnosis is most easily done. Hypnotic susceptibility is at its peak between the ages of eight and ten.[17] Children look up to adults with a vastly

[15] Even Clark Hull, a strident behaviorist, the first to perform really controlled experiments in hypnosis, and who scorned introspective data, was compelled to look on hypnosis as "prestige suggestion," perhaps with "a quantitative shift in the upward direction which may result from the hypnotic procedure." *Hypnosis and Suggestibility: An Experimental Approach* (New York: Appleton-Century-Crofts, 1933), p. 392.

[16] See Ernest Hilgard, *Hypnotic Susceptibility* (New York: Harcourt, Brace and World, 1965), p. 101. Those investigating glossolalia, discussed in III.2, have remarked that the person able to "speak in tongues" must have a very similar kind of trust in his charismatic leader. When such trust in such a leader diminishes, so does the phenomenon. It would be a simple matter, using cassette recordings for hypnotic induction procedures, to manipulate the variable of prestige and really demonstrate the importance of this factor in hypnosis.

[17] From the data of Theodore X. Barber and D. S. Calverley, "Hypnotic-Like Suggestibility in Children and Adults," *Journal of Abnormal and Social Psychology*, 1963, 66: 589–597. In a forthcoming book, I shall be discussing the development of consciousness in the child, suggesting that this age of greatest hypnotic susceptibility is just after the full development of consciousness.

greater sense of adult omnipotence and omniscience, and this thus increases the potentiality of the operator in fulfilling the fourth element of the paradigm. The more godlike the operator is to the subject, the more easily is the bicameral paradigm activated.

Evidence for the Bicameral Theory of Hypnosis

If it is true that the relationship of subject to operator in hypnosis is a vestige of an earlier relationship to a bicameral voice, several interesting questions arise. If the neurological model outlined in I.5 is in the right direction, then we might expect some kind of laterality phenomenon in hypnosis. Our theory predicts that in EEG's of a subject under hypnosis, the ratio of brain activity in the right hemisphere would be increased over that of the left, although this is complicated by the fact that it is the left hemisphere that to some extent must understand the operator. But at least we would expect proportionally more right hemisphere involvement than in ordinary consciousness.

At the present time we have no clear idea about even a usual EEG under hypnosis, such the conflicting findings of researchers. But there are other lines of evidence, even if they are unfortunately more correlational and indirect. They are:

ఴ Individuals can be categorized by whether they use the right or left hemisphere relatively more than others. A simple way of doing this is to face a person and ask questions and note which way his eyes move as he thinks of an answer. (As in I.5, we are speaking only of right-handed people.) If to his right, he is using his left hemisphere relatively more, and if to the left, his right hemisphere — since activation of the frontal eye fields of either hemisphere turns the eyes to the contralateral side. It has been recently reported that people who, in answering questions face to face, turn their eyes to the left, who are thus using their right hemisphere more than most others, are much more susceptible to hypnosis.[18] This can be interpreted as indicating that hypnosis may involve the right hemisphere in very special ways, that the more easily hypnotized person is the one who can 'listen to' and 'rely on' the right hemisphere more than others.

ॐ As we saw in I.5, the right hemisphere, which we have presumed to have been the source of divine hallucinations in earlier millennia, is presently considered to be the more creative, spatial, and responsible for vivid imagery. Several recent studies have found that individuals who manifest these characteristics more than others are indeed more susceptible to hypnosis.[19] These findings are consistent with the hypothesis that hypnosis is a reliance on right hemisphere categories, just as a bicameral man relied on his divine guidance.

ॐ If calling hypnosis a vestige of the bicameral mind is valid, we might also expect that those most susceptible to being hypnotized would be those most susceptible to other instances of the general bicameral paradigm. In regard to religious involvement, this appears to be true. Persons who have attended church regularly since childhood are more susceptible to hypnosis, while those who have had less religious involvement tend to be less susceptible. At least some investigators of hypnosis that I know seek their subjects in theological colleges because they have found such students to be more susceptible.

ॐ The phenomenon of imaginary companions in childhood is something I shall have more to say about in a future work. But it too can be regarded as another vestige of the bicameral mind. At least half of those whom I have interviewed remembered distinctly that hearing their companions speak was the same quality of experience as hearing the question as I asked it. True halluci-

---

[18] R. C. Gur and R. E. Gur, "Handedness, Sex, and Eyedness as Moderating Variables in the Relation between Hypnotic Susceptibility and Functional Brain Assymetry," *Journal of Abnormal Psychology*, 1974, 83: 635–643.

[19] Josephine R. Hilgard, *Personality and Hypnosis* (Chicago: University of Chicago Press, 1970), Ch. 7. The data on which the next three paragraphs are based also come from her important book, Chs. 5, 8, and 14 respectively.

nation. The incidence of imaginary companions occurs mostly between the ages of three and seven, just preceding what I would regard as the full development of consciousness in children. My thinking here is that, either by some innate or environmental predisposition to have imaginary companions, the neurological structure of the general bicameral paradigm is (to use a metaphor) exercised. If the hypothesis of this chapter is correct, we might then expect such persons to be more susceptible to the engagement of that paradigm later in life — as in hypnosis. And they are. Those who have had imaginary companions in childhood are easier to hypnotize than those who have not. Again it is a case where hypnotizability is correlated with another vestige of the bicameral mind.

꙰ If we can regard punishment in childhood as a way of instilling an enhanced relationship to authority, hence training some of those neurological relationships that were once the bicameral mind, we might expect this to increase hypnotic susceptibility. And this is true. Careful studies show that those who have experienced severe punishment in childhood and come from a disciplined home are more easily hypnotized, while those who were rarely punished or not punished at all tend to be less susceptible to hypnosis.

These laboratory findings are only suggestive, and there are quite different ways of understanding them, for which I refer the reader to the original reports. But together they do form a pattern which lends support to the hypothesis that hypnosis is in part a vestige of a preconscious mentality. Placing the phenomena of hypnosis against the broad historical background of mankind in this way gives them certain contours that they would not otherwise have. If one has a very definite biological notion of consciousness and that its origin is back in the evolution of mammalian nervous systems, I cannot see how the phenomenon of hypnosis can be understood at all, not one speck of it. But if we fully realize that consciousness is a culturally learned event, balanced over the suppressed vestiges of an earlier mentality, then we can see that consciousness, in part, can be culturally unlearned or arrested. Learned features, such as analog 'I,' can under the proper cultural imperative be taken over by a different initiative, and one such instance is what we call hypnosis. The reason that that different initiative works in conjunction with the other factors of the diminishing consciousness of the induction and trance is that in some way it engages a paradigm of an older mentality than subjective consciousness.

Objection: Does Hypnosis Exist?

Finally, I should briefly refer to possible alternative interpretations. But presently there are not so much theories of hypnosis as points of view, each correct as far as it goes. One view insists that imagination and concentration on what the hypnotist suggests, and the tendency of such an imagination to result in conforming action, are important.[20] They are. Another, that it is condition of monomotivation that counts.[21] Of course, that is a description. Another states that the basic phenomenon is simply the ability to enact different roles, the as-if nature of most hypnotic performances.[22] This certainly is true. Another correctly stresses the dissociation.[23] Another that hypnosis is a regression to a childlike relation to a parent.[24] And indeed this is often how

[20] Magda Arnold, "On the Mechanism of Suggestion and Hypnosis," *Journal of Abnormal and Social Psychology*, 1946, 41: 107–128.

[21] Robert White, "A Preface to the Theory of Hypnotism," *Journal of Abnormal and Social Psychology*, 1941, 16: 477–505.

[22] T. R. Sarbin, "Contributions to Role-Taking Theory." But see also his more recent paper with Milton Anderson "Role-Theoretical Analysis of Hypnotic Behavior," in J. E. Gordon.

[23] Ernest Hilgard, "A Neodissociation Interpretation."

[24] One of two psychoanalytic interpretations of hypnosis. See for example Merton M. Gill and Margaret Brenman, *Hypnosis and Related States* (New York: International Universities Press, 1959). The other, that hypnosis is a love relationship between operator and subject, is no longer taken seriously.

any vestige of the bicameral mind appears, since the bicameral mind itself is based on such admonitory experience.

But the main theoretical controversy — and it is a continuing one, and the one that is most important for us here — is whether or not hypnosis is really anything different from what happens every day in the normal state. For if this view is final, my interpretation in this chapter of a different mentality is utterly wrong. Hypnosis cannot be a vestige of anything since it does not really exist. All the manifestations of hypnosis, this position insists, can be shown to be simply exaggerations of normal phenomena. We can tick them off:

As for the kind of obedience to the operator, all of us do the same thing without thinking in situations *that are so defined,* as with a teacher or a traffic policeman, or perhaps the caller at a square dance.

As to such phenomena as suggested deafness, everyone has had the experience of 'listening' carefully to another person and yet not hearing a word. And so the mother who sleeps through a thunderstorm and yet hears and wakes to the cry of her baby is not engaging a different mechanism from that of the hypnotized subject who hears only the hypnotist's voice and is asleep to all else.

As for the induced amnesia which so astonishes an observer, who can remember what he was thinking five minutes ago? You must suggest to yourself a set or struction to remember at the time. And this the operator of the present day can do or not do, negating or enhancing the paraphrand of submersion, so that the subject does or does not remember.

As for the suggested paralysis under hypnosis, who has not been in discussion with a friend during a walk until, becoming more and more absorbed, both walk more slowly until you are standing still? Concentrated attention has meant arrest of movement.

As for hypnotic anesthesia, that most remarkable of hypnotic phenomena, who has not seen a hurt child distracted by a toy until the crying stops and the pain is forgotten? Or known of victims of accidents bleeding from unfelt wounds? And acupuncture may indeed be a related phenomenon.

And as for the "hidden observer," this kind of parallel processing goes on all the time. In ordinary conversation, we listen to someone and plan what we are going to say at the same time. And actors do this constantly, *always* acting as their own hidden observers; Stanislavski to the contrary, they are always able to criticize their performances. And many of the examples of nonconscious thought in I.1, or my description of driving a car and conversing which opened I.4, are further instances.

And as for the startling success of post-hypnotic suggestion, we all sometimes decide to react to some event in a certain way and then do so, even forgetting our prior reason. It is really not different from 'pre-hypnotic suggestion', as in the supposed paralysis of the dominant hand a few pages ago. It is a structuring of the collective cognitive imperative that can predetermine our reactions in very specific ways.

And so for other remarkable feats performed under hypnosis; all are exaggerations of everyday phenomena. Hypnosis, the argument runs, just seems different to an observer. The trance behavior is simply intense concentration as in the proverbial "absent-minded professor." Indeed a host of recent experiments have been aimed at showing that all hypnotic phenomena can be duplicated in waking subjects by simple suggestion.[25]

My reply, and it is the reply of others as well, is that this is not explaining hypnosis. It is explaining it away. Even though all of the phenomena of hypnosis can be duplicated in ordinary life (and I do not think they can), hypnosis can still be defined by distinct procedures, distinct susceptibilities which correlate with

[25] The most prominent and untiring researcher with this view is Theodore X. Barber. For Barber, "hypnosis" just does not exist as a state different from waking life, and the term should therefore always be written with quotation marks. Among his numerous papers, see his "Experimental Analysis of 'Hypnotic' Behavior: Review of Recent Empirical Findings," *Journal of Abnormal Psychology*, 1965, 70: 132–154.

other experiences as well as other vestiges of the bicameral mind, and by huge differences in the ease with which hypnotic phenomena can be reproduced with and without hypnotic induction. In any speculation about possible future changes in our mentality, this latter difference is extremely important. That is why I began this chapter as I did. If we are asked to be animals, five-year-olds, painless when pricked, color-blind, cataleptic, or show nystagmus to imagined whirlings of the visual field,[26] or to taste vinegar as champagne — it is enormously more difficult to do in our normal state of consciousness than when ordinary consciousness is absent under hypnosis. Such feats without rapport with an operator require grotesque efforts of persuasion and massive burdens of concentration. The full consciousness of the waking state seems itself like a huge wilderness of distracting closenesses that cannot easily be crossed to catch into such immediate control. Try looking out the window and pretending to be red-green color-blind to such an extent that those colors really do look like shades of gray.[27] It can be done to a certain extent, but it is much easier under hypnosis. Or get up now from where you are sitting and act like a bird, flapping your arms and emitting strange calls for for the next fifteen minutes, something easy to do under hypnosis. But there is not one reader of that last sentence who can do it — if he is alone. Whatever those sweaty feelings of foolishness or silliness are, the why-should-I's and the this-is-absurd's, they crowd in like careful tyrants jealous as a god of such a performance; you need the permission of a group, the authoriza-

[26] J. P. Brady and E. Levitt, "Nystagmus as a Criterion of Hypnotically Induced Visual Hallucinations," *Science*, 1964, 146: 85–86. But I do not agree with the authors that this proves the existence of true hallucinations.

[27] Normal subjects asked to respond to the Ishihara color-blindness test by trying not to see the color red and then by trying not to see green read some of the Ishihara cards in the manner expected from individuals with red or green color-blindness. This was shown by Theoder X. Barber and D. C. Deeley, "Experimental Evidence for a Theory of Hypnotic Behavior: I. 'Hypnotic Color-Blindness' without 'Hypnosis'," *International Journal of Clinical and Experimental Hypnosis*, 1961, 9: 79–86. But under hypnosis this pseudo-color-blindness is easier to obtain, as in Milton Erickson's "The Induction of Color-Blindness by a Technique of Hypnotic Suggestion," *Journal of General Psychology*, 1939, 20: 61–89.

tion of a collective imperative as well as the command of an operator — or a god — to achieve such obedience. Or put your hands on the table in front of you and make one of them distinctly redder; possible for you to do now, but much easier under hypnosis. Or raise both your hands for fifteen minutes without feeling any discomfort, a simple task under hypnosis but onerous without it.

What is it then that hypnosis supplies that does this extraordinary enabling, that allows us to do things we cannot ordinarily do except with great difficulty? Or is it 'we' that do them? Indeed, in hypnosis it is as if someone else were doing things through us. And why is this so? And why is this easier? Is it that we have to lose our conscious selves to gain such control, which cannot then be *by us?*

On another level, why is it that in our daily lives we cannot get up above ourselves to authorize ourselves into being what we really wish to be? If under hypnosis we can be changed in identity and action, why not in and by ourselves so that behavior flows from decision with as absolute a connection, so that whatever in us it is that we refer to as *will* stands master and captain over action with as sovereign a hand as the operator over a subject?

The answer here is partly in the limitations of our learned consciousness in this present millennium. We need some vestige of the bicameral mind, our former method of control, to help us. With consciousness we have given up those simpler more absolute methods of control of behavior which characterized the bicameral mind. We live in a buzzing cloud of whys and wherefores, the purposes and reasonings of our narratizations, the many-routed adventures of our analog 'I's. And this constant spinning out of possibilities is precisely what is necessary to save us from behavior of too impulsive a sort. The analog 'I' and the metaphor 'me' are always resting at the confluence of many collective cognitive imperatives. We know too much to command ourselves very far.

Those who through what theologians call the "gift of faith" can center and surround their lives in religious belief do indeed have different collective cognitive imperatives. They can indeed change themselves through prayer and its expectancies much as in post-hypnotic suggestion. It is a fact that belief, political or religious, or simply belief in oneself through some earlier cognitive imperative, works in wondrous ways. Anyone who has experienced the sufferings of prisons or detention camps knows that both mental and physical survival is often held carefully in such untouchable hands.

But for the rest of us, who must scuttle along on conscious models and skeptical ethics, we have to accept our lessened control. We are learned in self-doubt, scholars of our very failures, geniuses at excuse and tomorrowing our resolves. And so we become practiced in powerless resolution until hope gets undone and dies in the unattempted. At least that happens to some of us. And then to rise above this noise of knowings and really change ourselves, we need an authorization that 'we' do not have.

Hypnosis does not work for everyone. There are many reasons why. But in one particular group who find hypnosis difficult, the reason is neurological and partly genetic. In such people, I think that the inherited neurological basis of the general bicameral paradigm is organized slightly differently. It is as if they cannot readily accept the external authorization of an operator because that part of the bicameral paradigm is already occupied. Indeed, they often seem to the rest of us as if they were already hypnotized, particularly when confined in hospitals as they commonly are from time to time. Some theorists have even speculated that that is precisely their condition — a continuous state of self hypnosis. But I think such a position is a dreadful misuse of the term hypnosis, and that the behavior of schizophrenics, as we call them, should be looked at in another way — which is what we shall do in the next chapter.

CHAPTER 5

Schizophrenia

M OST OF US spontaneously slip back into something approaching the actual bicameral mind at some part of our lives. For some of us, it is only a few episodes of thought deprivation or an instance or two of hearing voices. But for others of us, genetically lacking an enzyme to easily break down the biochemical products of continued stress into excretable form, it is a much more harrowing experience — if it can be called an experience at all. We hear voices of impelling importance that criticize us and tell us what to do. At the same time, we seem to lose the boundaries of ourselves. Time crumbles. We behave without knowing it. Our mental space begins to vanish. We panic, and yet the panic is not happening to us. There is no us. It is not that we have nowhere to turn; we have nowhere. And in that nowhere, we are somehow automatons, unknowing what we do, being manipulated by others or by our voices in strange and frightening ways in a place we come to recognize as a hospital with a diagnosis we are told is schizophrenia. In reality, we have relapsed into the bicameral mind.

At least that is a provocative if oversimplified and exaggerated way of introducing an hypothesis that has been obvious in earlier parts of this essay. For it has been quite apparent that the views presented here suggest a new conception for that most common and resistant of mental illnesses, schizophrenia. This suggestion is that, like the phenomena discussed in the preceding chapters, schizophrenia, at least in part, is a vestige of bicamerality, a partial relapse to the bicameral mind. The present chapter is a discussion of this possibility.

The Evidence in History

Let us begin with a glance, a mere side-glance, at the earliest history of this disease. If our hypothesis is correct, there should first of all be no evidence of individuals set apart as insane prior to the breakdown of the bicameral mind. And this is true, even though it makes an extremely weak case, since the evidence is so indirect. But in the sculptures, literature, murals, and other artifacts of the great bicameral civilizations, there is never any depiction or mention of a kind of behavior which marked an individual out as different from others in the way in which insanity does. Idiocy, yes, but madness, no.[1] There is, for example, no idea of insanity in the Iliad.[2] I am emphasizing individuals *set apart* from others as ill, because, according to our theory, we could say that before the second millennium B.C., *everyone* was schizophrenic.

Secondly, we should expect on the basis of the above hypothesis that when insanity is first referred to in the conscious period, it is referred to in definitely bicameral terms. And this makes a much stronger case. In the *Phaedrus*, Plato calls insanity "a divine gift, and the source of the chiefest blessings granted to men."[3] And this passage preludes one of the most beautiful and

---

[1] Even the word found in I Samuel 13 that is sometimes brought forward as the first reference to schizophrenia is the Hebrew *halal*, which is better translated as foolish in the sense of an idiot.

[2] When E. R. Dodds suggests that a few places in the *Odyssey* refer to madness, I find his argument unconvincing. And when he concludes that there was a concept of mental disease common in Homer's time, "and probably long before," this is a completely unwarranted assertion. See E. R. Dodds, *The Greeks and the Irrational* (Berkeley: University of California Press, 1968), p. 67.

[3] *Phaedrus*, 244A.

soaring passages in all the *Dialogues* in which four types of insanity are distinguished: prophetic madness due to Apollo, ritual madness due to Dionysus, the poetic madness "of those who are possessed by the Muses, which taking hold of the delicate and virgin soul, and there inspiring frenzy, awaken lyrical and all other numbers," and, finally, erotic madness due to Eros and Aphrodite. Even the word for prophetic, *mantike,* and the word for psychotically mad, *manike,* were for the young Plato the same word, the letter *t* being for him "only a modern and tasteless insertion."[4] The point I am trying to make here is that there is no doubt whatever of the early association of forms of what we call schizophrenia with the phenomena that we have come to call bicameral.

This correspondence is also brought out in another ancient Greek word for insanity, *paranoia,* which, coming from *para + nous,* literally meant having another mind alongside one's own, descriptive both of the hallucinatory state of schizophrenia and of what we have described as the bicameral mind. This, of course, has nothing whatever to do with the modern and etymologically incorrect usage of this term, with its quite different meaning of persecutory delusions, which is of nineteenth-century origin. Paranoia, as the ancient general term for insanity, lasted along with the other vestiges of bicamerality described in the previous chapter, and then linguistically died with them about the second century A.D.

But even in Plato's own time, a time of war, famine, and plague, the four divine insanities were gradually shifting into the realm of the wise man's poetry and the plain man's superstition. The sickness aspect of schizophrenia comes to the fore. In later dialogues, the elderly Plato is more skeptical, referring to what we call schizophrenia as a perpetual dreaming in which some men believe "that they are gods, and others that they can fly,"[5] in

---

[4] Ibid., 244C.
[5] *Theaetetus,* 158.

which case the family of those so afflicted should keep them at home under penalty of a fine.[6]

The insane are now to be shunned. Even in the exotic farces of Aristophanes, stones are thrown at them to keep them away.

What we now call schizophrenia, then, begins in human history as a relationship to the divine, and only around 400 B.C. comes to be regarded as the incapacitating illness we know today. This development is difficult to understand apart from the theory of a change in mentality which this essay is about.

The Difficulties of the Problem

Before looking at its contemporary symptoms from the same point of view, I would make a few preliminary observations of a very general sort. As anyone knows who has worked in the literature on the subject, there is today a rather vague panorama of dispute as to what schizophrenia is, whether it is one disease or many, or the final common path of multiple etiologies, whether there exist two basic patterns variously called process and re-active, or acute and chronic, or quick-onset and slow-onset schizo-phrenia. The reason for this disagreement and its vagueness is because research in the area is as obstinate a tangle of control difficulties as can be found anywhere. How may we study schizo-phrenia and at the same time eliminate the effects of hospitaliza-tion, of drugs, of prior therapy, of cultural expectancy, of various learned reactions to bizarre experiences, or of differences in ob-taining accurate data about the situational crises of patients who, through the trauma of hospitalization, find it frightening to communicate?

It is beyond my effort here to sort out a way through these difficulties to any definitive position. Rather I intend to step around them with some simplicities on which there is wide agree-ment. These are, that there does exist a syndrome that can be

[6] *Laws*, 934.

called schizophrenia, that at least in the florid state it is easily recognized in the clinic, and that it is found in all civilized societies the world over.[7] Moreover, for the truth of this chapter, it is not really important whether I am speaking of *all* patients with this diagnosis.[8] Nor of the illness as it first appears, or as it develops subsequent to hospitalization. My thesis is something less, that *some of the fundamental, most characteristic, and most commonly observed symptoms of florid unmedicated schizophrenia are uniquely consistent with the description I have given on previous pages of the bicameral mind.*

These symptoms are primarily the presence of auditory hallucinations as described in I:4, and the deterioration of consciousness as defined in I:2, namely the loss of the analog 'I', the erosion of mind-space, and an inability to narratize. Let us look at these symptoms in turn.

Hallucinations

Again, hallucinations. And what I shall say here is merely adjunctory to my earlier discussion.

If we confine ourselves to florid unmedicated schizophrenics, we can state that hallucinations are absent only in exceptional cases. Usually they predominate, crowding in persistently and massively, making the patient appear confused, particularly when they are changing rapidly. In very acute cases, visual hallucinations accompany the voices. But in more ordinary cases, the patient hears a voice or many voices, a saint or a devil,

---

[7] "The Experiential World Inventory" developed by H. Osmond and A. El. Miligi at the Princeton Neuro-Psychiatric Institute, has been given to schizophrenics in different countries and cultures with very similar results.

[8] Nor of *just* such patients. There is a growing movement in psychiatry to distinguish diagnostic categories by the drugs specific to them, the schizophrenias by the phenothiazines and manic-depression by lithium. If this is correct, many patients formerly diagnosed as having paranoid schizophrenia are really manic-depressive since they respond only to lithium. In the manic phase, almost half of such patients have hallucinations.

a band of men under his window who want to catch him, burn him, behead him. They lie in wait for him, threaten to enter through the walls, climb up and hide under his bed or above him in the ventilators. And then there are other voices who want to help him. Sometimes God is a protector, at other times one of the persecutors. At the persecuting voices, the patients may flee, defend themselves, or attack. With helpful consoling hallucinations, the patient may listen intently, enjoy them like a festivity, even weeping at hearing the voices of heaven. Some patients may go through all sorts of hallucinated experiences while lying under the blankets in their beds, while others climb around, talk loudly or softly to their voices, making all kinds of incomprehensible gestures and motions. Even during conversation or reading, patients may be constantly answering their hallucinations softly or whispering asides to their voices every few seconds.

Now one of the most interesting and important aspects of all this in respect to the parallel with the bicameral mind is the following: auditory hallucinations in general are not even slightly under the control of the individual himself, but they are extremely susceptible to even the most innocuous suggestion from the total social circumstances of which the individual is a part. In other words, such schizophrenic symptoms are influenced by a collective cognitive imperative just as in the case of hypnosis.

A recent study demonstrates this very clearly.[9] Forty-five hallucinating male patients were divided into three groups. One group wore on their belts a small box with a lever which when pressed administered a shock. They were instructed to thus shock themselves whenever they began to hear voices. A second group wore similar boxes, were given similar instructions, but

[9] Arthur H. Weingaertner, "Self-administered aversive stimulation with hallucinating hospitalized schizophrenics," *Journal of Consulting and Clinical Psychology*, 1971, 36: 422–429.

pressing the lever did not give the patient a shock. A third group were given similar interviews and evaluation, but had no boxes. The boxes, incidentally, contained counters which recorded the number of lever presses, the frequency ranging from 19 to 2362 times over the fortnight of the experiment. But the important thing is that all three groups were casually led to expect that the frequency of hallucinations might diminish.

It was of course predicted on the basis of learning theory that the shocked group alone would improve. But alas for learning theory, all three groups heard significantly fewer voices. In some cases the voices vanished completely. And no group was superior to another in this respect, showing clearly the huge role of expectation and belief in this aspect of mental organization.

A further observation is a related one, that hallucinations are dependent on the teachings and expectations of childhood — as we have postulated was true in bicameral times. In contemporary cultures where an orthodox excessive personal relationship to God is a part of the child's education, individuals that become schizophrenic tend to hear strict religious hallucinations more than others.

On the British island of Tortola in the West Indies, for example, children are taught that God literally controls each detail of their life. The name of the Deity is invoked in threats and punishment. Churchgoing is the major social activity. When the natives of this island require any psychiatric care whatever, they invariably describe experiences of hearing commands from God and Jesus, feelings of burning in hell or hallucinations of loud praying and hymn-singing, or sometimes a combination of prayer and profanity.[10]

When the auditory hallucinations of schizophrenia have no particular religious basis they are still playing essentially the

[10] Edwin A. Weinstein, "Aspects of Hallucinations," *Hallucinations*, L. J. West, ed. (New York: Grune and Stratton, 1962), pp. 233–238.

same role as I have suggested was true for the bicameral mind, that of initiating and guiding the patient's behavior. Occasionally the voices are recognized as authorities even within the hospital. One woman heard voices that were mainly beneficial which she believed were created by the Public Health Service to provide psychotherapy. Would that psychotherapy could always be so easily accomplished! They constantly gave her advice, including, incidentally, not to tell the psychiatrist that she heard voices. They advised her on difficult pronunciations, or gave her hints on sewing and cooking. As she described it,

> When I am making a cake, she gets too impatient with me. I try to figure it out all by myself. I am trying to make a clothspin apron and she is right there with me trying to tell me what to do.[11]

Some psychiatric investigators, particularly of a psychoanalytic persuasion, wish to infer by the associations the patient uses that the voices can "in all instances . . . be traced to persons who were formerly significant in the patients' lives, especially their parents."[12] It is supposed that because such figures if recognized would produce anxiety, they are therefore unconsciously distorted and disguised by the patients. But why should that be so? It is more parsimonious to think that it is the patient's experiences with his parents (or other loved authorities) that become the core around which the hallucinated voice is structured, even as I have suggested was the case with the gods in the bicameral era.

I do not mean that parents do not figure in hallucinations. They often do, particularly in younger patients. But otherwise, the voice-figures of schizophrenia are not parents in disguise; they are authority figures created by the nervous system out of the patient's admonitory experience and his cultural expecta-

[11] A. H. Modell, "Hallucinations in schizophrenic patients and their relation to psychic structure," in West, pp. 166–173; the quotation is from p. 169.
[12] Modell, in West, p. 168.

tions, his parents of course being an important part of that admonitory experience.

One of the most interesting problems in hallucinations is their relation to conscious thought. If schizophrenia is partly a return to the bicameral mind, and if this is antithetical to ordinary consciousness (which it need not be in all cases), one might expect hallucinations to be the replacement of 'thoughts.'

In some patients at least, this is how hallucinations first appear. Sometimes, the voices seem to begin as thoughts which then transform themselves into vague whispers, which then gradually become louder and more authoritative. In other cases, patients feel the beginning of voices "as if their thoughts were dividing." In mild cases, the voices may even be under the control of conscious attention as are 'thoughts.' As one nondeluded patient described it:

> Here I have been in this ward for two years and a half and almost every day and every hour of the day I hear voices about me, sometimes sounding from the wind, sometimes from footsteps, sometimes rattling dishes, from the rustling trees, or from the wheels of passing trains and vehicles. I hear the voices only if I attend to them, but hear them I do. The voices are words that tell me one story or another, just as if they were not thoughts in my head, but were recounting past deeds — yet only when I think of them. The whole day through they keep on telling truly my daily history of head and heart.[13]

Hallucinations often seem to have access to more memories and knowledge than the patient himself — even as did the gods of antiquity. It is not uncommon to hear patients at certain stages of their illness complain that the voices express their thoughts before they have a chance to think them themselves. This process of having one's thoughts anticipated and expressed

[13] Gustav Störring, *Mental Pathology* (Berlin: Swan Sonnenschein, 1907), p. 27.

aloud to one is called in the clinical literature *Gedankenlaut-werden* and is approaching closely the bicameral mind. Some say they never get a chance to think for themselves; it is always done for them and the thought is *given* to them. As they try to read, the voices read in advance to them. Trying to speak, they hear their thoughts spoken in advance to them. Another patient told his physician that: "Thinking hurts him, for he can not think for himself. Whenever he begins to think, all his thoughts are dictated to him. He is at pains to change the train of thought, but again his thinking is done for him . . . In church he not infrequently hears a voice singing, anticipating what the choir sings . . . If he walks down the street and sees, say, a sign, the voice reads out to him whatever is on it . . . If he sees an acquaintance in the distance, the voice calls out to him, 'Look, there goes so and so,' usually before he begins to think of the person. Occasionally, though he has not the least intention of noticing passersby, the voice compels him to attend to them by its remarks about them."[14]

It is the very central and unique place of these auditory hallucinations in the syndrome of many schizophrenics which it is important to consider. Why are they present? And why is "hearing voices" universal throughout all cultures, unless there is some usually suppressed structure of the brain which is activated in the stress of this illness?

And why do these hallucinations of schizophrenics so often have a dramatic authority, particularly religious? I find that the only notion which provides even a working hypothesis about this matter is that of the bicameral mind, that the neurological structure responsible for these hallucinations is neurologically bound to substrates for religious feelings, and this is because the source of religion and of gods themselves is in the bicameral mind.

Religious hallucinations are particularly common in the so-

[14] Ibid., p. 30.

called twilight states, which are a kind of waking dream in many patients, varying in time from a few minutes to a few years, six months' duration being quite common. Invariably such states are characterized by religious visions, posturing, ceremony, and worship, a patient living with hallucinations just as in the bicameral state, except that the environment itself may be hallucinated and the hospital surroundings blotted out. The patient may be in contact with the saints in heaven. Or he may recognize doctors or nurses around him for what they are, but believe that they will prove to be gods or angels in disguise. Such patients may even cry with joy at talking directly with the inhabitants of heaven, may continually cross themselves as they converse with the divine voices or even with the stars, calling to them out of the night.

Often the paranoid, after a lengthy period of difficulties in getting on with people, may begin the schizophrenic aspect of his illness with an hallucinated religious experience in which an angel, Christ, or God speaks to the patient bicamerally, showing him some new way.[15] He becomes convinced therefore of his own special relationship to the powers of the universe, and the pathological self-reference of all the occurrences around him then becomes elaborated into delusional ideas which may be pursued for years without the patient's being able to discuss it.

Particularly illustrative of the tendency toward religious hallucinations is the famous case of Schreber, a brilliant German jurist around the close of the nineteenth century.[16] His own extremely literate retrospective account of his hallucinations while ill with schizophrenia is remarkable from the point of view of their similarity to the relationships of ancient men to their gods. His disease began with a severe anxiety attack during which he hallucinated a crackling in the walls of his house. Then one night,

[15] Eugen Bleuler, *Dementia Praecox or The Group of Schizophrenias*, Joseph Zinkin, trans. (New York: International Universities Press, 1950), p. 229.

[16] D. P. Schreber, *Memoirs of My Nervous Illness*, I. MacAlpine and R. A. Hunter, trans. and eds. (London: Dawson, 1955).

the cracklings suddenly became voices which he immediately recognized as divine communications and "which since then have spoken to me incessantly." The voices were continuous "for a period of seven years, except during sleep, and would persist undeterred even when I was speaking with other people."[17] He saw rays of light like "long-drawn-out filaments approaching my head from some vast distant spot on the horizon . . . Or from the sun or other distant stars that do *not* come towards me in a straight line, but in a kind of circle or parabola."[18] And these were the carriers of the divine voices, and could form into the physical beings of gods themselves.

As his illness progressed, it is of particular interest how the divine voices soon organized themselves into a hierarchy of upper and lower gods, as may be supposed to have occurred in bicameral times. And then, streaming down their rays from the gods, the voices seemed to be trying to "suffocate me and eventually to rob me of my reason." They were committing "soul-murder," and were progressively "unmanning" him, that is, taking away his own initiative or eroding his analog 'I'. Later in his illness, during more conscious periods, he narratized this into the delusion of being bodily turned into a woman. Freud, I think, overemphasized this particular narratization in his famous analysis of these memoirs, making the entire illness the result of repressed homosexuality that was erupting from the unconscious.[19] But such an interpretation, while possibly related to the original etiology of the stress that began the illness, is not very powerful in explaining the case as a whole.

Now, can we have the temerity to draw a parallel with such phenomena of mental illness and the organization of gods in antiquity? That Schreber also had voice-visions of "little men" is suggestive of the figurines found in so many early civilizations.

---

[17] Ibid., p. 225.

[18] Ibid., pp. 227–228.

[19] Sigmund Freud, "Psycho-analytic notes on an autobiographical account of a case of paranoia," in *Complete Psychological Works*, Vol. 12, James Strachey, trans. and ed. (London: Hogarth Press, 1958).

And the fact that, as he slowly recuperated, the tempo of speech of his gods slowed down and then degenerated into an indistinct hissing[20] is reminiscent of how idols sounded to the Incas after the conquest.

A further suggestive parallel is the fact that the sun as the world's brightest light takes on a particular significance in many unmedicated patients, as it did in the theocracies of bicameral civilizations. Schreber, for example, after hearing his "upper God (Ormuzd)" for some time, finally saw him as "the sun . . . surrounded by a silver sea of rays . . ."[21] And a more contemporary patient wrote:

> The sun came to have an extraordinary effect on me. It seemed to be charged with all power; not merely to symbolize God but actually to be God. Phrases like: "Light of the World," "The Sun of Righteousness that Setteth Nevermore," etc., ran through my head without ceasing, and the mere sight of the sun was sufficient greatly to intensify this manic excitement under which I was laboring. I was impelled to address the sun as a personal god, and to evolve from it a ritual sun worship.[22]

In no sense am I thinking here that there is innate sun-worship or innate gods in the nervous system that are released under the mental reorganization of psychosis. The reasons that hallucinations take the *particular* form they do lie partly in the physical nature of the world, but mostly in education and a familiarity with gods and religious history.

But I do mean to suggest

    (1) that there are in the brain aptic structures for the very existence of such hallucinations,

---

[20] Schreber, pp. 226, 332.

[21] Ibid., p. 269.

[22] J. Custance, *Wisdom, Madness and Folly* (New York: Pellegrini and Cudahy, 1952), p. 18.

(2) that these structures develop in civilized societies such that they determine the general religious quality and authority of such hallucinated voices, and perhaps organize them into hierarchies,

(3) that the paradigms behind these aptic structures were evolved into the brain by natural and human selection during the early civilizing of mankind, and

(4) are released from their normal inhibition by abnormal biochemistry in many cases of schizophrenia and particularized into experience.

There is a great deal more to say about these very real phenomena of hallucination in schizophrenia. And the need for more research here cannot be overstressed. We would like to know the life history of hallucinations and how this relates to the life history of the patient's illness; of this hardly anything is known. We would like to know more of how the particular hallucinatory experiences relate to the individual's upbringing. Why do some patients have benevolent voices, while others have voices so relentlessly persecuting that they flee or defend themselves or attack someone or something in an attempt to end them? And why do still others have voices so ecstatically religious and inspiring that the patient enjoys them like a festivity? And what are the language characteristics of the voices? Do they use the same syntax and lexicon as the patient's own speech? Or are they more patterned as we might expect from III.3? All these are problems that can be resolved empirically. When they are, they may indeed give us more insight into the bicameral beginnings of civilization.

The Erosion of the Analog 'I'

Of what transcending importance is this analog we have of ourselves in our metaphored mind-space, the very thing with which we narratize out solutions to problems of personal action, and see where we are going, and who we are! And when in schizophrenia it begins to diminish, and the space in which it exists begins to collapse, how terrifying the experience must be!

Florid schizophrenic patients all have this symptom in some degree:

> When I am ill I lose the sense of where I am. I feel 'I' can sit in the chair, and yet my body is hurtling out and somersaulting about 3 feet in front of me.

> It is really very hard to keep conversations with others because I can't be sure if others are really talking or not and if I am really talking back.[23]

> Gradually I can no longer distinguish how much of myself is in me, and how much is already in others. I am a conglomeration, a monstrosity, modeled anew each day.[24]

> My ability to think and decide and will to do, is torn apart by itself. Finally, it is thrown out where it mingles with every other part of the day and judges what it has left behind. Instead of wishing to do things, they are done by something that seems mechanical and frightening . . . the feeling that should dwell within a person is outside longing to come back and yet having taken with it the power to return.[25]

Many are the ways in which this loss of ego is described by patients who are able to describe it at all. Another patient has to sit still for hours at a time "in order to find her thoughts again." Another feels as if "he died away." Schreber, as we have seen, talked of "soul-murder." One very intelligent patient needs

[23] Both quotations from patients of Dr. C. C. Pfeiffer of the Brain-Bio Center of Princeton, New Jersey, where schizophrenia is regarded as several biochemical illnesses primarily treatable by brain nutrients.

[24] Storch as quoted by H. Werner, *Comparative Psychology of Mental Development* (New York: International Universities Press, 1957), p. 467.

[25] From E. Meyer and L. Covi, "The experience of depersonalization: A written report by a patient," *Psychiatry*, 1960, 23: 215–217.

hours of strenuous effort "to find her own ego for a few brief moments." Or the self feels it is being absorbed by all that is around it by cosmic powers, forces of evil or of good, or by God himself. Indeed, the very term schizophrenia was coined by Bleuler to point to this central experience as the identifying mark of schizophrenia. It is the feeling of 'losing one's mind', of the self 'breaking off' until it ceases to exist or seems to be unconnected with action or life in the usual way, resulting in many of the more obvious descriptive symptoms, such as "lack of affect" or abulia.

Another way in which this erosion of the analog 'I' shows itself is in the relative inability of schizophrenics to draw a person. It is, of course, a somewhat tenuous assumption to say that when we draw a person on paper, that drawing is dependent upon an intact metaphor of the self that we have called the analog 'I'. But so consistent has this result been that it has become what is called the Draw-A-Person Test (DAP), now routinely adminis- tered as an indicator of schizophrenia.[26] Not all schizophrenic patients find such drawings difficult. But when they do, it is extremely diagnostic. They leave out obvious anatomical parts, like hands or eyes; they use blurred and unconnected lines; sex- uality is often undifferentiated; the figure itself is often distorted and befuddled.

But the generalization that this inability to draw a person is a reflecting of the erosion of the analog 'I' should be taken with some circumspection. It has been found that older people some- times show the same fragmented and primitive drawings as do these schizophrenics, and it should also be noticed that there is a considerable inconsistency with this result and the hypothesis being examined in this chapter. We have stated in an earlier

[26] The first several years of research with the DAP have been reported in L. W. Jones and C. B. Thomas, "Studies on figure drawings," *Psychiatric Quarterly Supple- ment*, 1961, 35: 212–216.

chapter that the analog 'I' came into being toward the end of the second millennium B.C. If the ability to draw a person is dependent upon the drawer having an analog 'I', then we would expect no coherent pictures of humans before that time. And this most definitely is not the case. It is obvious that there are ways of explaining this discrepancy, but I prefer to simply record the anomaly at this time.

We should not leave this discussion of the erosion of the analog 'I' without mentioning the tremendous anxiety in our own culture that accompanies it, and the attempt, sometimes successful, sometimes unsuccessful, to arrest this terrifying fading-off of that most important part of our interior selves, the almost sacramental center of conscious decision. In fact, much of the behavior that has nothing to do with any reversion to a bicameral mind can be construed as an effort to combat this loss of the analog 'I'.

Sometimes, for example, there is what is called the "I am" symptom. The patient in trying to keep some control over his behavior repeats over and over to himself "I am," or "I am the one present in everything," or "I am the mind, not the body." Another patient may use only single words like "strength" or "life" to try to anchor himself against the dissolution of his consciousness.[27]

The Dissolution of Mind-Space

A schizophrenic not only begins to lose his 'I' but also his mind-space, the pure paraphrand that we have of the world and its objects that is made to seem like a space when we introspect. To the patient it feels like losing his thoughts, or "thought deprivation," a phrase which elicits immediate recognition from the schizophrenic. The effect of this is so bound up with the erosion

[27] Carney Landis, *Varieties of Psychopathological Experience* (New York: Holt, Rinehart and Winston, 1964).

of the analog 'I' as to be inseparable from it. Patients cannot easily think of themselves in the places that they are in and so they are unable to utilize information to prepare in advance for things that may happen to them.

One way this can be experimentally observed is in reaction-time studies. All schizophrenics of every type are much less capable than normally conscious people when they attempt to respond to stimuli presented to them at intervals of varying lengths. The schizophrenic, lacking an intact analog 'I' and a mind-space in which to picture himself doing something, is unable to "get ready" to respond, and, once responding, is unable to vary the response as the task demands.[28] A patient who has been sorting blocks on the basis of form may be unable to shift to sorting them for color when instructed to sort in a different way.

Similarly, the loss of the analog 'I' and its mind-space results in the loss of *as-if* behaviors. Because he cannot imagine in the usual conscious way, he cannot play-act, or engage in make-believe actions, or speak of make-believe events. He cannot, for example, pretend to drink water out of a glass if there is no water in it. Or asked what he would do if he were the doctor, he might reply that he is not a doctor. Or if an unmarried patient is asked what he would do if he were married, he might answer that he is not married. And hence his difficulty with the as-if behavior of hypnosis, as I mentioned at the end of the previous chapter.

Another way the dissolving of mind-space shows itself is in the disorientation in respect to time so common in the schizophrenic. We can only be conscious of time as we can arrange it into a spatial succession, and the diminishing of mind-space in schizophrenia makes this difficult or impossible. For example, patients may complain that "time has stopped," or that everything seems to be "slowed down" or "suspended," or more simply that they

[28] This is an interpretation of a widely held theory of David Shakow, "Segmental Set," *Archives of General Psychiatry*, 1962, 6: 1–17.

have "trouble with time." As one former patient remembered it after he was well:

> For a long time no days seemed to me like a day and no night seemed like a night. But this in particular has no shape in my memory. I used to tell time by my meals, but as I believed we were served sets of meals in each real day — about half a dozen sets of breakfast, lunch, tea, and dinner in each twelve hours — this was not much help.[29]

On the face of it, this may seem inconsistent with the hypothesis that schizophrenia is a partial relapse to the bicameral mind. For bicameral man certainly knew the hours of the day and the seasons of the year. But this knowing was, I suggest, a very different knowing from the narratization in a spatially successive time which we who are conscious are constantly doing. Bicameral man had behavioral knowing, responding to the cues for rising and sleeping, for planting and harvesting, cues so important that they were worshiped, as at Stonehenge, and were probably hallucinogenic in themselves. For someone coming from a culture where attention to such cues has been superseded by a different sense of time, the loss of that spatial successiveness leaves the patient in a relatively timeless world. It is interesting in this connection that when it is suggested to normal hypnotic subjects that time does not exist, a schizophrenic form reaction results.[30]

The Failure of Narratization

With the erosion of the analog 'I' and its mind-space, narratization becomes impossible. It is as if all that was narratized in the normal state shatters into associations subordinated to some gen-

[29] M. Harrison, *Spinners Lake* (London: Lane, 1941), p. 32.

[30] Bernard S. Aaronson, "Hypnosis, responsibility, and the boundaries of self," *American Journal of Clinical Hypnosis*, 1967, 9: 229–246.

eral thing perhaps, but unrelated to any unifying conceptive purpose or goal, as occurs in normal narratization. The logical reasons
cannot be given for behaviors, and verbal answers to questions do
not originate in any interior mind-space, but in simple associations or in the external circumstances of a conversation. The
whole idea that a person can explain himself, something which in
the bicameral era was distinctly the function of gods, can no
longer occur.

With the loss of the analog 'I', its mind-space, and the ability to
narratize, behavior is either responding to hallucinated directions, or continues on by habit. The remnant of the self feels like
a commanded automaton, as if someone else were moving the
body about. Even without hallucinated orders, a patient may
have the feeling of being commanded in ways in which he must
obey. He may shake hands normally with a visitor, but, asked
about this, reply, "I don't do it, the hand proffers itself." Or a
patient may feel that somebody else is moving his tongue in
speech, particularly as in coprolalia, when scatalogical or obscene
words are substituted for others. Even in early stages of schizophrenia, the patient feels memories, music, or emotions, either
pleasant or unpleasant, which seem to be forced upon him from
some alien source, and, therefore, over which 'he' has no control.
This symptom is extremely common and diagnostic. And these
alien influences often then develop into the full-blown hallucinations I have discussed earlier.

According to Bleuler, "conscious feelings rarely accompany the
automatisms which are psychic manifestations split off from the
personality. The patients can dance and laugh without feeling
happy; can commit murder without hating; do away with themselves without being disappointed with life . . . the patients
realize that they are not their own masters."[31]

Many patients simply allow such automatisms to take place.
Others, still able to narratize marginally, invent protective de-

[31] Bleuler, p. 204.

vices against such foreign control of their actions. Negativism itself, even, I think, in neurotics, is such. One of Bleuler's patients, for example, who was inwardly driven to sing, managed to get hold of a small block of wood which he would cram into his mouth in order to stop his mouth from singing. At present we do not know whether such automatisms and inner commands are always the result of articulate voices directing the patient in his actions, as a relapse to the bicameral mind would suggest. It may indeed be impossible to know, since the split-off fragment of the personality that is still responding to the physician may have suppressed the bicameral commands which are being 'heard' by other parts of the nervous system.

In many patients this appears as the symptom called Command Automatism. The patient obeys any and every suggestion and command coming from the outside. He is incapable of not obeying authoritative short orders, even when otherwise negativistic. Such orders must deal with simple activities and cannot apply to a long complicated task. The well-known waxy flexibility of catatonics may fall under this heading; the patient is really obeying the physician by remaining in any position in which he is placed. While not all such phenomena are, of course, characteristic of what we have called the bicameral mind, the underlying principle is. An interesting hypothesis would be that patients with such Command Automatism are those in whom auditory hallucinations are absent, and the external voice of the physician is taking its place.

Consistent with such an hypothesis is the symptom known as echolalia. When no hallucinations are present, the patient repeats back the speech, cries, or expressions of others. But when hallucinations are present, this becomes hallucinatory echolalia, where the patient must repeat out loud all that his voices say to him, rather than those of his environmental surroundings. Hallucinatory echolalia is, I suggest, essentially the same mental organization that we have seen in the prophets of the Old Testament, as well as the aoidoi of the Homeric poems.

Body Image Boundary Disturbance

It is possible that the erosion of the analog 'I' and its mind-space also results in what is called Boundary Loss in Rorschach studies of schizophrenia. This is a score for the proportion of images seen in the ink blots that have poorly defined, fuzzy, or inexistent boundaries or edges. Most interesting from our point of view here is that this measure is strongly correlated with the presence of vivid hallucinatory experiences. A patient high in Boundary Loss often describes it as a feeling of disintegration.

> When I am melting I have no hands, I go into a doorway in order not to be trampled on. Everything is flying away from me. In the doorway I can gather together the pieces of my body. It is as if something is thrown in me, bursts me asunder. Why do I divide myself in different pieces? I feel that I am without poise, that my personality is melting and that my ego disappears and that I do not exist anymore. Everything pulls me apart . . . The skin is the only possible means of keeping the different pieces together. There is no connection between the different parts of my body . . .[32]

In one study on Boundary Loss, the Rorschach was given to 80 schizophrenic patients. Boundary definiteness scores were significantly lower than in the group of normals and neurotics matched for age and socio-economic status. Such patients would commonly see in the ink blots mutilated bodies, animal or human.[33] This mirrors the breaking up of the analog self, or the metaphor picture that we have of ourselves in consciousness. In another study of 604 patients in Worcester State Hospital, it was specifically found that Boundary Loss, including, we may presume, the loss of the analog 'I', is a factor in the development of hallucinations. Patients who had more hallucinations were those

[32] P. Schilder, *The Image and Appearance of the Human Body* (London: Kegan Paul, Trench, Trubner, and Co., 1935), p. 159.

[33] S. Fisher and S. E. Cleveland, "The Role of Body Image in Psychosomatic Symptom Choice," *Psychological Monographs*, 1955, 69, No. 17, whole no. 402.

who were less successful in establishing "boundaries between the self and the world."[34]

Along the same line of thought, chronic schizophrenic patients are sometimes unable to identify themselves in a photograph, or may misidentify themselves, whether they are photographed individually or in a group.

The Advantages of Schizophrenia

A curious heading, certainly, for how can we say there are advantages of so terrifying an illness? But I mean such advantages in the light of all human history. Very clearly, there is a genetic inherited basis to the biochemistry underlying this radically different reaction to stress. And a question that must be asked of such a genetic disposition to something occurring so early in our reproductive years is, what biological advantage did it once have? Why, in the slang of the evolutionist, was it selected for? And at what period long, long ago, since such genetic disposition is present all over the world?

The answer, of course, is one of the themes I have stated so often before in this essay. The selective advantage of such genes was the bicameral mind evolved by natural and human selection over the millennia of our early civilizations. The genes involved, whether causing what to conscious men is an enzyme deficiency or other, are the genes that were in the background of the prophets and the 'sons of the nabiim' and bicameral man before them.

Another advantage of schizophrenia, perhaps evolutionary, is tirelessness. While a few schizophrenics complain of generalized fatigue, particularly in the early stages of the illness, most patients do not. In fact, they show less fatigue than normal persons and are capable of tremendous feats of endurance. They are not fatigued by examinations lasting many hours. They may move about day and night, or work endlessly without any sign of being tired. Catatonics may hold an awkward position for days that the

[34] L. Phillips and M. S. Rabinovitch, *Journal of Abnormal and Social Psychology*, 1958, 57: 181.

reader could not hold for more than a few minutes. This suggests that much fatigue is a product of the subjective conscious mind, and that bicameral man, building the pyramids of Egypt, the ziggurats of Sumer, or the gigantic temples at Teotihuacan with only hand labor, could do so far more easily than could conscious self-reflective men.

A further thing that schizophrenics do 'better' than the rest of us — although it certainly is no advantage in our abstractly complicated world — is simple sensory perception. They are more alert to visual stimuli, as might be expected if we think of them as not having to strain such stimuli through a buffer of consciousness. This is seen in their ability to block EEG alpha waves more quickly than normal persons following an abrupt stimulus, and to recognize projected visual scenes coming into focus considerably better than the normal.[35] Indeed, schizophrenics are almost drowning in sensory data. Unable to narratize or conciliate, they see every tree and never the forest. They seem to have a more immediate and absolute involvement with their physical environment, a greater *in-the-world-ness*. Such an interpretation, at least, could be put on the fact that schizophrenics fitted with prism glasses that deform visual perception learn to adjust more easily than the rest of us, since they do not overcompensate as much.[36]

The Neurology of Schizophrenia

If schizophrenia is in part a relapse to the bicameral mind, and if our earlier analyses have any merit, then we should find some kind of neurological changes that are consistent with the neurological model suggested in I.5. There I proposed that the halluci-

[35] See R. L. Cromwell and J. M. Held, "Alpha blocking latency and reaction time in schizophrenics and normals," *Perceptual and Motor Skills*, 1969, 29: 195–201; E. Ebner and B. Ritzler, "Perceptual recognition in chronic and acute schizophrenics," *Journal of Consulting and Clinical Psychology*, 1969, 33: 200–206.

[36] See E. Ebner, V. Broekma, and B. Ritzler, "Adaptation to awkward visual proprioceptive input in normals and schizophrenics," *Archives of General Psychiatry*, 1971, 24: 367–371.

nated voices of the bicameral mind were amalgams of stored admonitory experiences that were somehow organized in the right temporal lobe and conveyed to the left or dominant hemisphere over the anterior commissures and perhaps the corpus callosum.

Further, I have suggested that the advent of consciousness necessitated an inhibition of these auditory hallucinations originating in the right temporal cortex. But what precisely this means in a neuro-anatomical sense is far from clear. We definitely know that there are specific areas of the brain that are inhibitory to others, that the brain in a very general way is *always* in a kind of complicated tension (or balance) between excitation and inhibition, and also that inhibition can occur in a number of different ways. One way is an inhibition of an area in one hemisphere by excitation of an area in the other. The frontal eye fields, for example, are mutually inhibitory, such that stimulation of the frontal eye field on one hemisphere inhibits the other.[37] And we may suppose that some proportion of the fibers of the corpus callosum which connects the frontal eye fields are inhibitory themselves, or else excite inhibitory centers on the opposite hemisphere. In behavior, this means that looking in any direction is programmed as the vector resultant of the opposing excitation of the two frontal eye fields.[38] And this mutual inhibition of the hemispheres can be presumed to operate in various other bilateral functions.

But to generalize this reciprocal inhibition to asymmetrical unilateral functions is a more daring matter. Can we suppose, for example, that some mental process on the left hemisphere is paired in reciprocal inhibition with some different function on the

[37] A. S. F. Layton and C. S. Sherrington, "Observation on the excitable cortex of chimpanzees, orangutan, and gorilla," *Quarterly Journal of Experimental Physiology*, 1917, 11: 135.

[38] The phrasing here is that of Marcel Kinsbourne in "The control of attention by interaction between the cerebral hemispheres," *Fourth International Symposium on Attention and Performance*, Boulder, Colorado, August 1971.

right, so that some of the so-called higher mental processes could be the resultants of the two opposing hemispheres?

At any rate, the first step in bringing some credence to these ideas about the relationship of schizophrenia to the bicameral mind and its neurological model is to look for some kind of laterality differences in schizophrenics. Do such patients have different right-hemispheric activity from the rest of us? Research on this hypothesis is only beginning, but the following very recent studies are at least suggestive:

• In most of us, the total EEG over a long time period shows slightly greater activity in the dominant left hemisphere than in the right hemisphere. But the reverse tends to occur in schizophrenia: slightly more activity in the right.[39]

• This increased right hemisphere activity in schizophrenia is much more pronounced after several minutes of sensory deprivation, the same condition that causes hallucinations in normal persons.

• If we arrange our EEG machine so that we can tell which hemisphere is more active every few seconds, we find that in most of us this measure switches back and forth between the hemispheres about once a minute. But in those schizophrenics so far tested, the switching occurs only about every four minutes, an astonishing lag. This may be part of the explanation of the "segmental set" I have previously referred to, that schizophrenics tend to "get stuck" on one hemisphere or the other and so cannot shift from one mode of information processing to another as fast as the rest of us. Hence their confusion and often illogical speech and behavior in interaction with us, who switch back and forth at a faster rate.[40]

[39] Arthur Sugarman, L. Goldstein, G. Marjerrison, and N. Stoltyfus, "Recent Research in EEG Amplitude Analysis," *Diseases of the Nervous System*, 1973, 34: 162–181.

[40] This is the preliminary work on a few subjects of Leonide E. Goldstein, "Time Domain Analysis of the EEG: the Integrated Method," Rutgers Medical School preprint, 1975. I am grateful to him for discussing these suggestions with me.

• It is possible that the explanation of this slower switching in schizophrenia is anatomical. A series of autopsies of long-term schizophrenics have, surprisingly, shown that the corpus callosum which connects the two hemispheres is 1 mm. thicker than in normal brains. This is a statistically reliable result. Such a difference may mean more mutual inhibition of the hemispheres in schizophrenics.[41] The anterior commissures in this study were not measured.

• If our theory is true, any extensive dysfunction of the left temporal cortex due to disease, circulatory changes, or stress-induced alteration of its neurochemistry should release the right temporal cortex from its normal inhibitory control. When temporal lobe epilepsy is caused by a lesion on the left temporal lobe (or on both the left and right), thus (presumably) releasing the right from its normal inhibition, a full 90 percent of the patients develop paranoid schizophrenia with massive auditory hallucinations. When the lesion is on the right temporal lobe alone, fewer than 10 percent develop such symptoms. In fact this latter group tend to develop a manic-depressive psychosis.[42]

These findings need to be confirmed and explored further. But together they indicate without doubt and for the first time significant laterality effects in schizophrenia. And the direction of these effects can be interpreted as partial evidence that schizophrenia may be related to an earlier organization of the human brain which I have called the bicameral mind.

In Conclusion

Schizophrenia is one of our most morally prominent problems of research, such the agony of heart that it spreads both in those

[41] Randall Rosenthal and L. B. Bigelow, "Quantitative Brain Measurements in Chronic Schizophrenia," *British Journal of Psychiatry*, 1972, 121: 259–264.

[42] P. Flor-Henry, "Schizophrenic-like Reactions and Affective Psychoses Associated with Temporal Lobe Epilepsy: Etiological Factors," *American Journal of Psychiatry*, 1969, 126: 400–404.

afflicted and in those who love them. Recent decades have watched with gratitude a strong and accelerating improvement in the way this illness is treated. But this has come about not under the banners of new and sometimes flamboyant theories such as mine, but rather in the down-to-earth practical aspects of day-to-day therapy.

Indeed, theories of schizophrenia — and they are legion — because they have too often been the hobbyhorses of competing perspectives, have largely defeated themselves. Each discipline construes the findings of others as secondary to the factors in its own area. The socio-environmental researcher sees the schizophrenic as the product of a stressful environment. The biochemist insists that the stressful environment has its effect only because of an abnormal biochemistry in the patient. Those who speak in terms of information processing say that a deficit in this area leads directly to stress and counterstress defenses. The defense-mechanism psychologist views the impaired information processing as a self-motivated withdrawal from contact with reality. The geneticist makes hereditary interpretations from family history data. While others might develop interpretations about the role of schizophrenogenic parental influence from the same data. And so on. As one critic has expressed it, "Like riding the merry-go-round, one chooses his horse. One can make believe his horse leads the rest. Then when a particular ride is finished, one must step off only to observe that the horse has really gone nowhere.[43]

It is thus with some presumption that I add yet one more loading to this heavy roster. But I have felt impelled to do so, if only out of responsibility in completing and clarifying the suggestiveness of earlier parts of this book. For schizophrenia, whether one illness or many, is in its florid stage practically defined by certain characteristics which I have stated earlier were the salient characteristics of the bicameral mind. The presence of

---

[43] R. L. Cromwell, "Strategies for Studying Schizophrenic Behavior" (prepublication copy), p. 6.

auditory hallucinations, their often religious and always authoritative quality, the dissolution of the ego or analog 'I', and of the mind-space in which it once could narratize out what to do and where it was in time and action, these are the large resemblances.

But there are great differences as well. If there is any truth to this hypothesis, the relapse is only partial. The learnings that make up a subjective consciousness are powerful and never totally suppressed. And thus the terror and the fury, the agony and the despair. The anxiety attendant upon so cataclysmic a change, the dissonance with the habitual structure of interpersonal relations, and the lack of cultural support and definition for the voices, making them inadequate guides for everyday living, the need to defend against a broken dam of environmental sensory stimulation that is flooding all before it — produce a social withdrawal that is a far different thing from the behavior of the *absolutely* social individual of bicameral societies. The conscious man is constantly using his introspection to find 'himself' and to know where he is, relevant to his purposes and situation. And without this source of security, deprived of narratization, living with hallucinations that are unacceptable and denied as unreal by those around him, the florid schizophrenic is in an opposite world to that of the god-owned laborers of Marduk or of the idols of Ur.

The modern schizophrenic is an individual in search of such a culture. But he retains usually some part of the subjective consciousness that struggles against this more primitive mental organization, that tries to establish some kind of control in the middle of a mental organization in which the hallucination ought to do the controlling. In effect, he is a mind bared to his environment, waiting on gods in a godless world.

CHAPTER 6

The Auguries of Science

I HAVE TRIED in these few heterogeneous chapters of Book III to explain as well as I could how certain features of our recent world, namely, the social institutions of oracles and religions, and the psychological phenomena of possession, hypnosis, and schizophrenia, as well as artistic practices such as poetry and music, how all these can be interpreted *in part* as vestiges of an earlier organization of human nature. These are not in any sense a complete catalogue of the present possible projections from our earlier mentality. They are simply some of the most obvious. And the study of their interaction with the developing consciousness continually laying siege to them allows us an understanding that we would not otherwise have.

In this final chapter, I wish to turn to science itself and point out that it too, and even my entire essay, can be read as a response to the breakdown of the bicameral mind. For what is the nature of this blessing of certainty that science so devoutly demands in its very Jacob-like wrestling with nature? Why should we demand that the universe make itself clear to us? Why do we care?

To be sure, a part of the impulse to science is simple curiosity, to hold the unheld and watch the unwatched. We are all children in the unknown. It is no reaction to the loss of an earlier mentality to delight in the revelations of the electron miscroscope or in quarks or in negative gravity in black holes among the stars.

Technology is a second and even more sustaining source of the scientific ritual, carrying its scientific basis forward on its own increasing and uncontrollable momentum through history. And perhaps a deep aptic structure for hunting, for bringing a problem to bay, adds its motivational effluence to the pursuit of truth.

But over and behind these and other causes of science has been something more universal, something in this age of specialization often unspoken. It is something about understanding the totality of existence, the essential defining reality of things, the entire universe and man's place in it. It is a groping among stars for final answers, a wandering the infinitesimal for the infinitely general, a deeper and deeper pilgrimage into the unknown. It is a direction whose far beginning in the mists of history can be distantly seen in the search for lost directives in the breakdown of the bicameral mind.

It is a search that is obvious in the omen literature of Assyria where, as we saw in II.4, science begins. It is also obvious a mere half millennium later when Pythagoras in Greece is seeking the lost invariants of life in a theology of divine numbers and their relationships, thus beginning the science of mathematics. And so through two millennia, until, with a motivation not different, Galileo calls mathematics the speech of God, or Pascal and Leibnitz echo him, saying they hear God in the awesome rectitudes of mathematics.

We sometimes think, and even like to think, that the two greatest exertions that have influenced mankind, religion and science, have always been historical enemies, intriguing us in opposite directions. But this effort at special identity is loudly false. It is not religion but the church and science that were hostile to each other. And it was rivalry, not contravention. Both were religious. They were two giants fuming at each other over the same ground. Both proclaimed to be the only way to divine revelation.

It was a competition that first came into absolute focus with the late Renaissance, particularly in the imprisonment of Galileo in 1633. The stated and superficial reason was that his publications had not been first stamped with papal approval. But the true argument, I am sure, was no such trivial surface event. For the writings in question were simply the Copernican heliocentric theory of the solar system which had been published a century earlier by a churchman without any fuss whatever. The real division was more profound and can, I think, only be understood as a part of the urgency behind mankind's yearning for divine certainties. The real chasm was between the political authority of the church and the individual authority of experience. And the real question was whether we are to find our lost authorization through an apostolic succession from ancient prophets who heard divine voices, or through searching the heavens of our own experience right now in the objective world without any priestly intercession. As we all know, the latter became Protestantism and, in its rationalist aspect, what we have come to call the Scientific Revolution.

If we would understand the Scientific Revolution correctly, we should always remember that its most powerful impetus was the unremitting search for hidden divinity. As such, it is a direct descendant of the breakdown of the bicameral mind. In the late seventeenth century, to choose an obvious example, it is three English Protestants, all amateur theologians and fervently devout, who build the foundations for physics, psychology, and biology: the paranoiac Isaac Newton writing down God's speech in the great universal laws of celestial gravitation; the gaunt and literal John Locke knowing his Most Knowing Being in the riches of knowing experience; and the peripatetic John Ray, an unkempt ecclesiastic out of a pulpit, joyfully limning the Word of his Creator in the perfection of the design of animal and plant life. Without this religious motivation, science would have been mere technology, limping along on economic necessity.

The next century is complicated by the rationalism of the

Enlightenment, whose main force I shall come to in a moment. But in the great shadow of the Enlightenment, science continued to be bound up in this spell of the search for divine authorship. Its most explicit statement came in what was called Deism, or in Germany, *Vernumftreligion*. It threw away the church's "Word," despised its priests, mocked altar and sacrament, and earnestly preached the reaching of God through reason and science. The whole universe is an epiphany! God is right out here in Nature under the stars to be talked with and heard brilliantly in all the grandeur of reason, rather than behind the rood screens of ignorance in the murky mutterings of costumed priests.

Not that such scientific deists were in universal agreement. For some, like the apostle-hating Reimarus, the modern founder of the science of animal behavior, animal *triebe* or drives were actually the thoughts of God and their perfect variety his very mind. Whereas for others, like the physicist Maupertuis, God cared little about any such meaningless variety of phenomena; he lived only in pure abstractions, in the great general laws of Nature which human reason, with the fine devotions of mathematics, could discern behind such variety.[1] Indeed, the tough-minded materialist scientist today will feel uncomfortable with the fact that science in such divergent and various directions only two centuries ago was a religious endeavor, sharing the same striving as the ancient psalms, the effort to once again see the elohim "face to face."

This drama, this immense scenario in which humanity has been performing on this planet over the last 4000 years, is clear when we take the large view of the central intellectual tendency of world history. In the second millennium B.C., we stopped hearing the voices of gods. In the first millennium B.C., those of us who still heard the voices, our oracles and prophets, they too

---

[1] I discuss this more fully in my paper with William Woodward, "In the Shadow of the Enlightenment," *Journal of the History of the Behavioral Sciences*, 1974, 10: 3–15, 144–159.

died away. In the first millennium A.D., it is their sayings and hearings preserved in sacred texts through which we obeyed our lost divinities. And in the second millennium A.D., these writings lose their authority. The Scientific Revolution turns us away from the older sayings to discover the lost authorization in Nature. What we have been through in these last four millennia is the slow inexorable profaning of our species. And in the last part of the second millennium A.D., that process is apparently becoming complete. It is the Great Human Irony of our noblest and greatest endeavor on this planet that in the quest for authorization, in our reading of the language of God in Nature, we should read there so clearly that we have been so mistaken.

This secularization of science, which is now a plain fact, is certainly rooted in the French Enlightenment which I have just alluded to. But it became rough and earnest in 1842 in Germany in a famous manifesto by four brilliant young physiologists. They signed it like pirates, actually in their own blood. Fed up with Hegelian idealism and its pseudoreligious interpretations of material matters, they angrily resolved that no forces other than common physicochemical ones would be considered in their scientific activity. No spiritual entities. No divine substances. No vital forces. This was the most coherent and shrill statement of scientific materialism up to that time. And enormously influential.

Five years later, one of their group, the famous physicist and psychologist Hermann von Helmholtz, proclaimed his Principle of the Conservation of Energy. Joule had said it more kindly, that "the Great Agents of Nature are indestructible," that sea and sun and coal and thunder and heat and wind are one energy and eternal. But Helmholtz abhorred the mush of the Romantic. His mathematical treatment of the principle coldly placed the emphasis where it has been ever since: there are no outside forces in our closed world of energy transformations. There is no corner in the stars for any god, no crack in this closed universe of matter for any divine influence to seep through, none whatever.

All this might have respectfully stayed back simply as a mere working tenet for Science, had it not been for an even more stunning profaning of the idea of the holy in human affairs that followed immediately. It was particularly stunning because it came from within the very ranks of religiously motivated science. In Britain since the seventeenth century, the study of what was called "natural history" was commonly the consoling joy of finding the perfections of a benevolent Creator in nature. What more devastation could be heaped upon these tender motivations and consolations than the twin announcement by two of their own midst, Darwin and Wallace, both amateur naturalists in the grand manner, that it was evolution, not a divine intelligence, that has created all nature. This too had been put earlier in a kindlier way by others, such as Darwin's grandfather, Erasmus Darwin, or Lamarck, or Robert Chambers, or even in the exaltations of an Emerson or a Goethe. But the new emphasis was dazzling strong and unrelieving. Cold *Un*calculating Chance, by making some able to survive better in this wrestle for life, and so to reproduce more, generation after generation, has blindly, even cruelly, carved this human species out of matter, mere matter. When combined with German materialism, as it was in the wantonly abrasive Huxley, as we saw in the Introduction to this essay, the theory of evolution by natural selection was the hollowing knell of all that ennobling tradition of man as the purposed creation of Majestic Greatnesses, the elohim, that goes straight back into the unconscious depths of the Bicameral Age. It said in a word that there is no authorization from outside. Behold! there is nothing there. What we must do must come from ourselves. The king at Eynan can stop staring at Mount Hermon; the dead king can die at last. We, we fragile human species at the end of the second millennium A.D., we must become our own authorization. And here at the end of the second millennium and about to enter the third, we are surrounded with this problem. It is one that the new millennium will be working out, perhaps slowly, perhaps swiftly, perhaps even with some further changes in our mentality.

The erosion of the religious view of man in these last years of the second millennium is still a part of the breakdown of the bicameral mind. It is slowly working serious changes in every fold and field of life. In the competition for membership among religious bodies today, it is the older orthodox positions, ritually closer to the long apostolic succession into the bicameral past, that are most diminished by conscious logic. The changes in the Catholic Church since Vatican II can certainly be scanned in terms of this long retreat from the sacred which has followed the inception of consciousness into the human species. The decay of religious collective cognitive imperatives under the pressures of rationalist science, provoking, as it does, revision after revision of traditional theological concepts, cannot sustain the metaphoric meaning behind ritual. Rituals are behavioral metaphors, belief acted, divination foretold, exopsychic thinking. Rituals are mnemonic devices for the great narratizations at the heart of church life. And when they are emptied out into cults of spontaneity and drained of their high seriousness, when they are acted unfelt and reasoned at with irresponsible objectivity, the center is gone and the widening gyres begin. The result in this age of communications has been worldwide: liturgy loosened into the casual, awe softening in relevance, and the washing out of that identity-giving historical definition that told man what he was and what he should be. These sad temporizings, often begun by a bewildered clergy,[2] do but encourage the great historical tide they are designed to deflect. Our paralogical compliance to verb-

---

[2] Theologians are well aware of these problems. To enter into their discussions, one might start with Harvey Cox's *The Secular City* and then Mary Douglas' *Natural Symbols*, and then Charles Davis' "Ghetto or Desert: Liturgy in a Cultural Dilemma," in *Worship and Secularization*, ed. Wiebe (Vos, Holland: Bussum, 1970), pp. 10–27, and follow that with James Hitchcock's *The Recovery of the Sacred* (New York: Seabury Press, 1974).

ally mediated reality is diminished: we crash into chairs in our way, not go around them; we will be mute rather than say we do not understand our speech; we will insist on simple location. It is the divine tragedy or the profane comedy depending on whether we would be purged of the past or quickened into the future.

What happens in this modern dissolution of ecclesiastical authorization reminds us a little of what happened long ago after the breakdown of the bicameral mind itself. Everywhere in the contemporary world there are substitutes, other methods of authorization. Some are revivals of ancient ones: the popularity of possession religions in South America, where the church had once been so strong; extreme religious absolutism ego-based on "the Spirit," which is really the ascension of Paul over Jesus; an alarming rise in the serious acceptance of astrology, that direct heritage from the period of the breakdown of the bicameral mind in the Near East; or the more minor divination of the *I Ching*, also a direct heritage from the period just after the breakdown in China. There are also the huge commercial and sometimes psychological successes of various meditation procedures, sensitivity training groups, mind control, and group encounter practices. Other persuasions often seem like escapes from a new boredom of unbelief, but are also characterized by this search for authorization: faiths in various pseudosciences, as in scientology, or in unidentified flying objects bringing authority from other parts of our universe, or that gods were at one time actually such visitors; or the stubborn muddled fascination with extrasensory perception as a supposed demonstration of a spiritual surround of our lives whence some authorization might come; or the use of psychotropic drugs as ways of contacting profounder realities, as they were for most of the American native Indian civilizations in the breakdown of their bicameral mind. Just as we saw in III.2 that the collapse of the institutionalized oracles resulted in smaller cults of induced possession, so the waning of institutional religions is resulting in these smaller, more private religions of every description. And this historical process can be expected to increase the rest of this century.

Nor can we say that modern science itself is exempt from a similar patterning. For the modern intellectual landscape is informed with the same needs, and often in its larger contours goes through the same quasi-religious gestures, though in a slightly disguised form. These scientisms, as I shall call them, are clusters of scientific ideas which come together and almost surprise themselves into creeds of belief, scientific mythologies which fill the very felt void left by the divorce of science and religion in our time.[3] They differ from classical science and its common debates in the way they evoke the same response as did the religions which they seek to supplant. And they share with religions many of their most obvious characteristics: a rational splendor that explains everything, a charismatic leader or succession of leaders who are highly visible and beyond criticism, a series of canonical texts which are somehow outside the usual arena of scientific criticism, certain gestures of idea and rituals of interpretation, and a requirement of total commitment. In return the adherent receives what the religions had once given him more universally: a world view, a hierarchy of importances, and an auguring place where he may find out what to do and think, in short, a total explanation of man. And this totality is obtained not by actually explaining everything, but by an encasement of its activity, a severe and absolute restriction of attention, such that everything that is not explained is not in view.

The materialism I have just mentioned was one of the first such scientisms. Scientists in the middle of the nineteenth century were almost numbed with excitement by dramatic discoveries of how nutrition could change the bodies and minds of

---

[3] George Steiner in his articulate Massey Lectures of 1974 called these "mythologies" and discussed the point at greater length.

men. And so it became a movement called Medical Materialism, identified with relieving poverty and pain, taking to itself some of the forms and all of the fervor of the religions eroding around it. It captured the most exciting minds of its generation, and its program sounds distantly familiar: education, not prayers; nutrition, not communion; medicine, not love; and politics, not preaching.

Distantly familiar because Medical Materialism, still haunted with Hegel, matured in Marx and Engels into dialectical materialism, gathering to itself even more of the ecclesiastical forms of the outworn faiths around it. Its central superstition then, as now, is that of the class struggle, a kind of divination which gives a total explanation of the past and predecides what to do in every office and alarm of life. And even though ethnicism, nationalism, and unionism, those collective identity markers of modern man, have long ago showed the mythical character of the class struggle, still Marxism today is joining armies of millions into battle to erect the most authoritarian states the world has ever seen.

In the medical sciences, the most prominent scientism, I think, has been psychoanalysis. Its central superstition is repressed childhood sexuality. The handful of early cases of hysteria which could be so interpreted become the metaphiers by which to understand all personality and art, all civilization and its discontents. And it too, like Marxism, demands total commitment, initiation procedures, a worshipful relation to its canonical texts, and gives in return that same assistance in decision and direction in life which a few centuries ago was the province of religion.

And, to take an example closer to my own tradition, I will add behaviorism. For it too has its central auguring place in a handful of rat and pigeon experiments, making them the metaphiers of all behavior and history. It too gives to the individual adherent the talisman of control by reinforcement contingencies by which he is to meet his world and understand its vagaries. And even though the radical environmentalism behind it, of belief in a tabula rasa organism that can be built up into anything by reinforcement has long been known to be questionable, given the biologically evolved aptic structuring of each organism, these principles still draw adherents into the hope of a new society based upon such control.

Of course these scientisms about man begin with something that is true. That nutrition can improve health both of mind and body is true. The class struggle as Marx studied it in the France of Louis Napoleon was a fact. The relief of hysterical symptoms in a few patients by analysis of sexual memories probably happened. And hungry animals or anxious men certainly will learn instrumental responses for food or approbation. These are true facts. But so is the shape of a liver of a sacrificed animal a true fact. And so the Ascendants and Midheavens of astrologers, or the shape of oil on water. Applied to the world as representative of *all* the world, facts become superstitions. A superstition is after all only a metaphier grown wild to serve a need to know. Like the entrails of animals or the flights of birds, such scientistic superstitions become the preserved ritualized places where we may read out the past and future of man, and hear the answers that can authorize our actions.

Science then, for all its pomp of factness, is not unlike some of the more easily disparaged outbreaks of pseudoreligions. In this period of transition from its religious basis, science often shares with the celestial maps of astrology, or a hundred other irrationalisms, the same nostalgia for the Final Answer, the One Truth, the Single Cause. In the frustrations and sweat of laboratories, it feels the same temptations to swarm into sects, even as did the Khabiru refugees, and set out here and there through the dry Sinais of parched fact for some rich and brave significance flowing with truth and exaltation. And all of this, my metaphor and all, is a part of this transitional period after the breakdown of the bicameral mind.

And this essay is no exception.

* * *

Curiously, none of these contemporary movements tells us anything about what we are supposed to be like after the wrinkles in our nutrition have been ironed smooth, or "the withering away of the state" has occurred, or our libidos have been properly cathected, or the chaos of reinforcements has been made straight. Instead their allusion is mostly backward, telling us what has gone wrong, hinting of some cosmic disgrace, some earlier stunting of our potential. It is, I think, yet another characteristic of the religious form which such movements have taken over in the emptiness caused by the retreat of ecclesiastical certainty — that of a supposed fall of man.

This strange and, I think, spurious idea of a lost innocence takes its mark precisely in the breakdown of the bicameral mind as the first great conscious narratization of mankind. It is the song of the Assyrian psalms, the wail of the Hebrew hymns, the myth of Eden, the fundamental fall from divine favor that is the source and first premise of the world's great religions. I interpret this hypothetical fall of man to be the groping of newly conscious men to narratize what has happened to them, the loss of divine voices and assurances in a chaos of human directive and selfish privacies.

We see this theme of lost certainty and splendor not only stated by all the religions of man throughout history, but also again and again even in nonreligious intellectual history. It is there from the reminiscence theory of the Platonic *Dialogues*, that everything new is really a recalling of a lost better world, all the way to Rousseau's complaint of the corruption of natural man by the artificialities of civilization. And we see it also in the modern scientisms I have mentioned: in Marx's assumption of a lost "social childhood of mankind where mankind unfolds in complete beauty," so clearly stated in his earlier writings, an innocence corrupted by money, a paradise to be regained. Or in the Freudian emphasis on the deep-seatedness of neurosis in civilization and of dreadful primordial acts and wishes in both

our racial and individual pasts; and by inference a previous innocence, quite unspecified, to which we return through psychoanalysis. Or in behaviorism, if less distinctly, in the undocumented
faith that it is the chaotic reinforcements of development and the
social process that must be controlled and ordered to return man
to a quite unspecified ideal before these reinforcements had
twisted his true nature awry.

I therefore believe that these and many other movements of
our time are in the great long picture of our civilizations related
to the loss of an earlier organization of human natures. They are
attempts to return to what is no longer there, like poets to their
inexistent Muses, and as such they are characteristic of these transitional millennia in which we are imbedded.

I do not mean that the individual thinker, the reader of this
page or its writer, or Galileo or Marx, is so abject a creature as to
have any conscious articulate willing to reach either the absolutes
of gods or to return to a preconscious innocence. Such terms are
meaningless applied to individual lives and removed from the
larger context of history. It is only if we make generations our
persons and centuries hours that the pattern is clear.

As individuals we are at the mercies of our own collective
imperatives. We see over our everyday attentions, our gardens
and politics, and children, into the forms of our culture darkly.
And our culture is our history. In our attempts to communicate
or to persuade or simply interest others, we are using and moving
about through cultural models among whose differences we may
select, but from whose totality we cannot escape. And it is in this
sense of the forms of appeal, of begetting hope or interest or
appreciation or praise for ourselves or for our ideas, that our
communications are shaped into these historical patterns, these
grooves of persuasion which are even in the act of communication an inherent part of what is communicated. And this essay is
no exception.

No exception at all. It began in what seemed in my personal narratizations as an individual choice of a problem with which I have had an intense involvement for most of my life: the problem of the nature and origin of all this invisible country of touchless rememberings and unshowable reveries, this introcosm that is more myself than anything I can find in any mirror. But was this impulse to discover the source of consciousness what it appeared to me? The very notion of truth is a culturally given direction, a part of the pervasive nostalgia for an earlier certainty. The very idea of a universal stability, an eternal firmness of principle *out there* that can be sought for through the world as might an Arthurian knight for the Grail, is, in the morphology of history, a direct outgrowth of the search for lost gods in the first two millennia after the decline of the bicameral mind. What was then an augury for direction of action among the ruins of an archaic mentality is now the search for an innocence of certainty among the mythologies of facts.

Index

Index of Persons

(References in italics are to footnotes.)

Achilles, 69, 72, 73, 81, 94, 117, 259, 268, 289
Adkins, A. D. H., *260*
Agamemnon, 72, 73, 81, 258
Akurgal, Ekron, *153*
Albright, William F., *209*
Alcaeus, 284, 288
Aldred, Cyril, *186*
Alexander, S., 4
Allen, M. W., *122*
Amon of Thebes, 321
Amos, 278, 305, 311, 372
Angelergues, R., *122*
Apuleius, *334*
Archilochus, 283–285
Archimedes, 74
Aristides, Aelius, *327, 341*
Aristophanes, 407
Aristotle, *27, 45,* 289, 333
Arnold, Magda, *398*
Asclepius, *334,* 336
Ashurbanipal (king), 233, 237, 251
Atahualpa (Inca), 159–160
Athanasius, 346–347
Audberg, M. M., *88*
Augustine, 2, *2*

Baker, Ronald J., *359*
Balz, E., *351*
Barber, Theodore X., *394, 400, 401*
Barton, George A., *180, 181, 182, 229*
Benton, A. L., *122*
Benton, S., *272*
Bever, Thomas G., *368*
Bigelow, L. B., *430*
Binet, Alfred, *5,* 384, *384*
Birdsell, Joseph B., *129*
Bitterman, M. E., *7*
Blake, William, 375

Bleuler, Eugen, 88, *414,* 419, 423, 424
Bogen, Joseph E., *102, 107, 113, 114, 365*
Bohr, Nils, 53
Book, W. F., *33*
Brady, J. P., *401*
Brady, J. V., *94*
Bramwell, J. M., *384*
Braun, Ludwig, *266*
Brenman, Margaret, *398*
Brockma, V., *427*
Brook-Rose, Christine, *49*
Brown, F., *298*
Brumbaugh, Robert S., *212*
Bruun, R. D., *351*
Burklund, Charles W., *365*
Burland, C. A., *144, 167, 174*
Burnham, John C., *14*
Bushnell, G. H. S., *155, 167*
Butin, Romain F., *208*
Butzer, Karl W., *131, 138, 144*

Caillois, Roger, *239*
Callinus, 284
Callistratus, 336
Calverley, D. S., *394*
Carpenter, W. B., *25*
Carville, C. B., *125*
Chadwick, J., *80*
Chambers, Robert, 438
Chang Kwang-chih, *162*
Charcot, Jean Martin, 384
Chastenet, A.-M.-J., *383*
Chiarello, R. J., *368*
Childe, V. G., 138
Clark, Grahame, *136, 151, 166*
Clark, J. D., *131*
Clarkin, J., *351*
Cleveland, S. E., *425*

Cohen, John, *333*
Conrad, D. G., *94*
Constantine (emperor), 347
Covarrubias, *164*
Covi, L., *418*
Cox, Harvey, *439*
Cromwell, R. L., *427, 431*
Cyprian, 435

Darwin, Charles, 5, 9, 438
Darwin, Erasmus, 438
Davis, Charles, *439*
Day, Thomas, *364*
De Acosta, Father Joseph, *175*
Deeley, D. C., *401*
Democritus, 292
Demodocus, 372–373
Desborough, V. R. d'A., *69, 255*
Descartes, René, 16, 291
DeVore, Irven, *127*
Diomedes, 69
Dodds, E. R., *71, 162, 322, 330, 335, 344, 405*
Douglas, Mary, *439*
Dunlap, Knight, 14

Ebner, E., *427*
Edelstein, E. J., *334*
Edmonds, J. M., *282, 283*
Einstein, Albert, 44
Emerson, Ralph W., 438
Empson, William, quoted, 378
Engels, Frederick, 442
Erickson, Milton, *401*
Ettlinger, E. G., *105*
Euripides, 288

Féré, C., *384*
Finkelstein, J. J., *239*
Fisher, S., *425*
Flaubert, Gustave, *377*
Flor-Henry, Pierre, *430*
Frankfort, Henri, *184, 186, 191*
Frazer, Sir James, G., 166, *327*
Freud, Sigmund, 74, 415, 444

Galambos, R., *123*
Galileo, 434–435, 445

Galin, David, *119*
Gardiner, Alan H., *191*
Gardiner, Martin, *368*
Gardiner, W. Lambert, *35*
Gauss, C. F., 43
Gazzaniga, Michael S., *107, 113, 114, 115*
Gesenius, William, *298*
Gill, Merton M., *398*
Glaucus, 69, 72
Glucksberg, Sam, *49*
Goedicke, Hans, *194*
Goethe, J. W., 376–438
Goldstein, Leonide E., *429*
Goodman, Felicitas D., *353, 358, 359*
Gordon, Edmund I., *204*
Gordon, H. W., *116, 365*
Greenspoon, J., *35*
Greissman, Judith, *78*
Grunbaum, G. E. von, *239*
Gudea (king of Lagash), 170, 229
Guillaume, Alfred, *245, 294, 321, 363*
Gur, R. C., *396*

Hadamard, Jacques, *43*
Hagen, Victor W. von, *155, 159, 163, 172, 173*
Hall, Edward T., *97*
Hall, K. R. L., *127*
Hallo, W. W., *186*
Hammurabi, 198–200, 247–248, 250
Harford, R. A., *36*
Harnad, Stevan, *102, 121, 343*
Harper, Robert Francis, *198*
Harrison, M., *422*
Harshman, Richard A., *343*
Havelock, Eric A., 375
Heaney, Seamus, 57
Hécaen, H., *118, 122*
Hector, 70, 72, 74, 94
Hefferline, R. F., *36*
Hegel, G. W. F., 442
Heidel, Alexander, *162, 164, 234, 252, 295*
Held, J. M., *427*
Helmholtz, Hermann von, 43, 437
Hemming, John, *160*

Hennell, T., *89, 95*
Heraclitus, 2, 291, 322
Herodotus, 235, 251, 290, *326, 333*
Herrick, C. Judson, *13*
Herrnstein, Richard, *14*
Hesiod, 164, *267,* 278–279, *349,* 371–373
Hilgard, Ernest, *392, 394, 398*
Hilgard, Josephine R., *396*
Hinde, R. A., 7
Hitchcock, James, *439*
Hobbes, Thomas, 2
Hodgson, Shadworth, 11, *11*
Holloway, Julia, *337*
Homer, 71, 75–76, 272, 289; see also *Iliad* and *Odyssey* in Index of Subjects
Hooke, S. H., *183*
Housman, A. E., 376
Hull, Clark L., *394*
Hussey, Mary I., *244*
Huxley, Thomas Henry, 11, *11,* 438

Iamblichus, 334, *342,* 344, 346
Isaac, Glynn L., *129*

Jackson, J. Haughlings, 122, *123*
Jacobsen, Thorkild, *184*
James, William, 11, *11*
Janet, Pierre, *392*
Jaynes, Julian, *17, 132, 436*
Jayson, L. N., *96*
Jennings, H. S., 5, *13*
Jeremiah, 303–305, 311, 352
Joan of Arc, 73, 79, 180
Johnson, Samuel, 11
Jones, L. W., *419*
Josiah, King, 310, 336
Joule, James Prescott, 437
Julian (emperor), 331
Julianus, 331

Kant, Immanuel, 2
Keenan, B., *36*
Kihlstrom, John, *391*
Kildahl, John P., *359, 360*
Kimble, G. A., *32*
Kimura, Doreen, *368*

King, L. W., *248*
Kinsbourne, Marcel, *428*
Kirstein, Lincoln, *327*
Köhler, Wolfgang, 44
Konishi, M., *128*
Kraus, R. M., *49*

Lamarck, J., 438
Lamartine, A. M. L., 376
Lambert, W. G., *224*
Landa, 172, *173*
Landis, Carney, *420*
Layton, A. S. F., *428*
Leaf, Walter, *81, 270*
Leibnitz, G. W., *434*
Leichty, Erle, *238*
Levitt, E., *401*
Lewes, G. H., *3,* 12
Lewinsohn, P. M., *88*
Lewy, H., *228*
Linne, S., *155*
Lloyd, Seton, *153, 166*
Locke, John, 27, 66, 435
London, Perry, *386*
Lucian, 322, 334

McDougall, William, *11, 13*
McGuinness, EveLynn, *323*
Mach, Ernst, 2
McKenzie, John L., *299*
Magoun, H. W., *17*
Maimonides, *299*
Mallowan, M. E. L., *168, 169*
Marbe, Karl, 37–39
Marinatos, S., *213*
Marler, Peter, *128*
Marx, Karl, 442–445
Mason, F., 13
Mason, J. W., *94*
Maudslay, A. P., *166*
Maupertuis, 436
Mead, George Henry, 74
Mellaart, James, *139, 151, 166*
Mesmer, Anton, 381–384
Meyer, E., *418*
Miligi, A. El, *408*
Mill, James, 3
Mill, John Stuart, 12, *42*

Milner, Brenda, *118*
Milton, John, 375
Modell, A. H., *411*
Montagu, Ashley, *50*
Morant, G. M., *185*
Morgan, C. Lloyd, 12
Moses, 93, 174, 301–304, 363
Müller, Max, 30

Nargayoral, J., *243*
Nathan, P. E., *88*
Nathan, P. W., *124*
Nero, 334
Nevius, J. L., *363*
Newton, Sir Isaac, 380, 435
Nies, James B., *235*
Nijinsky, 26, 29
Nilsson, Martin P., *73*

Odysseus, 70, 81, 270, 286
Oesterreich, T. K., *323, 351*
Oldfield, R. C., *368*
Oppé, A. P., *323*
Oppenheim, A. Leo, *178, 239, 242, 244*
Orne, Martin, *385, 389, 390*
Ornstein, R. E., *119*
Osguc, Nimet, *210*
Osmond, Humphrey, *408*

Parmenides, 292
Parry, Milman, *78*
Pascal, Blaise, 434
Pattie, Frank A., 380
Paul (the Apostle), 96, 333, 357–358, 440
Pausanias, *327, 328, 333*
Peirce, C. S., 2
Penfield, Wilder, *101*, 108, *108, 108*, 112
Perot, Phanor, *108*, 112
Perrot, J., *139*
Petrie, Flinders, *166*
Pfeiffer, C. C., *418*
Pfeiffer, Robert H., *174, 244, 249*
Phillips, L., *426*
Philo, *341*
Picard, Charles, *327*
Pirgott, Stewart, *136, 151, 166*

Pindar, 282, 289, 291
Pizarro, Pedro, *159*
Plato, *164, 212*, 284, 291, 323, *340, 341*, 356, 370, 373, 405–407, 444
Plutarch, 279, 321–322, 330, *362*
Poincaré, Henri, 43
Pollit, Jerome J., *212*
Polyani, Karl, *210*
Porter, R. W., *94*
Ponzo, Mario, *265*
Porphyry, 345
Postman, Leo, *35*
Poulsen, F., *337*
Pressel, Esther, *353*
Prince, Morton, *392*
Pritchard, James B., *234*
Pumpelly, R., 137, *138*
Pythagoras, 290, 345, 434

Rainer, J. D., *91*
Rasmussen, T., *107*
Ray, John, 435
Razran, Gregory, *32*
Redford, Donald B., *295*
Reeves, D. L., *125*
Reimarus, H. S., 436
Remmington, Roger, *343*
Richards, I. A., *49*
Rignano, Eugenio, *30*
Rilke, Rainer Maria, 376
Ritzler, B., *427*
Roberts, Lamar, *101*
Rokeach, Milton, *391*
Rosenhan, David, *385*
Rosenthal, Randall, *430*
Rosenthal, Robert, *35*
Rosner, Burton, *123*
Rousseau, Jean Jacques, 444
Roux, George, *178*
Rowe, J. H., *158*
Ruggles, Howard E., *267*
Ryan, T. A., *32*
Ryle, Gilbert, 2

Saggs, H. W. F., *166, 178, 184, 195, 209, 214, 230, 233, 238, 251*
Sahagun, 164
Samarin, W. J., *359*

Samuel, 306–308
Sappho, 284–285
Sarbin, Theodore, R., *381, 393, 398*
Sarpedon, 69
Sassenrath, L., *35*
Saul (king of Israel), 307–308
Saul, R. E., *125*
Sawrey, W. L., *94*
Schaller, G., *128*
Schilder, P., *425*
Schliemann, Heinrich, 76
Schreber, D. P., 414–416, *414*
Sechan, Louis, *327*
Shakow, David, *421*
Shankweiler, D., *368*
Shannon, Jack, *121*
Shapiro, A. K., *351, 352*
Shapiro, H. L., *351*
Shelley, Percy Bysshe, 376
Sherrington, C. S., *428*
Shor, Ronald, *385*
Sidgewick, Henry, et al., *87*
Simpson, H. F., *88*
Simpson, W. K., *186*
Sinclair, J. H., *175*
Smith, Aaron, *107*
Smith, M. C., *124*
Smith, Sidney, *183*
Smith, William Stevenson, *215*
Snell, Bruno, *71*
Socrates, 292, 323, 340
Solon, 285–288, 290, 373
Sommer, Robert, *97*
Speiser, E. A., *228, 234*
Spencer, Herbert, 10
Sperry, R. W., *107, 113, 114, 115, 116, 119*
Stanford, W. B., *364*
Steiner, George, *441*
Storch, A., 418
Störring, Gustav, *412*
Strabo, *362*
Straus, Erwin W., *85, 97*
Suetonius, *334*
Sugarman, Arthur, *429*

Sully, J., *42*
Sumption, Jonathan, *337*

Tacitus, 327, 362
Terpander, 282–283
Thamyris, 377–378
Thomas, C. B., *419*
Thompson, J. Erik S., *156, 173*
Thucydides, 255
Titchener, E. B., 3, 5, 23
Toynbee, A. J., 138
Tukulti-Ninurta I, 223–228
Tyrtaeus, 284, 288

Ventris, M. C. F., *80*
Virgil, 331

Wada, J., 107, *107*, 365
Wallace, Alfred Russell, 9, *10,* 438
Warner, Randall, *78*
Washburn, Margaret Floy, *5*
Waskom, H. L., *34*
Watson, John B., 14
Watson, William, *162*
Watt, H. J., 38–40, *38*
Wayne, H. L., *351*
Webster, T. B. L., *80, 272, 370*
Weingaertner, Arthur H., *409*
Weinstein, Edwin A., *410*
Weisburg, R., *49*
Weiss, J. M., *94*
Weisz, J. D., *94*
Werner, H., *418*
West, D. J., *87*
Wheeler, Sir Mortimer, *162, 170*
Wheelwright, Phillip, *51*
White, Robert, *398*
Whitehead, Alfred North, 4
Wilson, John A., *186, 191*
Wilson, J. V. Kinnier, *238*
Witelson, Sandra F., *343*
Wolf, Theta, *384*
Woodward, William, *436*
Woodworth, Robert S., *28, 43, 264*
Woolley, Sir Leonard, *161,* 164, 196
Wundt, Wilhelm, 3

Index of Subjects

(References in italics are to footnotes.)

Admonition, experiences of, 106, 111–112, 279, 411–412
Adrenalin, 93, 262
Affect, and excerption, 62
Agriculture
  causes of, 137–138
  gods' decisions in, 180
  incipient at Eynan, 144
  Natufian, 139
  as primary subsistence, 144
Amos, 278, 305, 311, 372
Amulets, 232
Analog, defined, 54
Analog 'I', 65, 204, 271, 283, 287, 296, 375, 387, 415
  defined, 62
  in *Gilgamesh,* 253
  in hypnosis, 398
  loss of, in oracles, 328
  loss of, in schizophrenia, 417, 419–421, 423, 425
  origin of, in deceit, 219–220
  protects against impulsive behavior, 402
  and *thumos,* 263
Analog behavior, in *Iliad,* 82
Analog space, 65, 204
Anarchy, 211, 213
Andean civilizations, 156–158, 178. *See also* Incas
Angels, 233
  origin of, 230–231
Anterior commissures, *see* Brain
Aoidoi, 69, 76–78, 82, 215, 269, 277, 362
  change to *rhapsodes,* 369
  hallucinatory echolalia, 424
  and memory, 219
  in *Odyssey,* 272
  not possessed, 370

  as unity with past, 256
  verbal *Iliad,* 259
Aptic structures, 31, 39, 387, 443
  definition, *31*
  for hallucinations, 416–417
  for language, 50, 103
  for science, 434
  temporal priming of, 135
Architecture, 153, 155
Ashur, 209–210
Assimilation, 64–65
Associationism, 8
Assyria, 158
  bicameral breakdown in, 223–228
  cruelty of, 214
  dead called gods in, 164
  kings of, 249
  rise of, 209–212
  sortilege in, 240
Atlantis, 212. *See also* Thera
Augury, qualitative, 243–244
Auras, 74–75
Authoritarian governments, 205
Authorization
  archaic, 319, 331; general bicameral paradigm, 324; in glossolalia, 358–360; in hypnosis, 393–394
  and Christianity, 346–347
  in exorcism, 350
  idolatry as, 336
  poetry as, 363
  possession and hallucination, 342
  science and the church, 435
  Sibyls as, 332
  substitutes for ecclesiastical, 440
"Automatic inference," *42*
Autoscopic phenomena, 111, 287, 299
Aztecs, 174, 176

ba, 193–194, 290

Baboons, 127–130

Babylon, 224–225. *See also* Assyria

Babylonian kings, 249. *See also* Hammurabi

Baptism, 231

Bedouins, *245,* 294

Behavior, 66, 72
  and word changes, 292
  control of, by language, 134

Behaviorism, 13–15, 442, 445

Bible
  New Testament: spontaneous possession in, 346–347; use of *psyche,* 289. *See also* Christianity
  Old Testament: 118, 227, 229, 293, 299–313; Amos and Ecclesiastes compared, 295–297; bicameral children killed, 221; changes in I Samuel, 306–308; divination, *242;* inconsistency of bicameral voices among persons, 302–304; inconsistency within persons, 304; loss of bicameral mind, 313; loss of visual component, 300–302; nabiim, 299–313; orthological problem, 294–295; Pentateuch, 297–302; speech of idols, 174; spontaneous divination, 245; Tower of Babel legend, 235

Bicameral kingdoms, 149, 151–158, 194. *See also* Andean civilizations, Bicameral theocracies, Egypt, Hittites, Maya, Mesopotamia, Olmec
  boundary relations, 206–207
  hierarchy of priests, 207
  instability, 205–208

Bicameral man, 84–85, 117
  Amos, 295–296
  habit and voices, 213

Bicameral mind, 109, 194, 204. *See also* Consciousness
  auditory input, 208, 269. *See also* Hallucinations

breakdown of, 124; angels, 230–231; artistic expression, 377; consequences of, 227–228; divination, 236; erosion of religions, 439–441; evidence, 223–236; evil, idea of, 231–232; the Fall, 299; heaven, 233–235; increased physiological stress, 258–259; in *Odyssey,* 276; prayer, 228–230; punishment and redemption, 226; religious view of man, 439; science, 433–434; Shubshi, 225–226; time of, 197, 224

civilizing of mankind, 145

Code of Hammurabi, 200

confrontation of, with subjective, 158, 160

consistent with schizophrenic symptoms, 408, 413, 431–432

and decadence of oracles, 329–330

defined, 75

explanation of idols, 173

loss of, 294, 302

and music, 369

neurological model (illustrated), 104; brain organization, 122–125; cognitive function differences, 117–122; evidence, 106–125; hemispheric independence, 112–117; introduced, 105; language in hemispheres, 106–107; schizophrenia, 428–430; vestigial godlike function, 107–112

objections to theory of, 75–81

and poetry, 361, 377–378

reduced control, 201

reversion to, impossible, 216

as social control, 126, 205

tempo of development, 202

transilience to consciousness, 221, 259

Bicameral theocracies. *See also* Civilizations, Bicameral kingdoms
  god-king theocracy, 178, 185–194
  mansions for voices, 188–189; "Memphite Theology," 186;

Osiris, 187; theory of *ka,* 189–194

periodicity, 195

steward-king theocracy, 178–185
kings as gods, 184–185; mouth-washing ceremonies, 182–183; personal god, 183–184; selection by gods, 184

temporal changes, 194–201
idea of law, 197–201; increased complexity, 194–197

vestiges of, 320, 433
hypnosis, 396, 397, 401; imaginary companions, 396–397; schizophrenia, 405; support of culture, 355

voices. *See* Voices

Blind spot, 24–25, *25*

Body, the problem of, 71, 291
electrical stimulation of, 108;

Brain
anterior commissures (illustrated), 104–106

Broca's area, 101, 353, 374

consciousness, 16; and language 67

cerebral hemispheres
differences in function, 117–122; dominance, 100, 343; functions in brain-damaged, 118–119; hypnosis, 395–396; independent behavior of, 112–117; lateralization of music, 367–369; laterality effects in schizophrenia, 429–430; organization in Hammurabi, 200; speech and song, 365–366

early development of, 125

EEG: hemisphere function, 119, 343; hypnosis, 395; schizophrenia, 427, 429–430

electrical stimulation of, 108; failure of recognition, 112; passivity, 112; voices heard, 109–111

environmental changes, 117

general bicameral paradigm, 325

injury and exosomatic experiences, 46; and blindness, *25*

plasticity and redundancy, 122–124

reciprocal inhibition, 428–429

resiliency, 124

reticular formation, 17–18

right hemisphere: bicameral voices, 104; emotion, 116–117; godlike function, 107–112; involuntary inhibition of, 225; recognition of faces, 120–122; sortilege, 240; understanding language, 106–107; voices of gods, 106

sexual differences in function, 343–344

and speech, 100–104; areas (illustrated), 101

spontaneous possession, 350–353

Wernicke's area, 101–108, 366–367; contralateral, 106, 125, 353, 365–368, 374

Brain-damaged patients, 118–119

Broca's area. *See* Brain

Building inscriptions, 250–251

Burial practices. *See also* Dead
Egyptian, 188–189
Mesolithic midden-dwellers, 136
and names, 136
Natufian, 139
and voices, 141

Calls, intentional, 131–132

Causation, 64, 78–79, 259

Chance, 240, 305

Chaos, 209, 213, 214, 228–229, 256

China, 159, 162–163, *163*

Christianity, 318, 332, 346–347

Civilization
advent of agriculture, 137–138
beginning of, 144–145, 149
bicameral, 117; houses of gods, 150–160; idols, 165–175; and the individual, 79–81; living dead, 161–165; selective pressures, 103; writings of, 163–164

Civilization (*Cont.*)
  defined, 149
  diffusion of, 159, 163
  periodic breakdowns, 197
  pre-Columbian periodicity, 195
Collective cognitive imperative, 328,
    402–403, 445
  change in poets, 373–374
  decadence of oracles, 329
  decay of religions, 439
  and Delphic oracle, 324, 325
  in glossolalia, 358, 360
  in hypnosis, 385–386
  hysterical illness, 381
  learned consciousness, 340
  possession, 342, 348, 350
  schizophrenia, 409–410
Commands, 133
Commissurotomy, patients, 107, 113–
    119
Communication, 127–129
Concepts, 30, 31, 50
Conditioning, Pavlovian, 32–33
Conflict, 70, 94, 259
Consciousness. *See also* Subjectivity
  defined, 55
  versus actions, 11
  not association of elements, 8
  and biological evolution, 340
  causes of: Assyria, 209–212; con-
    quest, 214, 216; deceit, 219–
    220; epics, 217–219; failure of
    gods, 208–209; instability of bi-
    cameral kingdoms, 205–208;
    migrations, 213–215; natural
    selection, 220–221; observation
    of difference, 217; summarized,
    221; Thera, 212; trade, 206;
    writing, 208
  compatibilization, 65
  versus complex tasks, 25–27
  versus concept-formation, 30
  conciliation, 64–65
  conscious automaton theory, 11
  continuity, illusion of, 23–24
  not a copy of experience, 27
  cultural, not genetic, 220–222, 340

and Descartes, 16
diminished, and bicameral para-
    digm, 324
emergent evolution doctrine, 12,
    13
as epiphenomenon, 11
evolution of, 8, 67, 122
excerption, 61
extensiveness, illusion of, 21–23
in eye-to-eye contact, 169
in first human records, 68
generation of, by metaphor, 59
gods in place of, 72
growth in Greece, 256–292
helpless spectator theory, 10–12
problem of in *Iliad*, 69, 81–82
as learned, 221, 398
confused with learning, 6, 8, 31–
    36
location of, 16, 44–46
loss of, 353
matter, not property of, 4–5
metaphor, 58
metaphysical view, 9–10
morality coincident with, 286
narratization, 63
as operation, 65
and poetry, 58, 283–284, 287, 361–
    375
and possession, 339–342
distinct from reactivity, 22
reason, unnecessary for, 41
not reticular activating system, 16
as shift to visual mind, 269
spatialization in, 59–61
spatial quality and vision, 269
subjective, 24, 236, 276
thinking, unnecessary for, 36–37,
    39, 41
Titchener's designation of, 23
transilience to, 221. *See also*
    Greece, Hammurabi, Khabiru,
    Mesopotamia, Tukulti
use of the analog, 59
Cortex. *See* Brain
Culture
  change of norm, 222
  communication, 445

evidence of bicameral, 150
substrate of consciousness, 354
Cuneiform, 176–177
'heard,' 182
texts, 36, 180–184, 224–230
translation problems and inaccuracies, 177, 201, 246

Dancing, 282, 327
Daydreaming, 65
Dead
burial of, 136, 161–163
ghosts, 165
as gods, 163–165
grief for, 165
letters to, 189
in Mesolithic man, 136
in Neanderthal man, 136
prepared heads, 172
Death, survival after, 289
Deceit, 219
in *Odyssey*, 276
Deception, 160
in *Iliad*, 81
Decision-making
exopsychic. *See* Divination
aided by music, 369
and stress, 93–94. *See also* Stress
Delphic Oracle, 321–326, 341
decline of, 330–331
compared with Umbanda, 353–355
Plato on, 323
spoke in poetry, 362
as punishing, 156
authorization of Socrates, *323*
Demons, 231–233, 348
Devil, and Incas, 174–175
Dialectical materialism, 442
Dichotic listening, 368
dike, 280, 286–287
Dissociation in hypnosis, 392, 398
Divination, 236–246, *295,* 440. *See also* Omens
Amos, 296
augury, 242–244
institutionalized, 332
Saul, 307
sortilege, 239–242

spontaneous, 244–245; begins in bicameral voices, 305; by gods, 305–306; in Middle Ages, *245*
Dodona, Oracle at, 327, 340
Dominance hierarchy, 128–129
Dorian invasions, 214, 255–256, 266, 273, 278, 292–293
Dreams, 226, 229, 308, 328
continuity of consciousness, 23
dream books, 239
omens, 239
Druids, 327
Dualism
beginning of, 291
sustains idolatry, 335

Echolalia, 424
EEG. *See* Brain
Effigies, 165, 166. *See also* Idols, Figurines
Ego, 418–419
of Iliadic hero, 73
superego relationship, 74
Egypt, 143, 159
collapse of authority, 196–197
dynasties, 68
figurines, 166
god-king theocracy, 178
idols' role, 170
kings as gods, 185–194
Old Kingdom, 193
tombs, 163
Elohim, 297–298
Emotion, in commissurotomized. 116
Enlightenment, the, 436–437
Epics
as origin of narratization, 217–219
as response to havoc, 256
Epilepsy, 108, 113
Ethics, 71, 319
etor, 259, 266–269, 279
Evil, 231–232, 348
Evolution, 3–5, 151
Baldwinian, 221
of consciousness, 7–8, 122
continuity in, 10

Evolution (*Cont.*)
doctrine of emergent evolution,
12–13
of groups, 126–129
and hypnosis, 380
of language, 102, 126, 129–138
of learning, 7–8
and metaphysical forces, 10
of mind, 9
natural selection, 8, 10, 220–221
of speech areas, 103
Excerption
and affect, 62
feature of consciousness, 61
and memory, 62
Exodus of Israelites, 213
Exorcism, 233, 349
Exosomatic experiences, 46
Extispicy, 243–244
Eye index, 169–172
Eye-to-eye contact, 169
Eynan, 139–144, 160–161, 195, 438

Facial recognition, 120–122
Fall, the, 299, 444
Fatigue, 426–427
Figurines, 165–168. *See also* Idols,
Effigies
evolution of, 167
fertility cults, 166
as hallucinatory control, 166–167
as mnemonic devices, 167
Forgiveness, divine, 226
Free association, 37
Free will, 345. *See also* Volition

Gastro-intestinal stimuli, 267–268
Genetic basis, bicamerality, 311
Genetic disposition, schizophrenia,
426
General bicameral paradigm, 323–
327
in hallucinating from statues, 333–
337
explains Delphic Oracle, 325
in glossolalia, 360
basis of hypnosis, 379, 383, 394,
396

Genii, 231, 273, 321. *See also* Angels
gigunu, 179, 337
Gilgamesh, Epic of, 247, 251–253
Glossolalia, 357–360
God-carvers, 173
God-hero relationship, 74
God-houses, 151–152, 154, 157, 178–
179, 184
God-kings, 141–143, 158–159, 178,
191–192. *See also* Bicameral
theocracies, Osiris-Horus
God, search for, 434–437
Gods, 282–283. *See also* Hallucinations
absent, 223
angels, 230–231
and brain, 106–125
celestialization of, 233–235
commandments resisted, 220
as demons, 231–233
departure of, 224–227
failure of, 208–209
first (illustrated, 142), 138–144,
161
function of, 117
Greek and Hebrew, 74
and group size, 129
houses of, 150–160
in *Iliad,* 71–74
of *Iliad* and *Odyssey,* 273
in induced possession, 345–346
learning in, 217–218
and nervous system, 202
origin of, 126, 137–145, 163–165
as owners. *See* Bicameral theocracies
personal god, 183–184. *See also ili*
and *ka*
not poetic devices, 78
proliferation of, 196, 202
in schizophrenia, 414–416
silence and authorization, 320
silent, 231, 236
source of bicameral mind, 413
speech of, and brain, 103–106
speech of, renewed, 182–183
voices of, 106, 112, 118, 237, 436

as volition, 202
and written word, 208
Golden Age, 278
Good, idea of, 226, 275. *See also* morality
Graves, 161. *See also* Burial practices, Tombs
Great flood, 234
Greek terms analyzed. *See etor, ker, kradie, noos, phrenes, psyche, thumos*
Groups
evolution of, 126–129
and hallucinated king, 141

Hacilar culture, 151, 166
Hades, 289, 291
Hallucinations, 79. *See also* Voices
auditory, 85–91; admonitory, 111; authority of, 94–96; *ba,* 193–194; disappearance of, 227; effigies, 165–167; eye-to-eye, 169; hemispheric origin, 105; *ka,* 190–193; linguistic form, 105; origin, 134–135; and poets, 375–376; recognized, 137; as rulers, 181; social control, 140–144; stelae sources, 181–182
and city sites, 156
directed Trojan war, 75
gods as, 74
in hypnosis, 389–390
incidence of, 87
instigated by stress, 93
location of, 110
begin negatory possession, 348
versus possession, 342
in psychotics, 87–93
and reading, 218
in schizophrenia, 408–417
visual, 86, 91–92, 193
Hammurabi, 208, 214, 224, 296, 391
Code of (illustrated, 199), 198–200
letters of, 247–248, 250
Heart, 265–266
Hebrews. *See* Khabiru
Hemispheres, cerebral. *See* Brain

Heraldry, 176
He-who-is, 298–299, 301–307. *See also* Yahweh
Hieratic, 68, 176–177, 190
Hieroglyphics, 68, 176–177
History
has fixed patterns, 159
and *Iliad,* 76–78
invention of, 251
starts in omen texts, 239
selective emphasis, 228
Hittites, 153–154, 211, 213–214, 242, 293
Holocene Thermal Maximum, 145
Homer, existence of, 76. *See also* Index of Persons
Hunter-gatherer groups, 126
Hypnosis
changing nature of, 383–386
"demand characteristics," 385
evidence for theory, 395–398
existence questioned, 398–403
"hidden observer," 392, 400
hypnotist as authorization, 393–395
induction of, 386–387
parallel processing, 392
paraphrands of forces, 380–383
post-hypnotic suggestion, 328
susceptibility to, 395–397, 403
trance and compliance, 387–393
Umbanda trance state, 354
Hysterical illness, 382, 442–443

I Ching, 440
Iconography, 176
Identification, 5–6
Identity, 276–277
Idolatry today, 337–338
Idols, 153, 157, 165–175
animated, 336–337
conquests of, 248
destruction of, 310, 333, 336
eye idols (illustrated), 168
eye index of, 169
figurines, 165–168
of Hebrews, 307–310
Iamblichus on, 334

Idols (*Cont.*)
  of Incas, *173*
  king's corpses as, 144
  Mayan, 172–173
  Olmec, 171
  origin of idea of sacrifice, 243
  revival of, 332–338
  spectacle-idols, 168
  speech of, 173–175, 309, 333–337
  theory of, 169–173
ili, 184, 191
Iliad, 69–83, 117–118, 257–272, 280,
    289, 377
  authorship, 76
  beginning consciousness, 257–272
  bicameral mind theory, 75
  Code of Hammurabi, 200
  conscious mind, 72
  consciousness in, 81–82
  gods heard in, 180
  gods initiate action, 78, 180, 258
  as history, 76–78
  inconsistencies in, 81
  main action unconscious, 271
  no individual insanity, 405
  compared with *Odyssey*, 272
  psychology of hero, 73
Imaginary companions, 396–397
Immediate experience, 53
Incas, 158–160, 174–175, 416
Induction procedures
  and brain activity, 343
  cues for, 345
  in general bicameral paradigm,
    324
  in glossolalia, 358, 360
  in Hermetic literature, 334
  at Lebadea, 328
  and possession, 342
  stress as, 347–348
Indus Valley civilizations, 162, 170
Inquisition, 79
Insanity, 405–407. *See also* Schizo-
    phrenia
Insight, 43–44
Intercession by minor gods, 202, 230,
    233
Internalization, 270

Introspection, 4, 7, 27, 29, 37, 41, 44,
    60, 72, 432

Japan, 159, 178
Jeremiah, 303–305, 311
Jesus, 96, 289, 440
  idols of, 337
  religion for conscious men, 318
  and Yahweh, 347
Judaism, 318
Judgment, 37, 90, 199
Justice, origin of, 280, 285

ka (illustrated, 192), 90, 290
  new theory of, 189–194
ker, 268, 275
Khabiru, 294–295, 298, 306
  history, 295
  idols of, 308–310
Kings. *See also* Bicameral theocra-
    cies
  Assyrian and Babylonian, 248–249
  hallucinogenic, 140–141
kradie, 258, 265–266, 275, 279

Language. *See also* Metaphor,
    Speech
  and agriculture, 137–138
  and brain, 102–104, 106–107, 115,
    344
  consciousness, 66–67
  cortical processing code, 105
  evolution of, 67, 126, 129–138,
    202; names, 135–137
  generation of, 49
  of *Iliad*, 69, 78
  in *Memphite Theology*, 186
  as metaphor, 51
  and mind, 54, 55, 78
  as perception, 50
  understanding and obedience, 96
Lateralization. *See* Brain
Law, 312
  beginning of, 198
  binding into commonweal, 319
  Mosaic, 318
  as replacing voices, 301
Learning, 6–8, 31–36, 118, 386–387
  unconscious, 33–36

Lebadea, oracle at, 328–329
Literature
    ancient as poetry, 362
    bicameral and subjective, 312–313, 334
Lithium, *408*
Logic, and reason, 41
Lullabies, 368
Lungs. *See phrenes*
Lysergic acid diethylamide, 46

Magician, 303
Marxism, 442
Maya, 155–156
    breakdown of civilization, 197
    burial, 163
    glyphics, 176
    god-carvers, 173
    idols, 172–173
    sites inhospitable, 156
Medicine, and omens, 238
Medical Materialism, 442
Mediums, 344–346, 354–357
    training of, 355, 357
Memory, 6, 29, 371
    brain stimulation, 112
    excerption, 62
    introspection, 37
    later Greek poetry, 369
    and Muses, 371–372
    sources of, 219
    state-dependent, 387
"Memphite Theology," 186
mermerizein, 70
Metaphor, 48–52, 56, 268, 271
    in augury, 242
    as basis of sortilege, 241
    composition of, 56
    defined, 48
    in extispicy, 244
    in generation of language, 49
    and hypnosis, 380
    metaphier and metaphrand, 48–49
    paraphier and paraphrand, 56–58
    in spontaneous divination, 244
    as basis of understanding, 52

Metaphor 'me,' 387, 402
    defined, 63
Mesopotamia, 143, 152, 163–165, 218–219, 233, 246
    augury in, 242
    change in history of, 253
    cultures, 68, 166
    figurines, 166–168
    graves, 164
    idols, 168–170
    kingdoms, 80
    steward-king theocracy, 178–185; resiliency of, 197–198
Mimesis, 375, 377
Mind
    bicameral. *See* Bicameral mind
    cardiac, 266
    conscious, 55, 72, 79
    in *Iliad,* 69, 70, 257
    language of, 54–55
    mental acts, 66
    mind-body problem, 3
    of Solon, 285–288
    spatial analog, 66
    subjective: confrontation with bicameral, 158, 160; development of concept, 259–260
Mind-space, 46, 55, 59, 84, 254, 263, 265, 271, 283, 287, 291
    conciliation, 65
    in Ecclesiastes, 296
    in *Iliad,* 75, 82
    diminished in schizophrenia, 420–421
Mind-time, 65
Miracles, 303
Mnemonic aids, 166–167
Model, defined, 52
Monism, 4
Morality, beginning of, 275, 286–287
Moses, 93, 174, 301–304
Muses, 369–375
    and memory, 371–372
    sing together, *227,* 371
    and Thamyris, 377–378
Music. *See also* Singing
    from brain stimulation, 109, 365
    in dichotic listening, 368

Music (*Cont.*)
   function in early poetry, 369
   hallucinated, 378
   lateralization of, 367–368
Mycenae, 76, 215, 256, 281
   art of, 71
   empire of, 213
   minds of, 75
   society of, 80
   steward-king theocracy, 178
Mythological scenes, 231

Nabiim, 299–307, 310–312
Names, 135–137, 139, 184
Narratization, 29, 63–64
   in *Iliad*, 82
   omens approaching, 238
   origin of, 217–219
Natufians, 138–143
Neural plasticity, 123–125
noema, 284–285
noos (nous), 70, 79, 269–270, 276,
   279, 286, 291
Nouns, 133–134

Obedience as hearing, 97–99
Odyssey, 272–277, 327, 372–373
   compared with *Iliad,* 273–276
   and the Fall, 299
   gods in, 273
   public performances, 77
   souls in, 291
   toward consciousness, 277
Old Testament. *See* Bible
Olmec, 155–156
   burials, 163
   figurines, 166–167
   idols, 171
Omens, 232–233
   beginning science, 238–239, 434
   literature of, 236–239
   in *Odyssey,* 273
   origin of, 236
   types of, 238
Oracles, 232, 321–331, 333, 341
   collapse of, 440
   induction procedures, 386
   loss of consciousness, 341

mocked, 344
   stages of decadence, 329–330
Osiris-Horus relationship, 143, 187,
   189, 193

pankush, 154, 227
Paralogic compliance, 387–391, 440
Paraphrand, and paraphier
   create mind-space, 58
   defined, 56–57
   determine hypnosis, 380–383, 387–
      388
   generate idea of love, 57–58
Perses, 277–281, 286
Persona, gods as, 74
Phenothiazines, 408
Philistines, 308–309
phrenes, 69–70, 258, 263–265, 275,
   279, 283–284
Phrenology, 383–384
Physics, 5, 14, 38, 52
Pleistocene, 130, 134, 137
Poetry, 73, 78, 364
   ancient, and brain function, 366
   and the divine, 362–363
   Greek, 281–285. *See also Iliad,
      Odyssey,* Perses, Solon, *Works
      and Days*
   theory of, 374
   transformation of: from divine
      knowledge, 361–364; possession
      of poet, 370–375; relation to
      music, 364–370
Poets
   latter-day, 375–376
   mentality, 370–377; bicameral cre-
      ativity, 371–373; possession, 370,
      373–374
   and the theory of oracles, 370
Population, size problem, 129, 194–
   195
Possession, 339–360
   and Christianity, 346–347
   not hallucination, 342
   induced, 344–347, 440. *See also*
      Umbanda, Glossolalia; as a
      learned phenomenon, 353–355

loss of consciousness in, 339–342
in modern world, 353, 357
negatory, 347–353
neurology of, 341–342, 350–353
in poets, 370–374
sex differences in, 342–343, 350
spontaneous: demonization, 347; neurological basis, 350–353; utterances in meter, 363
Prayer, 228–230, 403
Preconscious hypostases
in early lyric and elegy, 281–285
in *Hesiod,* 277–280
in *Iliad,* 259–271
change in *Odyssey,* 273–276
in Solon, 285–288
temporal development of, 260–261
Prophecy, decline of, 312
Prophets, 156, 232, 282, 424. *See also* Nabiim
Protestantism, 435
psyche, 69, 270–271, 276, 279, 288–292
Psychoanalysis, 442
Psychology
associationism, 8, 31
behaviorism, 13, 15, 442, 445
faculty, 41
introspectionism, 6, 14
Würzburg School, 37
Psychosomatic illness, 94, 267, 268
Psychotropic drugs, 440
Puns in divination, 306
Pyramids, 155–156, 157, 161, 188–189, 427
Pyramid texts, 190
Purpose, absence of in early writing, 247

Reading as 'hearing' cuneiform, 182, 218, 247
Reasoning, 41–44, 319
Rebellion, possible, 227
Redemption, origin of idea, 226
Refugees, 213–215, 293–294. *See also* Khabiru
Regression, 388–389, 398
Religion

its beginning in Assyria, 226
as anguish for bicamerality, 297
Brazilian. *See* Umbanda
of Early Greeks, 71–75
in man today, 317–319
and science, 434
and scientisms, 441
source, 413
theme of lost certainty, 444
Religious attitudes, modern, 253
Religious belief, 396, 403, 410
Respiration, 263–265
Responsibility, 184, 286
Reticular activating system, 16–18
Right and wrong, 226, 313. *See also* Morality
Ritual, 179–180, 182–183, 233, 439
Rorschach ink-blot test, 68, 425

Sacrifice, 173, 232, 243
Samuel, 306–308
Schizophrenia
advantages of, 426–427
automatism, 423–424
boundary loss, 425–426
difficulties of problem, 407–408
dissolution of mind-space, 420–422
erosion of analog 'I,' 417–420
genetic basis, 311, 426
hallucinations in, 408–417; and aptic structures, 416–417; auditory, 73, 88–91, 95–96; authority of, 412–413; depend on childhood teaching, 410; and on collective cognitive imperative, 409–410; conscious thought, 412; in deaf, 91–92; incidence, 87; initiating and guiding behavior, 411; neurological relations, 413
historical evidence for theory, 405–407
hypnosis, 403, 421
and nabiim, 311
narratization failure, 422–424
negatory possession, 348–349
neurology of, 427–430
paralogic compliance in, 391

Schizophrenia (*Cont.*)
  as partial relapse to bicameral, 403–404, 427, 429–430
  perception, visual, 427
  reaction-time studies, 421
  and stress, 404, 426
  theories of, 431
  time disorientation, 421–422
Science
  beginnings in omens, 238–239, 434
  causes of, 433–434
  Enlightenment, 436–437
  as quest for authorization, 435, 437–438
  versus religious imperatives, 439
  rivalry with church, 434–435
  search for divinity, 435–437
  secularization of, 437
  theory of evolution, 438
Scientific materialism, 437, 441
Scientific Revolution, 318, 435
Scientisms, 441–444
Self, 62, 227, 291, 349, 391, 419. *See also* Analog 'I,' Metaphor 'me'
  creation of, 79
  in Greek poetry, 180
  develops in *Odyssey,* 276
  posited in others, 217
  preconscious hypostases, 260–261
  diminished in schizophrenia, 423, 425–426
  basis of treachery, 220
Self-reference, 276
Sexual differences in lateralization, 343–344, 350
Shrines, wayside, 196
Sibyls, 331–332
Sin, 226, 318
Singing. *See also* Music
  ancient poetry sung, 282, 364
  on right hemisphere, 365–366
  song laterality experiment, 366–367
  of Muses, 371, 373
  versus speech, 364
Skulls, remodeled, 151, 163, 165
Social control, 144
  bicameral, 205, 207

evolution of groups, 126–129
  hallucinatory, 194–195
  idols as, 144
  Natufian, 140
  rule by fear, 214
  writing as, 198
Social chaos. *See* Chaos
Social cohesion, 337
Social hierarchy, 302, 304
Social organization, 194–197
Solon, 285–288, 290, 373
soma, 71
Sortilege. *See* Divination
Soul, idea of, 69, 288–292
Sound, authority of, 94–97
Space
  analog, 65
  internal, 260–261. *See also* Mind-space; in Gilgamesh, 253
Spatialization. *See* Consciousness, spatialization
Speech, 27, 40, 231. *See also* Brain, Speech, and Language
  in early man, 130
  in *Iliad,* 73
  of possessed, 342
  schizophrenic, 73
Spirits, 355–356. *See also* Possession
Split-brain. *See* Commissurotomy
Statues, 150, 152, 155, 159–160, 169, 178–180, 198, 300, 325, 334–335, 337. *See also* Idols
Stelae, 156, 181, 198
Steward-kings. *See* Bicameral theocracies
Stonehenge, 422
Stress, 228
  of death, 141
  decision-stress, 93–94; bicameral mind breakdown, 258–259; hallucination in *Iliad,* 94
  distress and religion, 318
  and gods' voices, 209
  causes hallucinations, 86, 93, 258
  begins negatory possession, 347–349, 352
  and poetry, 361

in schizophrenia, 404, 426
and *thumos,* 262
Struction, defined, 39, *39*
Subjectivity. *See also* Consciousness
from bicamerality to, 246–254;
changes in *Gilgamesh,* 251–253;
comparisons of letters, 247–250;
spatialization of time, 249–251
Ecclesiastes, 295–296
evolutionary selection for, 311
Suicide, first historical, 308

tabula rasa refuted, 27–28
Temples, 153, 157, 159, 163, 179–
180. *See also* God-houses, Ziggurats
Temporal lobes. *See* Brain
Teotihuacan, 155, 167, 427
Theocracy, 80, 83. *See* Bicameral
theocracies
Theogony, 278, 369, 371–373
Thera, 212–213, 255, 293
Thinking
creative, 44
judgment, 37–39
thinking-about, 35
Thought deprivation, 420
thumos, 69, 258–259, 261–263, 274–
275, 278–279, 283–284
Time
in hypnotic trance, 391
in schizophrenia, 421
spatialization of: development of,
250–251; in Ecclesiastes, 296;
history, 251; justice, 280–281;
in *Odyssey,* 276
Tombs, 141–143, 161, 163–164
Tourette's Syndrome, 351–352
Trade, 206, 210
Trance
cues for, 344
in early Greek poetry, 369
part of general bicameral paradigm, 324
in glossolalia, 358–360
in hypnosis, 387–393
negatory possession, 348
in Umbanda, 354–355

Trance logic, 390. *See also* Paralogic
compliance
Treachery, 219–220
Troy, 75–78
Truth as nostalgia, 443, 446
tsunami, 212
Tukulti (illustrated, 224), 223–225,
229–230, *235,* 253
Twilight states, 92, 413

Umbanda, 353–357
Understanding, nature of, 52–53, 84
Upanishads, 313
Ur, 159, 161. *See also* Mesopotamia
eye idols, 168
figurines, 166
kings divine, 185
ziggurat, 152

Veda, 313, 362
Voices, 85–87, 122. *See also* Hallucinations
assimilation of, 193
authority of, 94–96, 98, 411
bicameral: in Amos, 296; children
with, killed, 311; competition
between, 303; from eye idols,
168; *ili,* 190; inconsistent, 304;
ka, 190; in Moses, 174; neural
tracts, 104; *ob,* 310; rationalization, 298; weakened in traders, 211; replaced by writing,
198, 302
in bicameral culture, 98
brain function, 106–125
of the dead, 161–165
figurines embodiments of, 167
of Joan of Arc, 73–74
and the king, 140–143
and mind, 79
Mycenean, 75
in novel situations, 83
Osiris, 187
prerequisite to consciousness, 79
Ptah's "tongue," 186
in schizophrenia, 88–91
and concept of soul, 290
sortilege as substitute, 240

Voices (*Cont.*)
  "true of voice," 189
  unnecesary with consciousness,
    288
  as volition, 202
  written down, 187
Volition, 11, 70, 75, 98–99, 105, 202

Wada test for hemispheric domi-
    nance, 107, *107,* 365
Wernicke's area. *See* Brain
Works and Days, 278–281, 287
Worship, idea of, 230
Writing
  versus auditory authority, 208
  beginning of law, 198
  results in breakdown of voices,
    302

civil direction, 198
defined, 176
first human, 68
pictograms, 176

Yahweh, 93, 117, 156, 235, 297, 311,
    349, 357
  and Jesus, 347
Yazilikaya, 153–154

Zen, 34
Ziggurat of Neo-Babylon, 235
Ziggurats, 143, 153, 179, 233–235,
    427
  change in concept of, 234–235
  origin of, at Eridu, 152

THE DRAWINGS

On pages 40, 101, 104, 120 by the author; on page 142 by Christiane Gillièron after a photograph by J. Perrot; on page 152 from J. Mellaart, *Earliest Civilizations of the Near East* (London: Thames and Hudson, 1965); on page 154 by kind permission of Ekrem Akurgal; on page 168 after Mellaart; on pages 170, 171, 224 by Susan Hockaday; on page 199 by Carol Goldenberg; on page 172 by kind permission of Francis Robicsek; on page 192 redrawn from Henri Frankfort, *Kingship and the Gods* (Chicago: University of Chicago Press, 1948).

The lines of verse on page 378 are from William Empson's "Doctrinal Point" and "The Last Pain," in *Collected Poems of William Empson*. Reprinted by permission of Harcourt Brace Jovanovich.